Thornton A. Jenkins

Telegraphic Dictionary of the United States Navy

Prepared by Authority of the Hon. Gideon Welles, Secretary of the Navy

Thornton A. Jenkins

Telegraphic Dictionary of the United States Navy
Prepared by Authority of the Hon. Gideon Welles, Secretary of the Navy

ISBN/EAN: 9783337201746

Printed in Europe, USA, Canada, Australia, Japan

Cover: Foto ©Andreas Hilbeck / pixelio.de

More available books at **www.hansebooks.com**

TELEGRAPHIC DICTIONARY

OF THE

UNITED STATES NAVY,

PREPARED BY AUTHORITY

OF THE

HON. GIDEON WELLES,

SECRETARY OF THE NAVY,

BY

COMMODORE THORNTON A. JENKINS, U. S. NAVY,

CHIEF OF BUREAU OF NAVIGATION.

WASHINGTON:
GOVERNMENT PRINTING OFFICE.
1868.

TELEGRAPHIC SIGNALS.

INTRODUCTION.

This TELEGRAPHIC DICTIONARY contains 11,106 words and sentences, in alphabetical order, and numbered regularly from 1 to 9999, followed by 01 to 0999, 001 to 0099, 0001 to 0009.

TELEGRAPHIC SIGNALS are only used when the desired sentence or sentences cannot be found in the Signal Book, or when such signals make recourse to the Telegraphic Dictionary necessary; each hoist may represent a letter of the alphabet, or word, or part of a sentence, and to facilitate the operation the entire sentence or sentences to be telegraphed should be written down in as concise language as possible, and the number corresponding to each letter, word, or part of the sentence is to be taken from the Telegraphic Dictionary and written above or opposite the letter, words, or parts of sentences which they represent in their proper order before exhibiting the first hoist of flags. Having all ready, run up the *cornet* at a different part of the vessel, (usually forward,) together with the first hoist of flags of the series, and keep it there until the last hoist is answered, when *it* and the signal flags of the last hoist are to be hauled down *together*. While the first hoist is being interpreted and answered, have the second one bent on to another set of halliards, and at the moment the first hoist is answered, haul it down and run up the second, then get the third ready, and so on through the entire series. The answering vessel, upon answering each signal, watches the *cornet*, and if it and the signal come down together she hauls down the answering pendant to the deck, otherwise only to the cross-trees or half way to the deck, to be ready to answer the next signal hoist by the time it reaches the truck.

CORNET.

The *Cornet*, hoisted at any part of a vessel at the same time with other signal flags exhibited at a different part of the same vessel, indicates that the signals displayed are *telegraphic*, and must be sought for in the Telegraphic Dictionary. The cornet is to be kept flying until the entire series of telegraphic signals is completed, and to be hauled down together with the last hoist of the series of signals.

NAVAL DAY SIGNALS MADE WITH FLAGS.

The first or upper signal flag of a hoist represents the first, the second flag the second, the third flag the third, and the fourth flag the fourth numeral of the hoist; and the signal is reported and read in that order.

When a signal number is composed of two or more numerals of the same name, the first flag hoisted representing that numeral will be repeated in its proper place by hoisting the repeating pendant answering to its position in the hoist—that is to say, the first flag of the hoist is repeated by the first repeating pendant, the second flag of the hoist by the second repeating pendant, and so on.

DAY SIGNAL SYMBOLS.

The day signal symbols for making *telegraphic signals* are: the ten numeral flags, the cornet, answering, interrogatory, geographical, first, second, and third repeating pendants, which are used in making naval general signals.

NIGHT SIGNAL SYMBOLS.

The naval night signal symbols consist of red, green, and white lights, and lights of combinations of those colors, representing, respectively, one of the ten numerals; the answering, geographical, interrogatory, numeral, and the preparatory signal lights.

The colors of the night signal lights, with the exception of the cipher, (0,) the preparatory and numeral signal lights, are assimilated to those of the day signal flags, and pendants—that is to say, red corresponds to red, blue to green, and white to white.

The white light represents the preparatory day signals, and the white signal flag represents the cipher when exhibited with other signal flags, and *Truce* when hoisted alone.

The numeral day pendant is represented at night by a green and red light.

NIGHT TELEGRAPHIC SIGNALS.

Telegraphic signals are made at night by hoisting and keeping up the vessel's night distinguishing lantern lights, burning the preparatory signal, and as soon as the preparatory signal is answered, by sending up a *rocket*. It will then be known that the signal to follow will be telegraphic. When a vessel desiring to communicate at night by signal has no night distinguishing lantern lights assigned to it, a white lantern light will be hoisted instead and kept up while the telegraphic signals are being made. The *Rocket* will represent the *Cornet* used by day to indicate telegraphic signals. Before commencing a series of night telegraphic signals, the numbers answering to the letters, words, or sentences to be telegraphed should be taken out of the Dictionary and written down in regular order and the lights representing them arranged in the same order for burning.

When the series of telegraphic signals is completed, as will be indicated by hauling down the lantern light or lights, if no answer is required, the answering light will be burned to show that the signals are understood.

PRIVATE DISTINGUISHING SIGNALS AND WATCHWORDS.

Private distinguishing signals and watchwords should be assigned to the different vessels composing a fleet, division, or squadron, and only to be used within the geographical limits of the command. They should be composed of letters or words in the Telegraphic Dictionary represented by their flags and the distinguishing pendant of the vessel by day, and by the lights representing them and the night distinguishing lanterns of the vessel by night. When the vessels pass within hail at night they should be used as watchwords and repeated as they pass. The private distinguishing signals and watchwords should always be employed to prevent enemies' vessels or intruders from passing through a fleet or convoy, especially at night.

SECRET SIGNALS.

TELEGRAPHIC SECRET SIGNALS may be made by applying the rules laid down in the Introduction to the Naval Signal Code to the Telegraphic Dictionary and to the Geographical List.

GEOGRAPHICAL LIST.

The geographical list of places arranged alphabetically and numbered in regular order, will be found at the end of the Telegraphic Dictionary.

The exhibition of the Geographical Pendant will indicate that the number made will be found in that list.

UNITED STATES ARMY SIGNALS, BY ALBERT J. MYER, COLONEL AND SIGNAL OFFICER OF THE ARMY.

The following Code of Signals, and instructions for working the same, are published for the information and use of all concerned.

The " General Service Code" is intended to be used for general communication between different vessels, or between vessels and parties on land. It is for the purpose of transmitting such messages only as may constantly occur in service, and concerning which it does not matter whether they are interpreted by the enemy or not.

Ciphers, either to be agreed upon by particular commanders or published generally through the command, must always be used in the transmission of messages of importance, or for any communication which might give information to an enemy.

Every signal officer ought to be able in a few minutes to devise a cipher for this purpose.

GENERAL SERVICE CODE.

A	22	P	1212
B	2112	Q	1212
C	121	R	211
D	222	S	212
E	12	T	2
F	2221	U	112
G	2211	V	1222
H	122	W	1121
I	1	X	2122
J	1122	Y	111
K	2121	Z	2222
L	221	&	1111
M	1221	ing	2212
N	11	tion	1112
O	21		

3—End of word.

33—End of sentence.

333—End of message.

22.22.22.3—"I understand," or "message is received and understood," or "I see your signals," or "affirmative generally."

22.22.22.333—Cease signaling.

121.121.121—Repeat.

212121—Error.

211.211.211—Move a little to the right.

221.221.221—Move a little to the left.

Flag waved successively from side to side until attention is attracted—"Attention, look for signals from this point."

1. 21112—Wait a moment.
2. 12221—Are you ready?
3. 22122—I am ready.
4. 22212—Use short pole and small flag.
5. 22221—Use long pole and large flag.
6. 12222—Work faster.
7. 11222—Did you understand?
8. 11112—Use white flag.
9. 11211—Use black flag.
10. 22222—Use red flag.

a—after.	b—before.	c—can.	h—have.
n—not.	r—are.	t—the.	u—you.
ur—your.	w—word.	wi—with.	

The signal for, "The address of the message is now complete," is made thus: the flag being in the first position is dropped to the front, and then waved in full circles twice to the right, then resumes the first position. The signal for, "The message is signed as follows," is made thus: the flag being in the first position, is dropped to the front, and then waved in full circles twice to the left, then resumes the first position.

INSTRUCTIONS FOR USING THE CODE.

The whole number opposite each letter, stands for that letter.

The numbers are made by motions of the flag or signal, to the right or left or in front of a vertical position.

POSITIONS AND MOTIONS.

There are one position and three motions. The FIRST POSITION is with the flag held directly above the head, the flag staff vertical. To make the FIRST MOTION or "one," or "1," the flag is waved to the ground to the right, and instantly brought to the first position. To make the SECOND MOTION or "two" or "2," the flag is waved to the ground to the left, and instantly brought to the first position. To make the THIRD MOTION "three," or "3," the flag is waved to the ground in front and instantly brought to the first position.

When the latter number consists of more than one figure, the motions of the flag for each figure follow each other without any pause between them.

Thus to make "A" or "two, two," or "twenty-two" or "22," the flag is waved without pause twice to the left and then brought to the first position. To make "B" or "two, one, one, two," or "twenty-one twelve" or "2112," the flag is waved without pause twice to the left, twice to the right, then to the left and then brought to the first position. That is, one "first motion" followed by two "second motions" followed by one "first motion," the flag not stopping between the motions. To make three "fronts," or "three, three, three," or "three thirty-three" or "333," the flag is waved directly to the front to the ground three times, and then returned to the first position.

At the end of each letter the flag is held in the first position about two seconds, to show that the letter is finished.

TO SEND A MESSAGE.

First call "attention" by waving the flag successively from side to side until it is seen and answered by the opposite station. The station called will "answer" by making 22.22.22.3, the general signal for assent or affirmation, to signify that it is ready to receive the message. The communicating station then makes 22.22.22.3, signifying "I see you are ready to receive the message," then proceeds to transmit the message, letter by letter. A pause is made at the end of each letter to show that the signal for that letter is finished. At the end of each word, the flag is waved to the ground directly in front, "3," to show that the word is finished. At the end of each sentence there is a pause, and the flag is waved to the ground twice directly in front, "33," to show that the sentence is finished. At the end of a message the flag is waved to the ground three times, directly in front, "333," showing that the message is finished.

When the signal "333," "end of message," is made, it indicates "my communication is complete; I await your answer." The station receiving the message will, upon noticing the signal "Message complete," if the message has been correctly received, immediately answer with the signal of assent, 22.22.22.3, and will then signal in turn such messages as it may have to communicate. If, however, the message or any part of it has not been correctly received, or is not understood, the receiving station will make the signal for "Repeat," 121. 121.121.3, followed by the part of the message to be repeated; as, 121.121.121.3, after or before the word—(here signal the word after or before which the repeat is required.) If the message is not understood at all, the signal "121.121.121.3," "all," is made. In commencing a repetition, the sending station will always commence by making the signal of assent, to show that the call for repeat is understood. This signal of assent, meaning "I understand," will be used habitually at the commencement of all communications.

RECORDING SIGNALS.

When circumstances render it necessary, a pause will be made at the end of each sentence to permit that sentence to be accurately written down. With skilled signalists such pauses are not necessary. Each signal number may be taken down with a pencil as soon as it is seen, and afterwards transmitted by reference to the code. When the signalist is accustomed to the code, this may be dispensed with, and only the words and sentences are written down during the pauses. When two men are together at a station, one man looks through the glass and calls the numbers as fast as they are seen to the other, who writes them down. Messages are thus recorded in the signal numbers composing them. This is done by writing for each letter the signal number which stands for it; thus, the word "W A S," written in signal numbers is, "1121 22 212," each letter in signal numbers being separated from the next by a small space. Each complete word is separated from the next by a dash, as "W A S—N O T," is in signal numbers, 1121 22 212—11 21 2.

When secret or cipher codes, codes devised for the occasion, or codes not before used, or when the commander wishes a message signaled of which he and his correspondent alone shall know the meaning, the message may be thus reduced to signal numbers before being placed in the hands of the signalist, who then becomes simply a medium for the transmission of the message, without knowledge of its contents. By this plan of reducing a message to its signal numbers written upon paper before it is sent, and of recording upon paper the signal numbers made by others as they are received, translating them afterwards by the code, it will be found that messages may be almost immediately exchanged by those having knowledge of the principles of the codes without the study or practice of any particular code.

In calling off from the glass signal numbers to be recorded in writing, each signal number should be given distinct and complete by itself, as for instance, "one twenty-one," "twenty-two," "one twelve," and so on.

When signals are made by a flagman detailed and practiced for the purpose, the flagman properly placed and equipped, and standing with the flag and staff in the "first position," each signal is ordered by calling off briskly, as an order, the numbers for that signal; the flagman making promptly, on hearing each order, those motions with the flag indicated by the signal numbers ordered. Each letter number must be called plainly, distinct, and clear by itself, that the flagman may know before commencing the signal what numbers are to be made together without pause, so that the motions may be made rapidly and well timed.

Thus in orders A "22," would be ordered "twenty-two," B "2112," "twenty-one twelve," C "121," "one twenty-one." Following the same general plan, it is evident that persons practiced as signalists need not be limited to the use of the signal equipments or of any apparatus. A handkerchief or hat held in the hand above the head and waved to the right for "one" "1," to the left for "two" "2," and lowered to the waist for "three" "3," can be readily used for any short distance. With a handkerchief attached to a walking-stick, or a boat flag on any staff, messages may be sent a mile or two, or even to greater distances. A man standing with his coat off, with his hands touching upon his breast for the first position, making a wave of his right arm for "one" "1," a wave of his left for "two" "2," dropping both hands to his side for "three" "3," returning always to the first position after each motion, can thus transmit any message.

The simple methods of application are numberless. Enough are here given to be suggestive to those whose duty it may be to study the subject.

To make clear the mode of signaling, let us suppose the word "Able" is to be signaled. There are made first the signal numbers of the letter "A" "22;" there is then a pause of two seconds, the flag being in the first position. The signal numbers of the letter "B" "2112," are then made, followed by another pause. Then the signal numbers of the letter "L" "221," succeeded by another pause. The signal numbers of the letter "E" "12," are then made, and the flag is then dropped to the front, "three" "3," returning to the first position, to indicate that the word is ended; and thus word by word until the message is completed.

NIGHT SIGNALS.

To be made with signal equipments; staff 12 feet long; flying torch 1½ inch in diameter; wicked, filled with turpentine, lighted and attached to upper extremity of signal staff by clamp screws. Copper foot torch two inches diameter, wicked, filled with turpentine, lighted and placed at the feet and in front of the flagman. The positions, orders, and motions for signaling at night are identical with those used in the day; the lighted foot torch being the "point of reference," in relation to which all motions are made. Each torch is fitted with an extinguisher. At the conclusion of each message the flying torch is extinguished. The foot light, or some other light in place of it, is left burning as long as signaling is continued, to the end that the communicating station may see to what point to direct their signals.

When, during the transmission of a message, the flying torch is lowered to the left and is there extinguished, it indicates that it is extinguished to be refilled, and so soon as filled and relighted the message will be resumed without any further intimation.

In night signaling, great care must be taken that the reference or foot light is always and certainly within view of the communicating station. To ascertain this, placing the eye on the level and in the place of the foot light, it must be noted whether the foot light at the communicating station can be thence seen; if not, the foot light must be raised or moved to a position certainly visible. This precaution should always be taken. The foot light must be always in front of the flagman and directly beneath the flying torch, when that is in the first position.

The torch should be refilled every fifteen minutes, and carefully trimmed after each message. When not in use the wick should be covered with the extinguisher.

Lanterns are sometimes substituted for the foot torch, especially on board of vessels where there is danger of fire. In this case, lanterns giving the most powerful light should be selected. Lanterns with reflectors can be used, taking care that the lantern is so placed as to throw the light upon the communicating station. A lantern may be substituted for the flying torch, and attached to the extremity of the staff in its stead. This will be found difficult, however. The light is not nearly so brilliant or so distinct as that given by the torch.

In signaling at short distances, lanterns may be used instead of torches; one lantern being placed stationary as the foot light, the other may be held directly above the head in the hand as the first position. The lantern is then waved to the right for "one" "1," to the left for "two" "2," and lowered to the waist for "three," "3," or pause signal.

Signals can be made in this way very conveniently for ship use, by placing one lantern upon the rail, and waving the other to its right or left to make any required signals, the general principles of the signals remaining the same. Signals made in this way are of convenient use in boats.

A convenient foot light is often made on shore by lighting a small fire near the feet of the signalist. With a single lantern then held in the hand or attached to a small staff, any message can be sent. Or if for any cause lanterns are not attainable, and fires can be kindled, a small fire may be used as a foot light while the signal motions are made with a brand from the fire, or a lighted pine knot or a piece of tarred rope, or with almost any combustible substance, capable of showing a flame and a light, held in the hand or attached to a staff and properly waved to either side or to the front to make the required signal motions.

[From Colonel Myer's Manual of Signals.]

SIGNALING IN CIPHER.

If signals are to be displayed in the presence of an enemy, they must be guarded by ciphers. The ciphers must be capable of frequent changes. The rules by which these changes are made must be simple. Ciphers are undiscoverable in proportion as these changes are frequent, and as the messages in each change are brief. When alphabet ciphers are used, the aim should be to never allow any letter to appear twice alike. The number of letters under each key is to be as small as possible. The terminations of words are to be concealed. The letters in each word ought to be made in unusual sequence. For this purpose a message to be enciphered may be wholly reversed; that is, written with the last word appearing first. Each word may also be reversed. It does not do away with the utility of ciphers that they may be sometimes deciphered, for we must often use them, conscious that, with sufficient time and the appliances, they can be interpreted; but knowing, also, that the time interpretation will require will render the message useless to an enemy. Simple devices, unused for such purposes, it is believed, before the war, have rendered it practicable to so exhibit signals that their interpretation becomes almost impossible. The entire code may change with every day, with every message, or with every word of every message.

The signal disk of the signal corps is as follows:

Description of signal disk.

On a small disk of card-board, or any other material, (Plate d, Fig. 1,) are written or printed the letters of the alphabet in irregular sequence, and arranged around the circumference of the disk. The letters are so placed that when the disk is properly held, all the letters are upright. On this small disk are also printed those combinations of letters which frequently occur in words, as "tion," "ing," "ous," &c., &c., and a sign to mark "the end of a word." On a larger disk are written or printed, arranged around its circumference in the same manner, either the letters of the alphabet or the symbolic numbers of signals which are to be used. The disks are fastened concentrically together in such manner that one may revolve upon the other, and that they may be clamped in any position. They are of such size that when so fastened, the letters, &c., upon the inner disk will each appear close to, and directly opposite one of the signal combinations upon the outer disk. (See Plate d, Fig. 1.) The figures "1" and "8" are sometimes used instead of the figures "1" and "2" to symbolize the elements "one" and "two," because the figure "8" is upright in most positions of the disks. Having a disk arranged and clamped, as at Fig. 1, in Plate d, it will be clearly understood by any signalist that so provided, he has before him an alphabetic code with every letter opposite its signal symbols; and he will comprehend that by referring to the disk he can transmit a message without the study of any particular code, and can transmit it in secret signals or cipher, by moving the disks upon each other, and so making changes in the code.

Thus to make "A" the combination "112," "one, one, two" is signaled; to make "C" the combination "1221," "one, two, two, one" is signaled; to make "T" the combination "211," "two, one, one" is signaled; to make "ing" the combination "2112," "two, one, one, two" is signaled; and there is so signaled the word "acting." To denote the end of the word, the common "pause signal," "3," "three," may be used, or whatever combination may be in the compartment opposite the character for "end of the word." This is arranged by preconcert, and so for any words. Clausus, &c., are made by repetitions of the pause signal. Now, it is evident that with any change of the relative positions of the disks made, as by rotating one upon the other, the whole code of alphabetic signals is changed. Thus, suppose the inner disk rotated until the letter "A" is opposite the combination "1112," "one, one, one, two." Then referring to the same figure in the plate to signal the word "acting:" "A" is "1112;" "C" is "2121," "T" is "22," "ing" is "2212." The signals do not in any way resemble those before exhibited for the same word. The signal for the "end of word" may also be different. These changes can be indefinitely varied. It is for making them that the disks are movable. Where different parties, as the officers of a corps or of an army, are to be in communication, rules for the changing of the disks issued to all, enable each to use them whenever they are in view of each other, each finding that his cipher will then correspond with that of the officer with whom he is signaling. And this may be, though the signalists have never met, and may be serving with detachments which have these communications with each other for the first time.

The following is a general rule for the use of signal disks. The signal disk is supposed to be arranged for a code of two elements. The communicating parties have disks similar, and like Fig. I.

RULES AND EXPLANATIONS FOR THE USE OF SIGNAL DISKS.

I.—EXPLANATION OF THE SIGNAL DISK.

The numerals on the outer rim of the disk represent the combinations to be made with a flag or torch. Each combination represents, when made, that letter on the inner disk which coincides with it.

II.—TO MAKE SIGNALS.

The signals for whatever code signals may be represented by the symbols upon the outer disks are made according to the rules heretofore given while treating of the different codes.

III.—THE ADJUSTMENT LETTER.

The adjustment letter is any letter selected on the inner disk which, together with a given combination on the outer disk, forms the cipher, and is the key to any communication sent in that particular cipher. The letter R is understood to be the adjustment letter, if no other letter is given.

The combination to be used with the adjustment letter is called the key number.

The adjustment letter and the signal combination being given, the inner disk will be turned so that the letter R will coincide with the combination. Example: The combination is "1212," adjustment letter R—the inner disk will be turned so that R will coincide with "1212." Any letter may be the adjustment letter. Any signal combination may be chosen for the key number. Example: the signal "1221—3—1122—333," would indicate that "W" was the adjustment letter, and "1122" the cipher combination. The disk would, in that case, be arranged as follows: "W" would be brought to coincide with "1122."

IV.—TO SEND A MESSAGE IN CIPHER.

Station "A" calls station "B" and gets "B's" acknowledgment. "A" gives "B" the cipher combination in which he intends to send the message. Example: "A" gives "B" "2122, (right, left, right, right,) 333;" "B" answers by repeating "22.22.22.3,—2122 333;" which indicates to "A" that "B" has got the correct cipher. "A" and "B" adjust their disks as follows: each turns the inner disk so that the letter R will coincide with the combination "2122" in the outer disk. (See plate Fig. I.) The disks of both parties are now alike, and the message commences.

To signal the word "pickets" in the foregoing cipher, station "A" would make "221-11-1221-2211-1212-211-122, 3"=Pickets. If "W" was the adjustment letter and "1122" the cipher combination, then "W" would coincide with "1122," and the word "Pickets" would be represented by "122-1211-212-2-2222-112-2111"=Pickets."

*   *   *   *   *   *   *   *

VI.—RECORD.

The officer receiving the message will have another officer or an enlisted man to write down the combinations as they are received, each being called off in its turn by the person at the glass. At the close of the message the officer will take the disk and decipher or translate the combinations thus written, acknowledging the receipt of the message in the usual manner.

To use the Naval Telegraphic Dictionary with the Army Symbols.

To do this, in daylight, exhibit the CORNET anywhere, except at one of the mastheads, to indicate that the Telegraphic Dictionary will be used, and call attention at the same time with the army signal flag.

The first nine letters of the alphabet will represent the nine digits, and the tenth letter the cipher. Thus:

No.	Symbol.	Value.
1	A	22
2	B	2112
3	C	121
4	D	222
5	E	12
6	F	2221
7	G	2211
8	H	122
9	I	1
0	J	1122

At night the call with the torches or lanterns and the prescribed night indications for telegraphing with Coston lights will apprise the lookout that the Telegraphic Dictionary will be used.

By using the Naval Telegraphic Dictionary with the army symbols, words and short sentences may be communicated instead of letters, and may be found in practice to be useful, especially at night and at short distances, when two lanterns may be used in place of torches or Coston lights.

Example: It is desired to communicate the word or sentence in the Telegraphic Dictionary answering to 159. Having called and been answered and the CORNET exhibited, proceed to make two, two,—one, two—one; or 22-12-1. The Naval General Signal Book may be used with the army symbols by calling in the usual manner, and when the call is answered make the letters S, B, U, and wait for an answer. The answering officer should reply by repeating the numbers answering to the letters S, B, U, which will indicate that he understands that the signals which will follow immediately thereafter will be from the Naval Signal Book. Or instructions may be issued to the different vessels, and to signal officers on shore if there be any to communicate with, that when a particular army signal flag is used it will indicate—

1st. Regular army signals.
2d. Telegraph Dictionary.
3d. Naval Signal Book.

The first might be a square Red flag with a white square in the centre;
The second a square Blue flag with a white square in the centre; and
The third a square Red flag.

The flags for army signaling should be as nearly of the same size as possible, and when used for calling should be waved or held so that the colors may be readily distinguished by the observer.

At night the colors of the position lantern lights would serve to indicate whether the signals were to be the Regular Army signals, from the Telegraphic Dictionary, or the Naval Signal Book.

First, a White Lantern light.
Second, a Green Lantern light.
Third, a Red Lantern light.

The disk may be used for secret combinations of numerals as well as for the letters of the alphabet.

Plate a.

ARMY SIGNALS.

First Position - or "Ready"

First Motion -"One" -"1"

Second Motion -"Two" -"2"

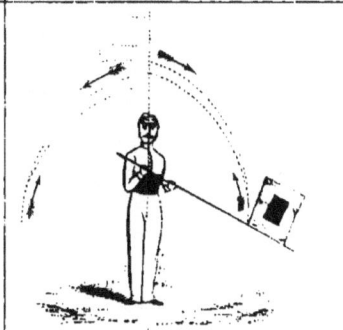

"Two" - "One" - "21"

"One -Two - One -Two" -"1212"

"Three" - "3" or "Front"

Bureau of Navigation. 1866

ARMY SIGNALS.

First Position - or "Ready"

First Motion - "One" - "1"

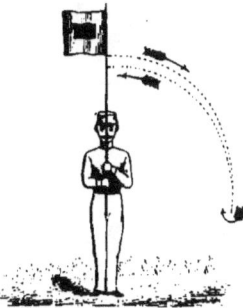

Second Motion - "Two" - "2"

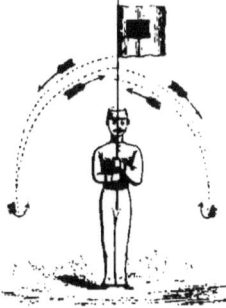

"One" - "Two" - "12"

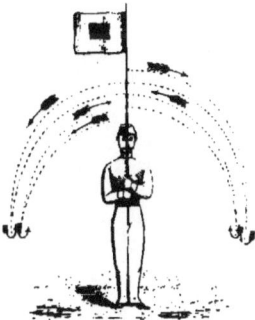

"Two - One - Two - One" - "2121"

"Three" - "3" or "Front"

Bureau of Navigation, 1866.

Plate c.

ARMY SIGNALS.

First Position - or "Ready,"
for Night Signals.

Bureau of Navigation.1866.

ARMY SIGNALS.

Figure 1.

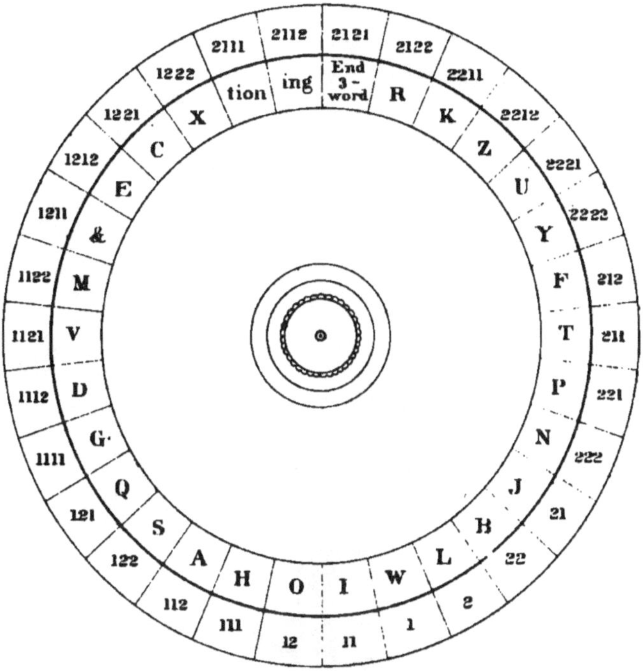

2111 2112 2121 2122
1222 tion ing End 3-word R 2211
1221 X K 2212
1212 C Z 2221
1211 E U 2222
1122 & Y
1121 M F 212
1112 V T 211
1111 D P 221
121 G· N 222
122 Q J 21
112 S B 22
111 A H O I W L 2
12 11 1

TWO DISCS.

Figure 2.

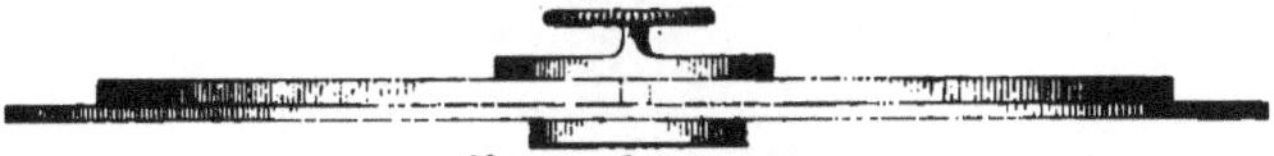

Vertical Section.

Bureau of Navigation, 1866.

ALPHABET NUMBERS.

Nos.	ALPHABET.	Nos.	ALPHABET.
1	A or an.	14	N.
2	B.	15	O.
3	C.	16	P.
4	D.	17	Q.
5	E.	18	R.
6	F.	19	S.
7	G.	20	T.
8	H.	21	U.
9	I.	22	V.
10	J.	23	W.
11	K.	24	X.
12	L.	25	Y.
13	M.	26	Z.

COMPASS SIGNAL NUMBERS.

Nos.	POINTS.	Nos.	POINTS.
27	North.	43	South.
28	North by East.	44	South by West.
29	North North East.	45	South South West.
30	North East by North.	46	South West by South.
31	North East.	47	South West.
32	North East by East.	48	South West by West.
33	East North East.	49	West South West.
34	East by North.	50	West by South.
35	East.	51	West.
36	East by South.	52	West by North.
37	East South East.	53	West North West.
38	South East by East.	54	North West by West.
39	South East.	55	North West.
40	South East by South.	56	North West by North.
41	South South East.	57	North North West.
42	South by East.	58	North by West.

Nos.	ABA	Nos.	ABS
59	Aback.	102	Aboard the wreck.
60	Abaft.	3	Abolish, *ed, ing.*
61	the beam.	4	Abominable, *y.*
62	fore channels.	5	Abortive, *ly.*
63	fore mast.	6	About.
64	main channels.	7	Above.
65	main mast.	8	the or this anchorage.
66	mizzen channels.	9	the bayou.
67	mizzen mast.	110	the city.
68	smoke stack.	1	the creek.
69	wheel house.	2	the entrance.
70	Abandon, *ed, ing, ment.*	3	the fleet.
71	the chase.	4	the fort, *s.*
72	the place.	5	the point.
73	the prize.	6	the sheers.
74	the wreck.	7	the wharf.
75	Abattis.	8	the yard.
76	Abdomen, *inal.*	9	Abreast.
77	Abduct, *ed, ing, ion.*	120	of the bayou.
78	Abeam.	1	of the creek.
79	Aberration.	2	of the entrance.
80	Abet, *ed, ing, tor, s.*	3	of the fleet.
81	Abeyance.	4	of the fort, *s.*
82	Abhor, *ring, red, rence.*	5	of the place.
83	Abide, *ing.*	6	of this ship.
84	Ability, *ies.*	7	of the town.
85	Abject, *ly.*	8	of the yard.
86	Abjure, *d, ing, ation.*	9	Abrogate, *d, ing.*
87	Able.	130	Abrupt, *ly, ness.*
88	Able-bodied men.	1	Abscess, *es.*
89	Able seaman, *men.*	2	Absent, *ing, ed, ce.*
90	Abnormal.	3	with leave.
91	Aboard.	4	without leave.
92	all are now.	5	Absentee, *s.*
93	all are not.	6	accounted for.
94	call everybody.	7	not accounted for.
95	come or go.	8	have returned.
96	send all.	9	have not returned.
97	the prize.	140	send for the.
98	the steamer.	1	wait for the.
99	the strange vessel.	2	do not wait for the.
100	the supply vessel.	3	send correct list of the.
101	the vessel indicated.	144	Absolute, *ly.*

3

Nos.	ACC	Nos.	ACR
145	Absorb, *ed, ing, ent, s.*		Account, *s, able, ability, ant, ing.*
6	Absorption, *ive.*	188	of men.
7	Abstain, *ed, ing, inence.*	9	of officers.
8	Abstemious.	190	of oil expenditures.
9	Abstract, *ed, ing.*	1	of dry provisions.
150	Abstracts.	2	of wet provisions.
1	Absurd, *ly, ity.*	3	of small stores.
2	Abundant, *ce, ly.*	4	of stores.
3	supply of provisions.	5	will be sent.
4	supply of water.	6	of water.
5	supply of wood.	7	Accounting officer, *s.*
6	Abuse, *s, d, ing, ive.*	8	Accrue, *d, ing, s.*
7	Academy.	9	Accumulate, *d, ing, ion, s.*
8	Accelerate, *ed, ing.*	200	Accurate, *ly, acy.*
9	Accept, *ed, ing, s, ance, able.*	1	Accuse, *d, ing, ation, r, s.*
160	my thanks.	2	Accustom, *ed.*
1	the thanks of.	3	Acetate, *s.*
2	Access, *ible.*	4	Acetic.
3	Accident, *s, al, ally.*	5	Ache, *s, ing.*
4	Acclimate, *ed, ing.*	6	Achieve, *d, ing, ment, s.*
5	Accommodate, *ed, ing, ion, s.*	7	Acid, *s, ity, ify, ied, ulated, ulous.*
6	Accompany, *ied, ing, ies.*	8	acetic.
7	Accomplice, *s.*	9	acitose.
8	Accomplish, *ed, ing.*	210	carbolic.
9	Accord, *ed, ance.*	1	carbonic.
170	According, *ly.*	2	citric.
1	Accost, *ed.*	3	muriatic.
2	Account, *s, able, ability, ant, ing.*	4	nitric.
3	conflicting.	5	sulphuric.
4	favorable.	6	tartaric.
5	reliable.	7	Acidi citrici syrup.
6	unfavorable.	8	Acknowledge, *d, ing, ment, s.*
7	unreliable.	9	A-cockbill.
8	book, *s.*	220	the anchor.
9	current.	1	the yards.
180	from the army.	2	Aconite.
1	have been received.	3	Aconiti, *rad., tinct.*
2	have been sent.	4	Acquaint, *ed, ing, ance.*
3	have not been received.	5	Acquiesce, *d, ing, ence.*
4	have not been sent.	6	Acquire, *d, ing, ment, s.*
5	of coal.	7	Acquisition, *s.*
6	of the enemy.	8	Acquit, *tal, ed, ing.*
187	of killed and wounded.	229	Across.

4

Nos.	ADI	Nos.	ADM
230	Across the bay.	273	Adjacent.
1	the country.	4	Adjoin, ed, ing.
2	the harbor.	5	Adjourn, ed, ment.
3	the river.	6	the Board, s.
4	the sound.	7	the Court, s.
5	Act.	8	has taken place.
6	at your own discretion.	9	will take place.
7	in concert with.	280	Adjudge, d.
8	independently of.	1	Adjudicate, d, ing, ion.
9	promptly.	2	Adjust, ed, ing, ment, s.
240	with great circumspection.	3	all difficulties.
1	Acts.	4	Adjutant, s.
2	of Congress.	5	General.
3	of the State Legislature, s.	6	A. A. General.
4	of war.	7	Administer, ed, ing.
5	Action.	8	Administration, tive.
6	avoid.	9	Admire, d, ing, ation, able, ably.
7	cease.	290	Admiral.
8	commence.	1	aid, send.
9	of the.	2	barge, send.
250	renew the.	3	cook, send.
1	withdraw from the.	4	coxswain, send.
2	Actions.	5	flag, hoist.
3	very suspicious.	6	flag, haul down.
4	of the strange vessel, s.	7	flagship.
5	Activity.	8	health.
6	Actor, s.	9	mail, send.
7	Actual, ly.	300	mail, send for.
8	Actuate, d, ing.	1	movements.
9	Acute, ly.	2	Rear.
260	Adapt, ed, ing, ation, ability.	3	servant, send.
1	Add, ed, ing, ition, itional, itive.	4	steward, send.
2	Addict, ed.	5	Vice.
3	Address, ed, ing.	6	Admiralty.
4	Adduce, d.	7	Court, s.
5	Adept, s.	8	decision, s.
6	Adequate, ly.	9	Judge, s.
7	Adhere, d, ing, ence.	310	jurisdiction.
8	to instructions.	1	limits.
9	to original plan.	2	proceedings.
270	Adhesion.	3	Admissible.
1	Adhesive, ly, ness.	4	Admission, s.
272	Adieu!	315	Admit, ed, ing, tance.

5

Nos.	ADM	Nos.	AFT
	Admit, *ed, ing, tance.*	358	Affix, *ed, ing.*
316	no one within the lines.	9	Afflict, *ed, ing, ive, ion.*
7	Admonish, *ed, ing.*	360	Affluent.
8	Admonition, *s.*	1	Afford, *ed, ing.*
9	Admonitory.	2	Affray, *s.*
320	Adobe, *s.*	3	Afire, *on fire.*
1	Adopt, *ed, ing, ion.*	4	Afloat.
2	Adorn, *ed, ing, s, ment, s.*	5	aft.
3	Adrift.	6	amidships.
4	Adroit, *ly, ness.*	7	at half tide.
5	Adult, *s.*	8	at high tide.
6	Adulterate, *d, ing, ion.*	9	at low tide.
7	Advance, *d, ing, ment, s.*	370	forward.
8	at full speed.	1	soon will be.
9	at half speed.	2	Afoot.
330	cautiously.	3	Aforesaid.
1	lookout, *s.*	4	Afoul.
2	picket, *s.*	5	Afraid.
3	slowly.	6	Africa, *n.*
4	take position in the.	7	coast.
5	Advantage, *ous, ously.*	8	cruise, *r.*
6	Adventure.	9	fever, *s.*
7	Adversary, *ies.*	380	trade, *r, s.*
8	Adverse, *ly.*	1	Aft, *abaft.*
9	Adversity, *ies.*	2	After.
340	Advert, *ed, ing.*	3	breakfast.
1	Advertise, *d, ing, ment, s.*	4	conviction.
2	Advice.	5	dark.
3	boat, *s.*	6	daylight.
4	vessel, *s.*	7	dinner.
5	Advise, *d, r, ing, ment.*	8	enquiry, *ies.*
6	Advocacy.	9	guard.
7	Advocate, *s, ed, ing.*	390	moonrise.
8	Adze, *s.*	1	nightfall.
9	carpenter's.	2	noon.
350	cooper's.	3	part.
1	Affable, *y.*	4	sail, *s.*
2	Affair, *s.*	5	sunrise.
3	Affect, *ed, ing.*	6	sunset.
4	Affidavit, *s.*	7	supper.
5	of the prisoner, *s.*	8	the moon sets.
6	of the witness, *es.*	9	the rain.
357	Affirm, *ed, ing, ation, ative, atively.*	400	the storm.

Nos.	AFT	Nos.	ALE
	After,		Ahead,
401	the tide changes.	443	of the danger.
2	yards.	4	of this division.
3	Afterwards.	5	of the enemy.
4	Again.	6	of the fleet.
5	Against.	7	of the line.
6	orders.	8	of this squadron.
7	regulations.	9	of the stranger.
8	usage.	450	of this vessel.
9	the law.	1	Aid, ed, ing.
410	the current.	2	me if possible.
1	the wind.	3	the stranger, s.
2	Age.	4	Aide-de-camp.
3	of the month.	5	Aim, ed, s, ing.
4	of the moon.	6	at the centre of the.
5	of the week.	7	in the direction shown by compass signal.
6	of the year.		
7	of the.	8	Air, y, ing, ed.
8	Agency, ies.	9	bedding.
9	Agent, s.	460	clothing.
420	of the Government.	1	passage, s.
1	of the underwriters.	2	pipe, s.
2	Aggravate, ed, ion, ing.	3	pump, s.
3	affair.	4	pump bucket, s.
4	circumstances.	5	pump crosshead, s.
5	Aggregate, s.	6	pump rod, s.
6	Aggress, or, ive, ing.	7	pump rod, s and link, s.
7	Aggrieve, ed.	8	pump side rod, s.
8	Agitate, d, ing, or, s.	9	pump valve, s.
9	Agonize, ed, ing.	470	space, s.
430	Agony, ies.	1	tight.
1	Agree, ed, ing, ment, s.	2	tube, s.
2	Agreeable, ly.	3	Alacrity.
3	news received.	4	Alarm, ed, ing, ist.
4	Aground.	5	signal–s.
5	aft.	6	Alas !
6	amidships.	7	Alaska.
7	fore and aft.	8	Alcohol, ic.
8	forward.	9	Aldebaran.
9	Ague, s.	480	Alderman, men.
440	Ague and fever.	1	Ale.
1	Ahead.	2	Alee.
442	of the.	483	Alert, ness.

Nos.	ALE	Nos.	AMB
484	Aleutian Islands.	527	Alligator, *s.*
5	Algebra, *ic, ical, ically.*	8	Ally, *ies, ied.*
6	Alias.	9	armies.
7	Alibi.	530	forces or fleets.
8	Alidade.	1	powers.
9	Alien, *s.*	2	Allot, *s, ment, s.*
490	Alienate, *d, ing, ation.*	3	Allow, *ance, ed, ing.*
1	Align, *s, ment, s.*	4	of provisions.
2	Alike.	5	of water.
3	Aliment, *al, ary.*	6	Alloy, *s.*
4	Alive.	7	Allude, *d, s.*
5	Alkali, *es, ne.*	8	Allusion, *s.*
6	All.	9	Almanac, *s,* American Nautical.
7	aback.	540	British Nautical.
8	abandoned.	1	Almost.
9	aboard.	2	Aloft.
500	afloat.	3	Alone.
1	aground.	4	Along.
2	along shore.	5	the shore.
3	day.	6	side.
4	discharged.	7	with.
5	embarked.	8	Aloof.
6	are, or have, gone, *disappeared.*	9	Alphabet, *ical, ically.*
7	hands.	550	Already.
8	I can learn.	1	Also.
9	is, or are, ready.	2	Alter, *able, ed, ation, s, ing.*
510	is lost.	3	Alterative.
1	is saved.	4	Altercation, *s.*
2	my boats.	5	Alternative, *s.*
3	night.	6	Although.
4	the assistance.	7	Altitude, *s.*
5	the news.	8	of the.
6	the papers.	9	of the moon.
7	the supplies.	560	of the north star.
8	the time.	1	of the sun.
9	will be ready at, or by.	2	Altogether.
520	your boats.	3	Alum.
1	your forces or command.	4	Always.
2	Allay, *ed, ing.*	5	Am.
3	Allegation, *s.*	6	Amalgam.
4	Allege, *d.*	7	Amaurosis.
5	Alleviate, *d, ing, ion.*	8	Amaze, *d, ing, ment, s.*
526	Alliance, *s.*	569	Ambassador, *s.*

Nos.	AMB	Nos.	ANN
570	Ambergris.	613	Ample, *y.*
1	Ambiguous, *uity.*	4	Amplitude, *s.*
2	Ambition.	5	of the sun.
3	Ambitious, *ly.*	6	Amputate, *ing, ion.*
4	Ambulance, *s.*	7	Amuse, *d, ing, ment, s.*
5	for the sick.	8	Anæsthetic.
6	for the wounded.	9	Analagous.
7	Ambuscade, *s.*	620	Analysis, *ses.*
8	Ambush, *ed.*	1	Analyze, *d, ing.*
9	Ameliorate, *ed, ing, ion.*	2	Anarchy.
580	Amenable.	3	Anatomical, *ly.*
1	Amend, *atory, ment, s.*	4	Anchor, *s, ed, ing.*
2	Amende honorable.	5	shackles.
3	America, *n.*	6	stock.
4	arms.	7	Anchorage.
5	army.	8	Ancient, *ly.*
6	boat, *s.*	9	And.
7	commerce.	630	Anemometer.
8	cruiser, *s.*	1	Aneroid barometer.
9	flag.	2	Aneurism.
590	man of war.	3	Anew.
1	mail steamer.	4	Anger.
2	merchantman, *men.*	5	Angle, *s.*
3	officer, *s.*	6	Angostura bark, bitters.
4	ship, *s*, vessel, *s.*	7	Angry, *ily.*
5	transport, *s.*	8	Anguish.
6	troops.	9	Angular, *ly.*
7	Amiability.	640	Animadvert, *ed, ing, sion.*
8	Amiable, *y.*	1	Animal, *s.*
9	Amicable, *y.*	2	Animalcule, *æ.*
600	Amid, *st.*	3	Animate, *d, ing.*
1	Amidships.	4	Animosity, *ies.*
2	Amiss.	5	Animus.
3	Amity.	6	Ankle.
4	Ammoniæ, *ac.*	7	bone.
5	carbonas.	8	joint.
6	liquor.	9	Anneal, *ed, ing.*
7	murias.	650	Annex, *ed, ing, ation.*
8	spts. aromat.	1	Annihilate, *d, ing.*
9	Ammunition.	2	the enemy.
610	Amnesty.	3	Anniversary, *ies.*
1	Among, *st.*	4	Announce, *d, ing, ment.*
612	Amount, *ed, ing, s.*	655	Annoy, *ance, ed, ing.*

Nos.	ANN	Nos.	ARB
656	Annual, *ly.*	699	Apparel.
7	Annul, *led, ling.*	700	Apparent, *ly.*
8	Anodyne, *s.*	1	altitude.
9	Anomalous, *ly.*	2	diameter.
660	Anomaly, *ies.*	3	distance.
1	Another.	4	time.
2	Answer, *ed, ing, s.*	5	Appeal, *ed, ing.*
3	Ant, *s.*	6	Appear, *ance, ed, ing.*
4	Antagonist, *s, ic.*	7	Appease, *d, ing.*
5	Antagonism.	8	Appellant. *s.*
6	Antarctic.	9	Appellate.
7	Antares.	710	Append, *ed, ing, age.*
8	Ante.	1	Appendix, *ces.*
9	meridian, (A. M.)	2	Appetite, *s.*
670	Antecedent, *s.*	3	Apple, *s.*
1	Anthracite coal.	4	Appliance, *s.*
2	Anti-bilious.	5	Applicable, *ly.*
3	Anticipate, *d, ing, ion.*	6	Applicant, *s.*
4	Antidote, *s.*	7	Application, *s.*
5	Antimonii et pottassæ tart.	8	Apply, *ied, ing.*
6	Antimony.	9	Appoint, *ed, ing, ment, s.*
7	Antipathy, *ies.*	720	Appraise, *ed, r, ment, s.*
8	Anti-scorbutic, *s.*	1	Appreciable, *y.*
9	Anti-septic, *s.*	2	Appreciate, *d, ing, ion.*
680	Anti-spasmodic, *s.*	3	Apprehend, *ed.*
1	Anvil, *s.*	4	Apprentice, *s.*
2	Anxiety, *ies.*	5	Apprise, *d, ing.*
3	Anxious, *ly.*	6	Approach, *ed, ing.*
4	Any.	7	Approbation.
5	Aorta.	8	Appropriate, *ly.*
6	Apartment, *s.*	9	Appropriation, *s.*
7	Apathy.	730	Approval.
8	Apeak.	1	Approve, *d.*
9	Aperient, *s.*	2	Approximate, *d, ing, ly.*
690	Aperture, *s.*	3	Appurtenance, *s.*
1	Apex.	4	April.
2	Apogee.	5	Apron, *s.*
3	Apologize, *ed, ing, s.*	6	Apt, *itude.*
4	Apology, *ies.*	7	Aquarius.
5	Apoplectic.	8	Aqueduct, *s.*
6	Apoplexy.	9	Arbitrarily.
7	Apothecary, *ies.*	740	Arbitrary.
698	Apparatus.	741	signal, *s.*

Nos.	ABC	Nos.	AS
742	Arc, *s.*		Armor, *ed.*
3	of a circle.	785	vessel, *s.*
4	of the heavens.	6	Armorer, *s.*
5	of the horizon.	7	mate, *e.*
6	Arch, *es, ed.*	8	gang, *s.*
7	Archipelago.	9	Armory, *ies.*
8	Archives.	790	Army, *ies.*
9	Arctic.	1	Arnica tinct.
750	coast.	2	Around.
1	ocean.	3	Arraign, *ed, ing, ment.*
2	region.	4	Arrange, *d, ing, ment, s.*
3	Arcturus.	5	Array, *ed, ing.*
4	Ardent, *ly.*	6	Arrear, *s, age.*
5	Arduous, *ly.*	7	Arrest, *ed, ing, s.*
6	Are.	8	Arrive, *d, ing.*
7	all the men.	9	Arrogance.
8	all the officers.	800	Arrogant.
9	all the supplies.	1	Arrogate, *d, ing.*
760	they not.	2	Arrow-root.
1	we not.	3	Arsenal, *s.*
2	you not.	4	Arsenic.
3	Areometer, *s.*	5	Arson.
4	Argand lamp, *s.*	6	Artery, *ies, ial.*
5	Argentine Confederation.	7	Artesian well.
6	Argument, *s.*	8	Articles.
7	Aries.	9	of agreement.
8	Aright.	810	of surrender.
9	Arithmetic, *al, ally.*	1	of trade.
770	Arm.	2	of war.
1	Arm, *ed, ing.*	3	Artifice, *s.*
2	Arms.	4	Artificial, *ly.*
3	Armament, *s.*	5	Artillerist, *s.*
4	of a ship of war.	6	Artillery.
5	of this ship.	7	As.
6	of your vessel.	8	he is.
7	of the strange vessel.	9	he is not.
8	Armature, *s.*	820	I am.
9	Armistice.	1	I am not.
780	agreed upon.	2	I have.
1	will commence.	3	I have not.
2	will expire.	4	I wish to.
3	Armor, *ed.*	5	I do not wish to.
784	plate, *s.*	826	it has been.

Nos.	AS	Nos.	ASS
	As,	869	Ashamed.
827	it has not been.	870	Ashore.
8	it is.	1	Asia, *tic.*
9	it is not.	2	Aside.
830	it may be.	3	Ask, *ed, ing.*
1	it may not be.	4	for information.
2	it ought to be.	5	for news, *papers.*
3	it ought not to be.	6	for what you need.
4	it should be.	7	permission.
5	it should not be.	8	Asleep.
6	it was.	9	Aspect.
7	it was not.	880	Asperity, *ies.*
8	it will be.	1	Asperse, *d, ing.*
9	it will not be.	2	Asphaltum.
840	many.	3	Asphyxia.
1	soon as.	4	Asperiant, *s.*
2	soon as possible.	5	Assail, *ed, ing.*
3	they are.	6	Assailant, *s.*
4	they are not.	7	Assassin, *s, ate, ated.*
5	they will.	8	Assassination.
6	they will not.	9	Assault, *ed, ing, s.*
7	we are.	890	of the army.
8	we are not.	1	of the enemy.
9	we will.	2	of the navy.
850	we will not.	3	of the place.
1	well as.	4	the works.
2	you are.	5	was made.
3	you are not.	6	will be made.
4	you will.	7	Assemblage, *s.*
5	you will not.	8	Assemble, *d, ing.*
6	Asafœtida.	9	Assembly, *ies.*
7	Ascend, *ed, ing, sion.*	900	Assent, *ed, ing.*
8	Ascendant.	1	Assert, *ed, ing, ion.*
9	Ascertain, *ed, ing.*	2	Assess, *ed, ing.*
860	Ash, *es.*	3	Assessment, *s.*
1	boards.	4	Assets.
2	bucket, *s,* or tub, *s.*	5	Assiduity.
3	hole, *s.*	6	Assiduous, *ly.*
4	pan, *s.*	7	Assign, *ed, ment, s.*
5	pit, *s.*	8	Assignee, *s.*
6	plank.	9	Assignor.
7	shoot, *s.*	910	Assimilate, *d, ing.*
868	timber.	911	Assist, *ed, ing, s, ance.*

Nos.	ASS	Nos.	ATE
912	Assistant, *s.*		At,
3	Engineer, *s.*	955	my suggestion.
4	Paymaster, *s.*	6	noon.
5	Secretary of the Navy.	7	once.
6	Secretary of State.	8	quarters.
7	Secretary of the Treasury.	9	slack water.
8	Secretary of War.	960	sunrise.
9	Surgeon, *s.*	1	sunset.
920	Associate, *d, ing.*	2	the expense of.
1	Assuage, *d, ing.*	3	the rendezvous.
2	Assume, *d, ing.*	4	the request of.
3	Assumption, *s.*	5	the same time.
4	Assurance.	6	the suggestion of.
5	Assure, *d, ing, edly.*	7	the time.
6	Astern.	8	the time fixed upon.
7	of the.	9	your convenience.
8	of the danger.	970	your expense.
9	of this division.	1	your service.
930	of the enemy.	2	your suggestion.
1	of the fleet.	3	Athwart.
2	of the line.	4	his hawse.
3	of the squadron.	5	my hawse.
4	of the stranger.	6	our hawse.
5	of this vessel.	7	the channel.
6	Asthma, *tic.*	8	the forefoot.
7	Astonish, *ed, ing, ment.*	9	the line.
8	Astound, *ed, ing.*	980	the line of fire.
9	Astringent, *s.*	1	Athwartships.
940	Astronomer, *s.*	2	Atlantic.
1	Astronomical, *ly.*	3	cable.
2	Astronomy.	4	coast.
3	Asylum.	5	ocean.
4	for the insane.	6	shore.
5	At.	7	squadron.
6	anchor.	8	States.
7	daylight.	9	Atlas, *es.*
8	headquarters.	990	Atmosphere.
9	high water.	1	Atmospheric, *al, ly.*
950	his expense.	2	Atone, *ing, ed, ment, s.*
1	his suggestion.	3	Atrip.
2	low water.	4	Atrocious, *ly.*
3	my own expense.	5	Atrocity.
954	my request.	996	Atrophy.

13

Nos.	ATT	Nos.	AZI
997	Attach, *ed, ing.*	1040	Authority, *ies.*
8	Attaché.	1	Authorize, *d, ing.*
9	Attack, *ed, ing.*	2	Autumn, *al.*
1000	commence, *d.*	3	equinox.
1	cease, *d.*	4	Auxiliary, *ies.*
2	took place at.	5	pump, *s.*
3	will cease.	6	Avail, *ed, ing.*
4	will commence.	7	Available, *ability.*
5	Attain, *ed, able, ment, s.*	8	Avarice, *ious.*
6	Attempt, *s, ed, ing.*	9	Avenge, *d, ing.*
7	Attend, *ed, ing, ance, ant, s.*	1050	Aver, *red, ring.*
8	Attention.	1	Average, *d, ing.*
9	Attentive, *ly.*	2	Averse.
1010	Attest, *ed, ing, ation.*	3	Avert, *ed, ing.*
1	Attitude.	4	Avidity.
2	Attorney, *ies.*	5	Avocation.
3	at law.	6	Avoid, *ed, ing.*
4	for the captor, *s.*	7	Avowal.
5	for the defense.	8	Avowedly.
6	for the Government.	9	Await, *ed, ing.*
7	for the prosecution.	1060	the arrival of.
8	General.	1	the return of.
9	Attract, *ed, ing.*	2	Awake.
1020	Attribute, *d, ing, able.*	3	Award, *ed, ing.*
1	Attrition.	4	Aware.
2	Auction, *eer.*	5	Away.
3	Audacious, *ly.*	6	Aweather.
4	Audacity.	7	Aweigh.
5	Audience, *s.*	8	Awful, *ly.*
6	with the authorities.	9	Awhile.
7	Auditor.	1070	Awkward, *ly, ness.*
8	Auger, *s.*	1	Awl, *s.*
9	Aught.	2	Awning, *s.*
1030	Augment, *ed, ing.*	3	fore and aft.
1	Augmentation.	4	stanchion, *s.*
2	August.	5	Axe, *s.*
3	Aurora australis.	6	handle, *s.*
4	borealis.	7	Axis, *es.*
5	Auspices.	8	Axle.
6	Auspicious, *ly.*	9	Axletree, *s.*
7	Authentic, *ate, ity.*	1080	Azimuth, *al.*
8	Author, *s.*	1	circle.
1039	Authoritative, *ly.*	1082	compass.

Nos.	AZU	Nos.	BAN
	Azimuth, *al.*	1125	Bake, *d, ing.*
1083	of the sun.	6	bread.
4	Azumuthal error.	7	oven, *s.*
5	Babbit, *metal.*	8	Baker, *s.*
6	Back, *ed, ing.*	9	Balance, *d, ing, s.*
7	and fill.	1130	Bale, *s.*
8	an anchor.	1	of cotton.
9	astern.	2	of flannel.
1090	stay, *s.*	3	of goods.
1	stay laniards.	4	of hemp.
2	your anchor.	5	Baleful, *ly.*
3	Backward, *ly, ness.*	6	Balk, *ed, ing.*
4	Bacon.	7	Ball, *s.*
5	Bad, *ly.*	8	and socket joint, *s.*
6	ammunition.	9	cartridge, *s.*
7	anchorage.	1140	cock, *s.*
8	condition.	1	proof.
9	conduct.	2	valves.
1100	lookout.	3	Ballast, *ed, ing.*
1	management,	4	Balloon, *s.*
2	news.	5	Baltic.
3	plan.	6	coast, *s.*
4	Badge, *s.*	7	fleet.
5	of distinction.	8	port, *s.*
6	of honor.	9	Banana, *s.*
7	of rank.	1150	Band, *s.*
8	Baffle, *d, ing.*	1	Band, *ed, ing.*
9	winds.	2	Bandage, *s, ed, ing.*
1110	Bag, *s.*	3	Banding, *plane.*
1	and hammock, *s.*	4	Bandit, *ti.*
2	Baggage.	5	Bane, *ful, fully.*
3	aboard.	6	Banian days.
4	ashore.	7	Banish, *ed, ing.*
5	has arrived.	8	Banishment.
6	has not arrived.	9	Bank, *s.*
7	Bagged.	1160	of clouds.
8	the enemy.	1	of fog.
9	the party.	2	of mud.
1120	Bagging.	3	of Newfoundland.
1	Bail, *ed, ing.*	4	of sand.
2	Bailiff, *s.*	5	your fires.
3	Bait, *ed, ing.*	6	Bank, *ed, ing.*
1124	Baize.	1167	Banked fires.

Nos.	BAR	Nos.	BAT
1168	Bar, *s.*		Barren, *ness.*
9	iron. .	1211	victory.
1170	steel.	2	Barricade, *s, ed, ing.*
1	of iron.	3	Barrier, *s.*
2	of steel.	4	Barrow, *s.*
3	Barred.	5	Barter, *ed, ing.* .
4	harbor.	6	Base, *d, ing, s.*
5	Barbadoes tar.	7	line.
6	Barbaric.	8	of the army.
7	Barbarism, *s.*	9	of the mountain.
8	Barbarity, *ies.*	1220	Basely, *ness.*
9	Barbarous, *ly.*	1	Bashaw, (Pacha.)
1180	Barber, *s.*	2	Basin, *s.*
1	Barbette.	3	Basket, *s.*
2	guns.	4	Bass.
3	Bare.	5	Bass horn.
4	poles.	6	Bastard file, *s.*
5	Barely.	7	Bastion, *ed, s.*
6	enough.	8	Batavian.
7	Bargain, *ed, ing.*	9	Bath, *s.*
8	Barge, *s.* '	1230	brick.
9	crew.	1	room, *s.*
1190	man, *men.* .	2	tub, *s.*
1	Bark, *barque.*	3	Battalion, *s.*
2	Bark, *ed.*	4	drill, *s.*
3	Barley.	5	formation, *s.*
4	Barnacles.	6	of cavalry.
5	Barometer, *s.*	7	of infantry.
6	mercurial.	8	of marines.
7	Barometric.	9	of seamen.
8	Barrack, *s.*	1240	of troops.
9	Barracoon, *s.*	1	Batten, *ed, ing.*
1200	Barrel, *s.*	2	down hatches.
1	of beef.	3	Batter, *ed, ing.*
2	of bread.	4	down the fort.
3	of flour.	5	down the place.
4	of oil.	6	down the town.
5	of pork.	7	Battery, *ies.*
6	of powder.	8	of the enemy.
7	of vegetables.	9	of this ship.
8	shaped.	1250	of your ship.
9	Barren, *ness.*	1	Battle, *s, ed, ing.*
1210	of result.	1252	array.

16

Nos.	BAT	Nos.	BEE
	Battle, *s, ed, ing.*		Bear, *s.*
1253	axe, *s.*	1295	off from the land.
4	axe frog, *s.*	6	up for.
5	field.	7	up under.
6	flag, *s.*	8	Bearing, *s.*
7	Bavarian.	9	a beam.
8	Bay, *s.*	1300	away.
9	shore.	1	down upon.
1260	side.	2	from.
1	steamer, *s.*	3	from me.
2	Bayonette, *s.*	4	is or are.
3	frog, *s.*	5	is or are not on.
4	drill.	6	in with the land.
5	sword.	7	off from the land.
6	Bayou, *s.*	8	of the chase.
7	Be.	9	of the enemy.
8	Beach, *ed, ing.*	1310	of the strange vessel.
9	is flat.	1	Beat, *ing.*
1270	is high.	2	the reveille.
1	is rocky.	3	the tattoo.
2	is sandy.	4	to windward.
3	is wooded.	5	Beaten.
4	Beacon, *s.*	6	the enemy.
5	Bead, *ed, ing.*	7	have beaten.
6	tool, *s.*	8	have been beaten.
7	Beak, *s, ed.*	9	Beautiful, *ly.*
8	iron.	1320	Becalm, *ed.*
9	of iron.	1	Became.
1280	of wood.	2	Because.
1	Beam, *s.*	3	Becket, *s, ed, ing.*
2	compass, *es.*	4	Bed, *ded, ding.*
3	engine, *s.*	5	bug, *s.*
4	ends.	6	clothes.
5	Bean, *s.*	7	plate, *s.*
6	Bear, *s.*	8	Bedaub, *ed, ing.*
7	a beam.	9	Bee block, *s.*
8	a hand.	1330	line.
9	away.	1	Beef, beeves.
1290	down upon.	2	Been.
1	from.	3	Beer.
2	from me.	4	barrels, *s.*
3	from you.	5	Beeswax.
1294	in with the land.	1336	Beet, *s.*

Nos.	BEF	Nos.	BET
1437	Befall, *en, ing.*	1380	Belting.
8	Befit, *ted, ting.*	1	leather.
9	Before.	2	Bench, *es.*
1340	hand.	3	mark, *s.*
1	long.	4	Bend, *s.*
2	now.	5	cable, *s.*
3	the beam.	6	fore and aft sails.
4	the mast.	7	light sails.
5	the wind.	8	sheet cable, *s.*
6	Beg, *ging, ged, s.*	9	square sails.
7	Began.	1390	topsails and courses.
8	Begin.	1	sails.
9	the movement.	2	Benefactor.
1350	Beginner, *s.*	3	Beneficence.
1	Beginning.	4	Beneficent, *ly.*
2	Behalf.	5	Beneficial, *ly.*
3	Behave, *d, ing.*	6	Benefit, *ed, ing.*
4	Behavior.	7	Benevolent, *ly.*
5	Behead, *ed.*	8	Bengal lights.
6	Beheld.	9	Benight, *ed.*
7	Behind.	1400	Bent.
8	hand.	1	plank.
9	time.	2	timber.
1360	the point.	3	Benumb, *ed, ing.*
1	the island, *s.*	4	Benzine.
2	the reef, *s.*	5	Bereave, *d, ing, ment.*
3	Behold.	6	Bereft.
4	Being.	7	Berlin blue.
5	Belaying cleat, *s.*	8	Berth, *ed, ing, s.*
6	pin, *s.*	9	deck.
7	Belie, *d.*	1410	Beseech, *ed, ing.*
8	Belief, *s.*	1	Beset, *ting.*
9	Believe, *ed, ing.*	2	Beside, *s.*
1370	Bell, *s.*	3	Besiege, *d, ing.*
1	buoy.	4	Besieger, *s.*
2	metal.	5	Besought.
3	Belladon., *extract.*	6	Bespeak, *ing.*
4	Belligerent, *s.*	7	Bespoke, *en.*
5	Bellows.	8	Best.
6	leather.	9	Bestial, *ly.*
7	Belong, *ed, ing.*	1420	Bestir.
8	Beloved.	1	Bestow, *ed, ing.*
1379	Below.	1422	Betel, *nut, s.*

Nos.	BET	Nos.	BIT
1423	Betimes.	1466	Bilious.
4	Betray, ed, ing.	7	Bill, s.
5	Betrayal.	8	hook, s.
6	Better.	9	of the anchor.
7	Between.	1470	of exchange.
8	daylight and dark.	1	of fare.
9	decks.	2	of health.
1430	Bevel, ed, ing.	3	of indictment.
1	angle, s.	4	of items.
2	gear, ing.	5	of lading.
3	Bewail, ed, ing.	6	of sale.
4	Beware.	7	Billet, s, ed, ing.
5	Bewilder, ed, ing.	8	head.
6	Bey.	9	moulding.
7	of Tripoli.	1480	Billows.
8	of Tunis.	1	Bimensal.
9	Beyond.	2	reports.
1440	range.	3	returns.
1	Bias, sed, sing.	4	Bind, ing.
2	Bible, s.	5	Binder, s.
3	Bicarbonate, s.	6	Binnacle, s.
4	Bichromate.	7	compass, es.
5	of potash.	8	light, s.
6	Bicker, ing, s.	9	Binocular glass, es.
7	Bickford's fuze, s.	1490	Biographical.
8	Bid, den.	1	dictionary.
9	Bidding.	2	Birch.
1450	Bide.	3	broom.
1	our time.	4	wood.
2	your time.	5	Bird, s.
3	Biennial, ly.	6	eye maple.
4	Big, ger, gest.	7	Birth, s, ing.
5	Bight, s.	8	day.
6	Bile.	9	Biscuit.
7	Bilge, s.	1500	Bisect, ed, ing.
8	cock, s.	1	Bismuth.
9	keel, s.	2	Bisextile year.
1460	keelson, s.	3	Bisulphate.
1	injection, s.	4	Bisulphuret.
2	plank, s.	5	Bit, ten.
3	pump, s.	6	Bite, ing.
4	way, s.	7	Bitter, ly.
1465	water.	1508	Bitumen.

Nos.	BIT	Nos.	BLO
1509	Bituminous coal.	1552	Bless, *ed, ing.*
1510	Bivalve, *s.*	3	Blew.
1	Bivouac.	4	Blight, *ed, ing.*
2	Bi-weekly.	5	Blind, *ed, ing.*
3	Black.	6	Blindly.
4	book, *s.*	7	Blindness.
5	flag, *s.*	8	Bliss, *ful, fully.*
6	lead.	9	Blister, *ed, ing.*
7	paint.	1560	steel.
8	smith, *s.*	1	Bloat, *ed.*
9	smith's forge.	2	Block, *ed, ing.*
1520	smith's tools.	3	house.
1	smith's work.	4	of wood.
2	varnish.	5	maker.
3	vomit.	6	tin.
4	Blacking.	7	Blockade, *d, ing.*
5	Bladder, *s.*	8	coast, *s.*
6	Blade, *s.*	9	harbor, *s.*
7	Blameable.	1570	runner, *s.*
8	Blame, *d, ing.*	1	Blockader, *s.*
9	Blameless.	2	Blood, *y.*
1530	Bland, *ness.*	3	Bloodshed.
1	Blandish, *ed, ing, ment, s.*	4	Blood vessel, *s.*
2	Blank, *s.*	5	Blot, *ted, ting.*
3	book, *s.*	6	Blow.
4	cartridge, *s.*	7	down boilers.
5	form, *s.*	8	off steam.
6	return, *s.*	9	off pipe.
7	Blanket, *s.*	1580	over.
8	Blaspheme, *d, ing.*	1	up.
9	Blasphemous.	2	valve, *s.*
1540	Blasphemy, *ies.*	3	Blower, *s.*
1	Blast, *ed, ing.*	4	engine, *s.*
2	furnace.	5	Blowing.
3	of a horn.	6	fresh.
4	of a or the steam whistle.	7	heavy, *ily.*
5	Blaze, *d, ing.*	8	too hard.
6	Bleach, *ed, ing.*	9	Blown.
7	Bleak, *ness, ly.*	1590	away.
8	Bled.	1	down.
9	Bleed, *ing.*	2	off shore.
1550	Blemish, *s, ed.*	3	over.
1551	Blend, *ed, ing.*	1594	up.

Nos.	BLU	Nos.	BOM
1595	Blue.		Boat, *s.*
6	bunting.	1638	signal, *s.*
7	cloth, *es.*	9	Boatswain, *s.*
8	flag, *s.*	1640	call, *s.*
9	flannel, *s.*	1	gang, *s.*
1600	light, *s.*	2	mate, *s.*
1	mass.	3	stores.
2	water.	4	Bobstay, *s.*
3	vitriol.	5	carried away.
4	Bluff, *s.*	6	laniard, *s.*
5	point.	7	plate, *s.*
6	Blunder, *ed, ing, s.*	8	Body, *ies.*
7	Blunt, *ed.*	9	Bog, *s, gy.*
8	Board.	1650	Boil, *s.*
9	of examiners.	1	Boiled.
1610	of survey.	2	linseed oil.
1	of trade.	3	Boiler, *s.*
2	of underwriters.	4	corrosion.
3	the enemy.	5	covering.
4	Boarders.	6	explosion.
5	Boarding.	7	iron.
6	boat, *s.*	8	jacket.
7	cutlass, *es.*	9	maker, *s.*
8	grapnel, *s.*	1660	plate, *s.*
9	netting, *s.*	1	scale.
1620	officer, *s.*	2	tube, *s.*
1	pike, *s.*	3	washer, *s.*
2	pistol, *s.*	4	Boiling.
3	Boat, *s.*	5	water.
4	anchor, *s.*	6	Boisterous, *ly.*
5	awning, *s.*	7	Bold, *ly, ness.*
6	capsized.	8	affair.
7	carriage, *s.*	9	shore.
8	crew, *s.*	1670	Boldest.
9	cushion, *s.*	1	Bolster, *s, ed, ing.*
1630	davit, *s.*	2	Bolt, *s, ed, ing.*
1	fall, *s.*	3	auger, *s.*
2	flag, *s.*	4	head, *s.*
3	grapnel, *s.*	5	iron.
4	hook, *s.*	6	of canvas.
5	howitzer, *s.*	7	rope, *s.*
6	lowering apparatus	8	Bomb, *s.*
1637	recall, *s.*	1679	proof, *s.*

Nos.	BOM	Nos.	BRA
	Bomb, *s.*	1721	Bound.
1680	shell, *s.*	2	down.
1	vessel, *s.*	3	eastward.
2	Bombard, *ed, ing.*	4	home.
3	'Bombardment.	5	in.
4	Bone, *s.*	6	on a cruise.
5	black.	7	out.
6	Bonfire, *s.*	8	north.
7	Bonnet.	9	south.
8	Booby.	1730	to.
9	Booby-hatch.	1	up.
1690	Book, *s.*	2	westward.
1	Boom, *s.*	3	Boundary, *ies.*
2	boat, *s.*	4	Boundless.
3	cover, *s.*	5	Bounty, *ies.*
4	foresail, *s.*	6	Bow.
5	iron, *s.*	7	and quarter.
6	mainsail.	8	and stern.
7	tackle, *s.*	9	chaser, *s.*
8	topping lift, *s.*	1740	line, *s.*
9	Boot, *s.*	1	timber, *s.*
1700	topping.	2	Bowels.
1	Booth, *s.*	3	Bower.
2	Booty.	4	anchor, *s.*
3	Borax.	5	cable, *s.*
4	Bore, *d, ing.*	6	Bowline, *s.*
5	Boring bitts.	7	bridle, *s.*
6	tools.	8	knot, *s.*
7	Bormann fuse, *s.*	9	' well out.
8	Born.	1750	Bowse, *ed.*
9	Borne.	1	Bowsprit.
1710	Borrow, *ed.*	2	'bees.
1	Botch, *ed, ing.*	3	bed.
2	Both.	4	cap.
3	bowers.	5	gammoning.
4	watches.	6	heel.
5	Bottle, *d, ing.*	7	is sprung.
6	Bottom.	8	saddle.
7	blow valve.	9	shrouds.
8	injection.	1760	netting.
9	Bought.	1	Boy, *s.*
1720	Boulder, *s.*	2	Brace, *d, ing, s.*
		1763	aback.

3

Nos.	BRA	Nos.	BRE
	Brace, *d, ing, s.*		Break, *ing.*
1764	about.	1806	ground.
5	block, *s.*	7	out.
6	by.	8	through the line, *s.*
7	pendant, *s.*	9	through the obstruction, *s.*
8	sharp up.	1810	Breakwater.
9	Brackish water.	1	Breaker, *s.*
1770	Brad, *s.*	2	ahead.
1	awl, *s.*	3	are seen to the.
2	Brail, *ed, ing.*	4	bear to the.
3	up the.	5	Breakfast, *ed, ing.*
4	Brain, *s.*	6	at daylight.
5	fever.	7	early.
6	Branch, *es, ed, ing.*	8	late.
7	of the stream.	9	with.
8	Brand, *s, ed, ing.*	1820	with me.
9	Brandy, *ies.*	1	with you.
1780	Brass.	2	Breast, *ed, ing.*
1	Brave.	3	deep.
2	Bravely.	4	fast, *s.*
3	Bravery.	5	high.
4	Braze, *d, ing.*	6	hook, *s.*
5	Brazier.	7	Breastwork, *s.*
6	Brazing solder.	8	Breath.
7	tool, *s.*	9	Breathless.
8	Brazilian, *s.*	1830	Breathe, *d, ing.*
9	Breach, *ed, ing.*	1	Breech, *ed.*
1790	in the wall.	2	heavy.
1	of the peace.	3	piece, *s.*
2	the wall.	4	pin, *s.*
3	Bread.	5	loader, *s.*
4	bag, *s.*	6	Breeching, *s.*
5	barrel, *s.*	7	Breed, *ing.*
6	room, *s.*	8	Breeze, *s.*
7	oven, *s.*	9	Breezing.
8	pans.	1840	Brevet, *ed, ing, s.*
9	Breadth.	1	1st Lieutenant.
1800	of the bay.	2	Captain.
1	of beam.	3	Major.
2	of the channel.	4	Lt. Colonel.
3	of the stream.	5	Colonel.
4	Break, *ing.*	6	Brig. General.
1805	bulk.	1847	Major General.

Nos.	BRE	Nos.	BUL
	Brevet, *ed, ing, s.*	1890	Broach, *ed, ing.*
1848	rank.	1	to.
9	Bribe, *d, ing, s.*	2	Broad.
1850	Bribery, *ies.*	3	axe, *s.*
1	Brick, *s.*	4	bay.
2	Bridal port, *s.*	5	mouth, *ed.*
3	Bridge, *d, ing, s.*	6	off.
4	Bridle, *s.*	7	off the bow.
5	Brief, *ly.*	8	pendant, *s.*
6	Brig, *s.*	9	side.
7	Brigantine, *s.*	1900	side guns.
8	Brigade, *s.*	1	sword exercise.
9	of artillery.	2	Broke, *n.*
1860	of cavalry.	3	backed.
1	of infantry.	4	Bronchial.
2	Brigadier, *s.*	5	Bronchitis.
3	Brigand, *s.*	6	Bronze, *d, ing.*
4	Bright.	7	powder.
5	light, *s.*	8	liquid.
6	Bright's disease.	9	Broom, *s.*
7	Brilliant, *ly.*	1910	Brought.
8	Brine.	1	Brow.
9	cock, *s.*	2	of the hill.
1870	pan, *s.*	3	Brown.
1	pump, *s.*	4	Bruise, *d, ing.*
2	Bring, *ing.*	5	Brunswick green.
3	back.	6	Brunt.
4	in.	7	Brush, *ed, ing.*
5	me.	8	Brushwood.
6	off.	9	Brushes.
7	out.	1920	Brutal, *ly.*
8	the.	1	Brutality.
9	them.	2	Bucket, *s.*
1880	to.	3	Bucklers.
1	Brink.	4	Buckskin, *s.*
2	Bristle, *s.*	5	Buff, *er, s.*
3	Bristol board.	6	Bugbear.
4	British.	7	Bugle, *s.*
5	flag.	8	Bugler, *s.*
6	goods.	9	Building, *s.*
7	interests.	1930	Built.
8	vessel, *s.*	1	Bulk, *y.*
1889	Brittle, *ness.*	1932	Bulkhead, *s.*

Nos.	BUL	Nos.	CAB
1933	Bulls-eye, *s.*		Bureau, *x.*
4	Bullet, *s.*	1976	of Steam Engineering.
5	mould, *s.*	7	of Yards and Docks.
6	proof.	8	Burglar, *s.*
7	Bullion.	9	Burglary, *ies.*
8	Bullock, *s.*	1980	Burial.
9	Bulwark, *s.*	1	ground, *s.*
1940	Bumpkin, *s, boomkin, s.*	2	service.
1	Bung, *s.*	3	of the dead.
2	Bungle, *d, ing, ly.*	4	Buried.
3	Bunk, *s.*	5	Burn, *ed, ing.*
4	Bunker, *s.*	6	Burnish, *ed, ing.*
5	Bunt, *s.*	7	Burst, *ing.*
6	cloth, *s.*	8	Burton, *s.*
7	gasket, *s.*	9	Bury.
8	jigger, *s.*	1990	the dead.
9	line, *s.*	1	Bush, *ed, ing.*
1950	line block, *s.*	2	Bushes.
1	whip, *s.*	3	Bushel, *s.*
2	Bunting.	4	Business.
3	black.	5	like manner.
4	blue.	6	hours.
5	green.	7	Busy, *ily.*
6	red.	8	But.
7	white.	9	Butcher, *ing.*
8	yellow.	2000	Butter.
9	Buoy, *s.*	1	Butt, *s.*
1960	black.	2	hinges.
1	red.	3	Butter-fly valve, *s.*
2	vertical striped.	4	Butting joint, *s.*
3	is in sight.	5	Button, *s.*
4	is not in sight.	6	Navy, large size.
5	does not watch.	7	Navy, medium size.
6	Buoyancy.	8	Navy, small size.
7	Buoyant, *ly.*	9	horn or bone.
8	Buoyed, *ing.*	2010	Buttress, *ed.*
9	Bureau, *x.*	1	Buy, *ing.*
1970	of Construction and Repair.	2	By.
1	of Equipment and Recruiting.	3	and by.
2	of Medicine and Surgery.	4	the wind.
3	of Navigation and Detail.	5	Cabal, *s.*
4	of Ordnance.	6	Cabbage, *s.*
1975	of Provisions and Clothing.	2017	Cabin, *s.*

25

Nos.	CAB	Nos.	CAN
	Cabin, *s.*	2060	Cam, *s.*
2018	boy, *s.*	1	movement, *s.*
9	cook, *s.*	2	Cambric.
2020	furniture.	3	Came.
1	mess, *es.*	4	Camel, *s.*
2	steward, *s.*	5	hair pencils.
3	stove, *s.*	6	Camp; *s, ed, ing.*
4	Cabinet.	7	bed, *s, ding.*
5	council.	8	equipage.
6	minister, *s.*	9	fire, s.
7	Cable, *s.*	2070	ground, *s.*
8	bitt, *s.*	1	kettle, *s.*
9	laid.	2	stool, *s.*
2030	laid rope.	3	Campaign.
1	length, *s.*	4	Camphene.
2	shackle, *s.*	5	lamp, *s.*
3	stopper, *s.*	6	Camphor.
4	swivel, *s.*	7	Can.
5	tier, *s.*	8	buoy, *s.*
6	Caboose, *camboose.*	9	hooks.
7	Cairn, *s.*	2080	reach.
8	Caisson, *s.*	1	see.
9	Calaboose.	2	spare.
2040	Calamitous.	3	the army?
1	Calamity, *ies.*	4	the fleet?
2	Calcine, *d, ing.*	5	the enemy?
3	Calcium light, *s.*	6	they not?
4	Calculate, *d, ing.*	7	we not?
5	Calculation, *s.*	8	you not?
6	Calendar, *s.*	9	you see?
7	Calf skin, *s.*	2090	Cannot.
8	Calibre, *s.*	1	reach.
9	Caliper, *s.*	2	see.
2050	compasses.	3	spare.
1	Call, *ed, ing.*	4	the army?
2	Calls, boatswains.	5	the fleet?
3	Callous, *ly.*	6	the enemy?
4	Calm, *s, ly.*	7	your vessel?
5	latitude, *s.*	8	Canadian, *s.*
6	weather.	9	Canal, *s.*
7	Calomel.	2100	boat, *s.*
8	Calumniate, *d, ing, ion.*	1	lock, *s.*
2059	Calumny, *ies.*	2102	Cancel, *led, ling.*

26

Nos.	CAN	Nos.	CAR
2103	Cancer, *s, ous.*	2146	Capricorn.
4	Candid, *ly.*	7	Capsici, tinct.
5	Candle, *s.*	8	Capsize, *d, ing.*
6	for running light lanterns.	9	Capstan, *s.*
7	moulds.	2150	bar, *s.*
8	Canister.	1	head.
9	Cannel coal.	2	pawl, *s.*
2110	Cannibal, *s, ism.*	3	spindle, *s.*
1	Cannon.	4	whelps.
2	ball, *s.*	5	Capsule, *s.*
3	range.	6	Captain, *s.*
4	Cannonade, *d, ing.*	7	boat.
5	Canoe, *s.*	8	General.
6	Canopus.	9	of the fleet.
7	Cant.	2160	of the merchantman.
8	hook, *s.*	1	of this ship.
9	lever, *s.*	2	of the vessel.
2120	timber, *s.*	3	of the yard.
1	Canted, *ing.*	4	Captious, *ly.*
2	Canteen, *s.*	5	Captive, *s.*
3	Cantharidis, pulv.	6	Captor, *s.*
4	tinct.	7	Capture, *s, d, ing.*
5	cerat.	8	Captured.
6	Cantonment, *s.*	9	boat, *s.*
7	Canvas.	2170	vessel, *s.*
8	cotton.	1	Car, *s.*
9	hemp.	2	Carbine, *s.*
2130	Caoutchouc.	3	ammunition.
1	Cap, *s.*	4	Carbolic acid.
2	cover, *s.*	5	Carbonic acid.
3	ornament, *s.*	6	Carbuncle.
4	ribbon, *s.*	7	Carbureted hydrogen.
5	shore, *s.*	8	Carcass, *es.*
6	square, *s.*	9	Card, *s.*
7	Capability, *ies.*	2180	Care, *d, ing.*
8	Capable.	1	Careen, *ed, ing.*
9	Capacious.	2	Career.
2140	Capacity, *ies.*	3	Careful, *ly.*
1	Cape, *s.*	4	Careless, *ly, ness.*
2	Capital.	5	Cargo, *es.*
3	punishment, *s.*	6	Carling, *s.*
4	Capitulate, *d, ing.*	7	Carmine.
2145	Capitulation.	2188	Carnage.

27

Nos.	CAR	Nos.	CAU
2189	Carouse, *ing.*		Cast, *ing.*
2190	Carpenter, *s.*	2232	to starboard.
1	gang, *s.*	3	Castigate, *d, ing.*
2	mate, *s.*	4	Castle, *s.*
3	tool, *s.*	5	Castor and Pollux.
4	work.	6	Castor oil.
5	Carpet, *s, ed.*	7	Casual, *ly.*
6	Carriage, *s.*	8	Casualty, *ies.*
7	Carrier, *s.*	9	Cat, *ted, ting.*
8	Carronade, *s.*	2240	Catback.
9	Carrot, *s.*	1	Catblock, *s.*
2200	Carry, *ies, ied, ing.*	2	Catface, *s.*
1	all sail.	3	Catgut.
2	away.	4	Catharpin, *s.*
3	Carrying trade.	5	Cathead, *s.*
4	Cart, *s, ed, ing.*	6	Catstopper, *s.*
5	Carte blanche.	7	Catalepsy.
6	Cartel, *s.*	8	Catalogue, *s.*
7	Cartilage, *s.*	9	Catamaran.
8	Cartridge, *s.*	2250	Catarrh, *s, al.*
9	box.	1	Catastrophe.
2210	cylinder.	2	Catch, *ing.*
1	paper.	3	Catechize, *d, ing.*
2	Carvel built boat.	4	Categorical.
3	Cascable, *s.*	5	Cater, *s, ed, ing.*
4	pin, *s.*	6	Caterer, *s.*
5	Case, *s, d.*	7	Cathartic, *s.*
6	Casemate, *ed.*	8	Catheter, *s.*
7	Case shot.	9	Catoptric, *s.*
8	Casing.	2260	Cattle.
9	Cash.	1	Caught.
2220	account, *s.*	2	Caulk, *ed, ing.*
1	book, *s.*	3	Caulker, *s.*
2	on hand.	4	gang, *s.*
3	Cashier, *ed, ing.*	5	Caulking.
4	Cask, *s.*	6	iron, *s.*
5	Cast, *ing.*	7	mallet, *s.*
6	away.	8	material, *s.*
7	iron.	9	Cause, *s, ed, ing.*
8	off.	2270	Caustic.
9	of the lead.	1	Cauterize, *d, ing.*
2230	steel.	2	Caution, *ed, ing.*
2231	to port.	2273	Cautious, *ly.*

28

Nos.	CAV	Nos.	CHA
2274	Cavalry.		Centre, *d, ing.*
5	arm, *s.*	2317	of metal.
6	camp, *s.*	8	of oscillation.
7	charge.	9	of percussion.
8	division, *s.*	2320	squadron.
9	Cavity, *ies.*	1	vessel.
2280	Cayenne pepper.	2	Century, *ies.*
1	Cease.	3	Ceremonial, *s.*
2	exercise, *s.*	4	Ceremony, *ies.*
3	firing.	5	Ceremonious, *ly.*
4	operations.	6	Certain, *ly, ty.*
5	Ceaseless, *ly.*	7	Certificate, *s.*
6	Cedar, *s.*	8	Certify, *ied, ing.*
7	log, *s.*	9	Cessation.
8	lumber.	2330	Chafe, *d, ing.*
9	timber.	1	Chafing gear.
2290	Cede, *d, ing.*	2	Chagrin, *ed.*
1	Celebrate, *d, ing.*	3	Chain, *s.*
2	anniversary.	4	armor, *ed.*
3	the day.	5	bolt, *s.*
4	Celebration, *s.*	6	cable, *s.*
5	Celebrity, *ies.*	7	compressor, *s.*
6	Celerity.	8	hook, *s.*
7	Cell, *s.*	9	locker, *s.*
8	Cemetery, *ies.*	2340	messenger, *s.*
9	Censorious, *ly, ness.*	1	plate, *s.*
2300	Censure, *d, ing.*	2	pump, *s.*
1	Census.	3	slings.
2	Cent, *s.*	4	stopper, *s.*
3	Centennial.	5	Chair, *s.*
4	Centigrade.	6	Chalk.
5	scale.	7	Chamber, *s.*
6	thermometer.	8	of commerce.
7	Central, *ly.*	9	Chambered gun, *s.*
8	Centralize, *d, ing.*	2350	Chamfer, *ed, ing.*
9	Centre, *d, ing.*	1	Chamois leather.
2310	bitt, *s.*	2	Chance, *s, ed, ing.*
1	boss.	3	of defeat.
2	column.	4	of success.
3	— division.	5	Chancre, *s.*
4	of attraction.	6	Change, *d, ing.*
5	of displacement.	7	of plan.
2316	of gravity.	2358	of formation.

Nos.	CHA	Nos.	CHI
	Change, d, ing.		Chase, d, ing.
2359	of wind.	2401	bore.
2360	of course.	2	gun, s.
1	of station or position.	3	the enemy.
2	of circumstances.	4	the strange vessel.
3	Changes.	5	Chaser, s.
4	Channel, s.	6	Chastise, d, ing.
5	buoy, s.	7	Cheap, er, est.
6	is narrow.	8	Cheaply.
7	is wide.	9	Cheat, ed, ing.
8	range, s.	2410	Check, ed, ing.
9	plates.	1	the enemy.
2370	Chapeau, x.	2	valve, s.
1	Chapel.	3	Check block, s.
2	Chapelling.	4	Cheer, s, ing, ed.
3	Chaplain, s.	5	ship.
4	Character, s.	6	Cheerful, ly, ness.
5	of the stranger, s.	7	Cheese.
6	Characterize, d, ing.	8	Chemical, ly.
7	Charcoal.	9	Chess-tree, s.
8	drying stove, s.	2420	Chevaux de frise.
9	Charges.	1	Chew, ed, ing, s.
2380	Charge, d, ing.	2	Chiccory.
1	Chargé d'affaires.	3	Chicken, s.
2	Charitable.	4	Chide, chid, chidden.
3	Charity, ies.	5	Chiding.
4	Chart, s.	6	Chief, s.
5	of the.	7	Chiefly.
6	of the coast of.	8	Chigre, s.
7	of this coast.	9	Chilblain, s.
8	of the bay of.	2430	Child.
9	of this bay.	1	Children.
2390	of the harbor of.	2	Chilian, s.
1	of this harbor.	3	Chill, ing, ed.
2	of the place.	4	shot.
3	of the locality.	5	Chills and fevers.
4	of this locality.	6	Chin.
5	of the world.	7	China.
6	Charter, ed, ing.	8	ware.
7	Chartered vessel, s.	9	Chinese.
8	Charter party.	2440	Chip, ped, ping, s.
9	Chase, d, ing.	1	Chisel, led, ling, s.
2400	bear, s.	2442	Chivalric.

Nos.	CHI	Nos.	CLA
2443	Chivalry.	2486	Cinnamon.
4	Chloride.	7	Cipher.
5	of lime.	8	Circle, *s, ed, ing.*
6	Chlorine.	9	Circuit, *ous.*
7	Chloroform.	2490	Circular, *s.*
8	Chock, *s.*	1	Circulate, *d, ing.*
9	of the bowsprit.	2	Circulation.
2450	of the rudder.	3	Circumference.
1	Chocolate.	4	Circumnavigate, *d, ing.*
2	Choice.	5	Circumpolar.
3	Choke, *d, ing.*	6	Circumscribe, *d, ing.*
4	Cholera.	7	Circumspect, *ly.*
5	morbus.	8	Circumstance, *s.*
6	Choose.	9	Circumstantial, *ly.*
7	Chop, *s, ped, ing.*	2500	Circumvallation.
8	Chopping block.	1	Circumvent, *ed, ing.*
9	sea.	2	Cirro cumulus.
2460	Chose, *en.*	3	Cirro stratus.
1	Chow-chow water.	4	Cirrus.
2	Christendom.	5	Cistern, *s.*
3	Christian, *s, ity, ize, ed.*	6	Citizen, *s.*
4	name.	7	Citizenship.
5	Christmas.	8	Citrate.
6	Chrome.	9	Citric acid.
7	green.	2510	City, *ies.*
8	orange.	1	authorities.
9	yellow.	2	court, *s.*
2470	Chronic.	3	government.
1	disease, *s.*	4	limits.
2	Chronometer, *s.*	5	Civil.
3	box, *es.*	6	authority, *ies.*
4	error.	7	court, *s.*
5	rate.	8	war, *s.*
6	time.	9	Civilize, *ed.*
7	Church.	2520	Civilization.
8	Churl, *ish.*	1	Civilian, *s.*
9	Churlishness.	2	Civility, *ies.*
2480	Cicatrize, *d, ing.*	3	Clack valve, *s.*
1	Cider.	4	Claim, *ed, ing, s.*
2	Cigar, *s.*	5	Claimant, *s.*
3	shaped.	6	Claim, *s.*
4	Cinder, *s.*	7	Clamor, *ed, ing.*
2485	Cinnabar.	2528	Clamorous, *ly.*

Nos.	CLA	Nos.	COA
2529	Clamp, *ed, ing.*	2571	Close.
2530	Claret wine.	2	aboard.
1	Clarify, *ied, ing.*	3	harbor.
2	Clash, *ed, ing.*	4	hauled.
3	Clasp, *ed, ing.*	5	order.
4	knife.	6	quarters.
5	Class, *ed, ing, es.*	7	reefed.
6	Classify, *ied, ing.*	8	in with the enemy.
7	Clause, *s.*	9	Closed, *ing.*
8	Clavicle.	2530	Closer.
9	Claw, *ed, ing.*	1	order.
2540	hammer.	2	quarters.
1	Claw off if possible.	3	to the shore.
2	Clay.	4	to the wind.
3	Clean, *ed, ing.*	5	Clothe, *s, d.*
4	bill of health.	6	Clothes line, *s.*
5	Cleanly.	7	Clothing.
6	Cleanliness.	8	Cloud, *s.*
7	Cleanse, *d, ing.*	9	Cloudy.
8	Clear, *ed, ing.*	2590	Club, *bed, bing.*
9	for action.	1	haul, *ed.*
2550	the land.	2	Clue, *s.*
1	the wreck.	3	Clump, *s.*
2	Cleat, *s.*	4	Clumsily.
3	Clemency.	5	Clumsy.
4	Clement, *ly.*	6	Cook, *s.*
5	Clergy, *man, men.*	7	Cooking.
6	Clerkship, *s.*	8	Cooking stove, *s.*
7	Clevis.	9	Coal, *s.*
8	Clew, *s, ed, ing.*	2600	anthracite.
9	Clew down.	1	bag, *s.*
2560	Clew garnets.	2	basket, *s.*
1	Clew lines.	3	blacksmith's.
2	Clew up.	4	bituminous.
3	Cliff's.	5	bucket, *s.*
4	Climate.	6	bunker, *s.*
5	Clinch, *ed, ing.*	7	cannel.
6	Cling.	8	cart, *s.*
7	Clung.	9	dust.
8	Clinker built boat, *s.*	2610	heaver, *s.*
9	Clip, *ped, ping.*	1	is bad.
2570	Clipper built vessel.	2	is good.
		2613	is nearly out.

Nos.	COA	Nos.	COM
	Coal, *s.*	2656	Cold weather.
2614	remaining.	7	Coldly.
5	shovels.	8	Colic.
6	tar.	9	Collapse, *ed, ing.*
7	trimmers.	2660	Collar, *ed, ing.*
8	vessel, *s.*	1	beam.
9	yard.	2	bone.
2620	Coaming, *s.*	3	Collation, *s.*
1	Coarse, *ness, ly.*	4	Collect, *ed, ing, ion.*
2	Coast, *ed, ing.*	5	Collective, *ly.*
3	Coast pilot, *s.*	6	Collide, *d, ing.*
4	Coaster, *s.*	7	Collision, *s.*
5	Coat, *s.*	8	Collodion.
6	of paint.	9	Collude, *d, ing.*
7	of varnish.	2670	Collusion.
8	Coating.	1	Colonel, *s, cy.*
9	Coax, *ed, ing.*	2	Colonial.
2630	Cock, *s.*	3	Colonist.
1	Cockpit.	4	Colonize, *d, ing.*
2	Cockroaches.	5	Colony, *ies.*
3	Cocoa.	6	Color, *ed, ing, s.*
4	Codfish.	7	Color guard.
5	Codlines.	8	Colorless.
6	Code.	9	Color sergeant.
7	of laws.	2680	Colt, *s.*
8	of signals.	1	carbine, *s.*
9	Coerce, *d, ing.*	2	Navy revolver, *s.*
2640	Coercion.	3	revolving rifle, *s.*
1	Coffee.	4	Colombia, *n.*
2	Coffee mill, *s.*	5	Columbiad, *s.*
3	Coffee pot, *s.*	6	Column, *s.*
4	Coffee, give to the men.	7	of companies.
5	Cofferdam, *s.*	8	of divisions.
6	Coffin, *s.*	9	of regiments.
7	Cognizant, *ance.*	2690	of squadrons.
8	Coil, *s, ed, ing.*	1	of twos.
9	Coin, *s.*	2	of threes.
2650	Coinage.	3	Colza oil.
1	Coincide, *d, ing.*	4	Combat, *ted, ting, s.*
2	Coincidence.	5	Combatant, *s.*
3	Coincident.	6	Combination, *s.*
4	Coke.	7	Combine, *d, ing.*
2655	Cold, *er, est.*	2698	Combustible, *s,*

Nos.	COM	Nos.	CON
2699	Combustion.	2742	Compass, *es.*
2700	Come, *in, g.*	3	bearing, *s.*
1	as soon as.	4	card, *s.*
2	near, *er.*	5	course, *s.*
3	on board.	6	deviation.
4	to an anchor.	7	variation of.
5	Comet, *s.*	8	Compel, *led, ling.*
6	Comfort, *ed, ing.*	9	Compensate, *d, ing, ion.*
7	Comfortable.	2750	Compete, *d, ing.*
8	Comity.	1	Competent.
9	Command, *s, ed, ing.*	2	Competition.
2710	Commandant.	3	Competitor, *s.*
1	of the station.	4	Complain, *ed, ing, t, s.*
2	of the yard.	5	Complainant, *s.*
3	Commander-in-Chief.	6	Complement, *s.*
4	Commemorate, *d, ing.*	7	of men.
5	Commence, *d, ing.*	8	of officers.
6	coaling.	9	of stores.
7	firing.	2760	Complete, *d, ing, ion, ly.*
8	Commencement.	1	Complicate, *d, ing.*
9	Commend, *ed, ing.*	2	Complicity.
2720	Commendable, *ly.*	3	Compliment, *ary, ed, ing, s.*
1	Comment, *ed, ing.*	4	Comply, *ing, ied.*
2	Commercial, *ly.*	5	Component.
3	code of signals.	6	Composition, *s.*
4	Commiserate, *d, ing, ion.*	7	nails.
5	Commission, *ed, ing, s.*	8	Comprehend, *ed, ing.*
6	officer, *s.*	9	Comprehensive.
7	Commit, *ted, ting.*	2770	Compressor, *s.*
8	Commodious, *ly.*	1	stopper, *s.*
9	Commodore, *s.*	2	Comprise, *d, ing.*
2730	barge.	3	Compromise, *d, ing, s.*
1	command.	4	Comptrol, *ler.*
2	pendant.	5	of the Treasury.
3	Commotion.	6	Compulsion.
4	Communicate, *d, ing.*	7	Compulsory.
5	Commute, *d, ing.*	8	Compute, *d, ing.*
6	Companion, *s.*	9	Con, *ned, ing.*
7	Company, *ies.*	2780	Conceal, *ed, ing, ment.*
8	Comparative, *ly.*	1	Conceive, *d, ing.*
9	Compare, *d, ing, ison.*	2	Concentrate, *d, ing.*
2740	watch.	3	fire.
2741	Compartment, *s.*	2784	forces.

Nos.	CON	Nos.	CON
2785	Concern, *ed, ing.*	2828	Conjuncture.
6	Concert, *ed, ing.*	9	Connect, *ed, ing.*
7	Conciliate, *d, ing, ion.*	2830	Connecting rod, *s.*
8	Concise, *ly, ness.*	1	link, *s.*
9	Conclude, *d, ing.*	2	Connive, *d, ing, ance.*
2790	Conclusion, *s.*	3	Conquer, *ed, ing, or, s.*
1	Conclusive.	4	Conscience, *tious, ly.*
2	Concord.	5	Conscious, *ness.*
3	Condemn, *ed, ing, ation.*	6	Consecutive, *ly.*
4	Condensation.	7	Consent, *ed, ing.*
5	of steam.	8	Consequence, *s, t, ly.*
6	Condense, *d, ing.*	9	Consider, *ed, ing, ation.*
7	apparatus.	2840	Considerable, *ly.*
8	Condenser, *s.*	1	Consist, *ed, ing.*
9	surface.	2	Consistent, *ly.*
2800	jet.	3	Console, *d, ing.*
1	Condition, *s, al, ally.*	4	Consolidate, *d, ing, ion.*
2	Conduce, *d, ing.*	5	Consonant, *ly.*
3	Conduct, *ed, ing.*	6	Consort, *ed, ing, s.*
4	Conduct book.	7	Conspicuous, *ly.*
5	Confer, *red, ring, ence.*	8	Conspiracy, *ies.*
6	Confess, *ed, ing, ion.*	9	Conspirator, *s.*
7	Confide, *d, ing.*	2850	Conspire, *d, ing.*
8	Confidence.	1	Constant, *ly.*
9	Confident, *ly, ial.*	2	Consternation.
2810	Confine, *d, ing.*	3	Constipate, *d, ing, ion.*
1	Confinement.	4	Constitute, *d, ing.*
2	Confirm, *ed, ing.*	5	Constitution.
3	Confiscate, *d, ing.*	6	Constrain, *ed, ing.*
4	Confiscation.	7	Constraint.
5	Conflict, *ed, ing.*	8	Construct, *ed, ing.*
6	Confluence.	9	Constructor, *s,*
7	Confluent small pox.	2860	Construction.
8	Conform, *ed, ing, ity, able.*	1	Construe, *d, ing.*
9	Confuse, *d, ing, ion.*	2	Consul, *s.*
2820	Confute, *d, ing.*	3	Consul General.
1	Congeal, *ed, ing, ation.*	4	Consulate.
2	Congest, *ed, ing, ion.*	5	Consult, *ed, ing.*
3	Congratulate, *d, ing, ion.*	6	Consultation, *s.*
4	Congress, *ional.*	7	Consume, *d, ing.*
5	of the U. S.	8	Consummate, *d, ing.*
6	Congreve rocket, *s.*	9	Consumption.
2827	Conjecture, *d, ing.*	2870	of coal.

Nos.	CON	Nos.	COR
	Consumption.	2913	Conveyance, *s.*
2871	of oil.	4	Convict, *ed, ing, ion, s.*
2	of provisions.	5	Convince, *d, ing.*
3	of supplies.	6	Convoy, *ed, ing.*
4	of water.	7	Convulsion, *s.*
5	Contagion.	8	Cook, *s, ed, ing.*
6	Contagious.	9	Cool, *ed, ing.*
7	Contemplate, *d, ing.*	2920	Cooler.
8	Contempt.	1	Coop, *s.*
9	Contend, *ed, ing.*	2	Cooper, *ed, ing, s, age.*
2880	Content, *ed, ing.*	3	.adze.
1·	Contention, *s.*	4	tools.
2	Contentious.	5	Coöperate, *d, ing, ion.*
3	Contentment.	6	Copaiba.
4	Contest, *ed, ing.*	7	Copal varnish.
5	Contingent, *ly.*	8	Copious, *ly.*
6	Continual, *ly.*	9	Copper, *ed, ing.*
7	Continue, *d, ing, ation.*	2930	bar, *s.*
8	Continuous, *ly.*	1	bolt, *s.*
9	Contraband.	2	nail, *s.*
2890	articles.	3	sheathing.
1	of war.	4	smith, *s.*
2	trade.	5	Copy, *ied, ing, ies.*
3	Contract, *s, ed, ing.*	6	Coral, *s.*
4	Contractor, *s.*	7	reef, *s.*
5	Contradict, *ed, ing, ion.*	8	Cord, *s.*
6	Contrary.	9	Cordage.
7	Contribute, *d, ing.*	2940	Core, *d.*
8	Contrition.	1	shot.
9	Contrive, *d, ing.*	2	Cork, *s.*
2900	Control, *led, ling.*	3	Corn, *ed.*
1	Controversy.	4	brooms.
2	Contumacious, *ly, ness.*	5	Coroner, *s.*
3	Contumacy.	6	Corporal, *s.*
4	Contuse, *d, ing.*	7	of the guard.
5	Contusion, *s.*	8	guard.
6	Convalesce, *ed, ing, ent.*	9	Corporeal, *ly.*
7	Convene, *d, ing.*	2950	Corps.
8	Convenience.	1	Corpse, *s.*
9	Convenient, *ly.*	2	Correct, *ed, ing, ly.*
2910	Conversation.	3	distance.
1	Converse, *d, ing.*	4	information.
2912	Convey, *ed, ing.*	2955	range.

36

Nos.	COR	Nos.	CRO
2956	Correction, *s.*	2999	Cowardly.
7	Correspond, *ed, ing, ent, s.*	3000	Coxswain, *s.*
8	Correspondence.	1	Craft.
9	Corroberate, *d, ing, ion.*	2	Cramp, *ed, ing,* iron.
2960	Corrode, *d, ing.*	3	Crane, *s.*
1	Corrosion.	4	Crank, *s.*
2	Corrosive sublimate.	5	brass, *es.*
3	Cost, *s, ly, liness.*	6	pin, *s.*
4	Coston's signal light, *s.*	7	shaft, *s.*
5	Cot, *s.*	8	Crazy.
6	Cotton.	9	Create, *d, ing.*
7	waste.	3010	Creature, *s.*
8	Cough, *ed, ing.*	1	Credence.
9	Could.	2	Credible.
2970	Council, *s.*	3	Credit, *ed, ing, able.*
1	of war.	4	Credibility.
2	Counsel, *s, led, ling.*	5	Credulous.
3	Count, *ed, ing.*	6	Creek, *s.*
4	Counteract, *ed, ing.*	7	Creep, *ed, ing.*
5	Counterbrace, *d, ing.*	8	Crept.
6	Counter-current.	9	Creosote.
7	Countermand, *ed, ing,*	3020	Crest, *s, ed.*
8	Counter-revolution.	1	Crevasse.
9	Counter-scarp.	2	Crew, *s.*
2980	Countersign, *ed, ing, s.*	3	Crime, *s.*
1	Country, *ies.*	4	Criminal, *s.*
2	Coup de main.	5	Criminate, *d, ing.*
3	Coup d' etat.	6	Cringle, *s.*
4	Couple, *d, ing.*	7	Cripple, *d, ing, s.*
5	gear.	8	Crisis.
6	pin.	9	Criterion.
7	Courage, *ous, ously.*	3030	Crockery.
8	Course, *s.*	1	Crook, *ed.*
9	Court, *s.*	2	Cross, *ed, ing.*
2990	martial.	3	Cross-bar, *s.*
1	of inquiry.	4	Cross examine, *d, ing.*
2	Cove, *s.*	5	Cross examination.
3	Cover, *ed, ing.*	6	Cross-head.
4	party.	7	Cross in the hawse.
5	Court, *ed, ing.*	8	Cross-jack yard.
6	Cow, *ed.*	9	Cross-piece.
7	Coward, *s.*	3040	Cross-tail, *s.*
2998	Cowardice.	3041	Cross-tide.

Nos.	CRO	Nos.	DAY
3042	Cross-tree, *s.*	3085	Cutlass, *es.*
3	Crowbar, *s.*	6	and revolver, *s* or pistols.
4	Crowd, *ed, ing, s.*	7	Cutter, *s.*
5	Crown of the anchor.	8	crew, *s.*
6	Cruel, *ly.*	9	Cutwater.
7	Cruelty, *ies.*	3090	Cwt., *hundred weight.*
8	Cruise, *d, ing, s.*	1	Cyclone, *s.*
9	Cruiser, *s.*	2	Cylinder, *s.*
3050	Crush, *ed, ing.*	3	bottom.
1	Cubebs.	4	escape valve, *s.*
2	Cubic, *al.*	5	face, *s.*
3	Cubic foot, *feet.*	6	head.
4	Cubic inch, *es.*	7	jacket, *s.*
5	Cul de sac.	8	Cylindric, *al.*
6	Culpable.	9	Cypress lumber, *plank or timber.*
7	Culpability.	3100	Dagger knee, *s.*
8	Culpably.	1	Daily.
9	Culprit, *s.*	2	Daily rate, *s.*
3060	Cumulo cirro stratus.	3	Daily routine.
1	Cumulo stratus.	4	Damage, *d, ing.*
2	Cumulus.	5	Damp, *ed, ing.*
3	Cup, *ped, ping, s.*	6	Dampness.
4	Cup valve.	7	Danger, *s.*
5	Curable.	8	Dangerous, *ly.*
6	Cure, *d, ing.*	9	Dark, *ness.*
7	Curious, *ly.*	3110	Darken, *ed, ing.*
8	Currency.	1	Dash, *ed, ing.*
9	Current, *ly.*	2	board, *s.*
3070	is strong.	3	pot, *s.*
1	is weak.	4	Dastard, *ly.*
2	Curtail, *ed, ing.*	5	Data, *datum.*
3	Curve, *d, ing, s.*	6	Date, *s, ed, ing.*
4	Cushion, *ed, ing, s.*	7	Daunt, *ed.*
5	Custody.	8	Dauntless.
6	Custom, *ary.*	9	Davit, *s.*
7	house, *es.*	3120	Day, *s.*
·8	house officer, *s.*	1	after.
9	Cut.	2	before.
3080	and run.	3	break.
1	away.	4	by day.
2	out.	5	labor, *er.*
3	through.	6	light.
3084	Cutaneous.	3127	time.

4

Nos.	DAY	Nos.	DEG
	Day, *s.*	3169	Declination.
3128	work.	3170	of the moon.
9	Dead.	1	of the needle.
3130	angle.	2	of the sun.
1	eye.	3	Decline, *d, ing.*
2	light, *s.*	4	Declinometer.
3	man, *men.*	5	Declivity, *ies.*
4	reckoning.	6	Decompose, *d, ing.*
5	Deadly.	7	Decorate, *d, ing, ion.*
6	Deafening.	8	Decoy, *ed, ing.*
7	Deal, *ing, s.*	9	vessel.
8	Dear, *ly.*	3180	Decrease, *d, ing.*
9	Death.	1	Decree, *d, ing.*
3140	blow.	2	of the court.
1	wound.	3	Deduct, *ed, ing.*
2	Debar, *red, ring.*	4	Deem, *ed, ing.*
3	Debate, *d, ing.*	5	Deep, *ly.*
4	Debilitate, *d, ing.*	6	sea lead, *s.*
5	Debility.	7	sea lead line, *s.*
6	Decay, *ed, ing.*	8	water.
7	Decrease, *d.*	9	Deepen, *ed, ing.*
8	Deceive, *d, ing.*	3190	water.
9	December.	1	Deeper.
3150	Decency, *ies.*	2	water.
1	Decent, *ly.*	3	Defame, *ed, ing, ion.*
2	Deception.	4	Defeat, *ed, ing, s.*
3	Decide, *d, ing.*	5	of the enemy.
4	Decimal, *s.*	6	of our forces.
5	Decimate, *d, ing, ion.*	7	Defect, *s, ive.*
6	Decipher, *ed, ing.*	8	Defection.
7	Decision, *s.*	9	Defence, *s.*
8	Decisive, *ly.*	3200	of the place.
9	Deck, *s.*	1	Defend, *ed, ing.*
3160	beam, *s.*	2	Defensible.
1	load.	3	Defensive.
2	plank, *s.*	4	Defer, *red, ring.*
3	pump, *s.*	5	Defiance.
4	stopper, *s.*	6	Defiant, *ly.*
5	tackle.	7	Deficiency, *ies.*
6	Declaration.	8	Define, *ed, ing.*
7	of war.	9	Defray, *ed, ing.*
3168	Declare, *d, ing.*	3210	Defy, *ied, ing.*
		3211	Degradation.

Nos.	DEG	Nos.	DES
3212	Degrade, *d, ing.*	3254	Depot, *s.*
3	Degree, *s.*	5	of army munitions.
4	of altitude.	6	of supplies.
5	of latitude.	7	Deprave, *d.*
6	of longitude.	8	Depravity.
7	De Hart on Courts Martial.	9	Deprecate, *d, ing.*
8	Delay, *ed, ing, s.*	3260	Depredate, *d, ing, ion.*
9	Deliberate, *d, ing, ly.*	1	Deprive, *d, ing, ation.*
3220	Deliberation, *s.*	2	Depth.
1	Delicate, *ly.*	3	of hold.
2	Delinquent, *s.*	4	of water.
3	Delirious.	5	Derange, *d, ing, ment.*
4	Delirium.	6	Derelict.
5	tremens.	7	Derive, *d, ing.*
6	Deliver, *ed, ing.*	8	Derogate, *d, ing, ion.*
7	Delivery.	9	Derogatory.
8	outboard.	3270	Derrick, *s.*
9	pump, *s.*	1	Describe, *d, ing.*
3230	valve, *s.*	2	Description, *s.*
1	Delusion.	3	Desert, *ed, ing.*
2	Delusive.	4	Deserter, *s.*
3	Demand, *ed, ing.*	5	Desertion, *s.*
4	Demi-bastion, *s.*	6	Deserve, *d, ing.*
5	Demi-lune, *s.*	7	Desiccated vegetables.
6	Demolish, *ed, ing.*	8	Design, *ed, ing.*
7	Demonstrate, *d, ing.*	9	Designate, *d, ing, ion.*
8	Demonstration.	3280	Desirable.
9	Demoralize, *d, ing.*	1	Desire, *d, ing.*
3240	Demurrage.	2	Desist, *ed, ing.*
1	Denial, *s.*	3	Desolate, *d, ing, ion.*
2	Dense, *ly.*	4	Despair, *ed, ing.*
3	fog.	5	Despatch, *es, ed, ing.*
4	Density, *ies.*	6	boat, *s.*
5	Deny, *ied, ing.*	7	flag.
6	Depart, *ed, ing.*	8	messenger, *s.*
7	Department, *al.*	9	vessel, *s.*
8	Departure, *s.*	3290	for the army.
9	Depend, *ed, ing.*	1	for the Commander-in-Chief.
3250	Dependence.	2	for the Department.
1	Deplorable, *ly.*	3	for the Government.
2	Deportment.	4	from the army.
3253	Deposition, *s.*	5	from the Commander-in-Chief.
		3296	Despicable, *ly.*

Nos.	DES	Nos.	DIS
3297	Destination.	3340	Die, *d.*
8	Destitute, *ion.*	1	Dying.
9	Destroy, *ed, ing.*	2	Diet, *ed, ing.*
3300	Destruction.	3	Differ, *ed, ing.*
1	Destructive.	4	Difference.
2	Detach, *ed, ing.*	5	of latitude.
3	officer, *s.*	6	of longitude.
4	officer, *s,* and men.	7	Difficult, *y, ies.*
5	squadron, *s.*	8	Digest, *ed, ing, ion.*
6	vessel, *s.*	9	Digestible.
7	Detachment.	3350	Dike, *d, ing.*
8	of troops.	1	Dilatory.
9	of vessels.	2	Dilemma.
3310	Detail, *ed, ing.*	3	Diligence.
1	officer, *s.*	4	Diligent, *ly.*
2	officer, *s,* and men.	5	Dim, *ly.*
3	working party, *ies.*	6	Dimension, *s.*
4	Detain, *ed, ing.*	7	Diminish, *ed, ing.*
5	Detect, *ed, ing.*	8	Diminution.
6	Detection.	9	Dimness.
7	Detention.	3360	Dine, *d, ing.*
8	Deter, *red, ring.*	1	Dinner.
9	Deteriorate, *d, ing, ion.*	2	Dip, *ped, ping.*
3320	Determinate, *ion.*	3	needle.
1	Detract, *ed, ing, ion.*	4	Diplomatic.
2	Detriment, *al.*	5	corps.
3	Develop, *ed, ing, ment, s.*	6	correspondence.
4	Deviate, *d, ing.*	7	Diplomatist, *s.*
5	Deviation, *s.*	8	Diptheria.
6	local, of the needle.	9	Direct, *ed, ing.*
7	Device, *s.*	3370	acting engine, *s.*
8	Devise, *d, ing.*	1	Direction, *s.*
9	Devolve, *d, ing.*	2	Dirt, *y.*
3330	Devote, *d, ing.*	3	Disability, *ies.*
1	Dew, *s.*	4	Disable, *d, ing.*
2	Dexterity.	5	engine, *s.*
3	Diabetes.	6	state.
4	Diagnosis.	7	vessel, *s.*
5	Diagram, *s.*	8	Disagree, *d, ing.*
6	Diameter, *s.*	9	Disagreeable.
7	Diarrhœa.	3380	Disallow, *ed, ing.*
8	Dictionary, *ies.*	1	Disappear, *ed, ing.*
3339	Did.	3382	Disappoint, *ed, ing, men ts.*

41

Nos.	DIS	Nos.	DIS
3383	Disapproval.	3426	Disencumber, *ed, ing.*
4	Disapprove, *d, ing.*	7	Disengage, *d.*
5	Disarm, *ed, ing.*	8	Disentangle, *d.*
6	Disarrange, *d, ing, ment.*	9	Disgrace, *d, ing, ful, fully.*
7	Disaster, *s.*	3430	Disguise, *d, ing, s.*
8	Disastrous, *ly.*	1	Dishearten, *ed, ing.*
9	Disavow, *ed, ing, al.*	2	Dishonest, *ly, y.*
3390	Disband, *ed, ing, ment.*	3	Dishonor, *ed, ing, able, ably.*
1	Disbelieve, *d, ing.*	4	Disinfect, *ed, ing.*
2	Disburse, *d, ing, ment, s.*	5	Disinfectant, *s.*
3	Disc crank, *s.*	6	Dislocate, *d, ing, ion.*
4	valve, *s.*	7	Dislodge, *d, ing.*
5	Discharge, *d, ing, s.*	8	the enemy.
6	Discipline, *d, ing.*	9	Disloyal, *ty, ly.*
7	Disclaim, *ed, ing, er.*	3440	Dismantle, *d, ing.*
8	Disclose, *d, ing.*	1	Dismast, *ed, ing.*
9	Disclosure, *s.*	2	Dismiss, *ed, ing, al.*
3400	Discolor, *ed, ing.*	3	from the service.
1	Discomfort, *s.*	4	Dismount, *ed, ing.*
2	Disconcert, *ed, ing.*	5	Disobedience.
3	Disconnect, *ed, ing.*	6	Disobedient, *ly.*
4	propeller.	7	Disobey, *ed, ing.*
5	Discontent, *ed.*	8	Disorder, *ed, ing, ly.*
6	Discontinue, *d, ing.*	9	Disorganize, *d, ing, er.*
7	coaling.	3450	Dispart, *s.*
8	firing.	1	sight, *s.*
9	Discord, *ant, antly.*	2	Dispensary, *ies.*
3410	Discourage, *d, ing, ment.*	3	Dispense, *d, ing.*
1	Discourteous, *ly.*	4	Disperse, *d, ing, ion.*
2	Discourtesy.	5	Displace, *d, ing, ment.*
3	Discover, *ed, ing,*	6	Display, *ed, ing.*
4	Discovery, *ies.*	7	Displease, *d, ing.*
5	Discredit, *ed, ing, able.*	8	Displeasure.
6	Discreet, *ly.*	9	Disposal.
7	Discrepancy, *ies.*	3460	Dispose, *d, ing.*
8	Discretion, *al, ary.*	1	Disposition, *s.*
9	Discriminate, *d, ing, ion.*	2	Dispossess, *ed.*
3420	Discuss, *ed, ing, ion.*	3	Disproportion.
1	Disease, *d, s.*	4	Disprove, *d, ing.*
2	Disembark, *ed, ing.*	5	Dispute, *d, ing.*
3	gun, *s.*	6	Disqualification, *s.*
4	stores.	7	Disqualify, *ied, ing.*
3425	troops.	3468	Disregard, *ed, ing.*

Nos.	DIS	Nos.	DRO
3469	Disreputable, *y*.	3512	Donkey boiler, *s*.
3470	Disrespect.	3	engine, *s*.
1	Dissatisfaction.	4	pump, *s*.
2	Dissatisfy, *ied*.	5	Dose, *d*, *ing*.
3	Disseminate, *d*, *ing*.	C	Double, *d*, *ing*.
4	Dissension, *s*.	7	Doubt, *ed*, *ing*.
5	Dissipate, *d*, *ing*, *ion*.	8	Doubtful, *ly*.
6	Dissolve, *d*, *ing*.	9	Down.
7	Dissuade, *d*, *ing*.	3520	all hammocks.
8	Distance, *d*, *ing*, *s*.	1	all bedding.
9	Distant, *ly*.	2	from aloft.
3480	Distinct, *ion*.	3	the bay.
1	Distinctly.	4	the river.
2	Distinguish, *ed*, *ing*, *able*	5	Dozen, *s*.
3	Distort, *ed*, *ing*, *ion*.	6	Drachm, *s*.
4	Distract, *ed*, *ing*.	7	Draft, *ed*, *ing*, *s*.
5	Distress, *ed*, *ing*.	8	Draftsman, *men*.
6	Distribute, *d*, *ing*.	9	Drag, *ged*, *ging*, *s*.
7	District, *s*,	3530	link, *s*.
8	court, *s*.	1	rope, *s*.
9	judge, *s*.	2	Dragoman.
3490	Distrust, *ed*, *ing*.	3	Drank.
1	Disturb, *ed*, *ing*, *ance*..	4	Draught.
2	Dive, *er*, *s*.	5	Draw.
3	Divert, *ed*, *ing*.	6	the charge, *s*.
4	Divide, *d*, *ing*.	7	the fire.
5	Divine service.	8	Drawing.
6	Diving.	9	knife, *ives*.
7	apparatus.	3540	Drawn.
8	dress, *es*.	1	battle.
9	Division, *al*.	2	Dread, *ed*, *ing*.
3500	Commander, *s*.	3	Dreadful, *ly*.
1	exercise, *s*.	4	Dress, *ed*, *ing*.
2	flag, *s*.	5	ship.
3	Do, *ing*.	6	ship fully.
4	Dock, *ed*, *ing*, *s*.	7	Drift, *ed*, *ing*.
5	yard.	8	of the current.
6	Doctor, *s*.	9	of the ship.
7	Document, *s*, *ary*.	3550	Drill, *ed*, *ing*.
8	Does.	1	Drink, *ing*.
9	Dollar, *s*.	2	Drop, *ped*, *ping*.
3510	Dominion, *s*.	3	astern.
3511	Done.	3554	down.

Nos.	DRO	Nos.	EIT
3555	Dropsy.	3598	Ease.
6	Drove, *driven.*	9	Easily.
7	Drown, *ed, ing.*	3600	East, *erly.*
8	Drug, *ged, s.*	1	course.
9	Drum, *med, ming.*	2	current, *s.*
3560	head, *s.*	3	drift.
1	Drunk, *en, enness.*	4	set.
2	Drunkard, *s.*	5	shore.
3	Dry, *ied, ing.*	6	Eastward, *ly.*
4	dock, *s.*	7	Eat, *able.*
5	holystone, *d, ing.*	8	Eating.
6	Duck.	9	Ebb, *ed, ing.*
7	Due.	3610	tide.
8	Dungaree.	1	Eccentric, *s.*
9	Dunnage.	2	gear.
3570	Dupe, *d, ing.*	3	hook, *s.*
1	Duplicate, *d, ing.*	4	rod, *s.*
2	report, *s.*	5	strap, *s.*
3	return, *s.*	6	wheel, *s.*
4	requisition, *s.*	7	Echelon.
5	Duplicity.	8	formation, *s.*
6	Durability.	9	movement, *s.*
7	Durable.	3620	Eclipse, *d, ing.*
8	Duration.	1	of the moon.
9	During.	2	of the sun.
3580	Dusk.	3	Economize, *d, ing.*
1	Dust, *y.*	4	Economy. *ical, ly.*
2	Dutch.	5	Eddy, *ied, ing, s.*
3	Dutiable.	6	current, *s.*
4	Duty, *ies.*	7	Edge, *d, ing.*
5	Dyke, *s.*	8	Edition, *s.*
6	Dysentery.	9	Effect, *ed, ing, ive, ively.*
7	Dyspepsia.	3630	Effectual, *ly.*
8	Each.	1	Efficacy, *cious.*
9	Eager, *ly, ness.*	2	Efficient, *ly.*
3590	Ear, *s.*	3	Effort, *s.*
1	Early.	4	Egg, *s.*
2	Earn, *ed, ing.*	5	Egress.
3	Earnest, *ly, ness.*	6	Egypt, *ian.*
4	Earth, *en.*	7	Eight, *th.*
5	Earthly.	8	Eighteen, *th.*
6	Earthquake, *s.*	9	Eighty, *th.*
3597	Earthwork, *s.*	3640	Either.

Nos.	ELA	Nos.	ENG
3641	Elapse, d, ing.	3684	Empress.
2	Elastic, ity.	5	Empty, ied, ing.
3	Elate, d.	6	Emulate, d, ing.
4	Elbow, s.	7	Emulous.
5	in the hawse.	8	Enable, d, ing.
6	Electric, al, ity.	9	Enact, ed, ing, ment, s.
7	telegraph, s.	3690	Engage, d, ing, ment, s.
8	Element, s, ary, al.	1	Encamp, ed, ing, ment, s.
9	Elevate, d, ing.	2	Encircle, d, ing.
3650	screw, s.	3	Enclose, d, ing, ure.
1	Elevation.	4	Encounter, ed, ing, s.
2	Eleven, th.	5	Encourage, d, ing, ment, s.
3	Elicit, ed, ing.	6	Encroach, ed, ing, ment.
4	Eligibility.	7	Encumber, ed, ing.
5	Eligible, y.	8	Encumbrance, s.
6	Elliptic compasses.	9	End, ed, ing.
7	Else.	3700	Endless.
8	Elude, d, ing.	1	Endanger, ed, ing.
9	Emaciate, d, ing, ion.	2	Endeavor, s, ed, ing.
3660	Emanate, d, ing, ion.	3	Endemic.
1	Embank, ed, ing, ment, s.	4	Endure, ance, d, ing.
2	Embargo, es.	5	Enemy, s, ies.
3	Embark, ed, ing, ation.	6	appears to be.
4	Embarrass, ed, ing, ment, s.	7	iron-clad, s.
5	. Embay, ed, ing.	8	movement, s.
6	Embezzle, d, ing, ment.	9	vessel, s.
7	Embolden, ed, ing.	3710	was defeated.
8	Embrace, d, ing, s.	1	was seen.
9	Embrasure, s.	2	Energetic.
3670	Embrocate, d, ing, ion.	3	Energy.
1	Embroil, ed, ing.	4	Enervate, d, ing.
2	Emerge, d, ing, ncy.	5	Enfeeble, d, ing.
3	Emery.	6	Enfilade, d, ing.
4	paper.	7	Enforce, d, ing.
5	cloth.	8	Engage, d, ing, ment, s.
6	Emetic, s.	9	with the enemy.
7	Emigrate, d, ing, ion.	3720	the enemy.
8	Eminent, ly.	1	the water battery, ies.
9	Emissary, ies.	2	the fort, s.
3680	Emperor, s.	3	Engine, s.
1	Emphatic, ally.	4	room, s.
2	Employ, ed, ing, ment.	3725	frame, s.
3683	Empower, ed, ing.		

Nos.	ENG	Nos.	ETC
3726	Engineer, *s.*	3769	Equal, *led, ling.*
7	of the fleet.	3770	Equalize, *d, ing.*
8	in-Chief.	1	Equally.
9	England.	2	Equation of time.
3730	English, *man, men.*	3	Equator, *ial.*
1	flag.	4	Equidistant.
2	fleet.	5	Equilibrium.
3	vessel, *s.*	6	Equinoctial.
4	Engrave, *d, ing, s.*	7	gale, *s.*
5	Enlarge, *d, ing, ment.*	8	Equinox, *es.*
6	Enlist, *ed, ing.*	9	Equip, *ped, ping, age.*
7	Eumity, *ies.*	3780	Equipment, *s.*
8	Enormity, *ies.*	1	Equitable, *ly.*
9	Enormous.	2	Equity.
3740	Enough.	3	Equivalent, *s.*
1	Enrage, *d.*	4	Equivocal, *ly.*
2	Enroll, *ed, ing, ment.*	5	Equivocate, *d, ing.*
3	Ensign, *s.*	6	Eradicate, *d, ing.*
4	Ensnare, *d, ing.*	7	Erase, *d, ing, rs.*
5	Entangle, *d, ing, ment.*	8	Erasure.
6	Enter, *ed, ing.*	9	Erect, *ed, ing.*
7	Entice, *d, ing.*	3790	Err, *ed.*
8	Entire, *ly.*	1	Errand, *s.*
9	Entrance.	2	Erroneous, *ly.*
3750	of the bay.	3	Error, *s.*
1	of the port.	4	Eruption.
2	of the river.	5	Escalade, *ing.*
3	Entrap, *ped, ping.*	6	Escape, *d, ing, ment.*
4	Entreat, *ed, ing, y.*	7	Escarp, *ed, ment, s.*
5	Enumerate, *d, ing, ion.*	8	Escort, *ed, ing, s.*
6	Envelop, *ed, ing.*	9	Especial, *ly.*
7	Envelopes.	3800	Espionage.
8	Environs.	1	Espouse, *d, ing.*
9	Envoy, *s.*	2	Esprit de corps.
3760	extraordinary.	3	Esquimaux.
1	Epaulettes.	4	Essential, *ly.*
2	Ephemeris.	5	Establish, *ed, ing, ment.*
3	Epidemic.	6	Esteem, *ed, ing.*
4	Epilepsy.	7	Estimable.
5	Epileptic.	8	Estimate, *d, ing, ion.*
6	Eprouvette.	9	Estrange, *d, ing, ment.*
7	Epsom salts.	3810	Estuary.
3768	Equable, *ly.*	3811	Etch, *ed, ing.*

46

Nos.	ETH	Nos.	EXP
3812	Ether.	3855	Exception, *al.*
3	Etiquette.	6	Excess.
4	Europe, *an.*	7	Exchange, *d, ing.*
5	Evacuate, *d, ing, ion.*	8	Exclude, *d, ing.*
6	Evade, *d, ing.*	9	Exclusion.
7	Evaporate, *d, ing, ion.*	3860	Exclusive, *ly.*
8	Evasion.	1	Excruciate, *d, ing.*
9	Evasive.	2	Exculpate, *d, ing, ion.*
3820	Even, *ly.*	3	Excusable, *ness.*
1	Evening, *s.*	4	Excuse, *d, ing.*
2	boat, *s.*	5	Execute, *d, ing, ion.*
3	gun.	6	Executive.
4	Event, *ful, s.*	7	officer, *s.*
5	Eventual, *ly.*	8	Exempt, *ed, ing, ion.*
6	Ever.	9	Exercise, *d, ing, s.*
7	Every.	3870	Exert, *ed, ing, ion.*
8	body.	1	Exhalation, *s.*
9	day.	2	Exhale, *d, ing.*
3830	effort.	3	Exhaust, *ed, ing, ion, ive.*
1	hour.	4	Exhibit, *ed, ing, ion, s.*
2	month.	5	Exigency, *ies.*
3	one.	6	Exist, *ed, ing, ence.*
4	thing.	7	Exonerate, *d, ing, ion.*
5	where.	8	Exorbitant, *ly.*
6	Evidence, *d, ing.*	9	Expansion.
7	Evident, *ly.*	3880	Expansive, *ly.*
8	Evil, *s.*	1	Ex parte.
9	Evince, *d, ing.*	2	Expect, *ed, ing, ation.*
3840	Evolution, *s.*	3	Expedient, *ly.*
1	Exact, *ed, ing, ion.*	4	Expedite, *d, ing.*
2	Exaggerate, *d, ing, ion.*	5	Expedition, *s.*
3	Examination.	6	Expeditious, *ly.*
4	of witness, *es.*	7	Expel, *led, ling.*
5	Examine, *d, ing.*	8	Expend, *ed, ing, iture, s.*
6	the deserter, *s.*	9	Expense, *s.*
7	the place, *s.*	3890	Expensive.
8	the vessel, *s.*	1	Experience, *d, ing.*
9	Example, *s.*	2	Experiment, *ed, ing.*
3850	Exasperate, *d, ing, ion.*	3	Experimental, *ly.*
1	Excavate, *d, ing, ion.*	4	Expert, *ly.*
2	Exceed, *ed, ing.*	5	Expiration.
3	Excellent, *ly.*	6	Expire, *d, ing.*
3854	Except, *ed, ing.*	3897	Explain, *ed, ing.*

Nos.	EXP	Nos.	FAT
3893	Explanation, *s.*		Eye, *s.*
9	Explanatory.	3941	sight.
3900	Explicit, *ly.*	2	witness, *es.*
1	Explode, *d, ing.*	3	Fabricate, *d, ing, ion.*
2	Exploit, *s.*	4	Face, *s, d, ing.*
3	Explore, *d, ing.*	5	Facilitate, *d, ing.*
4	Explosion, *s.*	6	Facility, *ies.*
5	Explosive.	7	Fact, *s.*
6	Export, *s, ed, ing, ation.*	8	Fagot, *s.*
7	Expose, *d, ing.*	9	Fahrenheit, *s,* scale.
8	Expostulate, *d, ing, ion.*	3950	thermometer.
9	Exposure.	1	Fail, *ed, ing.*
3910	Ex-President.	2	Failure, *s.*
1	Express, *ed, ing, ly, es.*	3	Fair, *ly, ness.*
2	messenger.	4	way.
3	Expressive.	5	weather.
4	Expulsion.	6	wind.
5	Extend, *ed, ing.*	7	Faithful, *ly.*
6	Extension.	8	Fall, *ing, en.*
7	Extensive, *ly.*	9	of the tide.
8	Extent.	3960	False, *ly.*
9	Extenuate, *d, ing, ion.*	1	alarm, *s.*
3920	Exterior.	2	hood, *s.*
1	Exterminate, *d, ing, ion.*	3	keel.
2	External, *ly.*	4	Falsify, *ied, ing.*
3	Extinguish, *ed, ing, ment.*	5	Falter, *ed, ing, s.*
4	Extort, *ed, ing, ion.*	6	Familiar, *ity.*
5	Extortionate.	7	Familiarize, *d, ing.*
6	Extra.	8	Family, *ies.*
7	Extract, *s, ed, ing, ion.*	9	Famine.
8	Extraordinary.	3970	Far.
9	Extravagance.	1	Fare, *d, ing.*
3930	Extravagant, *ly.*	2	Farewell.
1	Extreme, *ly, s.*	3	Farther.
2	breadth.	4	Farthest.
3	elevation.	5	Fasten, *ed, ing.*
4	length.	6	Fatal, *ly, ity.*
5	range.	7	Fate.
6	Extricate, *d, ing.*	8	Fathom, *s, ed, ing.*
7	Eye, *s.*	9	of chain.
8	bolt, *s.*	3980	Fatigue.
9	glass, *es.*	1	dress.
3940	piece, *s.*	3982	party, *ies.*

Nos.	FAU	Nos.	FIR
3983	Faucet, *s.*	4026	Feu de joie.
4	Fault, *s.*	7	Fever, *ish, s.*
5	Favor, *ed, ing, able.*	8	Few.
6	Favorite, *ism.*	9	Fid, *ded, ding.*
7	Fear, *ed, ing, s.*	4030	Fiddle, *d, ing.*
8	Fearful, *ly.*	1	Fidelity.
9	Fearless, *ly.*	2	Field, *s.*
3990	Fearnaught.	3	artillery.
1	Feasible.	4	book, *s.*
2	Feat, *s.*	5	carriage, *s.*
3	Febrifuge.	6	glass, *es.*
4	Febrile disease, *s.*	7	ice.
5	February.	8	officer, *s.*
6	Feeble, *ness, y.*	9	piece, *s.*
7	Feed, *ing.*	4040	work, *s.*
8	cock, *s.*	1	Fiend, *ish.*
9	pipe, *s.*	2	Fierce, *ly.*
4000	pump, *s.*	3	Fife, *s.*
1	water.	4	Fifer, *s.*
2	Feel, *ing.*	5	Fifteen, *th.*
3	Feet.	6	Fifth, *ly.*
4	Feign, *ed, ing.*	7	Fifty, *ieth.*
5	Feint.	8	Fight, *ing.*
6	Fell.	9	Figure, *s, d, ing.*
7	in with.	4050	File, *d, ing, s.*
8	Felon, *s.*	1	Fill, *ed, ing.*
9	Felonious, *ly.*	2	Filter, *ed, ing.*
4010	Felony, *ies.*	3	Filth, *y.*
1	Felt, *ing.*	4	Final, *ly.*
2	Felucca.	5	Finance, *s.*
3	Female, *s.*	6	Find, *ing.*
4	screw.	7	Fine.
5	Fender, *s.*	8	Finger, *s.*
6	Ferment.	9	Finish, *ed, ing.*
7	Ferocious, *ly.*	4060	Fire, *s, ed, ing.*
8	Ferocity.	1	alarm.
9	Ferret, *ed, ing.*	2	arms.
4020	Ferry, *ied, ing, s.*	3	brand, *s.*
1	Festival, *s.*	4	brick, *s.*
2	Festivity, *ies.*	5	brigade.
3	Fetid.	6	bucket, *s.*
4	Fetter, *ed.*	7	company, *ies.*
4025	Feud, *s.*	4068	engine, *s.*

Nos.	FIR	Nos.	FLO
	Fire, *s, ed, ing.*		Flat, *ly.*
4069	hose.	4111	floor.
4070	man, *men.*	2	Flaw, *s, y.*
1	quarters.	3	Flax, *en.*
2	raft, *s.*	4	Flaxseed.
3	room, *s.*	5	Flea, *s.*
4	ship.	6	Fled.
5	surface.	7	Flee, *ing.*
6	wood.	8	Fleet, *s.*
7	works.	9	Captain.
8	Firm, *ly, ness.*	4120	Engineer.
9	First.	1	evolution, *s.*
4080	Fish, *ing.*	2	formation, *s.*
1	block, *s.*	3	Paymaster.
2	boat, *s.*	4	Secretary.
3	davit, *s.*	5	Surgeon.
4	hook, *s.*	6	Flemish.
5	line, *s.*	7	eye.
6	tackle.	8	horse.
7	Fishes.	9	Flesh.
8	Fistula.	4130	Flexibility.
9	Fit, *ted, ting, s.*	1	Flexible.
4090	Fitment, *s.*	2	Flicker, *ed, ing.*
1	Five.	3	Flight.
2	Fix, *ed, ing.*	4	Flimsy.
3	ammunition.	5	Flinch, *ed, ing.*
4	Fixture, *s.*	6	Fling, *ing.*
5	Flag, *s.*	7	Flint, *y, s.*
6	of truce.	8	Flippant, *ly.*
7	ship.	9	Float, *ed, s.*
8	Flagrant, *ly.*	4140	at half tide.
9	Flame, *s.*	1	at high tide.
4100	Flange, *s.*	2	at low tide.
1	Flank, *ed, ing, s.*	3	Floating battery, *ies.*
2	of the army.	4	bridge.
3	of the enemy.	5	dock, *s.*
4	of the fleet.	6	light, *s.*
5	Flanker, *s.*	7	Flock, *s.*
6	Flannel.	8	Flag, *s.*
7	Flash, *ed, ing.*	9	Flood, *ed, ing.*
8	Flat, *ly.*	4150	tide, *s.*
9	aback.	1	Floor, *ing.*
4110	bottom, *ed.*	4152	cloth, *s.*

Nos.	FLO	Nos.	FOR
	Floor, *ing.*	4195	Foot, *ing.*
4153	timber, *s.*	6	band.
4	Flotilla, *s.*	7	cloth.
5	Flounder, *ed, ing, s.*	8	bridge.
6	Flour.	9	hold.
7	barrel, *s.*	4200	rope, *s.*
8	Flow, *ed, ing.*	1	rule.
9	Fluctuate, *d, ing, ion.*	2	shackle, *s, irons.*
4160	Flue, *s.*	3	valve, *s.*
1	Fluid, *ity.*	4	For.
2	compass.	5	Forage, *d, ing.*
3	Fluke, *s.*	6	Forbade.
4	Flush, *ed.*	7	Forbear, *ing, ance.*
5	of success.	8	Forbid, *ding, den.*
6	Fly, *ing.*	9	Forbore.
7	artillery.	4210	Force, *d, ing.*
8	block, *s.*	1	pump, *s.*
9	colors.	2	Forcible, *ly.*
4170	fish, *es.*	3	Ford, *ed, ing, able.*
1	jib.	4	Fore-arm.
2	jib-boom.	5	Forebode, *d, ing.*
3	jib halyards.	6	Fore boom, *s.*
4	Foam, *ed, ing.*	7	Fore brace, *s.*
5	Focal.	8	Forecast.
6	distance.	9	Forecastle.
7	Focus.	4220	Forefoot.
8	Foe, *s.*	1	Forego, *ing, ne.*
9	Fog, *gy.*	2	Fore guys.
4180	bank.	3	Forehead.
1	horn, *s.*	4	Foreign, *er.*
2	signal, *s.*	5	Fore lift, *s.*
3	whistle.	6	Foreman.
4	Foil, *ed, ing.*	7	Foremast.
.5	Fold, *ed, ing.*	8	Foremost.
6	Foliage.	9	Forenoon.
7	Follow, *ed, ing.*	4230	watch.
8	Follower, *s.*	1	Foreplane.
9	Folly, *ies.*	2	Fore royal.
4190	Foment, *ed, ing.*	3	mast.
1	Food.	4	yard.
2	Fool, *s, ed, ing, ish.*	5	Forerun, *ner.*
3	errand.	6	Foresail.
4194	hardy.	4237	Foresaw.

Nos.	FOR	Nos.	FRA
4238	Foresee, *ing.*	4281	Formidable.
9	Fore sheet.	2	Formula, *æ.*
4240	Fore shroud, *s.*	3	Forsake, *n.*
1	Foresight.	4	Forsook.
2	Forestall, *ed, ing.*	5	Fort, *s.*
3	Fore stay, *s.*	6	Forth.
4	Fore staysail.	7	coming.
5	Fore tack.	8	with.
6	Foretell, *ing.*	9	Fortieth.
7	Foretold.	4290	Fortification, *s.*
8	Fore top.	1	Fortified.
9	Fore topgallant mast.	2	Fortify, *ing.*
4250	Fore topgallant sail.	3	Fortitude.
1	Fore topgallant yard.	4	Fortnight, *ly.*
2	Fore topman, *men.*	5	Fortress.
3	Fore topmast.	6	Fortuitous, *ly.*
4	back stay.	7	Fortunate, *ly.*
5	shrouds.	8	Fortune.
6	stay.	9	of war.
7	staysail.	4300	Forty.
8	studding sail.	1	Forward, *ing, ed.*
9	topsail.	2	Foul, *ed, ing.*
4260	yard.	3	anchor.
1	Forewarn, *ed, ing.*	4	berth.
2	Fore yard, *s.*	5	bottom.
3	Forfeit, *ed, ing, s.*	6	hawse.
4	Forfeiture.	7	weather.
5	Forge, *d, ing.*	8	Found.
6	ahead.	9	Foundation, *s.*
7	Forgery, *ies.*	4310	Founder, *ed, ing.*
8	Forget, *ting, ful.*	1	Foundry, *ies.*
9	Forgave.	2	Four.
4270	Forgive, *n, ing.*	3	Fourteen, *th.*
1	Forlorn-hope.	4	Fourth, *ly.*
2	Form, *ed, ing.*	5	Fraction, *al.*
3	the line.	6	Fracture, *d, ing.*
4	the order of sailing.	7	Fragile.
5	the order of steaming.	8	Fragment, *s, ary.*
6	Formal, *ity, ies.*	9	Frail.
7	Formation, *s.*	4320	Frame, *d, ing.*
8	of the fleet.	1	timber, *s.*
9	of squadrons.	2	work.
4280	Former, *ly.*	4323	Franc, *s.*

Nos.	FRA	Nos.	FUN
4324	Frank, *ly.*	4367	Frigid, *ity.*
5	Frap, *ped, ping.*	8	zone.
6	Fraternal, *ly.*	9	Fringe, *d, ing.*
7	Fraternize, *d, ing.*	4370	Frivolous, *ly.*
8	Fraud, *s, ulent.*	1	Frock, *s.*
9	Fray, *ed, ing.*	2	Frog, *s.*
4330	Freak, *s.*	3	From.
1	Free, *d, ing.*	4	Front.
2	booter, *s.*	5	Frontier, *s.*
3	city.	6	Frost, *ed, ing.*
4	· port, *s.*	7	bitten.
5	Freeze, *ing.*	8	Frozen.
6	point.	9	Frugal, *ity, ly.*
7	Freight, *ed, ing.*	4380	Fruit, *s.*
8	money.	1	Fruition.
9	French.	2	Fruitless, *ly.*
4340	chalk.	3	Frustrate, *d.*
1	flag.	4	Fry, *ing.*
2	Frequent, *ed, ing.*	5	Fuel.
3	Fresh.	6	Fugitive, *s.*
4	breeze, *s.*	7	Fulfil, *led, ling, ment.*
5	force.	·8	Full.
6	water.	9	and by.
7	Freshen, *ed, ing.*	4390	dress, *ed.*
8	Freshet, *s.*	1	dress ship.
9	Fret, *ted, ting.*	2	manned.
4350	Fretful, *ly.*	3	moon.
1	Friction.	4	retreat.
2	clutch.	5	rigged ship.
3	coupling.	6	speed.
4	primer, *s.*	7	Fully.
5	roller, *s.*	8	Fulminate, *s.*
6	Friday.	9	of mercury.
7	evening.	4400	Fumigate, *d, ing, ion.*
8	morning.	1	Fun, *ny.*
9	night.	2	Function, *s, ary, aries.*
4360	noon.	3	Fund, *s.*
1	Friend, *s.*	4	Fundamental.
2	Friendly.	5	Funeral, *s.*
3	Friendship.	6	service, *s.*
4	Frigate, *s.*	7	· Funnel, *s.*
5	Fright.	4408	guy, *s.*
4366	Frighten, *ed, ing.*		

Nos.	FUR	Nos.	GAT
4409	Furious, *ly*.	4451	Gain, *ed, ing*.
4410	gale, *s*.	2	advantage.
1	Furl, *ed, ing*.	3	ground.
2	fore and aft sails.	4	on the chase.
3	light sails.	5	Gala day.
4	line, *s*.	6	Galaxy.
5	sails.	7	Gale, *s*.
6	Furlough, *ed*.	8	Gallot, *s*.
7	Furnace, *s*.	9	Gall, *ed, ing*.
8	door, *s*.	4460	Gallant, *ly, ry*.
9	Furnish, *ed, ing*.	1	Gallery, *ies*.
4420	Furniture.	2	Galley, *s*.
1	Further.	3	barge, *s*.
2	most.	4	Gallon, *s*.
3	orders.	5	of oil.
4	proof.	6	of water.
5	Fuse. *d, ing*.	7	Gallows.
6	composition.	8	frame, *s*.
7	plug, *s*.	9	Galvanic battery, *ies*.
8	stock.	4470	Gamble, *ing*.
9	wrench.	1	Gamboge.
4430	Fusible.	2	Gammoning.
1	Fusilade, *d, ing*.	3	scuttle.
2	Fusil oil.	4	Gang, *s*.
3	Fusion.	5	board, *s*.
4	Futile.	6	cask, *s*.
5	Futility.	7	way, *s*.
6	Futtock, *s*.	8	Gangrene, *d, ing*.
7	band.	9	Garble, *d, ing*.
8	plate, *s*.	4480	Garboard strake.
9	shroud, *s*.	1	Gargle, *d, ing*.
4440	stave, *s*.	2	Garland.
1	timbers.	3	Garlic.
2	Future.	4	Garment, *s*.
3	Gabble, *d, ing, er*.	5	Garrison, *ed, ing*.
4	Gabion, *s*.	6	Gash, *ed, es*.
5	Gaff, *s*.	7	Gasket, *s*.
6	end, *s*.	8	Gastric.
7	topsail, *s*.	9	Gate, *s*.
8	Gag, *ged, ging*.	4490	way, *s*.
9	Gage.	1	Gather, *ed, ing*.
4450	Gaiety, *ties*.	4492	way.

5

Nos.	GAU	Nos.	GNA
4493	Gauge, *d, ing.*	4536	Gill-net, *s.*
4	cock, *s.*	7	Gimbal, *s.*
5	point.	8	Gimlet, *s.*
6	rod, *s.*	9	Ginger.
7	Gauze.	4540	Ginseng.
8	Gear, *ed, ing.*	1	Gird, *ed, ing.*
9	engine.	2	Girtline, *s.*
4500	Gemini.	3	Gist.
1	Gendarme, *s, ry.*	4	Give, *ing.*
2	Gender.	5	chase.
3	General, *ly.*	6	Glacis.
4	average.	7	Glad, *ly, ness.*
5	order, *s.*	8	Gladden, *ed, ing.*
6	in chief.	9	Glare, *d, ing.*
7	signal, *s.*	4550	Glass, *es.*
8	rule.	1	gauge, *s.*
9	Generate, *d, ing, ion.*	2	Glaze, *d, ing.*
4510	Generosity.	3	Glazier, *s.*
1	Generous, *ly.*	4	Gleam, *ed, ing.*
2	Genial.	5	Glee, *ful.*
3	Genius.	6	Glide, *d, ing.*
4	Genoese.	7	Glimmer, *ed, ing.*
5	Gently.	8	Glimpse, *s.*
6	Geographical.	9	Glisten, *s, ed, ing.*
7	position.	4560	Glitter, *ed, ing, s.*
8	Geography.	1	Globe, *s.*
9	Geometrical.	2	Globular.
4520	German.	3	Globule, *s.*
1	silver.	4	Gloom, *y.*
2	Gesticulate, *d, ing.*	5	Glorify, *ied, ing.*
3	Get, *ting.*	6	Glorious, *ly.*
4	afloat.	7	news.
5	underway.	8	victory.
6	up stream.	9	Glory, *ied, ing.*
7	Giddiness.	4570	Gloss, *ed, ing, y.*
8	Giddy.	1	Glossary, *ies.*
9	Gift, *s.*	2	Glove, *s.*
4530	Gig, *s.*	3	Glow, *ed, ing.*
1	crew.	4	Glue, *d, ing.*
2	recall.	5	Glutinous.
3	Gigantic.	6	Glycerine.
4	Gild, *ed, ing.*	4577	Gnaw, *ed, ing.*
4535	Gill, *s.*		

55

Nos.	GO	Nos.	GRA
4578	Go, *ing.*	4621	Gout, *y.*
9	about.	2	Govern, *ed, ing.*
4580	ahead.	3	Government.
1	around.	4	dispatches.
2	back.	5	officer, *s.*
3	between.	6	Governor, *s.*
4	down.	7	Graceful, *ly.*
5	in.	8	Gracious, *ly.*
6	out.	9	Gradation, *al, s.*
7	through.	4630	Grade, *s.*
8	up.	1	Gradual, *ly.*
9	Goad, *ed, ing.*	2	Grain, *s.*
4590	Goal.	3	Grammar, *s.*
1	Goat, *s.*	4	Grammatical, *ly.*
2	God, *ly.*	5	Grampus.
3	God send.	6	Grand, *ly.*
4	Gold.	7	division, *s.* .
5	dust.	8	Grant, *ed, ing, s.*
6	lace.	9	Granulate, *d, ing, ion.*
7	mine, *s.*	4640	Grape, *s.*
8	smith, *s.*	1	shot.
9	wire.	2	Graphic, *al, ally.*
4600	Gone.	3	Grapnel, *s.*
1	Gong, *s.*	4	Grapple, *d, ing.*
2	Gonorrhœa.	5	Grasp, *ed, ing.*
3	Good.	6	Grass, *y.*
4	bye.	7	Grate.
5	coal.	8	bars.
6	condition.	9	Grateful, *ly.*
7	for nothing.	4650	Gratification.
8	luck.	1	Gratify, *ied, ing.*
9	morning.	2	Gratitude.
4610	night.	3	Gratuitous, *ly.*
1	opportunity.	4	Gratis.
2	sense.	5	Gratuity.
3	weather.	6	Gravamen.
4	will.	7	Grave, *s.*
5	Goosewing, *ed, s.*	8	Graving beach.
6	Gordian knot.	9	dock.
7	Goring cloths.	4660	yard.
8	Gossip, *ed, ing, y.*	1	Gravel, *ly.*
9	Got, *ten.*	2	Gravitate, *d, ing, ion.*
4620	Gouge, *s.*	4663	Gravity.

Nos.	GRA	Nos.	GUN
4664	Gray.	4707	Grumble, *d, ing, er.*
5	Graze, *d, ing.*	8	Guano.
6	Grease, *d, ing.*	9	Guarantee, *d, ing.*
7	Great, *er, est.*	4710	Guaranty.
8	guns.	1	Guard, *ed, ing.*
9	Grecian.	2	boat, *s.*
4670	Greek fire.	3	flag.
1	Green.	4	house.
2	hand, *s.*	5	ship.
3	paint, *s.*	6	Guardian.
4	wood.	7	Gudgeon, *s.*
5	Greet, *ed, ing.*	8	Guerilla, *s.*
6	Grenade, *s.*	9	warfare.
7	Gridiron, *s.*	4720	Guess, *ed, ing.*
8	pendulum.	1	Guess warp.
9	valve.	2	Guest, *s.*
4680	Grief, *s.*	3	Guidance.
1	Grievance, *s.*	4	Guide, *d, ing.*
2	Grieve, *d, ing.*	5	Guidon, *s.*
3	Grievous, *ly.*	6	Guileless.
4	Grind, *ing.*	7	Guilt, *y.*
5	stone.	8	Guiltless.
6	Gripe, *s, d, ing.*	9	Guinea, coast of.
7	Grit, *ty.*	4730	Guise.
8	Groan, *ed, ing, s.*	1	Gulf.
9	Grocer, *y, ies.*	2	stream.
4690	Grog, *gy.*	3	weed.
1	shop, *s.*	4	Gum, *med, ming, my.*
2	Groin, *s.*	5	arabic.
3	Grommet, *s.*	6	packing.
4	wad, *s.*	7	Gun, *s.*
5	Groove, *d, ing, s.*	8	barrel.
6	Grope, *d, ing.*	9	boat, *s.*
7	Gross, *ly.*	4740	carriage, *s.*
8	Ground, *ed, ing.*	1	cotton.
9	swell.	2	deck, *s.*
4700	tackle.	3	fire.
1	tier.	4	gear.
2	Groundless.	5	lock, *s.*
3	Grovel, *led, ling.*	6	metal.
4	Growl, *ed, ing.*	7	Gunner, *s.*
5	Grown.	8	mate, *s.*
4706	Growth.	4749	gang, *s.*

57

Nos.	GUN	Nos.	HAN
	Gunner, *s.*		Half.
4750	quadrant, *s.*	4792	hitch, *es.*
1	Gunnery.	3	pay.
2	Gunny bags.	4	pint, *s.*
3	Gun powder.	5	speed.
4	room.	6	starved.
5	shot wound.	7	tide.
6	sight, *s.*	8	way.
7	smith, *s.*	9	yearly.
8	stock, *s.*	4800	Halibut.
9	tackle, *s.*	1	Hall, *s.*
4760	wad, *s.*	2	Halliards.
1	Gunter's chain.	3	Halloo, *ed, ing.*
2	scale.	4	Hallucination.
3	Gust, *s.*	5	Halt, *ed, ing.*
4	of wind.	6	Halve, *d, ing, s.*
5	Gut, *ted, ting.*	7	Ham, *s.*
6	Gutta percha.	8	Hammer, *s, ed, ing.*
7	Guy, *s, ed, ing.*	9	Hammock, *s.*
8	Habeas corpus.	4810	cloths.
9	Habits.	1	nettings.
4770	Habitation, *s.*	2	Hamper, *ed, ing.*
1	Habitual, *ly.*	3	Hand, *s, ed, ing.*
2	Hack, *ed, ing, s.*	4	barrow, *s.*
3	Hackmatack.	5	basket, *s.*
4	Had.	6	car, *s.*
5	Hail, *s, ed, ing.*	7	cuff, *s.*
6	come within.	8	grenade, *s.*
7	the passing boat, *s.*	9	hole, *s.*
8	the stranger.	4820	hole plate.
9	the vessel.	1	Handily.
4780	Hair.	2	Hand-in-hand.
1	brained.	3	Handwork.
2	breadth.	4	Handlamp, *s.*
3	cloth.	5	Handle, *d, ing.*
4	Halcyon.	6	Hand lead, *s.*
5	Half.	7	pump, *s.*
6	and half.	8	over hand.
7	an hour.	9	saw, *s.*
8	breed.	4830	screw, *s.*
9	deck.	1	Handsome, *ly.*
4790	dollar, *s.*	4832	Handspike, *s.*
4791	eagle, *s.*		

Nos.	HAN	Nos.	HAV
4633	Hand tight.	4876	Harpy, *ies*.
4	writing.	7	Harsh, *ly*.
5	Handy billy.	8	Hartshorn.
6	Hang, *ed, ing*.	9	Has.
7	knee, *s*.	4880	Haste.
8	on.	1	Hasten, *ed, ing*.
9	Hank, *s*.	2	Hasty, *ily*.
4840	Hanoverian.	3	Hat, *s*.
1	Happen, *ed, ing*.	4	Hatch, *es*.
2	Happily.	5	Hatchet, *s*.
3	Happiness.	6	Hatch grating, *s*.
4	Happy.	7	tarpauline, *s*.
5	Harangue, *d, ing*.	8	Hatchway, *s*.
6	Harass, *ed, ing*.	9	Hate, *d, ing*.
7	Harbinger.	4890	Hatred.
8	Harbor, *ed, ing*.	1	Haughty, *iness*.
9	dues.	2	Haul, *ed, ing*.
4850	master.	3	aboard.
1	Hard, *er, est*.	4	aft.
2	and fast.	5	alongside.
3	a lee the helm.	6	by the wind.
4	a port the helm.	7	fire, *s*.
5	a starboard the helm.	8	line, *s*.
6	up the helm.	9	in.
7	Harden, *ed, ing*.	4900	out.
8	Hard fought.	1	off.
9	hearted.	2	on the wind.
4860	Hardihood.	3	the seine.
1	Hardly.	4	Have, *ing*.
2	Hardship, *s*.	5	furnished.
3	Hardware.	6	had.
4	Hard wood.	7	heard.
5	Hardy.	8	not.
6	Harm, *ed, ing*.	9	not had.
7	Harmless.	4910	not heard.
8	Harmonious, *ly*.	1	not seen.
9	Harmonize, *d, ing*.	2	not spoken.
4870	Harmony.	3	seen.
1	Harness.	4	spoken.
2	cask, *s*.	5	they.
3	Harp, *ed, ing*.	6	you.
4	Harping, *s*.	7	you heard.
4875	Harpoon, *ed, ing, s*.	4918	you seen.

Nos.	HAV	Nos.	HEI
	Have, *ing.*	4961	Health, *y.*
4919	you spoken.	2	climate.
4920	Havoc.	3	is bad.
1	Hawse.	4	is good.
2	buckler, *s.*	5	Hear, *ing.*
3	hole, *s.*	6	firing.
4	pipe, *s.*	7	Heart, *s, y.*
5	pendant, *s.*	8	Heartfelt.
6	plug, *s.*	9	Heartily.
7	Hawser, *s.*	4970	Heartrending.
8	Hazard, *ed, ing, s, ous.*	1	Heat, *ed, ing.*
9	Haze, *y.*	2	Heathen, *ish.*
4930	weather.	3	Heave, *ing.*
1	He.	4	ahead.
2	had.	5	astern.
3	had not.	6	down.
4	has.	7	the lead,
5	has not.	8	the log.
6	will.	9	short your cable.
7	will not.	4980	to your vessel.
8	Head, *ed, ing, s.*	1	up your anchor.
9	ache.	2	Heaven, *ly.*
4940	earing, *s.*	3	Heaver, *s.*
1	fast.	4	Heavily.
2	foremost.	5	Heavy.
3	gear.	6	cargo.
4	land.	7	firing.
5	line, *s.*	8	laden.
6	long.	9	metal.
7	most.	4990	sea.
8	of the mast.	1	spars.
9	off.	2	Heed, *ed, ing.*
4950	on.	3	Heel, *ed, ing.*
1	quarters.	4	lashing.
2	rails.	5	of the.
3	rope.	6	rope.
4	sail, *s.*	7	to port.
5	sea.	8	to starboard.
6	stays.	9	Height.
7	to wind.	5000	Heighten, *ed, ing.*
8	way.	1	Heinous, *ly.*
9	wind.	2	Heir, *ess.*
4960	Heal, *ed, ing.*	5003	apparent.

60

Nos.	HEL	Nos.	HIL
5004	Held.	5046	Herring, *s.*
5	Helix.	7	bone, *d, ing.*
6	Hell, *ish.*	8	fishery.
7	Helm.	9	Herself.
8	Helmsman, *men.*	5050	Hesitate, *d, ing, ion.*
9	Help, *ed, ing.*	1	Heterogeneous.
5010	Helpless, *ly.*	2	Hexagon, *al.*
1	Helpmate.	3	Hiatus.
2	Helter skelter.	4	Hiccough.
3	Helve, *d, ing.*	5	Hickory.
4	Hem, *med, ming.*	6	broom, *s.*
5	Hemisphere.	7	Hid, *den.*
6	Hemispherical.	8	Hide, *s.*
7	Hemlock.	9	Hideous, *ly.*
8	Hemorrhage.	5060	Hide rope.
9	Hemorrhoids.	1	Hiding.
5020	Hemp, *en.*	2	place.
1	cable.	3	High, *er, est.*
2	canvas.	4	and dry.
3	rope.	5	bluff, *s.*
4	waste.	6	handed.
5	Hen, *s.*	7	land, *s.*
6	coop, *s.*	8	latitude.
7	Hence.	9	Highly.
8	forth.	5070	Highminded.
9	Her. .	1	Highness.
5030	Herald, *ed, ing.*	2	High pressure.
1	Herb, *s.*	3	pressure engine.
2	Herculean.	4	price, *d, es.*
3	Here.	5	road.
4	Hereafter.	6	sea.
5	Herein.	7	speed.
6	Heresy.	8	steam.
7	Heretofore.	9	tone, *d.*
8	Herewith.	5080	treason.
9	Hermaphrodite brig.	1	water.
5040	Hermetical, *ly.*	2	water mark.
1	Hernia.	3	Highway, *s, man.*
2	Hero, *es.*	4	robber, *y.*
3	Heroic, *ally.*	5	Hilarity.
4	action.	6	Hill, *s, y.*
5045	Heroism.	7	Hillock, *s.*
		5088	Hilt, *ed.*

Nos.	HIM	Nos.	HOR
5089	Him.	5132	Hominy.
5090	Himself.	3	Homœopathic.
1	Hinder, *ed*, *ing*.	4	Homogeneous.
2	Hindmost.	5	Homograph, *s*, *ic*.
3	Hindoo, *s*.	6	signal, *s*.
4	Hindrance.	7	Honest, *y*, *ly*.
5	Hinge, *d*, *ing*.	8	Honor, *ed*, *ing*, *s*.
6	valve, *s*.	9	Honorable.
7	Hint, *s*, *ed*, *ing*.	5140	Honorably.
8	Hip, *s*.	1	Honorary.
9	joint, *s*.	2	member, *s*.
5100	Hire, *d*, *ing*.	3	Hood, *s*.
1	His.	4	ends.
2	Historic, *al*, *ably*.	5	wink, *ed*, *ing*.
3	History, *ies*.	6	Hook, *ed*, *ing*, *s*.
4	Hit, *ting*.	7	rope, *s*.
5	the enemy.	8	Hoop, *ed*, *ing*, *s*.
6	the target.	9	cough.
7	Hitch, *ed*, *es*.	5150	iron.
8	Hither.	1	Hope, *d*, *ing*, *ful*.
9	Hitherto.	2	Hopeless, *ly*.
5110	Hoarse, *ly*.	3	Horary.
1	Hobble, *d*, *ing*.	4	Horizon, *tal*.
2	Hog, *ged*.	5	glass, *es*.
3	brace, *s*.	6	Horn.
4	frame, *s*.	7	book of storms.
5	Hogshead, *s*.	8	card.
6	Hoist, *ed*, *ing*.	9	of the cross-trees.
7	gear.	5160	Horrible.
8	Hold, *ing*, *s*.	1	Horribly.
9	fast.	2	Horrid, *ly*.
5120	out as long as possible.	3	Horror, *s*.
1	ground.	4	Hors de combat.
2	Hole, *s*.	5	Horse, *s*.
3	Holiday, *s*.	6	artillery.
4	Hollow, *ed*.	7	back.
5	Holy.	8	block.
6	stone, *d*, *ing*, *s*.	9	car.
7	Homage.	5170	latitude, *s*.
8	Home, *s*.	1	mackerel.
9	squadron.	2	power.
5130	ward bound.	5173	shoe.
5131	Homicide, *s*.		

Nos.	HOS	Nos.	HYD
5174	Hose.		Howitzer, *s.*
5	carriage.	5217	boat carriage.
6	coupling, *s.*	8	field carriage.
7	Hospitable.	9	implements.
8	Hospitality.	5220	Howl, *ed, ing.*
9	Hospital, *s.*	1	Hub, *s.*
5180	nurse, *s.*	2	Huddle, *d, ing.*
1	steward, *s.*	3	Hug, *ged, ging.*
2	Hostage, *s.*	4	Huge, *ly.*
3	Hostile.	5	Hulk, *s.*
4	appearance, *s.*	6	Hull, *ed, ing.*
5	force, *s.*	7	down.
6	Hostility, *ies.*	8	Human.
7	Hot, *ly.*	9	nature.
8	flue.	5230	Humane.
9	headed.	1	Humanity.
5190	shot.	2	Humanize, *d, ing.*
1	water.	3	Humble, *d.*
2	well.	4	Humbug, *ged, ging, s.*
3	Hotel, *s.*	5	Humid, *ity.*
4	Hound, *s.*	6	Humiliate, *d, ing, ion.*
5	of the mast.	7	Humor, *ed, ing.*
6	Hour, *s, ly.*	8	Hundred.
7	angle.	9	Hundredth.
8	of the day.	5240	Hundred weight, C. W. T.
9	glass, *es.*	1	Hung.
5200	of the night.	2	Hunger.
1	House, *s, ed, ing.*	3	Hungry.
2	line.	4	Hunt, *ed, ing.*
3	of Representatives.	5	Hurt, *s, ing.*
4	topmast, *s.*	6	Hurricane, *s.*
5	topgallant mast, *s.*	7	deck.
6	Hove.	8	Hurry, *ied, ing.*
7	down.	9	Hurl, *ed, ing.*
8	short.	5250	Hurter, *s.*
9	to.	1	Husband, *ed, ing.*
5210	Hovel, *s.*	2	Hut, *s.*
1	Hover, *ed, ing.*	3	Hybrid.
2	How?	4	Hydrant, *s.*
3	do you do?	5	Hydraulic, *s.*
4	However.	6	press.
5	Howitzer, *s.*	7	ram.
5216	ammunition.	5258	Hydrogen.

Nos.	HYD	Nos.	ILL
5259	Hydrographer, *s.*	5301	If.
5260	Hydrographic.	2	he.
1	. office.	3	not.
2	Hydrography.	4	so.
3	Hydrometer, *s.*	5	the.
4	Hygiene.	6	they.
5	Hypochondriac.	7	we.
6	Hypocrisy.	8	you.
7	Hypocrite.	9	Igneous.
8	Hypocritical.	5310	Ignis fatuus.
9	Hypothetical.	1	Ignite, *d, ing, ion.*
5270	I am.	2	Ignoble.
1	I am not.	3	Ignominious.
2	I can.	4	Ignorance.
3	I cannot.	5	Ignorant, *ly.*
4	Ice.	6	Ignore, *d, ing.*
5	anchor, *s.*	7	Ill.
6	belt, *s.*	8	advised.
7	berg, *s.*	9	bred.
8	blink.	5320	breeding.
9	boat.	1	conducted.
5280	bound.	2	considered.
1	field, *s.*	3	deserved.
2	floe, *s.*	4	disposed.
3	Iceland, *ic.*	5	Illegal, *ity.*
4	I could.	6	Illegible.
5	I could not.	7	Illegitimate, *ly.*
6	Icy.	8	Ill fated.
7	Idea.	9	Illiberal.
8	Ideal, *ity.*	5330	Illicit, *ly.*
9	Identical, *ly.*	1	trade.
5290	Identify, *ied, ing.*	2	Illimitable.
1	Identity.	3	Illiterate.
2	Idiocy.	4	Ill judged.
3	Idiom, *s, atic.*	5	looking.
4	Idiosyncrasy.	6	luck.
5	Idiot, *s.*	7	manned.
6	Idle, *d, ing.*	8	mannered.
7	Idleness.	9	nature, *d.*
8	Idler, *s.*	5340	Illness.
9	Idol, *s, atry.*	1	Illogical.
5300	Idolize, *d, ing.*	2	Ill provided.
		5343	starred.

Nos.	ILL	Nos.	IMP
	Ill.	5386	Impair, *ed, ing*.
5344	temper, *ed*.	7	Impart, *ed, ing*.
5	time, *d*.	8	Impartial, *ly*.
6	Illuminate, *d, ing, ion*.	9	Impartiality.
7	Ill used.	5390	Impassable, *y, ility*.
8	Illusion.	1	Impassive.
9	Illustrate, *d, ing, ion*.	2	Impatience.
5350	Illustrious.	3	Impatient, *ly*.
1	Ill-will.	4	Impeach, *ed, ing, able*.
2	Image, *ry, s*.	5	Impeachment.
3	Imaginable.	6	Impede, *d, ing*.
4	Imaginary.	7	Impediment, *s*.
5	Imagination.	8	Impel, *led, ling*.
6	I may.	9	Impend, *ed, ing*.
7	I may not.	5400	Impenetrability.
8	Imbecile.	1	Impenetrable.
9	Imbecility.	2	Impenitent.
5360	Imbibe, *d, ing*.	3	Imperative, *ly*.
1	Imbroglio.	4	Imperceptible.
2	Imitable.	5	Imperfect, *ion, ly*.
3	Imitate, *d, ing, ion*.	6	Imperial, *ist*.
4	Immaterial.	7	Imperil, *led, ling*.
5	Immediate, *ly*.	8	Imperious, *ly*.
6	assistance.	9	Imperishable.
7	cause, *s*.	5410	Impertinence.
8	Immemorial.	1	Impertinent, *ly*.
9	Immense, *ly*.	2	Impervious.
5370	Immensity.	3	Impetuosity.
1	Immersion.	4	Impetuous, *ly*.
2	Immigrant, *s*.	5	Impetus.
3	Immigrate, *d, ing*.	6	Impinge, *d, ing*.
4	Imminent.	7	Implement, *s*.
5	Immobility.	8	Implicate, *d, ing, ion*.
6	Immoderate, *ly*.	9	Implicit, *ly*.
7	Immoral, *ly, ity*.	5420	Implore, *d, ing*.
8	Immortal, *ly*.	1	Imply, *ied, ing*.
9	Immortality.	2	Impolite, *ly*.
5380	Immortalize, *d, ing*.	3	Impolitic.
1	Immovable.	4	Import, *ed, ing*.
2	Immunity.	5	Importance.
3	Immure, *d*.	6	Important, *ly*.
4	Immutable.	7	Importation.
5385	Impact.	5428	Importer, *s*.

Nos.	IMP	Nos.	INC
5429	Importunate.	5472	Inaction.
5430	Importune, d, ing.	3	Inactive.
1	Importunity.	4	Inadequate, ly.
2	Impose, d, ing.	5	Inadmissible, ility.
3	Imposition.	6	Inadvertence.
4	Impossibility.	7	Inalienable.
5	Impossible.	8	Inanimate, d.
6	Imposter, s.	9	Inapplicable.
7	Imposture.	5480	Inappropriate, ly.
8	Impotence.	1	Inapt, itude.
9	Impotent.	2	Inarticulate.
5440	Impoverish, ed, ing.	3	Inasmuch.
1	Impracticability.	4	Inattention.
2	Impracticable.	5	Inattentive, ly.
3	Impregnability.	6	Inaudible, y.
4	Impregnable, y.	7	Inaugurate, d, ing.
5	Impregnate, d, ing.	8	Inauguration.
6	Impress, ed, ing.	9	Inauspicious, ly.
7	Impression.	5490	In board.
8	Impressive.	1	In boat, s.
9	Imprison, ed, ing.	2	Incalculable, y.
5450	Imprisonment.	3	Incandescence.
1	Improbable.	4	Incandescent.
2	Impromptu.	5	Incapability.
3	Improper, ly.	6	Incapable.
4	Impropriety, ies.	7	Incapacitate, d, ing.
5	Improve, d, ing, ment, s.	8	Incapacity.
6	Improvidence.	9	Incarcerate, d, ing, ion.
7	Improvident, ly.	5500	Incautious, ly.
8	Improvise, d, ing.	1	Incendiarism.
9	Imprudence.	2	Incendiary, ies.
5460	Imprudent, ly.	3	Incense, d, ing.
1	Impudence.	4	Incentive.
2	Impudent, ly.	5	Inception.
3	Impugn, ed, ing.	6	Incessant, ly.
4	Impulse, s, ive.	7	Inch, es.
5	Impunity.	8	board, s.
6	Imputation.	9	Incidence.
7	Impute, d, ing.	5510	Incident, ly, s, al.
8	In.	1	Incipient, ly.
9	Inability.	2	Incise, d, ing.
5470	Inaccurate, ly.	3	Incision, s.
5471	Inaccuracy, ies.	5514	Incite, d, ing.

Nos.	INC	Nos.	IND
5515	Inolvility, *ies.*	5558	Incorrect, *ly.*
6	Inclement.	9	Incorrigible, *y.*
7	Inclination, *s.*	5560	Incorrupt, *ible.*
8	Incline, *d, ing.*	1	Increase, *d, ing.*
9	engine, *s.*	2	distance.
5520	plane, *s.*	3	spread.
1	Include, *d, ing.*	4	Incredible, *y.*
2	Inclusive, *ly.*	5	Incredulity.
3	Incognito.	6	Incredulous, *ly.*
4	Incoherence.	7	Increment, *s.*
5	Incoherent, *ly.*	8	Incrust, *ed, ing, ation.*
6	Incombustible.	9	Incubus.
7	Income.	5570	Inculcate, *d, ing, ion.*
8	tax, *es.*	1	Inculpate, *d, ing, ion.*
9	Incoming.	2	Incumbent, *ly.*
5530	Incommode, *d, ing.*	3	Incur, *red, ring.*
1	Incommodious.	4	Incurable, *ly.*
2	Incomparable.	5	Incursion, *s.*
3	Incomparably.	6	Indebted, *ness.*
4	Incompatible.	7	Indecency, *ies.*
5	Incompetence.	8	Indecent, *ly.*
6	Incompetent.	9	Indecision.
7	Incomplete.	5580	Indecisive, *ly.*
8	Incomprehensible.	1	Indecorous.
9	Incompressible.	2	Indecorum.
5540	Inconceivable.	3	Indeed.
1	Inconclusive.	4	Indefatigable.
2	Incongruous.	5	Indefeasible, *ly.*
3	Incongruity.	6	Indefensible.
4	In consequence.	7	Indefinable, *ly.*
5	Inconsiderable, *y.*	8	Indefinite, *ly.*
6	Inconsiderate, *ly.*	9	Indelible, *y.*
7	In consideration of the.	5590	Indelicate, *ly.*
8	Inconsistency.	1	Indemnification.
9	Inconsistent, *ly.*	2	Indemnify, *ied, ing.*
5550	Inconsolable.	3	Indemnity, *ies.*
1	Inconstancy.	4	Indent, *ed, ing.*
2	Inconstant, *ly.*	5	Indentation, *s.*
3	Incontestable, *y.*	6	Indenture, *s.*
4	Inconvenience, *d, ing.*	7	Independence.
5	Inconvenient, *ly.*	8	Independence day.
6	Inconvertible, *y.*	9	Independent, *ly.*
5557	Incorporate, *d, ing, ion.*	5600	Indestructible.

Nos.	IND	Nos.	INF
5601	Indeterminate.	5644	In-door work.
2	Index, *indices.*	5	Indorse, *d, ing, ment, s.*
3	error.	6	In draught.
4	glass, *es.*	7	Indubitable, *y.*
5	hand.	8	Induce, *d, ing, ment, s.*
6	Indiaman.	9	magnetism.
7	India rubber.	5650	Induct, *ed, ing, ion.*
8	ink.	1	Inductive, *ly.*
9	Indian, *s.*	2	Indulge, *d, ing, ence.*
5610	Indicate, *d, ing.*	3	Indulgent, *ly.*
1	Indication, *s.*	4	Indurate, *d, ing.*
2	Indicative.	5	Industrial.
3	Indicator, *s.*	6	Industrious, *ly.*
4	Indict, *ed, ing, able.*	7	Industry.
5	Indictment, *s.*	8	Ineffective, *ly.*
6	Indifferent, *ly.*	9	Inefficiency.
7	Indigence.	5660	Inefficient.
8	Indigent.	1	Inelegant, *ly.*
9	Indigenous.	2	Ineligible, *y.*
5620	Indigestible.	3	Inequality.
1	Indigestion.	4	Inequilibrio.
2	Indignant, *ly.*	5	Inert, *ly.*
3	Indignation.	6	Inertia.
4	Indignity, *ies.*	7	Inestimable, *y.*
5	Indigo.	8	Inevitable, *y.*
6	Indirect, *ly.*	9	Inexcusable, *y.*
7	Indiscreet, *ly.*	5670	Inexhaustible, *y.*
8	Indiscretion.	1	Inexorable, *y.*
9	Indiscriminate, *ing, ly, ion.*	2	Inexpediency.
5630	Indispensable, *y.*	3	Inexpedient, *ly.*
1	Indispose, *d, ing.*	4	Inexpensive, *ly.*
2	Indisposition.	5	Inexperience, *d.*
3	Indisputable, *y.*	6	Inexplicable.
4	Indissoluble, *y.*	7	Inexpressible, *y.*
5	Indistinct, *ly.*	8	Inexpressive, *ly.*
6	Indistinguishable.	9	In extenso.
7	Indite, *d, ing.*	5680	Inextinguishable.
8	Individual, *s.*	1	Inextricable, *y.*
9	Individualize, *d, ing.*	2	Infallibility.
5640	Indivisible.	3	Infallible, *y.*
1	Indolence.	4	Infamous, *ly.*
2	Indolent, *ly.*	5	Infamy.
5643	Indomitable.	5686	Infancy.

Nos.	INF	Nos.	INN
5687	Infant, *s, ile.*	5730	Inhabit, *ed, ing, able.*
8	Infantry.	1	In harbor.
9	regiment, *s.*	2	In haste.
5690	Infatuate, *d, ing, ion.*	3	Inherent, *ly.*
1	Infect, *ed, ing, ion.*	4	Inherit, *ed, ing, ance.*
2	district.	5	Inhibit, *ed, ing.*
3	place.	6	Inhibition.
4	ship.	7	Inhospitable, *ly.*
5	Infectious.	8	Inhuman, *ity.*
6	disease, *s.*	9	Inimical, *ly.*
7	Infer, *red, ring, ence.*	5740	Inimitable, *y.*
8	Inferior, *ity, s.*	1	Iniquitous, *ly.*
9	force.	2	Iniquity, *ies.*
5700	speed.	3	Initial, *s.*
1	Infest, *ed, ing, s.*	4	velocity, *ies.*
2	Infinite, *ly, y.*	5	Initiate, *d, ing, ion.*
3	Infinitisimal.	6	Initiation.
4	Infirm, *ity, ities.*	7	Inject, *ed, ing.*
5	Inflame, *d, ing, mation, matory.*	8	Injection.
6	Inflammable.	9	cock, *s.*
7	Inflate, *d, ing, ion.*	5750	valve, *s.*
8	Inflexibility.	1	Injector.
9	Inflexible, *y.*	2	pipe, *s.*
5710	Inflict, *ed, ing, s, ion.*	3	Injudicious, *ly.*
1	Influence, *d, ing.*	4	Injunction, *s.*
2	Influential.	5	Injure, *d, ing.*
3	Influenza.	6	Injurious, *ly.*
4	Influx.	7	Injury, *ies.*
5	Inform, *ed, ing.*	8	Injustice.
6	Informal.	9	Ink, *ed, ing.*
7	Information.	5760	stand, *s.*
8	Informer, *s.*	1	Island.
9	Infraction.	2	In law.
5720	Infringe, *d, ing, ment.*	3	Inlet, *s.*
1	Infuriate, *d, ing.*	4	Inmate, *s.*
2	Infuse, *d, ing.*	5	Inmost, *innermost.*
3	Infusion.	6	Inn.
4	Ingenious, *ly.*	7	Innate, *ly.*
5	Ingenuity.	8	Inner.
6	Ingenuous, *ly.*	9	Innocence.
7	Inglorious, *ly.*	5770	Innocent, *ly.*
8	Ingredient, *s.*	1	Innocuous. *ly.*
5729	Ingulf, *ed, ing.*	5772	Innovate, *d, ing, ion.*

Nos.	INN	Nos.	INT
5773	Innuendo, *es*.	5815	Inspect, *ed, ing*.
4	Innumerable, *y*.	6	fleet.
5	Innoculate, *d, ing, ion*.	7	ship, *s*.
6	Inoffensive, *ly*.	8	the place.
7	Inopportune, *ly*.	9	Inspection, *s*.
8	In port.	5820	Inspiration.
9	In propria persona.	1	Inspire, *d, ing*.
5780	Inquest, *s*.	2	Install, *ed, ing, ation*.
1	Inquire, *d, ing*.	3	Instance, *d, ing, s*.
2	Inquiry.	4	Instant, *ly, aneous*.
3	Inquisitive, *ly*.	5	Instead.
4	Inquisitor, *ial*.	6	Instigate, *d, ing, ion*.
5	Inroad, *s*.	7	Instill, *led, ling*.
6	In safety.	8	Instinct.
7	Insane, *ly*.	9	Instinctive, *ly*.
8	Insanity.	5830	Institute, *d, ing, ion, s*.
9	Insatiable.	1	Instruct, *ed, ing*.
5790	Inscribe, *d, ing*.	2	Instruction.
1	Inscription, *s*.	3	Instructor, *s*.
2	Insect, *s*.	4	Instrument, *s*.
3	Insecure, *ly*.	5	Instrumentality.
4	Insecurity.	6	Insubordinate, *ly*.
5	Insensibility.	7	Insubordination.
6	Insensible, *y*.	8	Insufferable, *y*.
7	Inseparable, *y*.	9	Insufficient, *ly*.
8	Insert, *ed, ing*.	5840	Insular.
9	Insertion.	1	Insulate, *d, ing, ion*.
5800	Inshore.	2	Insult, *ed, ing*.
1	Inside.	3	Insuperable, *ly*.
2	bearings.	4	Insupportable, *y*.
3	track.	5	Insure, *d, ing*.
4	Insidious, *ly*.	6	Insurgent, *s*.
5	Insight.	7	Insurrection, *s, ary*.
6	Insignia.	8	Intact.
7	Insignificance.	9	Integral.
8	Insignificant, *ly*.	5850	Integrity.
9	Insincere, *ly, ity*.	1	Integument, *s*.
5810	Insinuate, *d, ing, ion*.	2	Intellect, *ual, ly*.
1	Insist, *ed, ing*.	3	Intelligence.
2	Insolence.	4	from home.
3	Insolent, *ly*.	5	of the enemy.
5814	Insoluble.	6	Intelligent, *ly*.
		5857	Intelligible, *ly*.

Nos.	INT	Nos.	INV
5858	Intemperance.	5901	Interruption, *s.*
9	Intemperate, *ly.*	2	Intersect, *ed, ing.*
5860	Intend, *ed, ing.*	3	Interstice, *s.*
1	Intense, *ly.*	4	Interval, *s.*
2	Intensity, *ies.*	5	Intervene, *d, ing.*
3	Intent, *ly.*	6	Intervention, *s.*
4	Intention, *al, ly.*	7	Interview, *s.*
5	Inter, *red, ring.*	8	Intestine.
6	Intercede, *d, ing.*	9	Intestines.
7	Intercept, *ed, ing.*	5910	Intimacy, *ies.*
8	Intercession.	1	Intimate, *d, ing.*
9	Interchange, *d, ing, able.*	2	Intimation, *s.*
5870	divisions.	3	Intimidate, *d, ing, ion.*
1	squadrons.	4	Into.
2	Intercourse.	5	action.
3	Interdict, *ed, ing.*	6	port.
4	Interest, *ed, ing.*	7	Intolerable, *y.*
5	news received.	8	Intolerance.
6	Interfere, *d, ing, ence.*	9	Intolerant, *ly.*
7	Interim.	5920	Intoxicate, *d, ing, ion.*
8	Interior.	1	Intractable.
9	Interline, *d, ing, ation.*	2	In transitu.
5880	Intermeddle, *d, ing.*	3	Intrench, *ed, ing, ment, s.*
1	Intermediate.	4	Intrepid, *ity, ly.*
2	Interment.	5	Intricacy, *ies.*
3	Interminable, *ly.*	6	Intricate, *ly.*
4	Intermit, *ted, ting.*	7	Intrigue, *d, ing, s.*
5	Intermittent.	8	Intrinsic, *al, ally.*
6	Internal, *ly.*	9	Introduce, *d, ing.*
7	affairs.	5930	Introduction.
8	discipline.	1	Intrude, *d, ing.*
9	rules and regulations.	2	Intrusion.
5890	International, *ality, ly.*	3	Intrusive, *ly.*
1	Internecine.	4	Intrust, *ed, ing.*
2	Interpolate, *d, ing, ion.*	5	Inundate, *d, ing, ion.*
3	Interpose, *d, ing.*	6	Inutility.
4	Interposition.	7	In vacuo.
5	Interpret, *ed, ing, ation.*	8	Invade, *d, ing.*
6	Interpreter, *s.*	9	Invader, *s.*
7	Interregnum.	5940	Invalid, *s, ed, ing.*
8	Interrogate, *d, ing, ion.*	1	Invalidate, *d, ing.*
9	Interrogative, *ly.*	2	Invaluable.
5900	Interrupt, *ed, ing.*	5943	Invariable, *y.*

Nos.	INV	Nos.	IT
5944	Invasion.	5987	Irreconcilable, *ly*.
5	Inveigle, *d, ing, ment*.	8	Irreconciled.
6	Invent, *ed, ing, ion*.	9	Irrefragable, *y*.
7	Inventor, *s*.	5990	Irregular, *ly, ity*.
8	Inventory, *ies*.	1	Irrelevant, *ly*.
9	Inverse, *ly, d*.	2	Irremediable, *y*.
5950	order.	3	Irreparable, *y*.
1	Inversion.	4	Irreproachable, *y*.
2	Invert, *ed, ing*.	5	Irresistible, *y*.
3	Invest, *ed, ing*.	6	Irresolute.
4	Investigate, *d, ing, ion*.	7	Irrespective, *ly*.
5	Inveterate, *ly*.	8	Irresponsible, *y*.
6	Invidious, *ly*.	9	Irrevocable, *y*.
7	Invigorate, *d, ing*.	6000	Irritability.
8	Invincible, *y*.	1	Irritable.
9	Inviolable, *y*.	2	Irritant, *s*.
5960	Inviolate, *d, ly*.	3	Irritate, *d, ing, ion*.
1	Invisible, *y*.	4	Is.
2	Invitation, *s*.	5	he.
3	Invite, *s, d, ing*.	6	he not.
4	Invoice, *d, s*.	7	it.
5	Invoke, *d, ing*.	8	it not.
6	Involve, *d, ing*.	9	not.
7	Invulnerable, *y*.	6010	she.
8	Inward, *s, ly*.	1	she not.
9	Iodide.	2	I should.
5970	Iodine.	3	have.
1	Iridium.	4	not.
2	Irksome.	5	not have.
3	Iron, *ed*.	6	Island, *s*.
4	bound.	7	Isothermal.
5	clad, *s*.	8	Issue, *d, ing*.
6	foundry.	9	clothing.
7	frame, *d*.	6020	provisions.
8	plate, *s, d, ing*.	1	Isthmus.
9	sheathed.	2	It.
5980	sick.	3	is.
1	side, *d*.	4	is not.
2	steamer, *s*.	5	may.
3	Iron work.	6	may not.
4	Irradiate, *d, ing*.	7	was.
5	Irrational, *ly*.	8	was not.
5986	Irreclaimable, *ly*.	6029	will.

Nos.	IT	Nos.	LAN
	It.	6072	Justify, *ied, ing.*
6030	will not.	3	Kedge, *s, d, ing.*
1	Itch.	4	Keelson.
2	Item, *s.*	5	Keep, *ing.*
3	Itself.	6	away.
4	Ivory black.	7	inside.
5	Jacket, *s.*	8	off.
6	Jack knife, *ves.*	9	outside.
7	Jack screw, *s.*	6080	Kept.
8	Jail, *s.*	1	Kettle, *s.*
9	Jalap.	2	Key, *ed, ing.*
6040	Jam, *med, ming, s.*	3	Key, *ing,* up.
1	January.	4	Kill, *ed, ing.*
2	Japanese.	5	Kind, *ness, ly.*
3	Jaundice.	6	Kingston valve.
4	Jaw, *s.*	7	Kit, *s.*
5	Jeopard, *ed.*	8	Kitchen, *s,* utensils.
6	Jeopardy.	9	Knee deep.
7	Jib.	6090	Knew.
8	Jib-boom.	1	Knoll, *s.*
9	Join, *ed, ing.*	2	Know, *ing.*
6050	me.	3	Knowingly.
1	the.	4	Knowledge.
2	the fleet.	5	Known.
3	Joiner, *s.*	6	Laborer, *s.*
4	Jointly.	7	Laboratory.
5	Journal, *s.*	8	Lack, *ed, ing.*
6	Judge, *d, ing, s.*	9	Lacker, *ed, ing.*
7	Advocate.	6100	Laden.
8	of the District Court.	1	Lag, *ged, ging.*
9	Judgment, *s.*	2	Lagoon, *s.*
6060	Judicial, *ly.*	3	Laid up.
1	Judicious, *ly.*	4	Lame, *d, ing, ly.*
2	July.	5	Lameness.
3	June.	6	Lament, *ed, ing, able.*
4	Junior, *s,*	7	Lamp, *s.*
5	Junk, *s.*	8	black.
6	Jurisdiction.	9	chimney, *ies.*
7	Jury mast.	6110	oil.
8	Jury rudder.	1	wicking.
9	Just, *ice.*	2	Lancet, *s.*
6070	Justifiable.	3	Land, *ed, ing.*
6071	Justification.	6114	Landsman, *men.*

73

Nos.	LAN	Nos.	LIF
6115	Land.	6157	Leather.
6	Language, *s.*	8	belting.
7	Lantern, *s.*	9	Leave, *ing.*
8	light, *s.*	6160	of absence.
9	Large, *ly.*	1	Led.
6120	Lash, *ed, ing.*	2	Ledge, *s.*
1	alongside.	3	Ledger, *s.*
2	securely.	4	Lee.
3	Lasso.	5	Left.
4	Last.	6	Leg, *s.*
5	Late, *ly.*	7	Legal, *ity, ly.*
6	action.	8	Legalize, *d, ing.*
7	news.	9	Legation.
8	Latitude.	6170	Legitimate.
9	and longitude.	1	Lemon, *s.*
6130	by account.	2	Lend, *ing.*
1	by observation.	3	Length, *s.*
2	is approximate.	4	Lengthen, *ed, ing.*
3	is correct.	5	Lenient, *ly.*
4	Latter, *ly.*	6	Lesion.
5	Laud, *ed, able.*	7	Less.
6	Laudanum.	8	Lessen, *ed, ing.*
7	Launch, *es, ed, ing.*	9	Let.
8	Launch's crew.	6180	Letter, *s.*
9	Launch's recall.	1	Levant, *er.*
6140	Law, *s.*	2	Levee.
1	book, *s.*	3	Level.
2	Lawful, *ly.*	4	Liable.
3	Lawless, *ly.*	5	Liberal, *ity.*
4	Law officer, *s.*	6	Liberally.
5	Laws of nations.	7	Liberate, *d, ing.*
6	Lax.	8	Liberty.
7	Lay, *ing.*	9	men.
8	Lay days.	6190	money.
9	Lazaretto.	1	Lice.
6150	Lead, *ing.*	2	Lie, *ing.*
1	Lead, *s.*	3	by.
2	Lead line, *s.*	4	off and on.
3	pencil, *s.*	5	Lieutenant, *s.*
4	Leadsman, *men.*	6	Commander.
5	Leak, *ed, ing, s.*	7	Life.
6156	Leakage.	6198	Lift, *s, ed, ing.*

Nos.	LIG	Nos.	LUN
6199	Light.	6242	Longitude.
6200	handed.	3	by account.
1	house, *s.*	4	by chronometer.
2	is fixed.	5	by lunar obs.
3	is revolving.	6	is approximate.
4	room, *s.*	7	is correct.
5	sails.	8	Look, *ed, ing.*
6	ship.	9	all around.
7	Lighten, *ed, ing.*	6250	out for.
8	Lighter, *s, age.*	1	out sharp.
9	Lightning.	2	Loom, *ed, ing.*
6210	conductors.	3	of the land.
1	Lignum vitæ.	4	Loose, *d, ing.*
2	Like, *d, ing.*	5	light sails.
3	Lumber, *s.*	6	sails to a bowline.
4	Lime, *s.*	7	Loot, *ing.*
5	juice.	8	Loose, *ing.*
6	Limit, *ed, ing.*	9	Loss, *es.*
7	Line, *s.*	6260	Lost.
8	Linguist, *s.*	1	Loud.
9	Link, *s.*	2	Lousy.
6220	motion.	3	Low.
1	Linseed oil.	4	land.
2	Lint.	5	pressure.
3	Liquor, *s.*	6	pressure engine.
4	List, *s.*	7	steam.
5	Litharge.	8	water.
6	Little.	9	Lower.
7	Live.	6270	rigging.
8	Live oak.	1	Lowest.
9	Load, *ed, ing.*	2	Loyal, *ty, ly.*
6230	Loaf, *loaves.*	3	Lubricant.
1	Local, *ly, ity.*	4	Lubricate, *d, ing.*
2	Lock, *s.*	5	Luck, *ily.*
3	Lodgement.	6	Lucky.
4	Log, *s, ged, ging.*	7	Luff, *ed, ing.*
5	book, *s.*	8	Luggage.
6	line, *s.*	9	Lugger, *s.*
7	reel, *s.*	6280	Lull, *ed, ing.*
8	slate, *s.*	1	Lumber.
9	Long.	2	Luminous.
6240	Longer.	6283	Lunacy.
6241	Longest.		

Nos.	LUN	Nos.	MAT
6284	Lunar, *s.*	6327	Male.
5	distance.	8	screw, *s.*
6	caustic.	9	Malefactor, *s.*
7	observation, *s.*	6330	Malicious, *ly.*
8	Lunatic, *s.*	1	Malignant, *ly.*
9	Lung, *s.*	2	Mallet, *s.*
6290	Lurch, *ed, ing, es.*	3	Malt liquors.
1	Luxury, *ies.*	4	Maltreat, *ed, ing, ment.*
2	Lymphatic.	5	Man, *ned, ning.*
3	Machine, *s.*	6	Manage, *d, ing, ment.*
4	Machinery, *s.*	7	Mangle, *d, ing.*
5	Machinist, *s.*	8	Mania a potu.
6	gang, *s.*	9	Maniac.
7	tool, *s.*	6340	Manilla.
8	Made.	1	Manly.
9	Magazine, *s.*	2	Manœuvre, *d, ing, s.*
6300	Magellan straits.	3	Man-of-war.
1	Maggot, *s, y.*	4	Man overboard.
2	Magnet, *s.*	5	Man servant.
3	Magnetic.	6	Manslaughter.
4	Magnify, *ied, ing.*	7	Manual.
5	Magnitude.	8	Many.
6	Mahogany.	9	Map, *ped, ping, s.*
7	Mail, *s.*	6350	March, *ed, ing.*
8	arrived.	1	Margin.
9	bag, *s.*	2	Marine, *s.*
6310	boat, *s.*	3	barometer, *s.*
1	messenger, *s.*	4	Mark, *ed, ing, s.*
2	Maim, *ed, ing.*	5	Market, *s, ing.*
3	Main, *ly.*	6	Marline.
4	centre boss.	7	spike, *s.*
5	connecting rod, *s.*	8	Marsh, *y.*
6	engine.	9	Martial.
7	engine journal.	6360	Mask, *ed, ing.*
8	engine shaft.	1	battery, *ies.*
9	shaft.	2	Mass, *ed, ing.*
6320	shaft journal.	3	Massacre, *d, ing.*
1	Maintain, *ed, ing.*	4	Massy, *s.*
2	Make, *ing.*	5	Mast, *s, ed, ing.*
3	Malady, *ies.*	6	Master, *s, ed, ing.*
4	Malaria.	7	at arms.
5	Malarious.	8	Mate, *s.*
6326	disease, *s.*	6369	of the watch.

Nos.	MAT	Nos.	MIS
6370	Material, *s.*	6412	Mess, *ed, ing.*
1	Mathematical, *ly.*	3	cook, *s.*
2	instrument, *s.*	4	furniture.
3	Matting.	5	Message, *s.*
4	Mattress, *es.*	6	Messenger, *s.*
5	Mature, *d, ing.*	7	Messmate, *s.*
6	Maul, *s.*	8	Met.
7	Maximum.	9	Metallic.
8	May.	6420	packing.
9	Mayor, *alty.*	1	Meteor, *s, ic.*
6380	McArthur's, Courts Martial.	2	Method, *s, ical.*
1	Me.	3	Metre.
2	Meal, *s.*	4	Mexican.
3	time.	5	Miasma, *tic.*
4	Mean, *s, ing.*	6	Mica.
5	time.	7	Mid.
6	Measles.	8	channel.
7	Measure, *s, d, ing.*	9	day.
8	Meat.	6430	night.
9	Mechanic, *s.*	1	watch.
6390	Mechanical.	2	way.
1	Medal, *s,* of honor.	3	Middle, *d, ing.*
2	Meddle, *d, ing, some.*	4	Midshipman, *men.*
3	Medical.	5	Might.
4	Medicine, *s.*	6	Mild, *ly.*
5	Mediterranean.	7	Milder.
6	Meet, *ing.*	8	Mildew, *ed, ing.*
7	Member, *s.*	9	Mile, *s.*
8	Men.	6440	Mileage.
9	Menace, *d, ing, s.*	1	Military.
6400	Mend, *ed, ing.*	2	Milk.
1	Merchant, *s.*	3	Mind.
2	Merchantman, *men.*	4	Minimum.
3	Mercurial.	5	Minister, *s.*
4	barometer.	6	plenipotentiary.
5	gauge.	7	Minor, *s.*
6	Mercury.	8	Minute, *s, ly.*
7	Meridian.	9	Mirage.
8	altitude.	6450	Miscarry, *ied, ing.*
9	distance.	1	Misconceive, *d, ing.*
6410	Merit, *ed, ing, s.*	2	Misconduct, *ed, ing.*
6411	Meritorious, *ly.*	3	Misconstrue, *d, ing.*
		6454	Misconstruction.

Nos.	MIS	Nos.	MUD
6455	Misdemeanor, *s.*		Mooring.
6	Misery.	6498	shackle, *s.*
7	Misfortune.	9	Mop, *s.*
8	Mislead, *ed, ing.*	6500	Moral, *s, ly.*
9	Mismanage, *d, ing, ment.*	1	Morass.
6460	Miss, *ed, ing.*	2	More.
1	Missile, *s.*	3	assistance.
2	Missing boat, *s.*	4	Morning.
3	vessel, *s.*	5	Morocco.
4	Mission.	6	Morphine.
5	Mistake, *ing.*	7	Mortal.
6	Mistook.	8	wound.
7	Misunderstand, *ing.*	9	Mortally.
8	Misunderstood.	6510	Mortar, *s.*
9	Mitigate, *d, ing.*	1	ammunition.
6470	Mizzen.	2	Mortification.
1	Moat, *s.*	3	Mortify, *ied, ing.*
2	Mob, *bed.*	4	Mortuary report, *s.*
3	Moderate, *d, ing, ly.*	5	Mosquito, *es.*
4	Moderation.	6	Most, *ly.*
5	Modification, *s.*	7	Mote.
6	Modify, *ied, ing.*	8	Motion.
7	Molasses.	9	Motive, *s.*
8	Molest, *ed, ing, ation.*	6520	Mould, *s, ed, ing.*
9	Moment, *ary, arily.*	1	Mount, *ed, ing, s.*
6480	Monday.	2	Mountain, *s, ous.*
1	evening.	3	Mouth, *s.*
2	morning.	4	of the creek.
3	night.	5	of the harbor.
4	noon.	6	of the river.
5	Money, *s.*	7	Movable, *s.*
6	Monitor, *s.*	8	Move, *d, ing.*
7	Monkey.	9	Movement, *s.*
8	wrench, *es.*	6530	of the Commander-in-Chief.
9	Monomaniac.	1	of the enemy.
6490	Monsoon, *s.*	2	Much.
1	Month, *s, ly.*	3	Mucilage.
2	Moon.	4	Mucous.
3	light.	5	membrane.
4	rise.	6	Mud.
5	Moor, *ed, ing, s.*	7	fort, *s.*
6	Mooring chocks.	8	Muddy.
6497	rings.	6539	bottom.

Nos.	MUF	Nos.	NAV
6540	Muffle, *d, ing.*	6582	Name, *d, ing, s.*
1	Municipal.	3	of the day, *s.*
2	Munition, *s.*	4	of the man or men.
3	Murder, *ed, ing.*	5	of the month.
4	Murderer, *s.*	6	of the officer, *s.*
5	Murderous.	7	of the place, *s.*
6	Muriatic acid.	8	of the vessel, *s.*
7	Music, *al.*	9	Naptha.
8	instrument, *s.*	6590	Narcotic, *s.*
9	Musician, *s.*	1	Narrate, *d, ing.*
6550	Musket, *s.*	2	Narrative, *s, ly.*
1	ball, *s.*	3	Narrow, *ed, ing, s.*
2	range.	4	Narrowly.
3	Musketry.	5	Nation, *s.*
4	Muslin.	6	National.
5	Must.	7	custom, *s.*
6	Mustard.	8	ensign.
7	Muster, *ed, ing.*	9	salute.
8	book.	6600	Nationality.
9	roll.	1	Native, *s.*
6560	the crew.	2	Nativity.
1	Mustering clothes.	3	Natural, *ly.*
2	Musty.	4	Naturalize, *d, ing.*
3	Mutilate, *d, ing, ion.*	5	Nature.
4	Mutineer, *s.*	6	Nausea.
5	Mutinous.	7	Nauseate, *d, ing.*
6	Mutiny, *ied, ing.*	8	Nauseous.
7	Mutton.	9	Nautical.
8	Mutual, *ly.*	6610	almanac, *s.*
9	Muzzle.	1	mile, *s.*
6570	My, *self.*	2	Naval.
1	Mysterious, *ly.*	3	academy.
2	Mystery.	4	affairs.
3	Nail, *ed, ing, s.*	5	committee, *s.*
4	4 penny.	6	depot, *s.*
5	6 do.	7	force, *s.*
6	8 do.	8	General Court Martial.
7	10 do.	9	hospital, *s.*
8	12 do.	6620	law, *s.*
9	24 do.	1	news.
6580	30 do.	2	order, *s.*
6581	Naked, *ness.*	3	regulation, *s.*
		6624	rendezvous.

Nos.	NAV	Nos.	NOI
	Naval.	6667	Neighborhood.
6625	service.	8	Neither.
6	station, *s.*	9	Nerve, *d, ing.*
7	Surgeon.	6670	Nervous, *ly, ness.*
8	supplies.	1	disease, *s.*
9	tactics.	2	temperament.
6630	Navigable.	3	Net, *s.*
1	Navigate, *d, ing.*	4	Nettle, *s.*
2	Navigation.	5	Net work.
3	Navigator, *s.*	6	Neuralgia.
4	Navy.	7	Neuralgic.
5	Department.	8	Neutral.
6	of the United States.	9	flag.
7	store ship.	6680	powers.
8	transport, *s.*	1	waters.
9	yard, *s.*	2	Neutrality.
6640	Neap tide, *s.*	3	Neutralize, *d, ing.*
1	Near, *ed, ing.*	4	Never.
2	Nearly.	5	Nevertheless.
3	Neat, *ly.*	6	New, *ly.*
4	Neat's foot oil.	7	moon.
5	Necessaries.	8	Newspaper, *s.*
6	Necessarily.	9	Next.
7	Necessary.	6690	Nigh, *er, est.*
8	Necessitate, *d.*	1	Night, *s, ly.*
9	Necessity, *ies.*	2	Nine.
6650	Neck.	3	Nineteen, *th.*
1	Need, *ed, ing.*	4	Ninety, *ieth.*
2	assistance.	5	Ninth, *ly.*
3	coal.	6	Nip.
4	provisions.	7	Nipper, *s, ed, ing.*
5	water.	8	Nitrate of silver.
6	Needle, *s.*	9	Nitre.
7	Needless, *ly.*	6700	Nitric acid.
8	Needy.	1	Nitrogen.
9	Negative, *d.*	2	No.
6660	Neglect, *ed, ing.*	3	further.
1	Neglectful.	4	nearer.
2	Negligence.	5	news.
3	Negligent, *ly.*	6	Noble.
4	Negotiate, *d, ing, ion.*	7	Nobly.
5	Negotiator, *s.*	8	Nobody.
6666	Negro, *es.*	6709	Noise.

Nos.	NOI	Nos.	OAT
6710	Noiseless, *ly*.	6753	Nothing.
1	Noisy.	4	in sight.
2	Nominal.	5	of importance.
3	horse power.	6	Notice, *d*, *ing*.
4	Non-appearance.	7	Noticeable.
5	Non-attendance.	8	Notification, *s*.
6	Non-combatant, *s*.	9	Notify, *ied*, *ing*.
7	Non-commissioned.	6760	Notwithstanding.
8	officer, *s*.	1	Nourish, *ed*, *ing*, *ment*.
9	Non compos mentis.	2	November.
6720	Non-concurrence.	3	Now.
1	Non-contagious.	4	Nowhere.
2	None.	5	Noxious.
3	on hand.	6	Nozzle, *s*.
4	to spare.	7	Nucleus.
5	Non-observance.	8	Nuisance.
6	Nook.	9	Number, *ed*, *ing*, *s*.
7	Noon.	6770	of guns.
8	Nor.	1	of the enemy.
9	Normal.	2	Numeral, *s*.
6730	condition.	3	Numerical, *ly*.
1	North.	4	order.
2	bank.	5	Nun buoy, *s*.
3	east, *er*, *erly*.	6	Nurse, *d*, *ing*, *s*.
4	Northerly.	7	Nut, *s*.
5	Northern, *most*.	8	bolt, *s*.
6	lights.	9	of safety valve lever.
7	Northing.	6780	Nutriment.
8	North shore.	1	Nutrition.
9	side.	2	Nutritious.
6740	star.	3	Nux vomica.
1	Northward, *ly*.	4	Oak, *s*, *en*.
2	Northwest, *er*, *erly*.	5	board, *s*.
3	North wind.	6	knee, *s*.
4	Nose.	7	plank, *s*, *ed*, *ing*.
5	Nostalgia.	8	timber, *s*.
6	Not.	9	Oakum.
7	Notability, *ies*.	6790	Oar, *s*.
8	Notable, *s*.	1	Oarsman, *men*.
9	Note, *d*, *ing*, *s*.	2	Oath, *s*.
6750	book, *s*.	3	of allegiance.
1	paper.	4	of office.
6752	worthy.	6795	Oat-meal.

Nos.	OBE	Nos.	OPP
6796	Obedience.	6839	Of.
7	to orders.	6840	Off.
8	Obedient, *ly*.	1	Off and on.
9	Obey, *ed, ing*.	2	Off duty.
6800	instructions.	3	Offence, *s*.
1	Object, *ed, ing, s*.	4	Offend, *ed, ing, er*.
2	Objection, *s*.	5	Offensive, *ly*.
3	Obligatory.	6	conduct.
4	Oblige, *d, ing*.	7	movement, *s*.
5	Oblique, *ly*.	8	Offer, *ed, ing*.
6	Obnoxious, *ly*.	9	Officer, *s, ed, ing*.
7	Obscene, *ly*.	6850	in charge.
8	Obscure, *d, ing*.	1	of the day.
9	Obsequies.	2	of the deck.
6810	Observance.	3	Official, *ly*.
1	Observation, *s*.	4	Offing.
2	for latitude.	5	Often, *er, est*.
3	for latitude and longitude.	6	Oil, *ed, ing, s*.
4	for longitude.	7	Old, *er, est*,
5	of the moon.	8	Omission, *s*.
6	of the polar star.	9	Omit, *ted, ting*.
7	of the sun.	6860	On.
8	Observatory, *ies*.	1	Once.
9	Observe, *d, ing*.	2	One.
6820	Observer, *s*.	3	One o'clock.
1	Obstacle, *s*.	4	Onerous.
2	Obstruct, *ed, ing, ion*.	5	Onion, *s*.
3	the channel.	6	Only.
4	the pass.	7	Ooze.
5	Obtain, *ed, ing, able*.	8	Open, *ed, ing*.
6	Obviate, *d, ing*.	9	Openly.
7	Obvious, *ly*.	6870	Operate, *ed, ing*.
8	Occasion, *ed, ing, s, al, ally*.	1	Operation, *s*.
9	Occultation, *s*.	2	of the enemy.
6830	Occupant, *s*.	3	Ophthalmia.
1	Occupy, *ied, ing*.	4	Opiate, *s*.
2	Occur, *red, ring*.	5	Opinion, *s*.
3	Occurrence, *s*.	6	Opportune, *ly*.
4	Ocean.	7	Opportunity, *ies*.
5	steamer, *s*.	8	Oppose, *d, ing*.
6	Octant, *s*.	9	Opposite, *ly*.
7	October.	6880	Oppress, *ed, ing*.
6838	Odd.	6881	Oppression.

Nos.	OPP	Nos.	OVE
6882	Oppresive, *ly.*	6925	Outfit, *s, ting.*
3	Opprobrious.	6	Outflank, *ed, ing.*
4	Opprobrium.	7	Outgeneral, *led, ling.*
5	Option, *al.*	8	Outlet, *s.*
6	Or.	9	of the bay.
7	Oral, *ly.*	6930	of the river.
8	Orange, *s.*	1	Outlying.
9	Ordeal.	2	Out of bread.
6890	Order, *s, ed.*	3	of coal.
1	book.	4	of line.
2	of battle.	5	of oil.
3	of sailing.	6	of provisions.
4	of steaming.	7	of range.
5	Orderly, *ies.*	8	of sight.
6	sergeant, *s.*	9	of the channel.
7	Ordinarily.	6940	of the way.
8	Ordinary seaman, *men.*	1	of trim.
9	Ordnance.	2	Outpost, *s.*
6900	bureau.	3	Outrage, *d, ing.*
1	circular, *s.*	4	Outrageous, *ly.*
2	depot, *s.*	5	Outsail, *ed, ing.*
3	instructions.	6	Outside.
4	officer, *s.*	7	planking.
5	returns.	8	Outward, *s.*
6	supplies.	9	bound.
7	Organization, *s.*	6950	Oven, *s.*
8	Organize, *d, ing.*	1	Over.
9	Origin, *al.*	2	Overawe, *d, ing.*
6910	Originate, *d, ing.*	3	Overbear, *ing.*
1	Orlop deck.	4	Overboard.
2	Oscillate, *ing.*	5	Overcharge, *d, ing.*
3	engine, *s.*	6	Overcoat, *s.*
4	Oscillation, *s.*	7	Overdue.
5	Other.	8	Overflow, *ed, ing.*
6	Ought.	9	Overhaul, *ed, ing.*
7	Ounce, *s.*	6960	the chase.
8	Our, *s, selves.*	1	Overland.
9	Out.	2	route.
6920	Outboard.	3	Overlap, *ped, ping.*
1	bearing.	4	Overload, *ed, ing.*
2	delivery.	5	Overlook, *ed, ing.*
3	building, *s.*	6	Overmasted.
6924	Outer, *most.*	6967	Overpower, *ed, ing, s.*

83

Nos.	OVE	Nos.	PAS
6968	Oversight, *s, ed, ing.*	7011	Painless.
9	Overstay, *ed, ing.*	2	Paint, *ed, ing, s.*
6970	Overstep, *ped, ping.*	3	and oils.
1	Overt, *ly.*	4	brush, *es.*
2	Overtake, *n, ing.*	5	oil, *s.*
3	Overture, *s, ing.*	6	ship.
4	Overwhelm, *ed, ing.*	7	work.
5	Overwork, *ed, ing.*	8	Painter, *s,*
6	Own, *ed, ing.*	9	gang.
7	Owner, *s.*	7020	Pair, *s, ed, ing.*
8	Ox, *en.*	1	Palisade, *d, ing, s.*
9	Oxalic acid.	2	Palliate, *d, ing, ion.*
6980	Oxidation.	3	Palliative.
1	Oxide.	4	Palm, *s, ed, ing.*
2	Oxygen.	5	of the anchor.
3	Oyster, *s.*	6	Paltry.
4	Pace, *s.*	7	Pampero, *s.*
5	Pacific.	8	Pan, *s.*
6	Pacify, *ied, ing.*	9	Panic, *s.*
7	Pack, *ed, ing, s.*	7030	stricken.
8	Package, *s.*	1	Paper, *s.*
9	Packet, *s.*	2	Parade, *d, ing.*
6990	day, *s.*	3	Parallax.
1	ship, *s.*	4	Parallel, *s, ed.*
2	steamer, *s.*	5	Paralysis.
3	Pack ice.	6	Paramount.
4	Packing box, *es.*	7	Parapet, *s.*
5	collar.	8	Pardon, *ed, ing, s.*
6	ring, *s.*	9	Parent, *s.*
7	rubber.	7040	Park, *s, ed, ing.*
8	Pack thread.	1	of artillery.
9	Paddle, *d, ing.*	2	Parley, *ed, ing.*
7000	arm, *s.*	3	Parole, *d, ing.*
1	box, *es.*	4	for the day.
2	float, *s.*	5	for the night.
3	shaft, *s.*	6	the prisoner, *s.*
4	shaft bearing.	7	Part, *ed, ing, s.*
5	steamer, *s.*	8	Particular, *ity, ly.*
6	Padlock, *s.*	9	Partner, *s.*
7	Paid.	7050	of the mast, *s.*
8	Pain, *ed, ing, s.*	1	Party, *ies.*
9	Painful, *ly.*	2	of the enemy.
7010	operation, *s.*	7053	Pass, *ed, ing, es.*

Nos.	PAS	Nos.	PER
7054	Passage, *s.*	7097	Pepper, *ed, ing.*
5	Passed Asst. Paymaster.	8	Perceptible, *ly.*
6	Passed Asst. Surgeon.	9	Percussion.
7	Passenger, *s.*	7100	cap, *s.*
8	Passive, *ly.*	1	fuse, *s.*
9	Passport, *s.*	2	gun, *s.*
7060	Password.	3	lock.
1	for the day.	4	powder.
2	for the night.	5	primer, *s.*
3	Past.	6	shell.
4	Patient, *ly.*	7	Peremptory, *ly.*
5	Patriotism.	8	order, *s.*
6	Patrol, *led, ling.*	9	Perfect, *ed, ing.*
7	Pattern, *s.*	7110	arrangements.
8	maker.	1	Perfectly.
9	Pay, *ing.*	2	accurate.
7070	Pay away.	3	Perforate, *d, ing.*
1	Paymaster, *s.*	4	Perform, *ed, ing:*
2	Pay-roll, *s.*	5	the duty.
3	Peace, *able.*	6	Performance.
4	is proclaimed.	7	Perhaps.
5	proclamation.	8	Peril, *led, ling, s.*
6	Peaceful, *ly.*	9	Perilous, *ly.*
7	Pea-jacket, *s.*	7120	undertaking.
8	Peak, *s.*	1	Perish, *ed, ing, able.*
9	Pebble, *s.*	2	Permanent, *ly.*
7080	Pebbly bottom.	3	Permission.
1	Pen, *s.*	4	is granted.
2	Penal.	5	is not granted.
3	offence.	6	Permit, *ted, ting, s.*
4	laws.	7	Pernicious, *ly.*
5	Penalty, *ies.*	8	Perplex, *ed, ing.*
6	of the law.	9	Perplexity.
7	Pencil, *led, ling, s.*	7130	Perseverance.
8	Pendant, *s.*	1	Persevere, *d, ing.*
9	Pending.	2	Persist, *ed, ing.*
7090	Penetrability.	3	Persistent, *ly.*
1	Penetrate, *d, ing, ion.*	4	Person, *s, age.*
2	Peninsula, *s.*	5	Personal, *ly.*
3	Penitentiary.	6	Personate, *d, ing.*
4	Pension, *ed, ing, er, ers.*	7	Personnel.
5	Penury.	8	Peruse, *ed, ing.*
7096	People.	7139	Peruvian.

Nos.	PER	Nos.	PLE
7140	Pervade, *d, ing.*	7153	Pintle, *s.*
1	Perversion.	4	Pipe, *d, ing, s.*
2	Pervert, *ed, ing.*	5	down.
3	Pestilence.	6	Piracy, *ies.*
4	Petroleum.	7	Pirate, *s.*
5	Petty.	8	Piratic, *al.*
6	officer, *s.*	9	Pistol, *s.*
7	officer's mess, *es.*	7190	Piston, *s.*
8	Phial, *s.*	1	packing.
9	Phosphate.	2	rod.
7150	Phosphorescent.	3	springs.
1	Phthisis.	4	Pitch, *ed, ing, s.*
2	Physical, *ly.*	5	of the propeller.
3	Physician, *s.*	6	ladle, *s.*
4	Pick, *ed, ing, s.*	7	Piteous, *ly.*
5	Pickaxe, *s.*	8	Pitiable.
6	Picket, *s, ed, ing.*	9	Pity, *ied, ing.*
7	boat, *s.*	7200	Pivot, *ed, ing, s.*
8	guard.	1	bolt, *s.*
9	the channel.	2	flag, *s.*
7160	vessel, *s.*	3	gun, *s.*
1	Pickle, *s.*	4	gun's crew.
2	Piece, *s.*	5	vessel, *s.*
3	of artillery.	6	Place, *d, ing, s.*
4	Pier, *s.*	7	Plague.
5	Pierce, *d, ing.*	8	Plain, *ly.*
6	through and through.	9	Plan, *s, ned, ning.*
7	Pike, *s.*	7210	of attack.
8	Pikeman, *men.*	1	of battle.
9	Pilfer, *ed, ing.*	2	of the enemy.
7170	Pillar block, *s.*	3	Plane table.
1	Pilot, *ed, ing, s.*	4	Plank, *s, ed, ing.*
2	Pilotage.	5	Plate, *d, ing.*
3	Pilot boat, *s.*	6	Plausible.
4	Pin, *s, ned, ning.*	7	Plead, *s, ed, ing.*
5	Pine, *s.*	8	guilty.
6	board, *s.*	9	not guilty.
7	timber.	7220	Pleasant.
8	wood.	1	Please, *d, ing.*
9	Pinion, *s.*	2	Pleasure.
7180	and rack, *s.*	3	Pledge, *d, ing.*
1	Pint, *s.*	4	Plenipotentiary.
7182	measure, *s.*	7225	Plentiful, *ly.*

Nos.	PLE	Nos.	POU
7226	Plenty.	7269	Populace.
7	Pleurisy.	7270	Population.
8	Plug, *ged, ging, s.*	1	Populous.
9	centre bit.	2	Pork.
7230	for boiler tubes.	3	Port, *s.*
1	the shot hole, *s.*	4	Portable.
2	Plumb.	5	engine.
3	Plumbago.	6	Port Admiral.
4	Plumber, *s.*	7	anchor, *s.*
5	block.	8	battery, *ies.*
6	Plunder, *ed, ing.*	9	beam.
7	Plunger, *s.*	7280	bow.
8	Plunging fire.	1	cullis.
9	rod, *s.*	2	fire.
7240	Pneumonia.	3	hole, *s.*
1	Pocket, *s.*	4	Portion, *ed, ing, s.*
2	compass.	5	Port quarter, *s.*
3	Point, *s, ed, ing.*	6	tack.
4	blank.	7	Portugese.
5	blank range.	8	Position, *s.*
6	of land.	9	of the buoy, *s.*
7	. of shoal.	7290	of the ship.
8	of the compass.	1	of the shoal.
9	Poison, *ed, ing.*	2	Positive, *ly.*
7250	Poisonous, *ly.*	3	Possess, *ed, ing.*
1	Polacre.	4	Possession.
2	Polar, *ity.*	5	Possibility.
3	Polarize, *d, ing.*	6	Possible.
4	Pole, *s.*	7	Possibly.
5	star.	8	Post, *s.*
6	Police.	9	Postage.
7	office, *s.*	7300	stamp, *s.*
8	officer, *s.*	1	Postmark, *ed.*
9	Pomp.	2	Post meridian.
7260	Pond, *s.*	3	mortem.
1	Pontoon, *s.*	4	mortem examination.
2	bridge.	5	office, *s.*
3	carriage.	6	Postpone, *d, ing, ment.*
4	Poop, *ed.*	7	Pot, *s.*
5	cabin.	8	Potash.
6	lantern.	9	Potato, *es.*
7	Poor.	7310	Pouch, *es.*
7208	Poppit valve, *s.*	7311	Poultry.

87

Nos.	POU	Nos.	PRI
7312	Pound, *s.*	7355	Premeditate, *d, ing, ion.*
3	Pour, *ed, ing.*	6	Premonitory.
4	Poverty.	7	symptoms.
5	Powder.	8	Preoccupy, *ied, ing.*
6	Power, *s.*	9	Preparation.
7	Powerful, *ly.*	7360	Preparatory.
8	Powerless.	1	pendant or light.
9	Practicability.	2	Prepare, *d, ing.*
7320	Practicable.	3	Prescribe, *d, ing, s.*
1	Practical, *ly.*	4	Prescription, *s.*
2	Practise, *d, ing.*	5	Presence.
3	Praise, *d, ing.*	6	of the enemy.
4	Praiseworthy.	7	Present, *ed, ing.*
5	Pratique.	8	Presentation.
6	Precaution, *ed, ing, ary.*	9	Preservation.
7	Precede, *d, ing.*	7370	Preserve, *d, ing.*
8	Precedence.	1	Preside, *d, ing, s.*
9	Precedent, *s.*	2	President, *s.*
7330	Precept, *s.*	3	and Cabinet.
1	of the court.	4	of the U. States.
2	Precipitate, *d, ing, ly.*	5	salute.
3	Precipitation.	6	Press, *ed, ing.*
4	Precipitous.	7	of business.
5	Precise, *ly, ness.*	8	of sail.
6	Precision.	9	of steam.
7	Preclude, *d, ing.*	7380	Pretext.
8	Preconcert, *ed, ing.*	1	Prevail, *ed, ing.*
9	Predatory.	2	Prevalence.
7340	Predecessor, *s.*	3	Prevalent, *ly.*
1	Predetermine, *d, ing.*	4	Prevaricate, *d, ing, ion.*
2	Predicament.	5	Prevent, *ed, ing, ion.*
3	Predispose, *d, ing.*	6	Preventer, *s.*
4	Predominate, *d, ing.*	7	Previous, *ly.*
5	Preëminent, *ly.*	8	Price, *s.*
6	Prefer, *red, ring.*	9	Prime, *d, ing.*
7	Preferable.	7390	Priming wire, *s.*
8	Preference.	1	Prince, *s.*
9	Preferment.	2	Princess, *es.*
7350	Prejudice, *d, ing, s.*	3	Principal, *ly.*
1	Prejudicial, *ly.*	4	Principle, *s.*
2	Preliminary, *ies.*	5	Printing press.
3	instructions.	6	Prior, *ity.*
7354	Premature, *ly.*	7397	Prison, *s.*

88

Nos.	PRI	Nos.	PRO
7398	Prisoner, *s.*	7440	Progress.
9	at large.	1	of our forces.
7400	counsel.	2	of the enemy.
1	defence.	3	of the siege.
2	of war.	4	Prohibit, *ed, ing, ion.*
3	Private, *ly, s.*	5	Prohibitory.
4	of marines.	6	Project, *ed, ing, s.*
5	signal, *s.*	7	Projectile, *s.*
6	signal key.	8	Projection.
7	soldier, *s.*	9	Prolong, *ed, ing.*
8	Privateer, *s.*	7450	the action.
9	Privateersman, *men.*	1	the war.
7410	Privation, *s.*	2	Promise, *d, ing.*
1	Privilege, *d, s.*	3	Promontory, *ies.*
2	Prize, *s.*	4	Promote, *d, ing.*
3	court, *s.*	5	good feeling.
4	crew, *s.*	6	the general welfare.
5	law, *s.*	7	Promotion, *s.*
6	list, *s.*	8	Prompt, *ed, ing, s.*
7	money.	9	Promptly.
8	property.	7460	Promptness.
9	Probability.	1	Promulgate, *d, ing, ion.*
7420	Probable, *ly.*	2	Pronunciamento.
1	Probation, *ary.*	3	Proof, *s.*
2	Proceed, *ed, ing, s.*	4	Propel, *led, ling.*
3	on service.	5	Propeller, *s.*
4	without delay.	6	blade, *s.*
5	Process.	7	shaft.
6	Procession, *s.*	8	Propensity, *ies.*
7	Proclamation, *s.*	9	Proper, *ly.*
8	Procrastinate, *d, ing, ion.*	7470	Property.
9	Procurable.	1	Prophylactic, *s.*
7430	Procure, *d, ing.*	2	Propitiate, *d, ing, ion.*
1	Produce, *d, ing.*	3	Propitious.
2	Productive, *ly.*	4	Proportion, *s, ed, ing.*
3	Profane, *d, ing, ly.*	5	Proportional.
4	Profanity.	6	Proposal, *s.*
5	Profess, *ed, ing.*	7	Propose, *d, ing.*
6	Profit, *ed, ing.*	8	Proposition, *s.*
7	Profitably.	9	Propriety.
8	Prognostic, *s.*	7480	Propulsion.
7439	Programme.	1	Proscribe, *d, ing.*
		7482	Proscription.

Nos.	PRO	Nos.	QUA
7483	Prosecute, *d, ing.*	7526	Punctual, *ly.*
4	Prosecution, *s.*	7	Punctuality.
5	Prospect, *s.*	8	Punish, *ed, ing.*
6	Prospective, *ly.*	9	Punishment, *s.*
7	Prostrate, *d, ing, ion.*	7530	Purchase, *d, ing, s.*
8	Protect, *ed, ing, ion, s.*	1	Pure.
9	Protection.	2	Purge, *d, ing.*
7490	Protectorate.	3	Purify, *ied, ing.*
1	Protest, *ed, ing, ation.*	4	Purloin, *ed, ing.*
2	Protract, *ed, ing.*	5	Purport, *ed, ing.*
3	Protractor, *s.*	6	Purpose, *d, ing, s.*
4	Prove, *d, ing, n.*	7	Pursuance.
5	Provide, *d, ing.*	8	Pursue, *d, ing.*
6	Provision.	9	Pursuer, *s.*
7	Provisions.	7540	Pursuit.
8	Provisional, *ly.*	1	Purveyor.
9	Provocation, *s.*	2	Pusillanimous.
7500	Provoke, *d, ing, s.*	3	Pusillanimity.
1	Provost Marshal.	4	Pustule, *s.*
2	Proximity.	5	Put, *ting.*
3	Proximo.	6	Putrefy, *ied, ing.*
4	Prudence.	7	Putrid.
5	Prudent, *ly.*	8	Putty.
6	Prudential, *ly.*	9	knife, *ives.*
7	Prussian blue.	7550	Pyrotechnics.
8	Prussian flag.	1	Quadrant, *s.*
9	Prussic acid.	2	Qualification, *s.*
7510	Public, *ly.*	3	Qualified.
1	Publication, *s.*	4	Qualify, *ing.*
2	Publicity.	5	Quality.
3	Public property.	6	Quantity, *ies..*
4	Publish, *ed, ing.*	7	Quarantine, *s.*
5	Pull, *ed, ing.*	8	flag.
6	Pulmonary.	9	physician.
7	Pulse, *s.*	7560	regulation, *s*
8	Pump, *ed, ing, s.*	1	station, *s.*
9	bolt, *s.*	2	Quarrel, *led, ling.*
7520	box, *es.*	3	Quarrelsome.
1	brake, *s.*	4	Quart, *s.*
2	gear.	5	Quarter, *ed, ing, s.*
3	tacks.	6	Quarterly.
4	valve, *s.*	7	description muster rolls.
7525	Punch, *ed, ing.*	7568	muster and pay rolls.

Nos.	QUA	Nos.	RAT
	Quarterly.	7605	Racksaw.
7569	report of aggregate of clothing expended.	6	Radiate, d, ing.
7570	report of articles condemned by board.	7	Radiation.
		8	Radiator.
1	report of bills of articles purchased.	9	Radius.
2	report of conditi'n of machinery and boilers.	7610	Raft, s, ed, ing.
		1	Raid, s, ed, ing.
3	report of conduct and attainments of officers.	2	Raiding party, ies.
		3	Rail, s.
4	report of firing, &c.	4	Railroad, s.
5	report of number and rating of crew.	5	Rain, ed, ing.
		6	Rain gauge, s.
6	report of ordnance stores.	7	Rain water.
7	report of provisions, clothing, &c., on hand, expended, &c.	8	Rainy.
		9	Raise, d, ing.
8	report of punishments.	7620	Raisins.
9	report of sick.	1	Rake, d, ing.
7580	report of stores expended.	2	fore and aft.
1	report of target practice.	3	of the masts.
2	steam log.	4	Rakish, ly.
3	synopsis of steam log and report.	5	Rally, ied, ing.
		6	Ram, s, med, ming.
4	Quartermaster, s.	7	at full speed.
5	Quarter, s.	8	Rammer, s.
6	Queen.	9	Ran.
7	Quell, ed, ing.	7630	Random.
8	Question, ed, ing.	1	Range, d, ing.
9	Quick, ly.	2	ahead.
7590	Quicken, ed, ing.	3	Rank, ed, ing, s.
1	Quicklime.	4	and file.
2	Quick-match.	5	Rap.
3	Quicksand, s.	6	full.
4	Quicksilver.	7	Raper's Navigator.
5	Quinine.	8	Rapid, ly.
6	Quire, s.	9	Rapids.
7	Quit, ting.	7640	Rapidity.
8	Quoin, s.	1	Rare, ly.
9	Rabbet, ed, ing.	2	Rash, ly, ness.
7600	joint.	3	Rasp.
1	plane.	3	Rat, s.
2	Race, d, ing.	4	Ratchet, s.
3	Rack, ed, ing.	5	brace, s.
7604	and pinion, s.	7646	wheel, s.

Nos.	RAT	Nos.	REC
7647	Rate, *s, d, ing*.		Recall, *ed, s*.
8	Rather.	7690	the boat, *s*.
9	Ratification.	1	Recapture, *d*.
7650	of the treaty.	2	Receipt, *s, ed, ing*.
1	Ratify, *ied, ing*.	3	of instructions.
2	the agreement.	4	Receive, *d, ing*.
3	the treaty.	5	information.
4	Ration, *s*.	6	on board.
5	for supernumeraries.	7	Receiving ship.
6	money.	8	Recent, *ly*.
7	Ratline, *s*.	9	Recipe.
8	stuff.	7700	Reciprocal, *ly*.
9	stuff, 12 thread.	1	Reciprocate, *d, ing*.
7660	stuff, 15 thread.	2	Reciprocity.
1	stuff, 18 thread.	3	Reckless, *ly, ness*.
2	stuff, 21 thread.	4	Reckon, *ed, ing*.
3	stuff, 24 thread.	5	is approximate.
4	Rattle, *d, ing*.	6	is correct.
5	down rigging.	7	Reclamation.
6	Ravage, *d, ing*.	8	Recognition.
7	Raw.	9	Recognizance.
8	hide, *s*.	7710	Recognize, *d, ing*.
9	Razor, *s*.	1	the coast.
7670	Reach, *ed, ing*.	2	the flag.
1	Readiness.	3	the ship.
2	Ready.	4	Recoil, *ed, ing*.
3	for action.	5	Recollect, *ed, ing, ion*.
4	Realize, *d, ing, ation*.	6	Recommence, *d, ing, ment*.
5	Ream, *s*.	7	Recommend, *ed, ing, ation*.
6	Rear.	8	Reconcile, *d, ing*.
7	Admiral.	9	Reconciliation.
8	Admiral's flag.	7720	Reconnoissance.
9	Admiral's salute.	1	Reconnoitre, *d, ing*.
7680	Reason, *ed, ing, able*.	2	the approaches.
1	Reassemble, *d, ing*.	3	the enemy.
2	Reassign, *ed, ing, ment*.	4	Reconsider, *ed, ing*.
3	Rebel, *led, ling, s*.	5	Record, *s, ed, ing*.
4	Rebellion.	6	Recover, *ed, ing*.
5	Rebellious, *ly*.	7	lost ground.
6	Rebut, *ted, ting*.	8	Recreation.
7	Recall, *ed, s*.	9	Recruit, *ed, ing, s*.
8	absentees.	7730	Recruiting officer, *s*.
7689	chasing vessel, *s*.	7731	Rectify, *ied, ing*.

Nos.	RED	Nos.	REM
7732	Red.	7775	Regard, *ed, ing*.
3	and green.	6	Regardless, *ly*.
4	and white.	7	of consequences.
5	buoy, *s*.	8	Regatta.
6	Redeem, *ed, ing*.	9	Regiment, *s, al*.
7	Red flag.	7780	of artillery.
8	lantern.	1	of cavalry.
9	lead.	2	of infantry.
7740	light, *s*.	3	Register, *s, ed, ing*.
1	Redouble, *d, ing*.	4	Regret, *ted, ting*.
2	Redoubt, *s*.	5	Regular, *ly, ity*.
3	Red paint.	6	Regulate, *d, ing, s*.
4	Redress, *ed, ing*.	7	movements by speed.
5	Reduce, *d, ing*.	8	Reinstate, *d, ing, ment*.
6	Reduction.	9	Reiterate, *d, ing, ion*.
7	Reef, *s, ed, ing*.	7790	Reject, *ed, ing*.
8	Reel, *ed, ing, s*.	1	Rejoice, *d, ing*.
9	Reëmbark, *ed, ing*.	2	Rejoin, *ed, ing*.
7750	" ammunition.	3	the Commander-in-Chief.
1	, artillery.	4	the fleet.
2	, force, *s*.	5	Relapse, *d, ing*.
3	Reënforce, *d, ing*.	6	Relax, *ed, ing, ation*.
4	Reënforcement, *s*.	7	Release, *d, ing*.
5	Reënlist, *ed, ing*.	8	the prisoner, *s*.
6	Reënlistment, *s*.	9	the vessel, *s*.
7	Reëstablish, *ed, ing, ment*.	7800	Reliability.
8	Reeve, *ing*.	1	Reliable.
9	Refer, *red, ring*.	2	Reliance.
7760	Refit, *ted, ting*.	3	Relief.
1	Reform, *ed, ing*.	4	in your power.
2	Refraction.	5	Relieve, *d, ing*.
3	Refractory.	6	the distressed vessel.
4	Refrain, *ed, ing*.	7	the guard vessel.
5	Refresh, *ed, ing, ment, s*.	8	the lookout, *s*.
6	Refuge.	9	Relieving tackle, *s*.
7	Refugee, *s*.	7810	Relinquish, *ed, ing*.
8	Refusal.	1	Reluctance.
9	Refuse, *d, ing*.	2	Reluctant, *ly*.
7770	the application.	3	Rely, *ied, ing*.
1	the offer.	4	Remain, *s, ed, ing*.
2	the terms.	5	Remark, *s, ed, ing, able*.
3	Refute, *d, ing*.	6	Remarkably.
7774	Regain, *ed, ing*.	7817	Remark book, *s*.

Re - Entering (handwritten annotation next to 7757)

Nos.	REM	Nos.	RES
7818	Remedial.	7861	Reproof.
9	Remedy, *ies, ied, ing.*	2	Repugnance.
7820	Remember, *ed, ing.*	3	Repulse, *d, ing.*
1	Remind, *ed, ing.*	4	Request, *s, ed, ing.*
2	Remiss.	5	cannot be granted.
3	Remit, *ted, ting.*	6	is granted.
4	Remittent.	7	Require, *d, ing, s, ments.*
5	Remonstrate, *d, ing.*	8	Requisite.
6	Remount, *ed.*	9	Requisition. *s.*
7	Remove, *d, ing.*	7870	for boatswain's stores.
8	Remunerate, *d, ing, ation.*	1	for carpenter's stores.
9	Render, *ed, ing, s.*	2	for clothing.
7830	Rendezvous.	3	for engineer's stores.
1	of the fleet.	4	for navigator's stores.
2	Renew, *ed, ing.*	5	for ordnance stores.
3	the attack.	6	for provisions.
4	Reopen, *ed.*	7	for small stores.
5	Reorganize, *d, ing, ation.*	8	for tobacco.
6	Repair, *ed, ing, s.*	9	Resalute.
7	damages.	7880	Rescind, *ed, ing.*
8	on board.	1	Rescue, *d, ing.*
9	Repeat, *ed, ing.*	2	persons in danger.
7840	the message.	3	Resemble, *s, d, ing.*
1	Repel, *led, ling.*	4	Resent, *ed, ing.*
2	all attempts.	5	Resentment, *s.*
3	the attack.	6	Reserve, *d, ing, s.*
4	Replace, *d, ing.*	7	Resident, *s,*
5	Reply, *ied, ing.*	8	minister, *s.*
6	Report, *s, ed, ing.*	9	Residue.
7	from home.	7890	Resign, *s, ed, ing.*
8	from the army.	1	his command.
9	has been sent.	2	his commission.
7850	latitude and longitude.	3	Resignation, *s.*
1	of officer, *s.*	4	Resist, *ed, ing.*
2	of survey.	5	Resistance.
3	particular, *s, of.*	6	Resolute, *ly.*
4	the name, *s, of.*	7	Resolve, *d, ing.*
5	the position of.	8	Resort, *ed, ing.*
6	Reprieve, *d, ing.*	9	Resource, *s.*
7	Reprimand, *ed, ing.*	7900	Respect, *ed, ing, s, able.*
8	by the Department.	1	Respectful, *ly.*
9	Reprisal, *s.*	2	Respective, *ly.*
7860	Reproach, *ed, ing, ful.*	7903	Respite, *d.*

Nos.	RES	Nos.	RIG
7904	Responsibility, *ies.*	7947	Revoke, *d, ing.*
5	Responsible.	8	Revolt, *ed, ing, s.*
6	Rest, *ed, ing.*	9	Revolution, *s, ary.*
7	Restoration.	7950	Revolutionize, *d, ing.*
8	Restorative, *s.*	1	Revolve, *d, ing.*
9	Restore, *d, ing.*	2	Revolving.
7910	Restrain, *ed, ing.*	3	light, *s.*
1	Restraint, *s.*	4	turret, *s.*
2	Restrict, *ed, ing, ion, s.*	5	Revolver, *s.*
3	Result, *ed, ing, s.*	6	ammunition.
4	Resume, *d, ing.*	7	Reward, *ed, ing, s.*
5	Retain, *ed, ing.*	8	Rheumatism.
6	Retake, *ing, n.*	9	Rhubarb.
7	Retaliate, *d, ing.*	7960	Rib, *s.*
8	Retaliation.	1	Ribbon, *s.*
9	Retard. *ed, ing, ation, s.*	2	Rice.
7920	Retention.	3	Ricochet.
1	Retire, *d, ing.*	4	Rid.
2	list.	5	Ride, *ing.*
3	officer, *s.*	6	out the gale at anchor.
4	Retract, *ed, ing, ion.*	7	Riding bitts.
5	Retreat, *ed, ing, s.*	8	Rifle, *s.*
6	Retreating force, *s.*	9	ammunition.
7	Retrench, *ed, ing, ment, s.*	7970	gun, *s.*
8	Return, *s, ed, ing.*	1	howitzer, *s.*
9	for the quarter.	2	howitzer, *s, ammunition.*
7930	mail.	3	musket ammunition.
1	the salute.	4	pit, *s.*
2	the visit.	5	projectile, *s.*
3	Reveille.	6	range.
4	Revenue cutter, *s.*	7	Rifleman, *men.*
5	flag, *s.*	8	Rig, *ged, ging, s.*
6	officer, *s.*	9	a jury mast.
7	Reverse, *d, ing.*	7980	a purchase.
8	bearing, *s.*	1	Rigger, *s.*
9	order of sailing.	2	gang, *s.*
7940	order of steaming.	3	Rigging loft.
1	Review, *ed, ing.*	4	screw.
2	the fleet.	5	stopper, *s.*
3	the troops.	6	Right.
4	Revise, *d, ing.*	7	abeam.
5	Revive, *d, ing.*	8	ahead.
7946	Revocation.	7989	astern.

Nos.	RIG	Nos.	RUD
	Right.	8032	Rocky.
7990	athwart.	3	bottom.
1	bank, *s.*	4	coast.
2	hand, *ed.*	5	landing.
3	side.	6	Rod, *s.*
4	tack.	7	Rode.
5	up and down.	8	Roll, *ed, ing, s.*
6	wing.	9	Roller, *s.*
7	Rightly.	8040	handspike, *s.*
8	Rigid, *ity.*	1	Rolling tackle, *s.*
9	Rigor.	2	Rope, *s.*
8000	Rigorous, *ly.*	3	Rough.
1	Rimbase, *s.*	4	Round, *s.*
2	Ring, *s.*	5	of ammunition.
3	bolt, *s.*	6	of canister.
4	of the anchor, *s.*	7	of grape.
5	stopper, *s.*	8	of shell.
6	leader, *s.*	9	shot.
7	Riot.	8050	Roundly.
8	Rioter, *s.*	1	Rout, *ed, ing.*
9	Riotous.	2	of our forces.
8010	Rip, *s.*	3	of the enemy.
1	Ripe.	4	Route.
2	Ripple, *d, ing.*	5	Routine.
3	Rise, *ing.*	6	Row, *ed, ing.*
4	Risk, *ed, ing, y.*	7	boat, *s.*
5	River, *s.*	8	guard.
6	bank.	9	Royal, *s.*
7	water.	8060	Rubber.
8	Rivet, *ed, s.*	1	hose.
9	Road, *s.*	2	packing.
8020	Roadstead, *s.*	3	Rudder, *s.*
1	Roar, *ed, ing.*	4	brace, *s.*
2	of battle.	5	case.
3	of surf.	6	chain, *s.*
4	Rob, *bed, bing.*	7	chock.
5	Roband, *s.*	8	head.
6	Robber, *s.*	9	is shipped.
7	Robbery, *ies.*	8070	is unshipped.
8	Rock, *s.*	1	pendant, *s.*
9	Rocket, *s.*	2	pintle, *s.*
8030	staff, *staves.*	3	stock.
8031	Rock shaft.	8074	Rude, *ly, ness.*

Nos.	RUI	Nos.	SCA
8075	Ruin, *ous*.	8118	Salt, *ed, ing*.
6	Rule, *s, ed, ing*.	9	Salt beef.
7	and regulation, *s*.	8120	Salt.
8	of the road.	1	Saltpetre.
9	Rumor, *ed, s*.	2	Salt pork.
8080	Run, *ning*.	3	Salt provision, *s*.
1	the battery, *ies*.	4	Salt water.
2	the blockade.	5	Salutary.
3	Runner, *s*.	6	Salute, *d, ing, s*.
4	Rupture, *d, ing, s*.	7	the Admiral.
5	Ruse de guerre.	8	the flag.
6	Russia leather.	9	the senior officer.
7	Russian.	8130	Salvo, *es*.
8	Rust, *ed, ing, s*.	1	Same.
9	Sabot, *s*.	2	Sample, *s*.
8090	Sabre, *s*.	3	Sanction, *ed, ing*.
1	bayonette, *s*.	4	Sand, *ed, ing*.
2	Sack, *s*.	5	bank, *s*.
3	Sacrifice, *d, ing*.	6	beach, *s*.
4	Sad, *ly*.	7	hill, *s*.
5	affair.	8	paper.
6	Sadden, *ed, ing*.	9	Sanguine.
7	Safe, *ly*.	8140	Sanitary.
8	anchorage.	1	Sap.
9	distance.	2	Sappers and miners.
8100	guard.	3	Satisfaction.
1	Safety.	4	Satisfactory.
2	valve, *s*.	5	arrangement, *s*.
3	Sag, *ged, ging*.	6	manner.
4	Said.	7	terms.
5	Sail, *ed, ing, s*.	8	Satisfy, *ied, ing, ies*.
6	by the wind.	9	Saturday.
7	Sailer, *s*.	8150	evening.
8	Sailing day.	1	morning.
9	directions.	2	night.
8110	Sailor, *s*.	3	noon.
1	Saleratus.	4	Sauce pan, *s*.
2	Sal ammoniac.	5	Save, *d, ing*.
3	Sale, *s*.	6	Saw.
4	Salient.	7	Sawyer, *s*.
5	Salinometer, *s*.	8	Say, *s*.
6	Salivate, *d, ing*.	9	Scabbard, *s*.
8117	Sally, *ied, ing*.	8160	Scald, *ed, ing*.

Nos.	SCA	Nos.	SEC
8161	Scale, *d, ing.*		Scrub, *bed, bing.*
2	boiler, *s.*	8204	paint work.
3	gun, *s.*	5	windsail, *s.*
4	Scaling ladder, *s.*	6	Scruple, *s.*
5	Scandalous.	7	Scrupulous.
6	conduct.	8	Scrutinize, *d, ing.*
7	Scar, *s.*	9	Scud, *ded, ding.*
8	Scarce.	8210	Scull, *s.*
9	Scarcely.	1	Scupper, *s.*
8170	Scarcity.	2	nail, *s.*
1	Scare, *d.*	3	Scurvy.
2	Scarf, *ed, ing.*	4	on board.
3	joint, *ed.*	5	Scuttle, *d, ing.*
4	Scarlet fever.	6	butt, *s.*
5	Scatter, *ed, ing.*	7	the vessel.
6	Schedule.	8	Sea.
7	Scheme, *s.*	9	Sea breeze, *s.*
8	School, *s.*	8220	Seafaring man, *men.*
9	book, *s.*	1	Seal, *s, ed, ing.*
8180	master, *s.*	2	Sealed orders.
1	Schooner, *s.*	3	Sealing wax.
2	Scissors.	4	Seam, *ed, ing, s.*
3	Scope.	5	Seaming needle, *s.*
4	of cable.	6	Seaman, *men.*
5	Scout, *ed, ing, s.*	7	Seamanship.
6	Scrap iron.	8	Seamanlike.
7	Scrape, *d, ing.*	9	Search, *ed, ing.*
8	Scraper, *s.*	8230	Sea room.
9	Screen, *s, ed, ing.*	1	Sea sick, *ness.*
8190	light, *s.*	2	Seaward, *ly.*
1	Screw, *s, ed, ing.*	3	Seaway.
2	bolt, *s.*	4	Seaworthy.
3	driver, *s.*	5	Second, *s, ed, ing.*
4	jack, *s.*	6	Secondary.
5	propeller, *s.*	7	Secrecy.
6	wrench, *es.*	8	Secret, *s.*
7	Scrub, *bed, bing.*	9	Secretary, *ies.*
8	decks.	8240	Secretary of.
9	and wash clothes.	1	of State.
8200	boats and their fixtures.	2	of the Interior.
1	brush, *es.*	3	of the Navy.
2	hammock, *s.*	4	of the Treasury.
8203	mess cloths.	8245	of War.

98

Nos.	SEC	Nos.	SHA
8246	Secrete, *d, ing.*	8289	Sentence, *d, ing, s.*
7	Secretely.	8290	Sentry, *ies.*
8	Secure, *d, ing.*	1	Separate. *d, ing.*
9	anchorage.	2	Separately.
8250	berth.	3	September.
1	Securely.	4	Sergeant.
2	Sediment.	5	at-arms.
3	Sedition, *s.*	6	of the guard.
4	Seditious, *ly.*	7	Serious, *ly.*
5	Seidlitz powder, *s.*	8	Servant, *s.*
6	See, *ing.*	9	Serve, *d, ing.*
7	Seek, *ing.*	8300	out provisions.
8	Seem, *s, ed, ing.*	1	out small stores.
9	Seen.	2	out clothing.
8260	Seine, *s.*	3	Service, *s.*
1	Seize, *d, ing, s.*	4	Serviceable.
2	the boat, *s.*	5	Serving mallet, *s.*
3	the property.	6	Session, *s.*
4	the vessel, *s.*	7	of the board.
5	Seizing stuff.	8	of the Court.
6	Seldom.	9	Set, *ting.*
7	Select, *ed, ing, ion.*	8310	all sail.
8	Self.	1	of the current.
9	Self preservation.	2	Settle, *d, ing.*
8270	Self-registering thermometer, *s.*	3	Settlement, *s.*
1	Selvagee, *s.*	4	Seven, *th.*
2	Semi-annual, *ly.*	5	bells.
3	Semi-barbarous.	6	Seventeen, *th.*
4	Semi-circle.	7	Seventy, *eth.*
5	Semi-diameter.	8	Several.
6	Senator, *s.*	9	Severe, *ly.*
7	Send, *ing.*	8320	Severity.
8	a boat.	1	Sew, *ing.*
9	an officer.	2	cotton.
8280	a messenger.	3	silk.
1	Senior, *s, ity.*	4	thread.
2	officer, *s.*	5	Sextant, *s.*
3	officer afloat.	6	Shackle, *d, ing, s.*
4	officer ashore.	7	pin, *s.*
5	officer's flag.	8	Shaft, *s.*
6	Sennit.	9	bearing, *s.*
7	Sensation, *al.*	8330	Shake, *d, ing.*
8288	Sent.	8331	out reefs.

Nos.	SHA	Nos.	SHO
8332	Shall.	8375	Ship-biscuit.
3	Shameful, *ly*.	6	Shipboard.
4	Sham fight.	7	Ship-carpenter, *s*.
5	Shank, *s*.	8	fever.
6	of the anchor.	9	joiner, *s*.
7	Shape, *d, ing*.	8380	keeper, *s*.
8	course for.	1	master, *s*.
9	Share, *d, ing, s*.	2	Shipping.
8340	Shark, *s*.	3	articles.
1	hook, *s*.	4	master, *s*.
2	Sharp.	5	office, *s*.
3	Sharpen, *ed, ing*.	6	Ship's boat, *s*.
4	Sharp lookout.	7	company.
5	shooters.	8	cook.
6	Sharp's breech loading carbine, *s*.	9	corporal.
7	Shatter, *ed, ing*.	8390	numbers.
8	She.	1	steward.
9	Sheave, *s*.	2	papers.
8350	Shed, *ded, ing*.	3	Shipwreck, *ed, ing*.
1	Sheep shank.	4	people.
2	skin, *s*.	5	Ship yard, *s*.
3	Sheer, *ed, ing*.	6	Shirt, *s*.
4	off.	7	Shoal, *ed, ing, s*.
5	Sheet, *ed, ing, s*.	8	water.
6	anchor, *s*.	9	Shock.
7	block, *s*.	8400	of an earthquake.
8	cable, *s*.	1	Shocked.
9	copper.	2	Shoe, *s*.
8360	iron.	3	maker, *s*.
1	lead.	4	Shore.
2	Shelf, *shelves*.	5	Short.
3	Shell, *ed, ing, s*.	6	distance.
4	room.	7	Shorten, *ed, ing*.
5	the place.	8	Short handed.
6	Shellac.	9	range.
7	Shelter, *ed, ing*.	8410	sail.
8	Shelve, *d, ing*.	1	tacks.
9	bank.	2	Shot, *s*.
8370	coast.	3	Should.
1	Shew, *ed, ing*.	4	Shoulder, *s*.
2	Shield, *ed, ing*.	5	Shove, *d, ing*.
3	Shift, *ed, ing*.	6	Shovel, *led, ling, s*.
8374	Ship, *ped, ping, s*.	8417	Show, *n, ing*.

Nos.	SHO	Nos.	SLO
8418	Shower, *s.*	8461	Sixty, *ieth.*
9	Shrapnel shell.	2	Size, *s.*
8420	Shrewdness.	3	Sketch, *ed, ing, s.*
1	Shrink, *ing, age.*	4	Skiff, *s.*
2	Shun, *ned, ning.*	5	Skilful, *ly.*
3	Shut.	6	Skill, *ed.*
4	Shy.	7	Skin, *s.*
5	Sick.	8	of the ship.
6	Sickly.	9	Skirmish, *ed, ing, es.*
7	Sickness.	8470	with artillery.
8	Side.	1	with boats.
9	light, *s.*	2	with cavalry.
8430	Siege, *s.*	3	with enemy.
1	Sight, *ed, ing.*	4	with infantry.
2	Sign, *ed, ing, s.*	5	Skirmisher, *s.*
3	Signal, *s.*	6	Skulk, *ed, ing, s.*
4	Signalled.	7	Skull, *s.*
5	Signalling.	8	Sky, *ies.*
6	Signature, *s.*	9	Slack, *ed, ing.*
7	Silence; *d, ing.*	8480	Slacken, *ed, ing.*
8	the battery, *ies.*	1	Slack water.
9	the enemy.	2	Slain.
8440	Silent, *ly.*	3	Slander, *ed, ing, s.*
1	Similar, *ly.*	4	Slanderous.
2	Similarity.	5	Slant, *s.*
3	Simple.	6	of wind.
4	formation, *s.*	7	Slate, *s.*
5	movement, *s.*	8	Slaughter, *ed, ing.*
6	Simplify, *ied, ing.*	9	Sleep, *ing.*
7	Simultaneous, *ly.*	8490	Sleepless, *ly.*
8	Since.	1	Sleepy.
9	Single, *d, ing.*	2	Sleet, *y.*
8450	anchor, *s.*	3	Slept.
1	stick, *s.*	4	Slice bar.
2	vessel, *s.*	5	Slide rod, *s.*
3	Singular, *ly.*	6	valve, *s.*
4	Sink.	7	Sliding joint.
5	the enemy.	8	Slight, *ly.*
6	Sinking.	9	Sling, *s.*
7	Situate, *d.*	8500	Slip, *ped, ping.*
8	Situation.	1	Sloop.
9	Six, *th.*	2	Slop, *s.*
8460	Sixteen, *th.*	8503	Slot, *s.*

Nos.	SLO	Nos.	SPA
8504	Slow, *ly*.	8547	Sodium.
5	down.	8	Sodomy.
6	match.	9	Solder, *ed, ing*.
7	movement, *s*.	8550	Soldier, *s, ly*.
8	rate of speed.	1	Sole.
9	Slower.	2	leather.
8510	Slush, *ed, ing*.	3	Solemn.
1	Small.	4	Solicit, *ed, ing, ation*.
2	arms.	5	Solicitous.
3	arm men.	6	Solicitude.
4	boat, *s*.	7	Solid, *ly*.
5	craft.	8	Solve, *d, ing*.
6	helm.	9	Some.
7	pox.	8560	Somebody.
8	pox hospital.	1	Somehow.
9	stuff.	2	Something.
8520	vessel, *s*.	3	Some time since.
1	Smaller.	4	Somewhere.
2	Smallest.	5	Soon.
3	Smell, *ing*.	6	Sooner.
4	Smith, *ery*.	7	Soonest.
5	Smoke, *d, ing*.	8	Sore, *ly*.
6	box.	9	Sorrow, *ed, ing, s*.
7	of steamer, *s*.	8570	Sorrowful, *ly*,
8	stack, *s*.	1	Sorry.
9	stack guys.	2	Sortie.
8530	Smooth.	3	Sought.
1	Smoothing plane.	4	Sound, *ed, ing, s*.
2	Smother, *ed, ing*.	5	at intervals of.
3	Smuggle, *d, ing*.	6	often.
4	liquor on board.	7	Sounding line.
5	Smuggler, *s*.	8	Soup.
6	Snag, *ged, ging, s*.	9	Source, *s*.
7	Snap, *ped*.	8580	South.
8	Snatch.	1	Southeast, *er, erly*.
9	Snifting valve, *s*.	2	Southerly.
8540	Snow, *ing*.	3	Southern.
1	So.	4	Southing.
2	Soak, *ed, ing*.	5	Southward.
3	Soap.	6	Southwest, *er, erly*.
4	Sober, *ed, ly*.	7	Southwestern.
5	Socket, *s*.	8	Sovereign, *ty*.
8546	Soda.	8589	Space, *d, ing, s*.

Nos.	SPA	Nos.	SQU
8590	Spade, *s.*	8633	Spirit, *s.*
1	Span, *ned, ning.*	4	Spittoon, *s.*
2	Spaniard, *s.*	5	Splendid, *ly.*
3	Spanish.	6	Splice, *d, ing.*
4	brown.	7	Splint, *s.*
5	dictionary.	8	Splinter, *ed, ing.*
6	Spanker, *s.*	9	netting.
7	Spar, *red, ring, s.*	8640	Split, *ting.*
8	deck.	1	Spoil, *ed, ing.*
9	deck battery, *ies.*	2	Spoken.
8600	Spare, *d, ing.*	3	Sponson, *s.*
1	anchor, *s.*	4	Spontaneous, *ly.*
2	spar, *s.*	5	combustion.
3	Spark, *s.*	6	Sprain, *ed, ing.*
4	Spasm, *s.*	7	Spray.
5	Spasmodic.	8	Spread, *ing.*
6	Speak, *ing.*	9	awnings.
7	the flag ship.	8650	Spree.
8	the strange vessel.	1	Spring, *s, ing.*
9	Speaking trumpet, *s.*	2	Sprung.
8610	Special, *ly.*	3	a leak.
1	messenger, *s.*	4	bowsprit.
2	Specie.	5	fore mast.
3	Specific.	6	fore topmast.
4	Specifically.	7	fore topgallant mast.
5	Specification, *s.*	8	main mast.
6	Specify, *ied, ing.*	9	main topmast.
7	Speck, *s.*	8660	main topgallant mast.
8	Speechless.	1	mizzen mast.
9	Speed.	2	mizzen topmast.
8620	Speedily.	3	mizzen topgallant mast.
1	Speedy.	4	Spun yarn.
2	Spell, *ed, ing.*	5	Spur.
3	Spent ball.	6	gearing.
4	Sperm.	7	shore, *s.*
5	candle, *s.*	8	wheel, *s.*
6	oil.	9	Spy, *ies.*
7	Spherical.	8670	glass, *es.*
8	Spike, *s, ed, ing.*	1	Squad, *s.*
9	the gun, *s.*	2	of recruits.
8630	Spill, *ed, ing.*	3	Squadron.
1	Spilling line, *s.*	4	Commander.
8632	Spindle, *s.*	8675	evolution, *s.*

Nos.	SQU	Nos.	STE
	Squadron.	8718	Starvation.
8676	sailing.	9	Starve, d, ing.
7	Squall, s.	8720	State, d.
8	of rain.	1	Statement, s.
9	of wind.	2	State prison, s.
8680	Squally.	3	prisoner, s.
1	weather.	4	room, s.
2	Square, d, ing.	5	Station, ed, ing, s.
3	rigged vessel, s.	6	bill, s.
4	Stab, bed, bing, s.	7	pointer, s.
5	Stability.	8	Stationary engine, s.
6	Stack, ed, ing.	9	Stationery.
7	Staff.	8730	Statistics.
8	corps.	1	Statute, s.
9	officer, s.	2	Stay, ed, ing, s.
8690	Stage, s, ing.	3	rod, s.
1	Stake, d, ing, s.	4	Steadily.
2	Stamp, ed, ing.	5	Steady.
3	Stamping machine.	6	Steal, ing.
4	Stanch, ed, ing.	7	Steam, ed, ing.
5	Stanchion, s.	8	chest.
6	Stand, s, ing.	9	engine, s.
7	Standard, s.	8740	frigate, s.
8	Standing backstay, s.	1	gauge, s.
9	order, s.	2	pipe, s.
8700	rigging.	3	power.
1	rule, s.	4	pump, s.
2	Starboard.	5	sloop-of-war.
3	anchor, s.	6	tight.
4	boat, s.	7	tug.
5	battery, ies.	8	whistle.
6	beam.	9	will be ready at.
7	bow.	8750	Steamer, s.
8	quarter.	1	Steel.
9	tack, s.	2	bar, s.
8710	watch.	3	pen, s.
1	Starlight.	4	spring, s.
2	Start, ed, ing.	5	yard, s.
3	Starting bar.	6	Steer, ed, ing.
4	gear.	7	Steerage.
5	point.	8	cook, s.
6	Startle, d, ing.	9	hammock, s.
8717	Startling news.	8760	mess, es.

Nos.	STE	Nos.	STR
	Steerage.	8803	Stole, n.
8761	officer, s.	4	Stomach, s.
2	steward, s.	5	pump, s.
3	way.	6	Stood.
4	Steering wheel.	7	off and on.
5	Steer small.	8	off shore.
6	straight.	9	towards the.
7	Stem, med, ming.	8810	Stop, ped, ping, s.
8	Step, ped, ping, s.	1	cock, s.
9	Sterling.	2	Stopper, s.
8770	Stern, s.	3	bolt, s.
1	board.	4	Stop valve, s.
2	chase.	5	Store, d, ing, s.
3	fast, s.	6	house, s.
4	frame, s,	7	ship, s.
5	most.	8	Storm, ed, ing, s.
6	of the ship.	9	sail, s.
7	port, s.	8820	staysail, s.
8	post.	1	trysail, s.
9	Stethoscope.	2	Storming party, ies.
8780	Steward, s.	3	Stormy.
1	Stick, ing.	4	weather.
2	Sticky.	5	Stout.
3	bottom.	6	Stove.
4	Stiff.	7	Stoves.
5	breeze, s.	8	Stow. ed, ing.
6	Stifle, d, ing.	9	everything snug.
7	Stigma.	8830	sheet anchor, s.
8	Stigmatize, d, ing.	1	Stowage.
9	Stimulant, s.	2	Straggler, s.
8790	Stimulate, d, ing.	3	Straight.
1	Stimulus.	4	Straighten, ed, ing.
2	Stink pots.	5	Strain, ed, ing, s.
3	Stipulate, d, ing, ion.	6	Strake, s.
4	Stir, red, ring.	7	Strand, ed, ing, s.
5	Stitch, ed, ing.	8	Stranded vessel, s.
6	Stock, s, ed, ing.	9	Strange, ly.
7	and fluke.	8840	Strange flag, s.
8	of the anchor, s.	1	Strange vessel, s.
9	with ammunition.	2	Stranger, s.
8800	with supplies.	3	Stranger's actions.
1	Stockade, s.	4	Strap, ped, ping, s.
8802	Stocking, s.	8345	of the block, s.

Nos.	STR	Nos.	SUB
	Strap, *ped, ping, s.*	8888	Struck.
8846	ornaments.	9	topmasts.
7	Stratagem.	8890	topgallant masts.
8	Strategetic.	1	lower yards.
9	Strategy.	2	Struggle, *d, ing, s.*
8850	Stratus.	3	Strychnine.
1	Straw color, *ed.*	4	Stubborn, *ly.*
2	Straw hat, *s.*	5	Stuck.
3	Stream, *s.*	6	Studding sail.
4	anchor, *s.*	7	boom, *s.*
5	cable, *s.*	8	boom iron, *s.*
6	Strength.	9	yard, *s.*
7	is inferior.	8900	Stuffing box, *es.*
8	is superior.	1	Stump topgallant masts.
9	of the enemy.	2	Stun, *ned, ning.*
8860	of the work, *s.*	3	Stupefy, *ied, ing.*
1	Strengthen, *ed, ing.*	4	Stupendous.
2	the defences.	5	achievement, *s.*
3	Strenuous, *ly.*	6	undertaking.
4	Stress of weather.	7	Stupid, *ity.*
5	Stretch, *ed, ing.*	8	blunder.
6	Stricken.	9	fellow.
7	Strict, *ly.*	8910	Stupor.
8	discipline.	1	Subaltern, *s.*
9	obedience.	2	Subdue, *d, ing.*
8870	order, *s.*	3	Subject, *ed, ing, s, ion.*
1	watch.	4	Subjugate, *d, ing, ion, s.*
2	Stricture, *s.*	5	Submarine armor.
3	Strife.	6	diver, *s.*
4	Strike, *ing.*	7	telegraph, *s.*
5	lower yards.	8	Submerge, *d, ing.*
6	sounding, *s.*	9	Submission.
7	topmasts.	8920	Submissive, *ly.*
8	topgallant masts.	1	Submit, *ted, ting.*
9	Stringent, *ly.*	2	Subordinate. *d, ing, s.*
8880	String piece, *s.*	3	Subordination.
1	Strip, *ped, ping, s.*	4	Suborn, *ed, ing.*
2	to a girtline.	5	Subpœna, *ed.*
3	Strive, *n, ing.*	6	Subsequent, *ly.*
4	Strong.	7	Subserve, *d, ing.*
5	Stronger.	8	Subservient, *ly.*
6	Strongest.	9	Subside, *d, ing.*
8887	Stronghold, *s.*	8930	Subsist, *ed, ing.*

Nos.	SUB	Nos.	SUP
8931	Subsistence.		Sunday, *s.*
2	Substantial, *ly.*	8974	morning.
3	Substantiate, *d, ing.*	5	night.
4	Substitute, *d, ing, ion.*	6	noon.
5	Subterfuge, *s.*	7	Sunk.
6	Subversive.	8	the boat.
7	of discipline.	9	the enemy.
8	Subvert, *ed, ing.*	8980	Sunken.
9	Succeed, *ed, ing.*	1	rock.
8940	Success, *ion.*	2	wreck.
1	Successful, *ly.*	3	Sunrise, *ing.*
2	Successor, *s.*	4	Sun's altitude.
3	Succor, *ed, ing.*	5	lower limb.
4	Such.	6	upper limb.
5	Suction.	7	centre.
6	Sudden, *ly.*	8	Sunset, *ting.*
7	attack.	9	Sunstroke.
8	death.	8990	Superannuate, *d, ing.*
9	shift of wind.	1	Superheated.
8950	Suffer, *ed, ing.*	2	steam.
1	Sufferer, *s.*	3	Superheater, *s.*
2	Sufficient, *ly.*	4	Superintend, *ed, ing.*
3	Suffocate, *d, ing, ion.*	5	Superintendence.
4	Sugar.	6	Superintendent.
5	Suggest, *ed, ing, ion.*	7	Superior, *s.*
6	Suggestive.	8	authority.
7	Suicidal.	9	calibre.
8	Suicide, *s.*	9000	force, *s.*
9	Suit, *ed, ing, s.*	1	number, *s.*
8960	Suitable, *ness.*	2	rank.
1	Sulphur.	3	skill.
2	Sulphuric acid.	4	speed.
3	ether.	5	Superiority.
4	Summary.	6	Supernumerary, *ies.*
5	court, *s*, martial.	7	rations.
6	punishment, *s.*	8	Supersede, *d, ing.*
7	Summer, *s.*	9	Supervise, *d, ing, ion.*
8	Summon, *ed, ing, s.*	9010	Supper.
9	witnesses.	1	time.
8970	Sun.	2	Supplicant, *s.*
1	Sunday, *s.*	3	Supplicate, *d, ing, ion.*
2	evening.	4	Supplies.
8973	inspection.	9015	for the army.

Nos.	SUP	Nos.	SWI
	Supplies.	9058	Survey, *ed, ing.*
9016	for the fleet.	9	has been made.
7	for the vessel, *s.*	9060	has been ordered.
8	Supply, *ied, ing.*	1	has condemned.
9	vessel, *s.*	2	of the.
9020	Suppose, *d, ing.*	3	ordered.
1	Supposition, *s.*	4	the approaches.
2	Suppress, *ed, ing.*	5	the coast.
3	Suppurate, *d, ing, ion.*	6	the harbor.
4	Supremacy.	7	will be ordered.
5	Supreme, *ly.*	8	Surveyor, *s.*
6	Surcharge, *d, ing.*	9	Survive, *d, ing.*
7	Sure, *ly.*	9070	Survivor, *s.*
8	Surf.	1	Suspect, *ed, ing.*
9	boat, *s.*	2	Suspend, *ed, ing.*
9030	is heavy.	3	from duty.
1	is light.	4	Suspense.
2	Surface, *s.*	5	Suspension.
3	blow, *s.*	6	bridge.
4	condenser, *s.*	7	from duty.
5	current, *s.*	8	of hostilities.
6	Surge, *d, ing.*	9	Suspicion, *s.*
7	Surgeon, *s.*	9080	Suspicious, *ly.*
8	apothecary, *ies.*	1	movements.
9	steward.	2	vessel, *s.*
9040	to assist.	3	Sustain, *ed, ing, s.*
1	Surgical.	4	Sustenance.
2	instrument, *s.*	5	Swab, *s, bed, bing.*
3	operation, *s.*	6	Swamp, *ed, ing, s.*
4	Surmise, *d, ing.*	7	Swash, *ed, ing.*
5	Surmount, *ed, ing.*	8	channel.
6	Surplus.	9	Sway, *ed, ing.*
7	Surprise, *d, ing.*	9090	Swear, *ing.*
8	the enemy.	1	Swedish.
9	Surrender, *ed, ing.*	2	Sweep, *s, ing.*
9050	the fleet.	3	Sweet.
1	the fort, *s.*	4	oil.
2	the place.	5	potato, *es.*
3	the vessel, *s.*	6	Swell, *ed, ing.*
4	Surround, *ed, ing.*	7	Swept.
5	the enemy.	8	for anchor.
6	the entrance.	9099	Swift, *ly.*
9057	the place.		

Nos.	SWI	Nos.	TAU
9100	Swifter, s, ed, ing.	9142	Take, ing, n.
1	in rigging.	3	account of.
2	Swiftly.	4	aim at.
3	Swim, med, ming.	5	charge of.
4	Swimmer, s.	6	departure.
5	Swinging boom, s.	7	distance.
6	Swivel, led, ling.	8	every precaution.
7	Sword, s.	9	on board.
8	bayonet, s.	9150	the place of.
9	belt, s.	1	your station, s.
9110	Swore.	2	Tale, s.
1	Sworn.	3	Tall.
2	Sympathetic.	4	Taller.
3	Sympathize, d, ing.	5	Tallest.
4	Sympathy.	6	Tallow.
5	Sympiesometer.	7	Tally, ies.
6	Symptom, s.	8	Tangent, s.
7	Syncope.	9	firing.
8	Syphilis.	9160	scale, s.
9	Syphilitic.	1	screw, s.
9120	Syphon, s.	2	Tank, s.
1	Syringe, s.	3	Tap, s, ped, ping.
2	Syrup.	4	and die, s.
3	System, s.	5	Tape.
4	Systematic.	6	measure, s.
5	Systematize, d, ing.	7	Taper, ed, ing.
6	Table, d, ing, s.	8	Tapioca.
7	land.	9	Tar, red, ring.
8	linen.	9170	down rigging.
9	money.	1	water.
9130	spoon, s.	2	Tardy.
1	spoonful, s.	3	Target, s.
2	Tack, ed, ing, s.	4	practice.
3	Tackle, d, ing, s.	5	Tarnish, ed, ing.
4	Tactic, s.	6	Tarpaulin, s.
5	of war.	7	for hatch, es.
6	Tactical.	8	Tartaric acid.
7	operation, s.	9	Task, s, ed, ing.
8	Taffrail, s.	9180	Taste, d, ing.
9	Tail, ed, ing, s.	1	Tasteless.
9140	Tailor, s, ed, ing.	2	Tattoo.
9141	Taint, ed.	3	Taught.
		9184	Taunt, ed, ing, s.

Nos.	TAU	Nos.	THA
9185	Taut, *en, ing.*	9228	Tenacious, *ly.*
6	bowline, *s.*	9	Tenacity.
7	leech, *es.*	9230	Tend, *ed, ing, s.*
8	Tax, *ed, ing.*	1	Tendency.
9	Tea, *s.*	2	Tender, *s, ed, ing.*
9190	Teach, *ing.*	3	assistance.
1	Teacher, *s.*	4	to the flag ship.
2	Teaspoon, *s, ful, s.*	5	Tenderly.
3	Tedious, *ly, ness.*	6	Tendon, *s.*
4	Teem, *ed, ing.*	7	Tenon, *s.*
5	Teeth.	8	Tensile.
6	Telegram, *s.*	9	force.
7	from the Admiral.	9240	strain.
8	from the Department.	1	Tension.
9	Telegraph, *ed, ing, s.*	2	Tent, *s, ed, ing.*
9200	Telegraphic.	3	Tepid.
1	cable, *s.*	4	Term, *s.*
2	dictionary, *ies.*	5	are accepted.
3	signal, *s.*	6	are rejected.
4	Telescope, *s.*	7	Terminate, *d, ing.*
5	Telescopic, *s.*	8	the truce.
6	smoke stack, *s.*	9	Termination.
7	Telltale.	9250	of the truce.
8	Temerity.	1	Terrestrial, *ly.*
9	Temper, *ed, ing.*	2	Terrible.
9210	Temperance.	3	conflict.
1	Temperate, *ly.*	4	consequence.
2	habits.	5	hurricane.
3	Temperature.	6	loss.
4	of the air.	7	Terribly.
5	of the water.	8	Terrific.
6	of the engine room.	9	gale.
7	Tempest, *s.*	9260	Terrify, *ied, ing.*
8	Tempestuous.	1	Territory, *ies.*
9	Temporary.	2	Terror, *s.*
9220	appointment.	3	stricken.
1	command.	4	Test, *s, ed, ing.*
2	service.	5	Testify, *ied, ing.*
3	Temporize, *d, ing.*	6	Testimonial, *s.*
4	Temptation, *s.*	7	Testimony.
5	Ten, *th.*	8	Tetanus.
6	Ten-penny nails.	9	Tête-de-pont.
9227	Tenable.	9270	Than.

Nos.	THA	Nos.	THU
9271	Thank, *s.*		Third, *ly.*
2	you.	9314	rate.
3	you for.	5	Thirst, *ed, ing.*
4	Thankful, *ly.*	6	Thirsty.
5	Thankless.	7	Thirteen, *th.*
6	Thanksgiving.	8	Thirty, *eth.*
7	That.	9	This.
8	Thaw, *ed, ing.*	9320	Thole pin, *s.*
9	The.	1	Thorough.
9280	Theft, *s.*	2	investigation.
1	Their.	3	understanding.
2	Them.	4	Thoroughly.
3	Themselves.	5	Those.
4	Then.	6	Though.
5	Theodolite, *s.*	7	Thought, *s.*
6	Theory, *ies.*	8	Thoughtful, *ly.*
7	There.	9	Thousand, *th.*
8	Therefore.	9330	Thrash, *ed, ing.*
9	Therein.	1	Thread, *s, ed, ing.*
9290	Thereupon.	2	Threat, *s.*
1	Thermal.	3	Threaten, *ed, ing, s.*
2	Thermometer, *s.*	4	the enemy.
3	Farenheit, *s.*	5	Threatening.
4	Centigrade.	6	appearance.
5	Reaumur, *s.*	7	movements.
6	graduated to 600° Fahrenheit.	8	weather.
7	Thermometric.	9	Three.
8	data.	9340	Threw.
9	observation, *s.*	1	Thrill, *ed, ing.*
9300	These.	2	Throat, *s.*
1	They.	3	Throttle, *d, ing, s.*
2	Thick, *ly.*	4	valve, *s.*
3	Thicken, *ed, ing.*	5	Through.
4	Thief, *ieves.*	6	and through.
5	Thievish, *ly.*	7	out.
6	Thigh, *s.*	8	Throw, *ing.*
7	Thimble, *s.*	9	away.
8	Thin, *ned, ning.*	9350	out of gear.
9	Thing, *s.*	1	overboard.
9310	Think, *ing.*	2	Trim, *med, ming.*
1	Thinly.	3	Thrust bearings.
2	Third, *ly.*	4	Thumb.
9313	cutter.	9355	cleat, *s.*

Nos.	THU	Nos.	TOP
	Thumb.	9398	Timidity.
9356	stall, *s.*	9	Tin.
7	Thump, *ed, ing, s.*	9400	Tinware.
8	Thunder, *ed, ing.*	1	Tincture.
9	Thunder shower, *s.*	2	Tinder-box, *es.*
9360	Thursday.	3	Tip.
1	evening.	4	Tire, *d.*
2	morning.	5	Tiresome.
, 3	noon.	6	Tissue.
4	night.	7	paper.
5	Thus.	8	Title, *s.*
6	Thwart, *ed, ing.*	9	To.
7	Tibia.	9410	Tobacco.
8	Ticklish.	1	To-day.
9	Tidal.	2	Toe, *s.*
9370	Tide, *s.*	3	Together.
1	gauge, *s.*	4	Toggle, *d, s.*
2	is ebb.	5	Told.
3	is flood.	6	Tolerable.
4	is high.	7	Tolerably.
5	is low.	8	Tolerate, *d, ing, ion.*
6	rip, *s.*	9	Tomato, *es.*
7	table, *s.*	9420	To-morrow.
8	way.	1	evening.
9	Tidings.	2	morning.
9380	Tidy.	3	noon.
1	Tier, *s.*	4	Tompion, *s.*
2	Tierce, *s.*	5	Ton, *s.*
3	Tight, *ly.*	6	of coal.
4	Tighter.	7	of freight.
5	Tightest.	8	Tongue, *ed.*
6	Tighten, *ed, ing.*	9	Tonic, *s.*
7	Tiller, *s.*	9430	Tonnage.
8	head.	1	Too.
9	rope.	2	far ahead.
9390	Timber, *s.*	3	far astern.
1	Time.	4	Took.
2	ball.	5	Tool, *s.*
3	fuse, *s.*	6	chest, *s.*
4	of night.	7	Tooth, *ed.*
5	Times.	8	Top, *ped, ping, s.*
6	Timely.	9	block, *s.*
9397	Timid, *ly.*	9440	chains.

Nos.	TOP	Nos.	TRA
9441	Topgallant.		Topsail, *s.*
2	backstay, *s.*	9484	schooner, *s.*
3	brace, *s.*	5	sheet, *s.*
4	buntline, *s.*	6	tye, *s.*
5	clewline, *s.*	7	tye block, *s.*
6	crosstrees.	8	Top tackles.
7	forecastle.	9	tackle pendants.
8	halliards.	9490	timbers.
9	mast.	1	Torch, *es.*
9450	rigging.	2	light.
1	sail, *s.*	3	Tore.
2	sheets.	4	Torment, *ed, ing.*
3	stay, *s.*	5	Torn.
4	staysail.	6	Tornado, *es.*
5	studding sail, *s.*	7	Torpedo, *es.*
6	studding sail boom, *s.*	8	boat, *s.*
7	tye, *s.*	9	fuze, *s.*
8	yard, *s.*	9500	Torpid, *ity.*
9	Top hamper.	1	Torpidly.
9460	heavy.	2	Torpor.
1	Topic, *s.*	3	Torrent, *s.*
2	Toplight, *s.*	4	Torrid.
3	Topman, *men.*	5	Tortuous, *ly.*
4	Topmast, *s.*	6	Torture, *d, ing.*
5	backstay, *s.*	7	Torturous.
6	shrouds.	8	Toss, *ed, ing.*
7	stay, *s.*	9	Total, *ly.*
8	staysail.	9510	Touch, *ed, ing.*
9	studding sail, *s.*	1	hole, *s.*
9470	studding sail boom, *s.*	2	Tough.
1	Topmost, *s.*	3	Tourniquet, *s.*
2	Topographer, *s.*	4	Tow, *ed, ing, s.*
3	Topographical, *ly.*	5	Towage.
4	survey.	6	Towards.
5	Topography.	7	Tow boat, *s.*
6	Topping lift, *s.*	8	Towel, *s, ling.*
7	Top rim, *s.*	9	Tower, *s, ed, ing.*
8	rope, *s.*	9520	Tow line, *s.*
9	Topsail, *s.*	1	Town, *s.*
9480	brace, *s.*	2	Trace, *d, ing, s.*
1	buntline, *s.*	3	Trachea.
2	clewline, *s.*	4	Tracing paper.
9483	halliard, *s.*	9525	Track, *ed, ing, s.*

Nos.	TRA	Nos.	TRE
9526	Trackless.	9569	Translator, *s.*
7	Tract, *s.*	9570	Transmit, *ted, ting.*
8	Tractable.	1	Transom.
9	Trade, *d, ing, s.*	2	knees.
9530	wind, *s.*	3	Transparent, *ly.*
1	Tradition, *al.*	4	Transpire, *d, ing.*
2	Traduce, *d, ing.*	5	Transport, *s, ed, ing.*
3	Traffic, *ked, king.*	6	ammunition.
4	Tragedy.	7	artillery.
5	Tragical, *ly.*	8	fleet.
6	Trail, *ed, ing.*	9	provisions.
7	Train, *ed, ing.*	9580	service.
8	on the enemy.	1	supplies.
9	tackle, *s.*	2	troops.
9540	Trait, *s.*	3	vessel, *s.*
1	Traitor, *s.*	4	Transporting blocks.
2	Traitorous.	5	trucks.
3	Trajectory, *ies.*	6	Transportation.
4	Trammel, *led, ling.*	7	of ammunition.
5	Trample, *d, ing.*	8	of artillery.
6	Train road.	9	of provisions.
7	Trance.	9590	Tranship, *ped, ping.*
8	Tranquil, *ly.*	1	Transhipment, *s.*
9	Tranquillity.	2	Transverse, *d, ing.*
9550	Tranquilize, *d, ing.*	3	section.
1	Transact, *ed, ing.*	4	Traveler, *s.*
2	Transaction, *s.*	5	Traverse, *d, ing.*
3	Trans-Atlantic.	6	board.
4	Transcribe, *d, ing.*	7	sailing.
5	Transcript.	8	table, *s.*
6	Transfer, *red, ring.*	9	Trawl, *ing.*
7	accounts.	9600	net.
8	men.	1	Treacherous, *ly.*
9	officer, *s.*	2	conduct.
9560	Transferable.	3	Treachery.
1	Transform, *ed, ing, ation.*	4	Treason.
2	Transgress, *ed, ing, ion.*	5	Treasonable.
3	the law, *s.*	6	Treasure, *d, ing, s.*
4	Transit.	7	Treasury.
5	instrument, *s.*	8	Department.
6	Transition, *s.*	9	instructions.
7	Translate, *d, ing.*	9610	of the United States.
9568	Translation, *s.*		

Nos.	TRE	Nos.	TRO
9611	Treat, *ed, ing, s.*	3653	Triatic stay.
2	with the enemy.	4	purchase.
3	with us.	5	Tribe, *s.*
4	the prisoners.	6	Tribunal, *s.*
5	Treatise, *s.*	7	Tributary, *ies.*
6	on Courts Martial.	8	Trice, *d, ing.*
7	on Gunnery.	9	up awnings.
8	on International law.	9660	up bedding.
9	on Marine Engines.	1	up clothes lines.
9620	on Maritime law.	2	up hammocks.
1	on Ship Building.	.3	Tricing line, *s.*
2	Treatment.	4	Trick.
3	Treaty, *ies.*	5	Tricky.
4	been signed.	6	Tri-color, *ed.*
5	not been signed.	7	Triennial.
6	ratified.	8	Trim, *med, ming, s.*
7	not ratified.	9	the ballast.
8	making.	9670	by the head.
9	making power, *s.*	1	the sails.
9630	Treble, *d.*	2	by the stern.
1	Tree, *s.*	3	the ship for best speed.
2	Treenail, *s.*	4	Trimmer, *s.*
3	Tremble, *d, ing.*	5	Trip, *ped, ping.*
4	Tremendous, *ly.*	6	the anchor, *s.*
5	Tremor.	7	Tripping line, *s.*
6	Tremulous, *ly.*	8	Triple, *d, ing.*
7	Trench, *ed, ing, es.*	9	Triplicate, *s, d, ing.*
8	Trend, *s, ed, ing.*	9680	Tripod, *s.*
9	of the coast.	1	Triumph, *ed, ing, s.*
9640	of the chain.	2	Triumphant, *ly.*
1	Trespass, *ed, ing.*	3	Trivial, *ly.*
2	Trestle.	4	Troop, *s.*
3	tree, *s.*	5	of horse, *cavalry.*
4	work.	6	ship, *s.*
5	Trial, *s.*	7	Trophy, *ies.*
6	by Court Martial.	8	of the battle, *s.*
7	will commence.	9	Tropic, *s.*
8	will not commence.	9690	Tropical, *ly.*
9	Triangle, *s.*	1	fruits.
9650	Triangular, *ly.*	2	productions.
1	Triangulation.	3	Trouble, *d, ing, s.*
9652	Triangulate, *d, ing.*	4	Troublesome.
		9695	Trough of the sea.

Nos.	TRO	Nos.	TWE
9696	Trowsers.		Tuesday.
7	Troy weight.	9739	night.
8	Truce, *s.*	9740	noon.
9	boat.	1	Tug, *ged, ging, s.*
9700	has ended.	2	boat, *s.*
1	is broken.	3	Tumbling sea.
2	will terminate at.	4	Tumor, *s.*
3	Truck, *s.*	5	Tumult, *s.*
4	Truckle, *d, ing.*	6	Tumultuous, *ly.*
5	Truculent.	7	Tun, *s, tons.*
6	True.	8	Turbid, *ly.*
7	Truly.	9	stream.
8	Trumpet, *s, ed, ing.*	9750	Turbulence.
9	Trunk, *s.*	1	Turbulent, *ly.*
9710	engine, *s.*	2	Turkish.
1	Trunnion, *s.*	3	man-of-war.
2	plate, *s.*	4	Turk's head.
3	ring, *s.*	5	Turmoil, *s.*
4	Truss, *ed, ing, es.*	6	Turn, *ed, ing, s.*
5	band, *s.*	7	away.
6	Trust, *ed, ing.*	8	in the hawse.
7	Trustworthy.	9	of the tide.
8	Trusty.	9760	the hands up.
9	Truth, *s.*	1	Turning in rigging.
9720	Truthful, *ly.*	2	lathe.
1	Try, *ied, ing.*	3	point.
2	again.	4	Turnip, *s.*
3	my best.	5	Turnpike, *s.*
4	your best.	6	Turpentine.
5	Trysail, *s.*	7	can, *s.*
6	boom, *s.*	8	Turpitude.
7	brail, *s.*	9	Turret, *s, ed.*
8	gaff, *s.*	9770	is disabled.
9	mast, *s.*	1	was disabled.
9730	Tub, *s.*	2	guns.
1	Tube, *s.*	3	Turreted vessel, *s.*
2	for boiler, *s.*	4	Turtle, *s.*
3	for condenser, *s.*	5	eggs.
4	Tubercles.	6	fishing.
5	Tubular boiler, *s.*	7	Twelve, *th.*
6	Tuesday.	8	days.
7	evening.	9	day of the month.
9738	morning.	9780	fathoms.

Nos.	TWE	Nos.	UNA
	Twelve, *th*.	9823	Ulcer, *s*.
9781	feet.	4	Ulcerate, *d, ing, s*.
2	hours.	5	Ulceration.
3	hundred.	6	Ulterior.
4	knots.	7	motive.
5	miles.	8	object, *s*.
6	months.	9	Ultimate, *ly*.
7	o'clock.	9830	Ultimatum.
8	penny nails.	1	Ultra.
9	Twenty, *ieth*.	2	Umber.
9790	Twice.	3	Umbilical.
1	Twilight.	4	Umbrage.
2	Twine.	5	Umbrella tree.
3	Twist, *ed, ing, s*.	6	Umpire, *s*.
4	Two.	7	Unabated, *ing*.
5	blocks.	8	Unable.
6	days.	9	Unaccommodating.
7	fathoms.	9840	Unaccountable.
8	feet.	1	Unaccustomed.
9	foot rule.	2	Unacquainted.
9800	hours.	3	Unadvisable.
1	hundred.	4	Unadvised, *ly*.
2	knots.	5	Unaffected.
3	knot current.	6	Unallowable.
4	masted.	7	Unalterable.
5	miles.	8	Unalterably.
6	months.	9	Unambitious, *ly*.
7	o'clock.	9850	Unamiable.
8	Tye.	1	Unanimity.
9	block	2	Unanswerable.
9810	Type, *s*.	3	Unapproachable.
1	Typhoid fever.	4	Unarm, *ed, ing*.
2	Typhoon.	5	Unarmed vessel, *s*.
3	Typhus fever.	6	Unasked.
4	Typographic, *al*.	7	Unassailable.
5	error, *s*.	8	Unassigned.
6	Tyrannical, *ly*.	9	Unassumed, *ing*.
7	Tyrannize, *d, ing*.	9860	Unattached.
8	Tyranny.	1	Unattainable.
9	Ubiquity, *ous*.	2	Unattended.
9820	Ugly.	3	Unauthorized.
1	business.	4	action.
9822	weather.	9865	Unavailable.

Nos.	UNA	Nos.	UND
9866	Unavailing.	9909	Uncompromising.
7	Unavoidable.	9910	Unconcern, ed.
8	delay.	1	Unconditional, ly.
9	Unaware.	2	surrender.
9870	Unbearable.	3	Uncongenial.
1	Unbecoming.	4	Unconnected.
2	an officer.	5	Unconquerable.
3	conduct.	6	Unconquered.
4	Unbend, ing.	7	Unconquerably.
5	chain, s.	8	Unconscious, ly.
6	sails.	9	Unconstitutional, ly.
7	Unbent.	9920	Unconstrained, ly.
8	Unblemished.	1	Unconsumed.
9	character.	2	Uncontradicted.
9880	Unbidden.	3	Uncontrollable.
1	Unbind, ing.	4	Uncontrolled.
2	Unbit, ted, ting.	5	Unconvicted.
3	cable.	6	Uncorrupt, ed, ing.
4	Unbound, ed.	7	Uncouple, d, ing.
5	Unbroken.	8	propeller.
6	chain of evidence.	9	Uncourteous, ly.
7	Unburied.	9930	Uncover, ed, ing.
8	Unbusiness-like.	1	Uncultivated.
9	Uncared for.	2	land.
9890	Unceasing, ly.	3	Uncurrent.
1	Unceremonious, ly.	4	Undecayed.
2	Uncertain.	5	Undeceive, d, ing.
3	Uncertainty, ies.	6	Undecided.
4	Unchain, ed, ing.	7	what next to do.
5	Unchangeable.	8	Undefeated.
6	Unchanged, ing.	9	Undefended.
7	Uncharitable, ly, ness.	9940	Undefiled.
8	Uncivilized.	1	Undefined.
9	Unclaimed.	2	Undelayed.
9900	Unclean, ly.	3	Undeniable, y.
1	Unclothed.	4	Under.
2	Uncoil, ed, ing.	5	bare poles.
3	Uncomfortable, ly.	6	brush.
4	quarters.	7	current, s.
5	situation.	8	foot.
6	Uncommon, ly.	9	way.
7	Uncomplaining, ly.	9950	way get.
9908	Uncomplimentary.	9951	Undergo, ing.

118

Nos.	UND	Nos.	UNE
9952	Undergrowth.	9995	Undulate, d, ing.
3	Underhand, ed.	6	Undulatory.
4	Underlay, ing, underlaid.	7	motion.
5	Underlie, ing.	8	Unearth, ed, ing.
6	Undermost.	9999	Unearthly.
7	Underneath.	01	Uneasily.
8	Underpart, s.	2	Uneasy.
9	Underrate, d, ing.	3	Unemployed.
9960	Under restraint.	4	Unended.
1	Underrun, ning.	5	Unending.
2	the cable or hawser.	6	Unendurable.
3	Under sail.	7	Unengaged.
4	sail and steam.	8	vessel, s, or boat, s.
5	Understand, ing.	9	Unenlightened.
6	signal, s.	010	understanding.
7	your instructions.	1	Unequal, ly.
8	Understate, d, ing.	2	combat.
9	Under steam.	3	distribution of.
9970	Undertake, n, ing.	4	force, s.
1	Under the lee.	5	Unequally divided.
2	the lee of the land.	6	Unequipped.
3	Undervalue, d, ing.	7	Unequivocal, ly.
4	Underway.	8	conduct.
5	Undeserved, ly.	9	Unerring.
6	Undesigned, ly.	020	aim.
7	Undesirable.	1	guide.
8	Undetermined.	2	Unessential.
9	Undeviating.	3	Uneven, ly.
9980	Undiminished.	4	Uneventful.
1	Undisciplined.	5	Unexamined.
2	Undisputed.	6	Unexcelled.
3	right.	7	Unexceptionable.
4	territory, ies.	8	conduct.
5	Undistinguishable.	9	Unexecuted.
6	Undistributed.	030	orders.
7	Undisturbed, ly.	1	Unexpected, ly.
8	Undo, ing, undid.	2	arrival.
9	Undock, ed, ing.	3	departure.
9990	Undoubted, ly.	4	disaster.
1	Undoubting.	5	movement, s.
2	Undress, ed, ing.	6	news.
3	ship.	7	orders.
9994	Undue.	038	Unexplained.

Nos.	UNE	Nos.	UNI
039	Unextinguishable.	082	Unfurnished.
040	Unextinguished.	3	Ungenerous, *ly.*
1	Unfading.	4	Ungentlemanly.
2	Unfailing.	5	Ungovernable.
3	Unfair, *ly.*	6	Unguarded, *ly.*
4	dealings.	7	Unguided.
5	Unfaithful, *ly.*	8	Unhandsome, *ly.*
6	Unfaithfulness.	9	Unhandy.
7	Unfamiliar, *ly.*	090	Unhappily.
8	Unfasten, *ed, ing.*	1	Unhappy, *iness.*
9	Unfathomable.	2	Unharmed.
050	Unfavorable.	3	Unhealthy.
1	circumstances.	4	Unheard of.
2	report, *s.*	5	conduct.
3	weather, *s.*	6	Unheeded.
4	wind, *s.*	7	Unhesitating, *ly.*
5	Unfeeling.	8	Unholy.
6	Unfeigned, *ly.*	9	Unhook, *ed, ing.*
7	Unfetter, *ed, ing.*	0100	Unhung.
8	Unfinished.	1	Uniform, *s.*
9	Unfit, *ted, ting.*	2	cap.
060	for service.	3	circular, *s.*
1	for use.	4	coat, *s.*
2	Unfix, *ed, ing.*	5	dress.
3	bayonets.	6	pantaloons.
4	Unforbidden.	7	rate of speed.
5	Unforseen.	8	regulation.
6	accident, *s.*	9	sword, *s.*
7	circumstance, *s.*	0110	Uniformity.
8	Unforgiven.	1	Uniformly.
9	Unforgotten.	2	Unimpaired.
070	Unfortified.	3	Unimpeachable.
1	harbor.	4	Unimportant.
2	Unfortunate, *ly.*	5	Uninfluenced.
3	circumstance, *s.*	6	Uninformed.
4	individual, *s.*	7	Unimportant.
5	Unfounded.	8	news.
6	Unfriendliness.	9	particulars.
7	Unfriendly.	0120	Uninhabitable.
8	behavior.	1	place.
9	people.	2	Uninhabited.
080	Unfruitful, *ly.*	0123	Uninjured.
081	Unfurl, *ed, ing.*		

120

Nos.	UNI	Nos.	UNO
0124	Unintelligible.	0166	Unlimited.
5	communication, *s.*	7	authority.
6	manœuvre, s.	8	Unload, *ed, ing.*
7	Unintentional, *ly.*	9	coal vessel.
8	neglect.	0170	ordnance vessel.
9	Uninteresting.	1	storeship.
0130	Uninterpreted.	2	the vessel.
1	communication, *s.*	3	Unlock, *ed, ing.*
2	Uninvited.	4	Unlooked for.
3	Uninviting.	5	Unluckily.
4	appearance.	6	Unlucky.
5	Uninvolved.	7	Unman, *ned.*
6	Union, *s.*	8	Unmanageable.
7	down.	9	Unmanly.
8	flag, *s.*	0180	Unmannerly.
9	Unison.	1	Unmarked.
0140	Unit, *s.*	2	Unmarried.
1	Unite, *d, ing.*	3	officer, *s.*
2	United States of America.	4	Unmask, *ed, ing.*
3	of Colombia.	5	enemy.
4	Unity.	6	the battery, *ies.*
5	Universal, *ly.*	7	Unmeaning, *ly.*
6	custom.	8	Unmerciful, *ly.*
7	Unjoint, *ed, ing.*	9	treatment.
8	Unjust, *ly.*	0190	Unmerited.
9	accusation.	1	rebuke.
0150	punishment.	2	Unmindful, *ly.*
1	suspicions.	3	Unmistakable.
2	Unjustifiable.	4	Unmixed.
3	Unkind, *ly, ness.*	5	Unmoor, *ed, ing.*
4	Unknown.	6	ship.
5	coast.	7	Unmoved.
6	quantity.	8	Unnatural, *ly.*
7	vessel, *s.*	9	conduct.
8	Unlaid.	0200	Unnavigable.
9	Unlash, *ed, ing.*	1	Unnavigated.
0160	Unlawful, *ly.*	2	Unnecessarily.
1	meeting.	3	Unnecessary.
2	Unlay, *ing.*	4	noise.
3	Unless.	5	trouble.
4	Unlike, *ly.*	6	Unnerve, *d.*
0165	Unlimber, *ed, ing.*	7	Unnoticed.
		0208	Unobjectionable.

Nos.	UNO	Nos.	UNS
0209	Unobserved.	0252	Unreasonable, y.
0210	Unobserving.	3	Unrebuked.
1	Unobstructed.	4	Unrecalled.
2	Unobtainable.	5	Unrecommended.
3	Unobtrusive, ly.	6	Unreconciled.
4	Unoccupied.	7	Unreel, ed, ing.
5	Unoffending.	8	Unreeve, ing.
6	Unofficial, ly.	9	Unreflected.
7	action.	0260	Unrelenting.
8	correspondence.	1	Unreliable.
9	Unopened.	2	data.
0220	Unopposed.	3	information.
1	Unorganized.	4	observation, s.
2	body.	5	Unrelieved.
3	crew.	6	Unremitting, ly.
4	force, s.	7	vigilance.
5	Unpack, ed, ing.	8	Unreported.
6	Unpalatable.	9	Unresisting.
7	Unparalleled.	0270	Unrestrained.
8	audacity.	1	Unrevealed.
9	effort, s.	2	Unrevoked.
0230	Unpardonable.	3	Unrewarded.
1	Unpleasant, ly.	4	Unrig, ged, ging.
2	Unpractised.	5	Unrighteous, ly.
3	Unprecedented.	6	Unripe.
4	Unprejudiced.	7	Unrivalled.
5	Unprepared.	8	Unrivet, ed, ing.
6	for battle.	9	Unruly.
7	for sea.	0280	Unsafe, ly.
8	Unpretending.	1	anchorage.
9	Unprincipled.	2	condition.
0240	Unprofessional, ly.	3	Unsanctioned.
1	Unprofitable, y.	4	Unsatisfactory.
2	Unpromising.	5	result, s.
3	Unprotected.	6	Unsatisfied.
4	Unprovided.	7	Unscathed.
5	Unprovoked.	8	Unscrew, ed, ing.
6	Unpublished.	9	Unscrupulous, ly.
7	Unqualified, ly.	0290	Unseal, ed, ing.
8	Unquestionable.	1	Unsealed orders.
9	Unquestionably.	2	Unseasonable.
0250	Unquestioned.	0293	Unseasonably.
0251	Unravel, led, ling.		

Nos.	UNS	Nos.	UNW
0294	Unseaworthy.	0337	Untidy.
5	condition.	8	Until.
6	Unseemly.	9	after dark.
7	conduct.	0340	after sunrise.
8	Unseen.	1	after sunset.
9	danger, s.	2	next week.
0300	Unserviceable.	3	to-morrow.
1	Unsettle, d, ing.	4	Untimely.
2	Unshackle, d, ing.	5	Unto.
3	Unshaken.	6	Untold.
4	Unsheltered.	7	Untouched.
5	Unship, ped, ping.	8	Untoward, ly.
6	Unsightly.	9	Untranslated.
7	Unsigned.	0350	Untried.
8	Unskilful, ly.	1	Untrue.
9	Unskilled.	2	Untrustworthy.
0310	Unsling.	3	Untruth, s.
1	Unsociable.	4	Untruthful, ly.
2	Unsoldierly.	5	Unusual, ly.
3	conduct.	6	appearance.
4	Unsound.	7	conduct.
5	Unsparing, ly.	8	excitement.
6	Unstable.	9	phenomena.
7	Unsteadiness.	0360	Unvaried.
8	Unsteady.	1	Unvarying.
9	Unsubdued.	2	Unventilate, d, ing.
0320	Unsuccessful, ly.	3	Unwarily.
1	Unsuitable.	4	Unwarlike.
2	Unsullied.	5	Unwarrantable.
3	Unsupplied.	6	Unwarranted.
4	Unsupported.	7	Unwary.
5	Unsupporting.	8	Unwavering.
6	Unsurpassed.	9	Unwearied, ly.
7	Unsurveyed.	0370	Unwelcome.
8	Unsuspected.	1	news.
9	Unsuspecting.	2	Unwell.
0330	Unsustained.	3	Unwholesome.
1	Unsystematic.	4	food.
2	Untoward.	5	water.
3	Untenable.	6	Unwieldy.
4	position.	7	Unwilling, ly, ness.
5	Unterrified.	8	Unwise, ly.
0336	Unthinking, ly.	0379	Unworthily.

Nos.	UNW	Nos.	VAL
0380	Unworthy.	0423	Usurp, *ed, ing.*
1	Unwritten.	4	Usurpation.
2	Unyielding, *ly.*	5	Utensil, *s.*
3	Up.	6	Utility.
4	anchor, *s.*	7	Utilize.
5	and down.	8	Utmost.
6	boats.	9	difficulty.
7	the bay.	0430	Utter, *ed, ing.*
8	the river.	1	Utterance, *s.*
9	the stream.	2	Uttermost.
0390	Upbraid, *ed, ing.*	3	Vacancy, *ies.*
1	Upheld.	4	Vacant, *ly.*
2	Uphill.	5	Vacate, *d, ing.*
3	Uphold, *ing.*	6	Vaccinate, *d, ing.*
4	Uphroe.	7	all on board who have not already been.
5	Upon.		
6	Upper.	8	all on board have been.
7	deck, *s.*	9	Vaccination.
8	hand.	0440	Vaccine.
9	works.	1	Vacillate, *d, ing.*
0400	Upright, *ly.*	2	Vacillation.
1	Uprise, *ing.*	3	Vacuum.
2	Uproar, *ing.*	4	gauge.
3	Upset, *ting.*	5	Vade mecum.
4	Upside down.	6	Vagabond, *s.*
5	Upton's Maritime Warfare and prize.	7	Vagary, *ies.*
6	Uptown.	8	of the imagination.
7	Upward, *s.*	9	Vague, *ly.*
8	Uranus.	0450	Vain, *ly.*
9	Urge, *d, ing.*	1	effort, *s.*
0410	Urgency.	2	glorious.
1	Urgent, *ly.*	3	glory.
2	Urinary.	4	Valerian.
3	Urinate.	5	Valiant, *ly.*
4	Urine.	6	Valid, *ity.*
5	Ursa Major.	7	reason, *s.*
6	Us.	8	Valley, *ies.*
7	Usage.	9	Valor, *ous.*
8	of the service.	0460	Valuable.
9	Use, *d, ing.*	1	information.
0420	Useful, *ly.*	2	prize.
1	Useless, *ly.*	3	Valuation, *s.*
0422	Usual, *ly.*	0464	Value, *d, ing, s.*

Nos.	VAL	Nos.	VER
0465	Valve, *s.*		Veer, *ed, ing.*
6	box.	0508	to the left.
7	casing.	9	to the right.
8	door.	0510	Vegetable, *s.*
9	gear.	1	Vehemence.
0470	opening.	2	Vehement, *ly.*
1	seat.	3	Vein, *y, s.*
2	stem.	4	Velocity, *ies.*
3	Van.	5	Venal, *ity.*
4	division.	6	Venerable.
5	of the army.	7	Venerate, *d, ing, ion.*
6	of the fleet.	8	Venereal.
7	squadron.	9	Vengeance.
8	Vane, *s.*	0520	Venial.
9	Vang, *s.*	1	Venison.
0480	Vanguard.	2	Venom.
1	Vanish, *ed, ing.*	3	Venomous, *ly.*
2	Variety, *ies.*	4	Vent.
3	Vanquish, *ed, ing.*	5	bit.
4	Vapor, *s.*	6	brace.
5	Variable, *ly.*	7	drill.
6	current, *s.*	8	field.
7	weather.	9	hole.
8	winds.	0530	plug.
9	Variance, *s.*	1	is stopped.
0490	Variation.	2	Ventilate, *d, ing, ion.*
1	chart, *s.*	3	Ventilator, *s.*
2	of the compass.	4	Venture, *d, ing.*
3	Varicocele.	5	Venus.
4	Varicose veins.	6	Veracity.
5	Variegation.	7	Verbal, *ly.*
6	Variety.	8	directions.
7	Variola.	9	instructions.
8	Varioloid.	0540	message.
9	Various, *ly.*	1	Verdict.
0500	Varnish, *ed, ing.*	2	is guilty.
1	Vary, *ied, ing.*	3	is not guilty.
2	Vast, *ly.*	4	Verdigris.
3	Vattel's laws of nations.	5	Verification.
4	Vaunt, *ed, ing.*	6	Verify, *ied, ing.*
5	Veer, *ed, ing.*	7	Veritable.
6	away.	8	Vermicelli.
0507	cable.	0549	Vermilion.

Nos.	VER	Nos.	VIT
0550	Vermin.	0593	Victimize, *d, ing.*
1	Vernal equinox.	4	Victor, *s.*
2	Vernier.	5	Victorious, *ly.*
3	Version, *s.*	6	Victory.
4	Vertical, *ly.*	7	must be ours.
5	Vertigo.	8	Victual, *led, ling, s.*
6	Very.	9	Vie, *d, ing.*
7	bad.	0600	View, *ed, ing.*
8	badly done.	1	Vigilance.
9	bad weather.	2	Vigilant, *ly.*
0560	fast.	3	Vigor.
1	good.	4	Vigorous, *ly.*
2	good opportunity.	5	Vile, *ly.*
3	much.	6	Villain, *s.*
4	much better.	7	Villany, *ies.*
5	sick.	8	Vindicate, *d, ing.*
6	slow.	9	Vindication.
7	strange.	0610	Vindicator, *s.*
8	well.	1	Vindictive, *ly.*
9	well done.	2	Vinegar.
0570	Vessel, *s.*	3	Viol block, *s.*
1	of war.	4	Violate, *d, ing.*
2	Vestige.	5	regulations of the service.
3	Veteran, *s.*	6	the regulations of the port.
4	Veto, *ed, ing, es.*	7	the laws.
5	Vex, *ed, ing, es.*	8	Violation, *s.*
6	Vexation, *s.*	9	Violence.
7	Vexatious.	0620	Violent, *ly.*
8	Vial, *s.*	1	Violin, *s.*
9	Vibrate, *d, ing, s.*	2	Vertical, *ly.*
0580	Vibration, *s.*	3	Virtue.
1	Vice.	4	Virtuous, *ly.*
2	Admiral.	5	Virulence.
3	Admiralty.	6	Virulent.
4	Consul.	7	Virus.
5	Presidency.	8	Visible, *y.*
6	President.	9	Vision.
7	Viceroy.	0630	Visionary, *ies.*
8	Vice royalty.	1	Visit, *ed, ing, s.*
9	Vicinity.	2	Visitor, *s.*
0590	Vicious, *ly.*	3	Vital, *ly.*
1	Vicissitude, *s.*	4	importance.
0592	Victim, *s.*	0635	Vitality.

Nos.	VIT	Nos.	WAR
0636	Vitals.	0679	Wait, *ed, ing, s.*
7	Vitiate, *d, ing.*	0680	Waiter, *s.*
8	Vitriol.	1	Waive, *d, ing.*
9	Vituperate, *d, ing, ion.*	2	all claim.
0640	Vivid, *ly.*	3	Wake, *d, ing.*
1	Vividness.	4	Wakeful.
2	Vocabulary, *ies.*	5	Waken, *ed.*
3	Voice.	6	Wales.
4	Void, *ed, ing.*	7	Walk, *ed, ing, s.*
5	Volatile.	8	Walking beam.
6	Volcanic.	9	Wall sided.
7	Volcano, *es.*	0690	Walnut timber.
8	Volition.	1	Wane, *d, ing.*
9	Volley, *s.*	2	Want, *ed, ing, s.*
0650	of musketry.	3	Wanton, *ly.*
1	Volume, *s.*	4	War, *red, ring.*
2	Voluminous.	5	Department.
3	Voluntary.	6	has commenced.
4	Volunteer, *s, ed, ing.*	7	has ended.
5	for hazardous service.	8	Ward, *s, ed, ing.*
6	Vomit, *ted, ting, s.*	9	Wardroom.
7	black vomit.	0700	boat, *s.*
8	Vortex.	1	boys.
9	Vouch, *ed, ing.*	2	cook.
0660	Vow, *ed, ing, s.*	3	furniture.
1	Voyage, *d, ing, s.*	4	mess.
2	Voyager, *s.*	5	officers.
3	Vulcanize, *d, ing.*	6	steward, *s.*
4	India rubber hose.	7	Warfare.
5	India rubber.	8	Warlike.
6	Vulnerable.	9	Warm, *ed, ing.*
7	Wad, *s.*	0710	hearted.
8	Wad hook.	1	weather.
9	Wade, *d, ing, s.*	2	work.
0670	Wafer, *s.*	3	Warmly.
1	Wage, *d, ing.*	4	Warmth.
2	Wages.	5	Warn, *ed, ing.*
3	Wagon, *s.*	6	the vessel, *s.*
4	Waif, *s.*	7	Warning signal.
5	Wail, *ed, ing.*	8	Warp, *ed, ing, s.*
6	Waist, *s.*	9	Warrant, *s, ed, ing.*
7	anchor, *s.*	0720	officer, *s.*
0678	boat, *s.*	0721	officers' mess.

Nos.	WAR	Nos.	WEA
0722	Warranty.		Water, *s, ed, ing.*
3	Warrior, *s.*	0765	works.
4	Wary, *ily.*	6	worn.
5	Was.	7	Wave, *d, ing, s.*
6	Wash, *ed, ing.*	8	of the hand.
7	clothes.	9	of the lantern.
8	stand.	0770	to the left.
9	Washer, *s.*	1	to the right.
0730	Washer woman, *en.*	2	Waver, *ed, ing.*
1	Waste, *d, ing.*	3	Wax.
2	for machinery.	4	Way, *s.*
3	pipe.	5	and means.
4	water.	6	We.
5	Wasteful, *ly.*	7	are.
6	Watch, *ed, ing, es.*	8	are not.
7	and watch.	9	can.
8	bill.	0780	cannot.
9	house.	1	ought.
0740	maker, *s.*	2	ought not.
1	number.	3	shall.
2	Watchful, *ly.*	4	shall not.
3	Watchman, *men.*	5	Weak, *ly.*
4	Watchword.	6	force.
5	for the night is.	7	handed.
6	Water, *s, ed, ing.*	8	Weaken, *ed, ing.*
7	battery, *ies.*	9	Weakness.
8	cask, *s.*	0790	Wealth.
9	closet, *s.*	1	Wealthy.
0750	cock, *s.*	2	Weapon, *s.*
1	course, *s.*	3	Wear.
2	craft.	4	and tear.
3	gauge, *s.*	5	ship.
4	level.	6	short round.
5	line, *s.*	7	Wearing.
6	logged.	8	Wear, *ing,* out.
7	man, *men.*	9	Wear, *ing,* ship.
8	mark.	0800	Wearied.
9	proof.	1	Weariness.
0760	spout, *s.*	2	Wearisome.
1	tank, *s.*	3	Weary, *ing.*
2	tight.	4	Weather.
3	way, *s.*	5	beam.
0764	wheel, *s.*	0806	beaten.

Nos.	WEA	Nos.	WHI
	Weather.		Westerly.
0807	bit your cable.	0849	drift.
8	bound.	0850	set.
9	bow.	1	wind.
0810	gauge.	2	Western.
1	glass, (barometer.)	3	Westernmost.
2	helm.	4	West Indies.
3	is looking better.	5	Westing.
4	quarter.	6	Westward, *ly*.
5	shore.	7	Wet, *ting*.
6	side.	8	bulb thermometer.
7	tide.	9	provisions.
8	wise.	0860	Whale, *s*.
9	Weatherly.	1	boat, *s*.
0820	Weathermost.	2	bone.
1	Wedge, *d, ing*.	3	fishery.
2	Wednesday.	4	Whaler, *s*.
3	evening.	5	Whaling fleet.
4	morning.	6	Wharf.
5	noon.	7	Wharfage.
6	night.	8	What.
7	Week, *s*.	9	day.
8	Weekly.	0870	news.
9	exercise.	1	time.
0830	report, *s*.	2	Whatever.
1	routine.	3	Wheaton's Laws of Nations.
2	Weevil, *s*.	4	Wheel.
3	Weevilly.	5	and pinion.
4	bread.	6	barrow, *s*.
5	Weigh, *ed, ing*.	7	rope, *s*.
6	anchor.	8	Whelp, *s*, of the capstan.
7	Weight, *s*.	9	When.
8	of metal.	0880	Whence.
9	Weights and measures.	1	Whenever.
0840	Welcome, *d, ing*.	2	Where.
1	Weld, *ed, ing*.	3	Whereas.
2	Welfare.	4	Whereby.
3	Well.	5	Wherefore.
4	Were.	6	Wherein.
5	West.	7	Wherever.
6	Westerly.	8	Which.
7	current, *s*.	9	While.
0848	course.	0890	Whip, *ped, ping, s*.

Nos.	WHI	Nos.	WIT
0891	Whipping twine.	0934	Wilful, *ly.*
2	Whirl, *ed, ing.*	5	Will.
3	Whirlpool.	6	Willingly.
4	Whirlwind.	7	Wilt, *ed, ing.*
5	Whisker, *s.*	8	Win, *ning.*
6	Whiskey.	9	Winch, *es.*
7	Whistle, *d, ing.*	0940	Wind, *s.*
8	White.	1	and water.
9	and black.	2	bound.
0900	cap, *s.*	3	gauge.
1	frock, *s.*	4	is ahead.
2	lead.	5	is fair.
3	paint, *s.*	6	rode.
4	trowsers.	7	sail, *s.*
5	Whiten, *ed, ing.*	8	Windage.
6	White squall.	9	Windlass.
7	swelling.	0950	Windward.
8	wash, *ed, ing.*	1	Windy.
9	water.	2	Wing, *s, ed, ing.*
0910	Whiting.	3	and wing.
1	Whitworth gun, *s.*	4	of the army.
2	Who.	5	of the fleet.
3	Whoever.	6	Winged out.
4	Whole.	7	Winter, *ed, ing.*
5	Wholesome.	8	Wipe, *d, ing.*
6	food.	9	Wiper, *s.*
7	fruit.	0960	Wire, *s.*
8	Wholly.	1	cloth.
9	Whom.	2	gauze.
0920	Whose.	3	rope.
1	Whosoever.	4	rigging.
2	Why.	5	Wisdom.
3	Wick, *s.*	6	Wise, *ly.*
4	Wicked, *ly.*	7	Wiser.
5	Wickedness.	8	Wisest.
6	Wide, *ly.*	9	Wish, *ed, ing, es.*
7	channel.	0970	With.
8	spread.	1	a will.
9	stream.	2	difficulty.
0930	Widely.	3	the sun.
1	Width.	4	Withdraw, *ing.*
2	Wild, *ly.*	5	from action.
0933	firing.	0976	Withdrew.

Nos.	WIT	Nos.	YAR
0977	Wither, *ed, ing.*	0021	Workmanship.
8	Withheld.	2	Workshop, *s.*
9	Withhold, *ing.*	3	World.
0980	Within.	4	Worm, *s.*
1	Without.	5	and scraper, *s.*
2	day.	6	Wormy.
3	difficulty.	7	Worn.
4	Withstand, *ing.*	8	out.
5	Withstood.	9	Worry, *ied, ing.*
6	Witness, *ed, ing.*	0030	Worse.
7	Witnesses.	1	Worst.
8	Women.	2	Worth.
9	Won.	3	Worthless, *ness.*
0990	Wood, *ed.*	4	Worthy.
1	Wooden.	5	Would.
2	ship, *s.*	6	Wound, *ed, ing, s.*
3	Wood ends.	7	Wounded men.
4	Woodlock, *s.*	8	Wounded officer, *s.*
5	Woodwork.	9	Wreck, *ed, ing, s.*
6	Woof.	0040	master.
7	Wool.	1	Wrecked people.
8	Woold, *ed, ing.*	2	vessel, *s.*
0999	Woolen.	3	Wretch, *ed, es.*
001	clothing.	4	Wretchedness.
2	Word, *ed, s.*	5	Write, *ing.*
3	Wore.	6	Written.
4	Work, *ed, ing.*	7	Writer, *s.*
5	against.	8	Writing paper.
6	at.	9	Wrong, *ed, ing.*
7	down.	0050	Wrongful, *ly.*
8	house.	1	Wrote.
9	in.	2	Wrought.
0010	night and day.	3	iron.
1	out.	4	iron nails.
2	to windward.	5	iron plate, *s.*
3	up.	6	Xebec.
4	Working beam.	7	Yacht, *s, ing.*
5	class, *es.*	8	Yam, *s.*
6	day.	9	Yard, *s.*
7	drawings.	0060	arm, *s.*
8	party, *ies.*	1	arm and yard arm.
9	Workman or men.	2	across.
0020	Workmanlike.	0063	rope, *s.*

Nos.	YAR	Nos.	ZOU
	Yard, *s.*	0086	Yet.
0064	tackle, *s.*	7	Yield, *ed, ing.*
5	whip, *s.*	8	You.
6	Yarn, *s.*	9	are.
7	Yaw, *ed, ing.*	0090	are not.
8	Yawl, *s.*	1	must.
9	Year, *s.*	2	should.
0070	Yearly.	3	will.
1	Yellow.	4	Your.
2	bunting, *s.*	5	distinguish'g pendants or lights.
3	fever.	6	number.
4	fever on board.	7	station.
5	ochre.	8	Yourself, *selves.*
6	paint.	0099	Zeal.
7	Yeoman, *s, men.*	0001	Zealous, *ly.*
8	account, *s.*	2	Zenith.
9	stores.	3	distance.
0080	store room, *s.*	4	Zero.
1	Yes.	5	Zinc paint.
2	Yesterday.	6	sheet, *s, of.*
3	afternoon.	7	Zodiac, *al.*
4	evening.	8	Zone, *s.*
0085	morning.	0009	Zouave, *s.*

GEOGRAPHICAL LIST.

Nos.	AAL	Nos.	ALB
1	Aalborg, Denmark.	43	Africa, Coast of.
2	Aalesund, Norway.	4	Africa, East Coast of.
3	Aarhaus, Denmark.	5	Africa, West Coast of.
4	Abaco, Bahamas.	6	Agamenticus Hills, Maine, U. S.
5	Abaco L. H., Bahamas.	7	Agde Harbor, France.
6	Abacou Point, Hayti, W. I.	8	Agde, Mount, France.
7	Abacou Great Island, Bahamas.	9	Agia Maria Cape, Asia Minor.
8	Abbeville, France.	50	Agenhu Island, Loo-Choo Islands.
9	Aberaron, Wales.	1	Aggermore Rock.
10	Aberdeen, Scotland.	2	Agincourt Island.
1	Abergeley, Wales.	3	Agio Strati Island, Greek Archip'ago.
2	Aberystwith, Wales.	4	Aglionby Point.
3	Abo, Russia.	5	Agnes, St., England, West Coast.
4	Aboukir, Egypt.	6	Agnes Island.
5	Abrolhos Shoals, Coast of Brazil, S. A.	7	Aguada Bay.
6	Absecom Inlet, New Jersey, U. S.	8	Aguadilla Bay.
7	Absecom Light-house, Coast of New Jersey, U. S.	9	Agua del Key.
8	Abydos, Asia Minor.	60	Aguas Calientes, Mexico.
9	Abyssinia, East Africa.	1	Aguilas, Spain.
20	Acapulco, Mexico.	2	Agugas Point.
1	Accomac, Coast of, Virginia, U. S.	3	Agulha Point, Madeiras.
2	Accra, Guinea.	4	Ahus, Sweden.
3	Acheen, Sumatra.	5	Aiges Mortes, France.
4	Acheen Head, N. W. Point Sumatra.	6	Air, Point of, Coast of Wales.
5	Achil Head, Ireland.	7	Aix, France.
6	Acklin Island, Bahamas.	8	Aix-la-Chapelle, Prussia.
7	Acre, Syria.	9	Ajaccio, Corsica.
8	Adalia, Asiatic Turkey.	70	Ajon Reef.
9	Adalia, Gulf of, Karamania.	1	Ajuero.
30	Adelaide, Australia.	2	Akabah, Gulf of, Red Sea.
1	Aden, Arabia.	3	Akarua, New Zealand.
2	Admiral's Cove.	4	Akrotiri Cape, Greek Archipelago.
3	Admiralty Islands, South Pacific.	5	Akyab, Bengal.
4	Admiralty Sound, Terra del Fuego.	6	Alacranes, Gulf of Mexico.
5	Adour River, France.	7	Aland Isles, Russia.
6	Adore Matte Atoll, Maldive Island.	8	Alamaquan Island, Mariana Islands.
7	Adra, Spain.	9	Alang Point, Clove Island.
8	Adrianople, Turkey.	80	Alargate Reef, Mosquito Coast.
9	Adriatic Sea, Mediterranean.	1	Alaya, Asiatic Turkey.
40	Adramitti, Asia Minor.	2	Albatross Island, Bass Straits.
1	Adventure Bay.	3	Albatross Islands, Brazil.
42	Affghanistan, Asia.	4	Albemarle Sound, N. Carolina, U. S.
		85	Alberton, Australia.

Nos.	ALB	Nos.	AMB
86	Albion Bank.	127	Al-Kalah, Barbary.
7	Alboran Island, Mediterranean.	8	Alkmaar, Holland.
8	Alcantara, Spain.	9	Allas Straits, Malay Archipelago.
9	Alcatrases Shoals, Cuba.	130	Allanis Hole.
90	Alcatraz Island, Coast of Africa.	1	Allegranza, Canary Islands.
1	Alcatrazes, Brazil.	2	Allerton, Australia.
2	Alceste Island, Yellow Sea.	3	Alligator Reef, Jamaica, W. I.
3	Alcoutra.	4	Alligator Rock, S. E. Coast of China.
4	Alcoy Island.	5	Alligator River, N. Coast Australia.
5	Aldabra Island, Indian Ocean.	6	Alligator Pond Key.
6	Aldborough, England.	7	Alligator River, North Carolina, U. S.
7	Alden's Rock, Maine, U. S.	8	All Saints Bay, Brazil.
8	Alderney, English Channel.	9	All Saints, West Indies.
9	Aleutian Islands.	140	Almadies Rocks, Senegambia.
100	Alexander, Cape, Barrow's Straits.	1	Almeria, Spain.
1	Alexander, Cape, N. Coast America.	2	Almirante Bay.
2	Alexander, Cape, Choiseul Island, South Pacific.	3	Almirante Islands.
		4	Almafedas, Brazil.
3	Alexander Island, Antarctic Ocean.	5	Almunecar, Spain.
4	Alexander, Mount, Gulf Carpentaria.	6	Alnemouth, England.
5	Alexander, Port, West Coast Africa.	7	Alofa, South Pacific Ocean.
6	Alexander Shoal, China Sea.	8	Aloupo Cape, Karamania.
7	Alexandretta, Karamania.	9	Alphonse Island, Almirante Isles.
8	Alexandria, Port of, Egypt.	150	Alpreck Point, N. W. Coast France.
9	Alexandria, Potomac River, Virginia, U. S.	1	Alsen, Baltic Sea.
		2	Alta Vela, South Coast St. Domingo.
110	Alfraques, Port, East Coast of Spain.	3	Altamaha Sound, Georgia, U. S.
1	Alfred Shoal, Celebes.	4	Althorpe Is., Spencer Gulf, Australia.
2	Algarroba Point.	5	Altona, Germany.
3	Algeciras, Gibraltar Bay, Spain.	6	Altowaba.
4	Alghero, Island of Sardinia.	7	Alvarado, Gulf of Mexico.
5	Algiers, Africa.	8	Amak Island, N. W. Coast America.
6	Algoa Bay, Cape of Good Hope.	9	Amakirima Island, Loo-Choo group.
7	Alhucemas, Morocco.	160	Amanu, South Pacific Ocean.
8	Alicante, Spain.	1	Amargura Island, S. Pacific Ocean.
9	Alicante, Gulf of, Spain.	2	Amastro, Black Sea.
120	Alicota, Island of Sicily.	3	Amatigneh Id., N. W. Coast America.
1	Alice Point, Naples.	4	Amazon River, South America.
2	Aliceedi Island, Lipari Islands.	5	Ambas Bay, Bight of Biafra.
3	Aliguai Island, Mindinao, Philippine Islands.	6	Ambatiki Island, S. Pacific Ocean.
		7	Ambelie, Low Id., Celebes, E. Coast.
4	Alijos Rocks, Galapagos Islands.	8	Amber Cape, Madagascar.
5	Alipata Point, Leyte, Philippine Is.	169	Ambergris Bay, West Indies.
126	Alippee, Hindostan.		

Nos.	AMB	Nos.	ANG
170	Amblaw Island, Bouro.	212	Anaa, Low Archipelago, So. Pacific Ocean.
1	Amboina, Island, Ceram.		
2	Ambolon Island, Mindoro.	3	Anachoretes, South Pacific Ocean.
3	Amberg Bay, N. W. Coast of Borneo.	4	Analaboo, S. W. Coast of Sumatra.
4	Amboroo Bank, Senegambia.	5	Anambas, China Sea.
5	Ambryna Land, China Sea.	6	Anamour Cape, Karamania.
6	Ambriz, Africa.	7	Ananes Rocks, Greek Archipelago.
7	Ambrose, St., Island, S. Pacific Ocean.	8	Anapa, Circassia.
8	Ambrym Island, New Hebrides.	9	Anaphi Island, Greek Archipelago.
9	Ameland, North Sea.	220	Anasco Bay.
180	Amelia Island, Florida, U. S.	1	Annsi Island, Greek Archipelago.
1	Amelia Sound, Georgia, U. S.	2	Anastasia Island, Coast Florida, U. S.
2	Ameni, Lacadive Islands.	3	Anntaxan Island, Mariana Islands.
3	Amherst, Gulf of Martaban.	4	Anatolia, Asia Minor.
4	Amherst Island, Magdalen Islands.	5	Anchor Cay, Torres Straits.
5	Amherst Rocks, Pescadores Islands.	6	Anchor Point, N. America, W. Coast.
6	America, North.	7	Ancboras Islands, Brazil, East Coast.
7	America, South.	8	Anciola Point, Iviza, Balearic Isles.
8	America, East Coast.	9	Ancona, Italy.
9	America, South Coast.	230	Ancutta, Lacadive Islands.
190	America, West Coast of.	1	Andalusia Bank, China Sea.
1	America, N. W. Coast of.	2	Andamans, Bay of Bengal.
2	American Shoal, Florida Reefs.	3	Andema Island, N. Pacific Ocean.
3	Amet Island.	4	Andöe, Norway.
4	Amlia Island, Aleutian Isles.	5	Andrava Bay, Madagascar.
5	Amo Iguian Islet, Philippine Islands.	6	Andre, St., Philippine Islands.
6	Amorgo Island, Greek Archipelago.	7	Andrea Cape, Island Cyprus.
7	Amorgo Poulo Island, Greek Arch'go.	8	Andrea, St., Adriatic.
8	Amoughta Island, Aleutian Isles.	9	Andrew, St., Cape, Madagascar.
9	Amoor River, Asia, Okotsk Sea.	240	Andrew, St., Island, North Pacific.
200	Amorgos, Greece.	1	Andrew's, St., Maine, U. S.
1	Amourang Bay, Celebes, North Coast.	2	Andrew's, St., East Coast Scotland.
2	Amoy, China, South East Coast.	3	Andrew's, St., Bay, Florida, U. S.
3	Amphinome Shoals, Australia, N. W. Coast.	4	Andrew's, St., Isl., Mosquito Coast.
4	Amphitrite Island, China Sea.	5	Andrew's, St., Sound, Georgia, U. S.
5	Amrum, Denmark.	6	Andros Island, Bahamas, W. I.
6	Amsterdam, Holland.	7	Andros Island, Greek Archipelago.
7	Amsterdam, Dutch Guiana.	8	Anegada, Virgin Isles.
8	Amsterdam, Venezuela.	9	Angar Island, Persian Gulf.
9	Amsterdam Island, Dampier Straits.	250	Angau Island, Feejee Islands.
210	Amsterdam Island, Indian Ocean.	1	Angeles Point, Chili.
211	Amtschitka Island, America, N. W. Coast.	2	Angelica Reef, South of Celebes.
		253	Angelo, St., Mount, W. Coast Adriatic.

138

Nos.	ANG	Nos.	ANT
254	Angelo, St., Cape, Greece.	297	Anne, St., Bay, Marquesas Islands.
5	Angelo, St., Mount, Naples.	8	Anne, St., Isl., Seychelle Archipelago.
6	Angenweel Harbor, India, W. Coast.	9	Anne, St., Mountains, Gulf of St.
7	Angerstein Rocks.		Lawrence.
8	Anglesea, North Wales.	300	Annenkov Island, Sandwich Islands.
9	Angola, West Africa.	1	Annisquam, Massachusetts, U. S.
260	Angostura, South America.	2	Annobona, Bight of Biafra.
1	Angour Island, Pelew Islands.	3	Ano Nuevo Point, Mexico.
2	Angoza Island, Mozambique.	4	Anouda, Feejee Isl., S. Pacific Ocean.
3	Angra, Azores.	5	Anse a Chouchou Bay.
4	Angra Pequena, South Africa.	6	Anse a Claire.
5	Angria Bank, West Coast of India.	7	Anse a Galet.
6	Anguilla Isl., West Indies, Bahamas.	8	Anse a Pitres.
7	Anguilla, Island, Virgin Isles.	9	Anse, Great, Antilles.
8	Anguille, Cape, Labrador, W. Coast.	310	Anson Bay, Corea.
9	Anguila Point, Iviza, Balearic Isles.	1	Anson Bay, Ladrones.
270	Anhatomirim, Brazil, S. E. Coast.	2	Antarctic Ocean.
1	Anholt Island, Denmark.	3	Antibes, France.
2	Aniva Cape, Penins. of Sagalin.	4	Anticosti Island, Gulf St. Lawrence.
3	Anjediva Island, Malabar Coast.	5	Anticosti, East Point.
4	Anjenga, Ceylon.	6	Anticosti, West Point.
5	Anjer, Strait of Sunda.	7	Antigozzo, Candia.
6	Anjol, Cape, S. Coast of Java.	8	Antiqua Island, West Indies.
7	Ann, Cape, Massachusetts, U. S.	9	Antimille, Antemilo, Greek Archip'go.
8	Ann, Cape, New Britain.	320	Antioch, Karamania.
9	Ann, Cape, Harbor, Mass., U. S.	1	Antioco, St., Island, Sardinia.
280	Ann's Reef, Lipari Islands.	2	Antiparos, Greek Archipelago.
1	Ann, St., Cape, Coast of Liberia.	3	Antipaxo Island, Ionian Isles.
2	Ann, St., Island, E. Coast of Brazil.	4	Antipsara, Asia Minor.
3	Ann, St., Shoals, Gulf of Guinea.	5	Antique, Philippine Isles.
4	Ann, St., Bay, Jamaica, W. I.	6	Antivari, Albania.
5	Ann, St., Harbor, Cape Breton Island.	7	Antonio, Cape, Spain, E. Coast of.
6	Ann, St., Lights, Coast of Wales.	8	Antonio, Port, Jamaica, W. I.
7	Anna, Pulo, North Pacific Ocean.	9	Antonio, St., Azores.
8	Anna, St., Island, Brazil.	330	Antonio, St., Bay, Bight of Biafra, Africa.
9	Anna, St., Island, Solomon Islands.	1	Antonio, St., Cape, Brazil, S. A.
290	Anna, Santa.	2	Antonio, St., Cape, Buenos Ayres, S.A.
1	Anna, Santa, de Chaves.	3	Antonio, St., Cape, Cuba, W. I.
2	Annamoaka Island, S. Pacific Ocean.	4	Antonio, St., Mountains, Bermudas.
3	Anuam, Isle of Man.	5	Antonio, St., Reef, South Africa.
4	Annapolis, Chesapeake Bay.	6	Anton, St., Port, Iviza Island, Mediterranean.
5	Annapolis, Nova Scotia.		
296	Annatom Island, S. Pacific Ocean.	337	Antonio, St., Port, Patagonia, S. A.

Nos.	ANT	Nos.	ARF
338	Anton Lizardo, Mexico, Coast of.	380	Arcadia, Greece, West Coast.
9	Anthony, St., Cape, Arabia, Red Sea.	1	Arcas, Gulf of Mexico.
340	Antony, St., Light, English Coast.	2	Arcé Island, Patagonia, East Coast.
1	Antwerp, Belgium.	3	Archangel, White Sea.
2	Anvil, Porto Rico Island, W. I.	4	Archangel Island, S. Pacific Ocean.
3	Anzo, Port, Gulf of Genoa, Mediter'n.	5	Arch. Gabriel Bank, Kamschatka.
4	Aor, Pulo, Sumatra.	6	Arched Rock, South Africa.
5	Aotia, New Zealand, N. E. Coast of.	7	Archimedes B'k, Rio de la Plata, S. A.
6	Aoura, North Pacific Ocean.	8	Archipelago, Aleutian, N. W. Coast of America.
7	Aour, Marshall Is., N. Pacific Ocean.		
8	Apamama, South Pacific Ocean.	9	Archipelago, Buccaneer.
9	Aparri, Babuyanes Islands.	390	Archipelago, Chayos.
350	Apataki, South Pacific Ocean.	1	Archipelago, Dampier.
1	Apee Island, New Hebrides.	2	Archipelago, Grecian.
2	Apenrade, Denmark.	3	Archipelago, Louisade.
3	Api Head, Flores.	4	Archipelago, Low.
4	Apia, New Hebrides.	5	Archipelago, Malay.
5	Apia Harbor, New Hebrides.	6	Archipelago, Santa Cruz.
6	Apolima Island, Navigator's Islands.	7	Archipelago, Solomon's.
7	Apollonia, Ivory Coast, Africa.	8	Archipelago, Sooloo.
8	Apollos Island, Japan Islands.	9	Arcuento, Mt., Sardinia.
9	App Shoal, Palawan.	400	Arctic Ocean.
360	Appalachee Bay, Florida, U. S.	1	Ardasier Shoal, N. W. of Borneo.
1	Appalachicola, Florida, U. S.	2	Ardassier Islet, Gilolo Passage.
2	Aprouak River, Guiana, S. A.	3	Arden Island, Torres Straits.
3	Aquia Creek, Potomac River, Virginia, U. S.	4	Ardglass, Ireland.
4	Arab's Tower, Egypt.	5	Ardjuno Mt., Java, South Coast.
5	Arabat, Black Sea.	6	Ardrossan, Scotland.
6	Arabia.	7	Arecife, Port Naos, Madeiras.
7	Arabian Sea, Gulf.	8	Arecifos Island, N. Pacific Ocean.
8	Aracan, Coromandel Coast.	9	Areemba Head, Mozambique, South Africa.
9	Aracati, Brazil.		
370	Arahi Point, New Zealand.	410	Arena Island, Mindanao, Philippine Islands.
1	Araish, Africa, N. W. Coast.	1	Arena Point, California.
2	Arakamchechen, North Coast Asia.	2	Arena Point, Peru.
3	Arakcheyeff Island.	3	Arenas Cay, Gulf of Mexico.
4	Aransas Bay, Texas, U. S.	4	Arenas Point, Mosquito Coast.
5	Aransas Pass, Texas, U. S.	5	Arendal, Norway.
6	Aratica, South Pacific Ocean.	6	Arensberg, Russia.
7	Arauco, Chile, S. A.	7	Arentes, Java Sea.
8	Arbolado Point, Gulf of California.	8	Arequipa, Peru.
379	Arbroath, Scotland.	9	Arfak Mount'ns, New Guinea, North Coast.

Nos.	ARG	Nos.	ASS
420	Argentine Confederation.	461	Arnold Id., Australia, N. E. Coast.
1	Argent Mountain, Guiana, S. A.	2	Arrabida Fort, Portugal.
2	Argentario Mountain, Gulf of Genoa, Italy.	3	Arracan River, Bay of Bengal.
		4	Arran Islands, Galway Bay.
3	Argentera Cape, Minorca, Mediter'n.	5	Arrar, Ras, Arabia, South Coast.
4	Argentiera Island, Greek Archip'ago.	6	Arroa S., Strait of Malacca.
5	Argentino Fort, Buenos Ayres.	7	Arrogant Rock, Java Sea.
6	Argonaut Island, Coast of Tartary.	8	Arrowsmith's Is., N. Pacific Ocean.
7	Argostoli Port, Ionian Isles.	9	Arru Islands, Banda Sea.
8	Arguello Point, Mexico.	470	Arsenal Point, Potomac River, U. S.
9	Arguin Bank, Africa, N. W. Coast.	1	Arta, Gulf of, Ionian Sea.
430	Argyle Island, Georgia, U. S.	2	Arthur Island, South Pacific Ocean.
1	Arholma, East Coast of Sweden.	3	Arthur Islet, Marshall Islands, Nor. Pacific Ocean.
2	Ari Atoll, Maldive Isles.		
3	Ariadne Bank, Society Islands, Sou. Pacific Ocean.	4	Arthur, Mt., Van Dieman's Land, North Coast.
4	Ariadne Rocks, Pescadores Islands.	5	Arthur, Port, Van Dieman's Land, South Coast.
5	Aringa Island, N. W. & N. of Gilolo.		
6	Arichat, Cape Breton Isles.	6	Artibonite River.
7	Arichat Harbor.	7	Arubah Cape, Beloochistan.
8	Arica, Peru.	8	Arutua, South Pacific Ocean.
9	Arid Cape, Recherche Archipelago, Australia.	9	Arvoredo Island, Brazil, S. E. Coast.
440	Aride Island, Seychelle Archipelago.	480	Arzenie, Persian Gulf, S. Coast.
1	Ariel Reef, New Zealand.	1	Arzeu, Morocco.
2	Arimoa Isles, New Guinea, N. Coast.	2	Asaua Group, South Pacific Ocean.
3	Aris Island, New Guinea, N. Coast.	3	Ascalon, Syria.
4	Arish, El, Syria.	4	Ascension Bay, Gulf of Mexico.
5	Aristazabal Cape, Patagonia, E. Coast.	5	Ascension Island, Caroline Islands.
6	Arki, Greek Archipelago.	6	Ascension Island, South Atlantic.
7	Arklow, Ireland.	7	Ashnpee Harbor.
8	Arkona, Baltic Sea.	8	Ashmore Shoal, Australia.
9	Arlagnuk, Arctic Ocean.	9	Asia.
450	Armegon Hill, Coromandel Coast.	490	Asia Minor.
1	Armenia, Asia.	1	Asia Island, Dampier Strait.
2	Armi, Cape del, Gulf of Genoa, Italy.	2	Asia Light, Black Sea.
3	Armi, Cape del, Naples, Italy.	3	Asia Rock, Peru, S. A.
4	Armiansk, Black Sea.	4	Asinara, Sardinia.
5	Atmstrong Island, N. Pacific Ocean.	5	Aspinwall or Colon, Central America.
6	Armuyden Bank, Strait of Sunda.	6	Aspo Beac, Gulf of Finland.
7	Arnheim Bay, Gulf of Carpentaria.	7	Aspo Island, Norway.
8	Arnheim Cape, Gulf of Carpentaria.	8	Aspotogon Harbor.
9	Arno, Norway.	9	Assam, India.
460	Arno River, Italy.	500	Assateague Island, U. S.
		501	Assateague Inlet, U. S.

Nos.	ASS	Nos.	AVE
502	Assens, Denmark.	545	Attwick Rock, Strait of Gaspar.
3	Asses' Ears, China, S. Coast.	6	Attwood's Cay, Bahamas, W. I.
4	Asses' Ears, Japan Islands.	7	Auckland, China Sea.
5	Asses' Ears, Persian Gulf.	8	Auckland, New Zealand.
6	Assini River, Ivory Coast, Africa.	9	Auckland Islands, S. Pacific Ocean.
7	Assumption Island, Ladrones.	550	Audierne, France.
8	Assumption Island, Mozambique.	1	Auflaka, Sea of Marmora, Turkey.
9	Astola Island, Beloochistan.	2	Augusta, Port, Sicily.
510	Astoria, New York, U. S.	3	Augusta, Maine, U. S.
1	Astoria, Oregon, U. S.	4	Augusta, Georgia, U. S.
2	Astova, Mozambique Channel.	5	Augusta River.
3	Astrolabe Cape, Solomon Islands.	6	Augustin, St., Bay, Madagascar.
4	Astrolabe Creek, Solomon Islands.	7	Augustin, St., Cape, Brazil.
5	Astrolabe Island, New S. Shetland.	8	Augustin, St., Cape, Philippines.
6	Astrolabe Reef, Feejee Islands.	9	Augustin, St., Harbor, Florida, U. S.
7	Astrolabe Reefs, Loyalty Isles.	560	Augustin, St., Isl., S. Pacific Ocean.
8	Astrolabe Road, New Zealand.	1	Augustin, St., Mt.,N. Amer.,W. Coast.
9	Astrolabe Rock.	2	Augustus Island, Australia.
520	Astropalaia, Greek Archipelago.	3	Augustus, Mt., Torres Straits.
1	Asuad, Ras al, Barbary.	4	Aura Island, South Pacific Ocean.
2	Asuad, Ras al, East Africa.	5	Aureed Island, Torres Straits.
3	Asuncion, Paraguay, South America.	6	Aulona, or Valona, Adriatic Sea.
4	Asuncion Island, Gulf of California.	7	Aurora Bank, Gilolo Passage.
5	Atacames, U. S. Colombia, S. A.	8	Aurora Island, Low Archipelago.
6	Atalaia Point, River Amazon.	9	Aurora Island, New Hebrides.
7	Atangota Island, Navigators' Islands.	570	Auskery Island, Orkney Isles.
8	Atcha, N. W. Coast of America.	1	Australia.
9	Atchafalaya, Louisiana, U. S.	2	Australia, North.
530	Atchafalaya River, U. S.	3	Australia Reef, N. W. of Australia.
1	Aterra Cape, Ionian Isles.	4	Australia, South.
2	Athens, Greece.	5	Australia, Western.
3	Athens, Gulf of, Greece.	6	Australian Bight.
4	Athos, Cape, Greek Archipelago.	7	Australind, Australia, S. W. Coast.
5	Athos, Mount, Greek Archipelago.	8	Austria, Europe.
6	Atiou, Cook Islands.	9	Aux Cayes, St. Domingo, N. Coast.
7	Atlantic Island, N. Pacific Ocean.	580	Ava, Japan.
8	Atlantic Coast.	1	Avarena Point, St. Domingo, S. Coast.
9	Atlantic, North.	2	Avatcha Bay, Kamtchatka.
540	Atlantic, South.	3	Avatcha Islands, Kamtchatka.
1	Atooi Isl., Sandwich Isl's, N. Pacific.	4	Aveiro, Portugal.
2	Atrato River, U. S. Colombia, C. A.	5	Averdi, Cape, Solomon Islands.
3	Atrevida, Mexico, West Coast of.	6	Aves Island, Windward Islands,W. I.
544	Attou, N. W. Coast of America.	587	Aves Islands, Coast of Venezuela.

Nos.	AVI	Nos.	BAL
588	Avinoff, Cape, N. W. Coast America.	631	Baffin Island.
9	Avlona, Adriatic, East Coast.	2	Baffin's Bay.
590	Avola, Sicily.	3	Baffin's Islands.
1	Avon Islands, N. W. of Australia.	4	Bagamango Island.
2	Avova, Cape, Karamania.	5	Baglan.
3	Avranches, France.	6	Bagnan Island.
4	Awa, Cape, Islands of Japan.	7	Bahamas, W. I.
5	Awakalo, Feejee Islands.	8	Bahama, Great Bank, W. I.
6	Awath, Ras, East Africa.	9	Bahama Island, W. I.
7	Axim, Ivory Coast, Africa.	640	Bahama, Little Bank, W. I.
8	Ayas, Karamania.	1	Bahama Channel, Old, W. I.
9	Ayer Bongy, Sumatra.	2	Bahama, Cuba, W. I.
600	Ayr, Point of, Isle of Man.	3	Bahia, Brazil.
1	Ayr, or Ayre Harbor, Scotland.	4	Bahia, Alejandro.
2	Ayre Island, Minorca.	5	Bahia Blanca.
3	Azafoun, Mt., Algiers, Africa.	6	Bahia Honda, Cuba.
4	Azamor, Morocco, Africa.	7	Bahia Honda, Florida.
5	Azata, Viti Archepelago, S. Pacific.	8	Bahia Honda, Guatemala.
6	Azof, or Azov, Russia, Black Sea.	9	Bahia Honda, U. S. Colombia.
7	Azof, Sea of.	650	Bahia Falsa, Brazil.
8	Azores, North Atlantic.	1	Baie de Ferret.
9	Baagoe.	2	Baie de Flammands.
610	Baba.	3	Baie du Mesle.
1	Babà Cape.	4	Bahrein Island.
2	Babel Islands.	5	Baia.
3	Bab el Mandeb, Straits.	6	Bailey Island.
4	Babi Island.	7	Bailey Islands.
5	Babi Pulo, Aru Islands.	8	Bailique Island, River Amazon, S. A.
6	Babi Pulo, Java.	9	Bairout (or Beyrout), Syria.
7	Babi Pulo, Sumatra.	660	Bajo Gallardo.
8	Babily Pulo.	1	Bajo Navidad.
9	Babor Mount.	2	Bajo Seco.
620	Babuyanes Islands.	3	Bajoli, Cape.
1	Babuyan, New.	4	Baker's Island, Maine, U. S.
2	Bacalhao Island.	5	Baker's Island, Mass., U. S.
3	Back Point.	6	Baker Point.
4	Back River, Massachusetts.	7	Balabac Island.
5	Back River, Virginia.	8	Balabalak.
6	Back River Light-house, Virginia.	9	Balabea Island.
7	Back River Point.	670	Balade Harbor, New Caledonia.
8	Badagry.	1	Balagonan Point.
9	Badgley Point.	2	Balambangan Island.
630	Baffa.	673	Balandra Bay.

Nos.	BAL	Nos.	BAN
674	Balasore River.	717	Bancoot River, British India.
5	Balbi Mount.	8	Bancowan.
6	Balbriggan.	9	Banculin Point.
7	Bald Cape.	720	Banda Island, Molucca Archipelago.
8	Bald Head I. and L. H., N. Carolina.	1	Banda Sea.
9	Bald Head, Australia.	2.	Banda Straits.
680	Bald Head, Maine, U. S.	3	Bande de l'Arier Bay.
1	Balearic Islands, Mediterranean.	4	Banditte Island.
2	Baleine Bank.	5	Bandol.
3	Baleine Shoal.	6	Bandoras Bay.
4	Baleira, Morocco.	7	Bane Harbor.
5	Balintang Islands.	8	Bane's Port, Cuba, W. I.
6	Baline Cove.	9	Banff.
7	Balize, Honduras.	730	Bangay Island.
8	Balize, Delta of the Mississippi.	1	Banglores.
9	Balize Rock.	2	Banguey Is., Borneo, N. E. Coast.
690	Ball's Pyramid.	3	Banguey Is., Borneo, N. W. Coast.
1	Ball's Rocks.	4	Bangor, Ireland.
2	Ball's Creek.	5	Bangor, Maine, U. S.
3	Ballina, Ireland.	6	Banham Islands.
4	Ballard, Cape.	7	Baniak Island.
5	Ballard Point.	8	Banistre Cays.
6	Ballena Point.	9	Banjar Massin, Borneo.
7	Balleny Islands.	740	Banjoar.
8	Ballones Cape.	1	Banka Island, Malay Archipelago.
9	Bally Island, Malay Archipelago.	2	Bankel Island.
700	Bally Strait, Malay Archipelago.	3	Baukok, Siam.
1	Bally Cottin, Ireland.	4	Banks' Cape.
2	Bally Shannon, Ireland.	5	Banks' Island.
3	Balta Island.	6	Banks' Islands.
4	Balona Shoals, Cuba.	7	Banks' Land.
5	Baltic.	8	Banks' Peninsula.
6	Baltic Port.	9	Bauks' Point.
7	Baltimore, Maryland, U. S.	750	Banks', Sir J., Group.
8	Baltimore, Ireland.	1	Banks' Straits, Bass' Straits.
9	Bampton Shoal.	2	Banks of Florida, U. S.
710	Bancawang.	3	Banks of Newfoundland.
1	Bana Point.	4	Banna, Ras.
2	Bananas Islands.	5	Bannister Road.
3	Bancn, Celebes.	6	Bantam.
4	Banca, Indian Archipelago.	7	Banton Island.
5	Bancawan Island.	8	Bantoncillo Island.
716	Bancoongong.	759	Bantry Bay, Ireland.

Nos.	BAP	Nos.	BAR
760	Bappang Shoal.	803	Barn Islands.
1	Baracoa, Cuba, W. I.	4	Barnegat Inlet, New Jersey, U. S.
2	Barahona.	5	Barnegat L. H.
3	Barancas, Pens'cola Bay, Florida, U.S.	6	Barnouic Rocks.
4	Barataria Bay, Louisiana, U. S.	7	Barnett's Harbor.
5	Barawally Bay, W. I.	8	Barneveldt, Fort.
6	Barbados Island, W. I.	9	Barneveldt Islands.
7	Barbaios.	810	Barnstable.
8	Barbara, St.	1	Barnstable Bay, Massachusetts, U. S.
9	Barbara, Santa, Island.	2	Barnstable, England.
770	Barbara, St., Port.	3	Barquero.
1	Barbarie Point.	4	Barra Head.
2	Barbas Cape.	5	Barra Island, Hebrides.
3	Barbe, St.	6	Barracoa.
4	Barbe Islands.	7	Barra Ciega, Mexico.
5	Barbuda, W. I.	8	Barracouta Island.
6	Barbukit Hill.	9	Barracouta Point.
7	Barbour's River.	820	Barracouta Shoals.
8	Barburet Islands.	1	Barra del Tordo.
9	Barcelona.	2	Barra de Santa Anna.
780	Barclay Cape.	3	Barra de Santander, Mexico.
1	Barclay de Tolly Island.	4	Barra Velha.
2	Bard Head.	5	Barren Cape.
3	Bardia Pulo.	6	Barren Island, Andamans.
4	Bardsey Island.	7	Barren Islands, China Sea.
5	Barebush Cay.	8	Barren Islands, Madagascar.
6	Bareedy Cape.	9	Barren Island, Furneaux.
7	Barellah, Pulo.	830	Barren Island, Maryland, U. S.
8	Barfleur Cape, France.	1	Barren Islands, China.
9	Bari.	2	Barren Islands, N.W. Coast America.
790	Barima Point.	3	Barren Mount, East.
1	Baring Islands.	4	Barren Inlet.
2	Baring Shoals.	5	Barrier Cape.
3	Barker Islands.	6	Barrier Islands.
4	Bariay Harbor, Cuba, W. I.	7	Barrier Great Reefs.
5	Barilla River.	8	Barrington.
6	Barletta.	9	Barrington Bay.
7	Barmosa Kebir.	840	Barrister Bay.
8	Barmouth.	1	Barroinee Point.
9	Barnhill, India.	2	Barrow Cape.
800	Barnhill, Persian Gulf.	3	Barrow Harbor.
1	Barn Island.	4	Barrow Hill.
802	Barn Island Harbor.	845	Barrow Island, South Pacific.

Nos.	BAR	Nos.	BAX
846	Barrow Island, Low Archipelago.	889	Batacarang Point.
7	Barrow Point, Australia.	890	Batag Island.
8	Barrow Point, North America.	1	Batalin Island.
9	Barrow Point, N. W. America.	2	Batan Island.
850	Barry Head.	3	Batang Port.
1	Barrysway Bay.	4	Batang Reef.
2	Barsalore Peak.	5	Batangan, Cape.
3	Barthol, St., Island, New Guinea.	6	Batangas.
4	Barthol, St., Island, New Hebrides.	7	Batavanan Island.
5	Barthol, St., Islands.	8	Batavano.
6	Barthol, St., Port.	9	Batavia, Java.
7	Barton Shoal.	900	Batchian.
8	Bartlett's Reef.	1	Bate.
9	Bartlett's Creek.	2	Bateepow Rock.
860	Barwell Island.	3	Bateman's Hill.
1	Bas, Isle de, France.	4	Bath, Maine, U. S.
2	Baseelan Island.	5	Bathurst, Cape.
3	Bashee Islands, Philippines.	6	Bathurst Island, Australia.
4	Basil Bay.	7	Bathurst Island, Barrow Strait.
5	Basil, Cape.	8	Bathurst Har., Van Dieman's Land.
6	Basin Bark.	9	Bathurst Low, River Gambia.
7	Basiluzza Island.	910	Bathy.
8	Baskerville, Cape.	1	Baticolo, Ceylon.
9	Basque Harbor.	2	Batigui Island.
870	Bass Harbor.	3	Baton Rouge, Louisiana, U. S.
1	Bass Harbor Isle.	4	Batoubara.
2	Bass Rock, Greenland.	5	Batou Gadi.
3	Bass Rock, Scotland.	6	Batou Pegge.
4	Bass Harbor L. H., Maine, U. S.	7	Batou Palo.
5	Bass Rip, Coast, U. S.	8	Batoum, Cape, Asiatic Turkey.
6	Bass Strait.	9	Battanta.
7	Bassadore Bank.	920	Battle Islands.
8	Bassa, Grand.	1	Battoo Point.
9	Bassania Point.	2	Battoo Barra River.
880	Bassas Rocks.	3	Batty Malve.
1	Bassas da India.	4	Baubelthouap.
2	Bassas de Pedro.	5	Bauer, Cape.
3	Bassean River.	6	Bauld, Cape.
4	Basse Terre.	7	Baxo del Comboy.
5	Bassin d'Arcachon, N. Coast of Spain.	8	Baxo de Galardo.
6	Bastia.	9	Baxo Nicolas Shoal, Cuba, W. I.
7	Bastimente Harbor.	930	Baxo, Nuevo, Gulf of Mexico.
888	Bat Island.	931	Baxo, Nuevo, Pedro Bank.

Nos.	BAX	Nos.	BED
932	Baxo Negro.	975	Bayonne, France.
3	Bay of Good Hope.	6	Bayou, St. John's, Louisiana, U. S.
4	Bay City.	7	Bazarouto Islands.
5	Bay de l'Eau.	8	Beach of Destretto.
6	Bay de los Esteros, California.	9	Beach Channel, Charleston, S.C., U.S.
7	Bay de Portage.	980	Beach Channel, Florida, U. S.
8	Bay d'Omar.	1	Beach of Pernambuco, Brazil.
9	Bay l'Argent.	2	Beach of Torres.
940	Bay of Acul.	3	Beachy Head, England.
1	Bay of All Saints.	4	Beachy Point.
2	Bay of Biscay.	5	Beacon Bluff.
3	Bay of Bulls.	6	Beacon Island.
4	Bay of Cortez, Cuba.	7	Beacon Inlet.
5	Bay of Cutteau.	8	Beagle Bank.
6	Bay of Despair.	9	Beagle Island.
7	Bay of Fair and False.	990	Beagle Reef.
8	Bay of Fundy.	1	Beak Point.
9	Bay of Ilha Grande.	2	Bear Bay.
950	Bay of Islands, Newfoundland.	3	Bear Haven.
1	Bay of Islands, New Zealand.	4	Bear Island.
2	Bay of Juliana.	5	Bear Islands, Hudson's Bay.
3	Bay of Lort.	6	Bear Island, North Asia.
4	Bay of Neyba.	7	Bear Island, Maine.
5	Bay of Ocoa, Cuba.	8	Bear Inlet.
6	Bay of Perlas.	9	Bear's Cove.
7	Bay of Rencontre.	1000	Bearn Cape.
8	Bay of Rocks.	1	Beata Island, West Indies.
9	Bay of Rotte.	2	Beauchene Island.
960	Bay of San Christoval.	3	Beaufort, North Carolina, U. S.
1	Bay of St. Anthony.	4	Beaufort, South Carolina, U. S.
2	Bay of St. Barbe.	5	Beaufort Inlet.
3	Bay of St. Genevieve.	6	Beaufort Islands.
4	Bay of St. John.	7	Beaumaris, North Wales.
5	Bay of St. Joseph.	8	Beaupré Islands.
6	Bay of St. Louis.	9	Beaver Harbor, Lake Michigan, U. S.
7	Bay of Thurin.	1010	Beaver Tail, Rhode Island, U. S.
8	Bay of Truxillo.	1	Bec du Raz.
9	Bay New Brunswick.	2	Bedeque Bay.
970	Bay Roberts.	3	Bedford Cape.
1	Bay Ronde, Louisiana, U. S.	4	Bedford, New, Mass., U. S.
2	Bay Verte.	5	Bedford Reef, Long Isl'd Sound, U.S.
3	Bayport, Florida, U. S.	6	Bedoo, Ras.
974	Bayonnaise Bank.	1017	Bedout Cape.

Nos.	BED	Nos.	BER
1018	Bedout Island.	1061	Bellona Island,
9	Bedra Island.	2	Bellona Shoal.
1020	Beechey Point.	3	Bellow's Rock.
1	Beehive Mountain.	4	Beloochistan.
2	Beehive Rock.	5	Belo Poulo Island.
3	Bees, St., Head.	6	Belt Little, Denmark.
4	Behague, Cape.	7	Belt Great, Denmark.
5	Behague Island.	8	Belvidere Shoals.
6	Behring, Cape.	9	Bembatooka Bay, Madagascar.
7	Behring Island.	1070	Bembridge Light, Isle of Wight.
8	Behring's Straits.	1	Bemini Islands.
9	Bejaren Island, Celebes.	2	Benares Shoal.
1030	Bejaren Island, Gilolo.	3	Benass Ras.
1	Bel Air, Port of.	4	Bench Island.
2	Belawan.	5	Bencoolen.
3	Belcher's Sound.	6	Bencoonat.
4	Belette Point.	7	Ben Davis' Point.
5	Belfast, Maine, U. S.	8	Benedicito Island.
6	Belfast, Ireland.	9	Benedict.
7	Belgica, Fort.	1080	Benevento.
8	Belgium.	1	Bengal, Asia.
9	Belize, Mississippi River, U. S.	2	Bengal, Bay of.
1040	Belk Island.	3	Benguela, West Africa.
1	Bell Beacon.	4	Bengazi.
2	Bell Beacon Island.	5	Bengut, Cape.
3	Bell Beacon Point.	6	Benicarlo.
4	Bell Point.	7	Benicia, California, U. S.
5	Bell Rock.	8	Benidorme Island.
6	Bell Rock, Bass Straits.	9	Benin River, W. Africa.
7	Bell Rock, Scotland.	1090	Benin, Bight of, W. Africa.
8	Bell Sound.	1	Benito, San, Islands.
9	Bellaco Rock.	2	Ben Jawad, Ras.
1050	Bellavista, Cape.	3	Bennett's Cape.
1	Bellavista, Ireland.	4	Bennet's Creek.
2	Belle Harbor.	5	Ben More.
3	Belle Islands.	6	Ben Norris.
4	Belle Isle, St. Lawrence, N. A.	7	Ben Tuirck.
5	Belle Isle, France.	8	Bentinck Island.
6	Belle Isle, Salvador.	9	Bequia Island, Caribbee Islands.
7	Belle Isle, Straits of.	1100	Bequia Granadines.
8	Bellingham Bay, N. W. Coast U. S.	1	Berbera.
9	Bellingshausen Island.	2	Berbice, British Guiana.
1060	Bell of Quillota.	1103	Berck Point.

Nos.	BER	Nos.	BIR
1104	Berdiansk, Cape.	1147	Bickerton Harbor.
5	Berdistan Shoal.	8	Bickerton Island.
6	Beregis Reef.	9	Bicquetto Island, St. Lawrence.
7	Berezan Island.	1150	Biddulph Islands.
8	Berenice, Egypt.	1	Bideford Bay, England.
9	Berg River.	2	Bidstone Light, England.
1110	Bergen, Norway.	3	Big Annemessix, Chesapeake Bay.
1	Bergen, Prussia.	4	Big Pelican Island.
2	Bergen Island.	5	Bieloi.
3	Bergen op Zoom.	6	Bielosarai, Cape.
4	Berkely Sound, Falkland Islands.	7	Bigali Island.
5	Bermija Island.	8	Bigar Islands.
6	Bermudas, North Atlantic.	9	Bight of Benin.
7	Bernal Chico Islands.	1160	Bight of Biafra.
8	Bernardin Bay.	1	Bighude Point.
9	Bernardin, Cape.	2	Bijouga Islands.
1120	Bernardino, St.	3	Bijourtier Island.
1	Bernardo Islands.	4	Bilboa, Spain.
2	Bernardo, San, Islands.	5	Biliran.
3	Bernera Island.	6	Billingsgate Island.
4	Bernier, Cape.	7	Billiton Island, Dutch Guiana.
5	Bernier Island.	8	Billiton Straits.
6	Bernouilli, Cape.	9	Billool, Ras.
7	Berry Head.	1170	Bill's Rock.
8	Berry Islands, Bahamas.	1	Biloxi, Mississippi, U. S.
9	Bertier Rock.	2	Bima.
1130	Bertrand Island.	3	Bingham Point.
1	Berwick, North Scotland.	4	Bintang Hill.
2	Berwick's Bay, Louisiana, U. S.	5	Biorko.
3	Besuki.	6	Bir, Ras.
4	Betanzos, Spain.	7	Birch Island.
5	Betra-par.	8	Birch Point.
6	Beveridge Reef.	9	Bird's Ferry.
7	Beverly, Mass., U. S.	1180	Bird Island, Banda Sea.
8	Beware Point.	1	Bird Island, Falkland Islands.
9	Beyrout, or Bairout, Syria.	2	Bird Island, Ladrones.
1140	Bexley, Cape.	3	Bird Island, Low Archipelago.
1	Bianco, Cape, Africa.	4	Bird Island, New Guinea.
2	Bianco, Cape, Cyprus.	5	Bird Island, Sandwich Islands.
3	Bianco, Cape, Ionian Isles.	6	Bird Island, Seychelles.
4	Bianco, Cape, Sicily.	7	Bird Island, West Africa.
5	Biafra, Bight of, West Africa.	8	Bird Islands, Australia.
1146	Biarritz, France.	1189	Bird Islands, East Africa.

149

Nos.	BIR	Nos.	BLE
1190	Bird Islands, Magdalen Islands.	1233	Black Rock, Connecticut, U. S.
1	Bird Key, Morant Keys.	4	Black Rock Point.
2	Bird Rock, West Indies.	5	Black Rock, Mergui Archipelago.
3	Bird Rocks.	6	Black Rock, New Brunswick.
4	Birkenhead, England.	7	Black Rock, N. W. of Borneo.
5	Birmah, Asia.	8	Black Rocks.
6	Birmingham, England.	9	Black Rock Bay.
7	Birnie Island.	1240	Black Sea.
8	Biscay, Bay of.	1	Blacknear Point.
9	Bisceglia, Naples.	2	Blackman's Bluff.
1200	Biscayen's Hook.	3	Black Walnut Cove.
1	Biscayno Cay, Florida Coast.	4	Black Water Bank.
2	Bisco Islands.	5	Blackwood Point.
3	Bishop Island, North Pacific.	6	Blair Harbor.
4	Bishop Island, South Pacific.	7	Blakely Harbor, Washingt'n T., U.S.
5	Bishop S. Rock.	8	Blaize, St., Cape.
6	Bishops & Clerks.	9	Blanca Island.
7	Bishop's Lagoon.	1250	Blanche Point, Lurga Island.
8	Bissao, Senegambia.	1	Blancherotte.
9	Biva Island.	2	Blanco, Cape, Africa.
1210	Bizerta.	3	Blanco, Cape, Asia Minor.
1	Bjorneborg.	4	Blanco, Cape, Guatemala.
2	Bjuroklubb.	5	Blanco, Cape, Majorca.
3	Black Bay, Louisiana, U. S.	6	Blanco, Cape, Patagonia.
4	Blackbeard Island.	7	Blanco, Cape, Peru.
5	Black Comb.	8	Blanco, Cape, Spain.
6	Black Head, Australia.	9	Blanco, Cape, Syria.
7	Black Head, Baffin's Bay.	1260	Blanco, Cape, N. Africa.
8	Black Head, England.	1	Blanco Peak.
9	Black Head, Ireland.	2	Blanco Point, Guatemala.
1220	Black Head. Labrador.	3	Blanco Point, Peru.
1	Black Head, New Zealand.	4	Blanguilla Island.
2	Black Head Bay.	5	Blankenberg Light.
3	Black Island.	6	Blanquilla Island.
4	Black Pagoda.	7	Blanquilla Shoal.
5	Black Point, South Atlantic.	8	Blanquilla, Leeward Isles.
6	Black Point, Spitsbergen.	9	Blas, San, Cape.
7	Black River.	1270	Blas, St., Cape.
8	Black River, Mosquito Coast.	1	Blas, San, Point.
9	Black Rock, Sligo Bay.	2	Blaze, Mt.
1230	Black Rock-Bay, Ireland.	3	Blaze Point.
1	Black Rock Harbor.	4	Bledas Islands.
1232	Black Rock, Massachusetts, U. S.	1275	Blenheim Reef.

11

Nos.	BLE	Nos.	BOM
1276	Blewfields, Mosquito Coast	1319	Boca Mona.
7	Bligan Cape.	1320	Boca Navios.
8	Bligh Island.	1	Boca Valliente.
9	Bligh's Cape.	2	Boca Tigre.
1280	Bligh's Entrance.	3	Boca Yuma.
1	Bligh's Lagoon Island.	4	Bocas Islands, West Indies.
2	Blind Bay.	5	Bock Point.
3	Block Island, Rhode Island, U. S.	6	Boddam Island.
4	Blockhouse Island.	7	Bodega Bay.
5	Blomoe Island.	8	Bodoe, Norway.
6	Blonde Rock.	9	Body's Island, North Carolina, U. S.
7	Blooborra Point.	1330	Bodkin Point, Maryland, U. S.
8	Bloody Bay.	1	Bodkin Swash, Maryland, U. S.
9	Bloody Farland Harbor.	2	Boele Comba.
1290	Bloodsworth Island.	3	Bogatshua Cape.
1	Blosseville Island.	4	Boggy's Peak.
2	Blowing Rock.	5	Bogoslov Island.
3	Bluefields or New Legovia, C'tl Amer.	6	Bogskar Island.
4	Bluefield's Bay.	7	Bogota, U. S. Colombia.
5	Bluefield's Lagoon.	8	Bogue Banks, North Carolina, U. S.
6	Bluehill Bay.	9	Bogue Inlet.
7	Blue Pinion Harbor.	1340	Bohemia Riv'r, Ches'peake Bay, U. S.
8	Bluff Cape.	1	Bohanderos Islands.
9	Bluff Point.	2	Bohol Island.
1300	Blyth, England.	3	Boidi.
1	Blyth Island.	4	Boileau Cape.
2	Board Island.	5	Bois-Blanc Island, Lake Huron.
3	Boat Harbor.	6	Bajador Cape.
4	Boat Extreme.	7	Bolbones, Mt.
5	Boat Rock.	8	Bold Head.
6	Boca Chica.	9	Bolhessoo Island.
7	Boca de Cumayaa.	1350	Bolinao Cape.
8	Boca de Majello.	1	Bolingbroke Point.
9	Boca de Nigua.	2	Bolio.
1310	Boca de Nixao.	3	Bolivar Point, Texas, U. S.
1	Boca de Quiabon.	4	Bolivia.
2	Boca del Toro.	5	Bolongo Island.
3	Boca de Za.	6	Bolaheretsky.
4	Boca de Romana.	7	Bolthead.
5	Boca Grande.	8	Bolushead.
6	Boca Grande Harbor, Florida, U. S.	9	Bom Abrigo.
7	Boca Grande Key, Florida, U. S.	1360	Bomba.
1318	Boca Huero.	1361	Bombay.

Nos.	BOM	Nos.	BOU
1362	Bombay Castle.	1405	Boon Island, Maine, U. S.
3	Bombay Hook, Delaware River.	6	Booring Islands.
4	Bombay Shoal.	7	Boot Island.
5	Bombonon Point.	8	Boot Reef.
6	Bomige Islands.	9	Boothia, Gulf of.
7	Bommelöe.	1410	Bootes Rock.
8	Bomosa Island.	1	Boguerones Point.
9	Bompas Point.	2	Bora-bora Island.
1370	Bon, Cape.	3	Borcum Light, North Sea.
1	Bona.	4	Borda, Cape.
2	Bonobé.	5	Bordeaux, France.
3	Bonacca Island.	6	Bordelaise Island.
4	Bonaventura Island.	7	Boreel, Cape.
5	Bonavista Bay, Newfoundland.	8	Borja Bay.
6	Bonavista Cape.	9	Borlase Warr Cape.
7	Bona Vista, Cape de Verdes.	1420	Borneo City.
8	Bond Reefs.	1	Borneo River.
9	Bonden.	2	Borneo Shoal.
1380	Bonetta Cove.	3	Borneo Coral Islands.
1	Bon Fouca.	4	Bornholm, Baltic.
2	Boni, Caribbee Islands.	5	Borodino Islands.
3	Boni Island.	6	Borracha Island.
4	Bonifacio, Corsica.	7	Borracha Cay.
5	Bonifacio Straits, Corsica.	8	Bosbouroun, Cape.
6	Bonin Islands, North Pacific.	9	Boscawan Island.
7	Bonne Bay.	1430	Bosphorus.
8	Bonny River.	1	Bossut, Cape.
9	Bonoa.	2	Bostanch, Ras.
1390	Bonpland Point.	3	Boston, England.
1	Bonqueron.	4	Boston, U. S.
2	Bontekoe.	5	Boston Bay, U. S.
3	Bonthian, Mt.	6	Boston Island.
4	Bonvet's Island.	7	Boston Islands.
5	Bonvouloir Islands.	8	Botany Bay, New South Wales.
6	Boo Islands.	9	Botany Island.
7	Boobooan.	1440	Botel Tobago.
8	Booby Island.	1	Botel Tobago Light.
9	Booby Shoal.	2	Bothnia, Gulf of, Russia.
1400	Boolanbow Hill.	3	Bottle Island.
1	Booleelooyan Point.	4	Bottomless Bay.
2	Boompjes.	5	Bottomless Pit.
3	Boom Rock.	6	Boubouang Point.
1404	Boon Island, Ceram.	1447	Bouc, Port de.

Nos.	BOU	Nos.	BRE
1448	Bousan Point.	1490	Brabant, Cape.
9	Boucher Island.	1	Bradley Reef.
1450	Boudeuse Island, Admirante Isles.	2	Bradore Hills.
1	Boudeuse Island, S. Pacific.	3	Brace's Cove, Mass., U. S.
2	Boudroom, Anatolia.	4	Brackman Bluff.
3	Bougainville, Cape, Australia.	5	Brador Bay.
4	Bougainville, Cape, Van Dieman's Land.	6	Braganza Shoal.
		7	Braha Harbor.
5	Bougainville Island.	8	Brahestad.
6	Bougainville, Mt.	9	Brala Pulo.
7	Bougainville Shoal.	1500	Brama Point.
8	Bouja.	1	Branca.
9	Bouka Island.	2	Branco, Cape.
1460	Boulanga Island.	3	Brandon Head.
1	Boulang Pulo.	4	Brandy Rocks.
2	Bouldyr Island.	5	Brandywine Shoal.
3	Boulogne, France.	6	Brangman's Bluff.
4	Boungo, Cape.	7	Brant Island.
5	Bountiful Islands.	8	Brant Point.
6	Bounty Islands.	9	Branford Reef.
7	Bourbon Island.	1510	Bras d'Or.
8	Bourgas, Turkey.	1	Bras, St., Cape.
9	Bouro Island, Banda Sea.	2	Brasse, Pulo.
1470	Bouro Island, Sumatra.	3	Brava, Cape de Verdes.
1	Bouton Islands, Celebes.	4	Brava, East Africa.
2	Bouton Islands, Malacca Strait.	5	Bravo del Norte.
3	Bouvard, Cape.	6	Brazil.
4	Bouvet's Island.	7	Brazil Rock.
5	Bow Island.	8	Brazza Island.
6	Bowbear Harbor.	9	Brazos Santiago, Texas, U. S.
7	Bowditch Island.	1520	Brazos River Entrance.
8	Bowditch Ledge, Mass., U. S.	1	Brea Head.
9	Bowen, Cape, Australia.	2	Breaker Point.
1480	Bowen, Cape, Baffin's Bay.	3	Breakheart Point, Newfoundland.
1	Bowen Rocks.	4	Breakneck Passage.
2	Bowles Bank.	5	Breaksea Island.
3	Bowling Green, Cape.	6	Breaksea Spit.
4	Boxeador, Cape.	7	Breakwater.
5	Boxey Harbor.	8	Breakwater L. H.
6	Boyanna Bay.	9	Brebes Point.
7	Boydtown.	1530	Brekat Point.
8	Boyne River, Ireland.	1	Bremen.
1489	Boyne River, Australia.	1532	Bremerhaven.

Nos.	BRE	Nos.	BRO
1533	Bremer Light.	1576	Britomart.
4	Bremer Mount.	7	Briton Harbor.
5	Brenton's Bay.	8	Britto Shoal.
6	Brenton's Reef.	9	Broa Bay, Cuba.
7	Brent's Point.	1580	Broad Haven.
8	Bressou Fort.	1	Broad Road.
9	Brest, France.	2	Broad Sound, Boston Bay, U. S.
1540	Brett, Cape.	3	Brocken Island.
1	Brewster, Cape.	4	Brockelsby River.
2	Briars Point.	5	Brodie Rocks.
3	Bridgeman Island.	6	Broer Ruys, Cape.
4	Bridgeport, Connecticut, U. S.	7	Brogden Point.
5	Bridgeport L. H.	8	Brogle, Cape.
6	Bridgetown.	9	Broken Bay, New South Wales.
7	Bridgewater, Cape.	1590	Broken Island.
8	Bridgewater Reef.	1	Brondolo Port.
9	Bridlington.	2	Brono Neck.
1550	Bridport, England.	3	Brooklyn, New York, U. S.
1	Brielle.	4	Brookline, Boston, Mass., U. S.
2	Brieuc, St.	5	Brother, West Indies.
3	Brig Rock.	6	Brothers, Andamans.
4	Brigadier's Island, Maine, U. S.	7	Brothers, Bight of Biafra.
5	Brigantine Bay.	8	Brothers, China.
6	Brighton.	9	Brothers, China East.
7	Brigus Bay.	1600	Brothers, China Sea.
8	Brigus Harbor.	1	Brothers, East Africa.
9	Brill Shoal.	2	Brothers, Greece.
1560	Brilliante Shoal.	3	Brothers, Hainan.
1	Brindisi, Adriatic, Italy.	4	Brothers, Hudson's Bay.
2	Bringen Pulo.	5	Brothers, Macas Strait.
3	Brisbane River, New South Wales.	6	Brothers, Mergui Archipelago.
4	Bristol, England.	7	Brothers, New Guinea.
5	Bristol, Rhode Island, U. S.	8	Brothers, Red Sea.
6	Bristol Channel, England.	9	Brothers, Sumatra.
7	Bristol Bay.	1610	Brough of Birsa.
8	Bristol Island.	1	Broughton Bay.
9	Bristow Island.	2	Broughton, Cape.
1570	Bristow Rock.	3	Broughton Island.
1	Britannia Island.	4	Broughton Reef.
2	Britannia Rook.	5	Broughton Rocks.
3	British Columbia, N. W. America.	6	Brouwers Shoal.
4	British Guiana, South America.	7	Brown's Head, U. S.
1575	British Sound, E. Coast of Africa.	1618	Brown's Head Light-house, U. S.

Nos.	BRO	Nos.	BUR
1619	Brown's Shoal, West Indies.	1662	Buddoness.
1620	Brown Mt.	3	Budua.
1	Brown Point.	4	Buen Ayre Island, Leeward Isles.
2	Brown Shoals.	5	Buenos Ayres, S. A.
3	Brown's Inlet.	6	Buenaventuro, U. S. Colombia.
4	Brown's Range.	7	Buenavista Point, Cuba, W. I.
5	Brown's Strait.	8	Buey Inlet.
6	Brownston Head.	9	Buffa, Guinea.
7	Brownsville, Texas, U. S.	1670	Buffalo, New York, U. S.
8	Browse Island.	1	Buffalo Island.
9	Brue Rock.	2	Buffalo Peak. .
1630	Bruges, Belgium.	3	Buffalo Point.
1	Brunai, Borneo.	4	Buffaloe River, South Africa.
2	Brune Bank, Jamaica, W. I.	5	Bugiaron Cape.
3	Brune Island, Van Dieman's Land.	6	Bugio.
4	Brunet Island.	7	Buia, Cape.
5	Bruny Island.	8	Buia Point.
6	Brury Island.	9	Bujijo del Gato.
7	Brunswick, Georgia, U. S.	1680	Buka Bay.
8	Brule Shoals.	1	Bulacabl Point.
9	Brush Key.	2	Bulagao Mt.
1640	Brussels, Belgium.	3	Bulalagui Point.
1	Brüsteort.	4	Bull Rock.
2	Bruzzano, Cape.	5	Bullen, Cape, Arctic Ocean.
3	Bryan Island.	6	Bullen, Cape, Bight of Biafra.
4	Bryantown.	7	Buller, Cape.
5	Bryer's Island.	8	Bullock Island.
6	Bryon Island.	9	Bull's Bay, South Carolina, U. S.
7	Buachil Island.	1690	Bull Point.
8	Bucalemo Head.	1	Bultig Island.
9	Bucalisse Island.	2	Bulungan.
1650	Buccaneer's Archipelago.	3	Bulusan Volcano.
1	Buccleugh Shoal.	4	Bumbo Island.
2	Buchaness, Scotland.	5	Buncrana.
3	Buchon Mt.	6	Bunder Abbas.
4	Buck's Harbor, Maine, U. S.	7	Bunga Pulo.
5	Buck's Island, West Indies.	8	Bungelow Island.
6	Buck's Port, Maine, U. S.	9	Bunker's Group.
7	Buckingham's Shoal.	1700	Bunker's Island.
8	Buckland Mt.	1	Bunker's Ledge, Maine, U. S.
9	Budd Island, Feejee Islands.	2	Bunwut Island.
1660	Budd Island, Java Sea.	3	Buppan Bluff.
1661	Budd Island, Moluccas.	1704	Burela Cape.

Nos.	BUR	Nos.	CAC
1705	Burford Island.	1748	Buzzard's Bay, Massachusetts, U. S.
6	Burgeo Islands.	9	Buzzard's Roost Island.
7	Burgh Head.	1750	Byam Martin I., Barrow's Straits.
8	Burias Island.	1	Byam Martin I., Low Archipelago.
9	Burica Point.	2	Byers' Island.
1710	Burin Bay.	3	Byramgore Reef.
1	Burin Inlet.	4	Byron Bay.
2	Burkha.	5	Byron Cape, Australia.
3	Burlings.	6	Byron Cape, New Ireland.
4	Burlington Bay, Lake Ontario, U. S.	7.	Byron Cape, South Pacific Ocean.
5	Burmah, Asia.	8	Byron Island.
6	Burnam Pulo.	9	Cabagan River, Cuba.
7	Burney Island.	1760	Cabaleria Cape, Minorca.
8	Burning Island.	1	Caballo Point, Spain, N. Coast.
9	Burnt Island, Arabian Gulf.	2	Caballones Channel, Cuba.
1720	Burnt Island, Terra del Fuego, S. A.	3	Cabane Bay.
1	Burnt Island Light-house, U. S.	4	Cabbage Island.
2	Buro, Cape.	5	Cabedello Fort, Brazil, E. Coast.
3	Burra Ness.	6	Cabelete Island, Luzon, E. Coast.
4	Burra Voe Ness.	7	Cabes, Africa.
5	Burrow Head.	8	Cabeza de Bondo, Philippine Islands.
6	Burrow's Island.	9	Cabeza de Toro.
7	Burt Fort.	1770	Cabezo.
8	Buruhan.	1	Cabicunga Point, Luzon.
9	Bush Cay.	2	Cabingan Is., Borneo, N. E. Coast.
1730	Busheab Island.	3	Cable Island, South Pacific Ocean.
1	Bushire, Persia.	4	Cabo Falso.
2	Bushy Island.	5	Cabonica Harbor, Cuba.
3	Busi Island.	6	Cabossa Island, Gulf of Martaban, British India.
4	Busios Islands.		
5	Buskar Light.	7	Cabot, St. Lawrence River.
6	Bussorah, Asiatic Turkey.	8	Cabra Island, West Indies.
7	Busto, Cape.	9	Cabras Island, Africa, W. Coast.
8	Busvagon Island.	1780	Cabras Island, Philippine Islands.
9	Butler's Hole, Massachusetts, U. S.	1	Cabras Port, Canary Islands.
1740	Butt of Lewis.	2	Cabrera Island, Baleares.
1	Button Island.	3	Cabrera Island, Greece.
2	Button Island Gt.	4	Cabron Cape, St. Domingo, N. Coast.
3	Button Islands, Marshall Islands.	5	Cabrutee, Lacadive Islands.
4	Button Islands, North America.	6	Caburiahan.
5	Buttons.	7	Cabuli Island, China Sea.
6	Buyer's Island.	8	Caccia Cape, Sardinia.
1747	Buyuk Dereh.	1789	Cacheo Fort, Senegambia.

156

Nos.	CAC	Nos.	CAL
1790	Cachipour Cape, Brazil, N. Coast.	1833	Calcasieu River, Louisiana, U. S.
1	Cadaques, Spain.	4	Calcutta, India.
2	Cader Idris, Wales.	5	Caldeira Island, South Africa.
3	Cadiz, Spain.	6	Caldera, La, Mindanao, Philippine Islands.
4	Caermarthan, South Wales.		
5	Caernarvou, North Wales.	7	Caldera Port, Peru.
6	Caernarvon Bay, North Wales.	8	Caldera Point, St. Domingo, S. Coast.
7	Cafferelli I., Buccaneer's Archip'ago.	9	Calderoni Is., Grecian Archipelago.
8	Caffraria, S. E. Africa.	1840	Caldmian Islands, Philippine Is.
9	Cagayan, Philippine Islands.	1	Caldy Island, South Wales.
1800	Cagayan, Sooloo Islands.	2	Calebar, New, R., Bight of Biafra.
1	Cagayanes Islands, Philippine Is.	3	Calebar, Old, R., Bight of Biafra.
2	Cagio River, Cuba.	4	Calebasse Creek, Maraca I., River Amazon.
3	Cagliari, Sardinia.	5	Calebra, Carribbee Islands.
4	Cahil Rock.	6	Caledon Mount, Australia.
5	Caicos Islands, Bahamas.	7	Caledonia Bay, Central America.
6	Caicos Bank, Bahamas.	8	Caleton, St. Domingo.
7	Caicos Channel, Bahamas.	9	Calf of Man, Irish Sea.
8	Caicos Shoal, Pensacola Bay, U. S.	1850	Calf, S. Point, Isle of Man.
9	Caillon Bay, Louisiana, U. S.	1	Calf Rock, Ireland, W. Coast.
1810	Caiman Point, Luzon, W. Coast.	2	Calibogue Sound, S. Carolina, U. S.
1	Caios Point, Spain.	3	Calicut, British India.
2	Cairncross Island, Australia.	4	California, U. S.
3	Cairo, Illinois, U. S.	5	California, Gulf of, Mexico.
4	Cairo, Egypt.	6	Calingapatam, British India.
5	Cairoçu Point, Brazil.	7	Calitura, Ceylon.
6	Caite Islands, Brazil, N. Coast.	8	Callagouk Island, Gulf of Martaban, British India.
7	Cajeli Bay, Bouro, Banda Sea.	9	
8	Calaan Point, Luzon, E. Coast.		Callao, Peru.
9	Calaan Point, Luzon, W. Coast.	1860	Calliagua Bay.
1820	Calabar River, Upper Guinea.	1	Callohiji Is., Strait of Macassar.
1	Calafiguera Cape, Majorca.	2	Calm Point, Russian America.
2	Calais, France.	3	Caloltong Point, Luzon, E. Coast.
3	Calamianes Islands, China Sea.	4	Caloni Island, Asia Minor.
4	Calamita Mount, Italy, W. Coast.	5	Caloombyan Harbor, Sunda Strait.
5	Calamity Har., Banks' I., N. Pacific.	6	Calpentyn Fort, Ceylon.
6	Calangaman Island, Philippine Is.	7	Calshot Light, Isle of Wight.
7	Calava Cape, Sicily.	8	Calumpan Point, Samar, Philipp'e Is.
8	Calavina Harbor.	9	Calusa, Philippine Islands.
9	Calavite Mt., Mindoro, Philip'ine Is.	1870	Calvada Island, Brazil, E. Coast.
1830	Calavite Pt., Mindoro, Philip'ine Is.	1	Calventura Rocks, British India.
1	Calayan Island, Philippine Islands.	2	Calvert Islands, N. Pacific Ocean.
1832	Calcanhar Point, Brazil, E. Coast.	1873	Calvi, Corsica.

Nos.	CAL	Nos.	CAN
1874	Calymere Point, Ceylon.	1917	Camrant Harbor, Cochin China.
5	Camana Mount, Peru.	8	Camtoos River, South Africa.
6	Camaran Island, Red Sea.	9	Cana (or Cani) Rocks, Tunis.
7	Camarat Cape, France.	1920	Canada, North America.
8	Camaroens Cape, Africa, W. Coast.	1	Canada East, North America.
9	Camaron Cape, Honduras Coast.	2	Canada West, North America.
1880	Cambay, India.	3	Canada Bay, Newfoundland.
1	Cambing Island, Banda Sea.	4	Canadian Channel, Mouth of St. Lawrence River.
2	Cambir, Pulo, China Sea.		
3	Cambodia, Siam.	5	Canal de la Hacha, Cuba.
4	Cambodia Cape, Siam.	6	Canalle, France.
5	Cambodia River, Siam.	7	Cananea, Brazil, E. Coast.
6	Cambridge, England.	8	Cananore Point, Malabar Coast.
7	Cambridge, Maryland.	9	Cananova, Cuba.
8	Cambridge, Massachusetts.	1930	Canary Islands, North Atlantic.
9	Cambridge Gulf, Australia.	1	Canary Grand, Canary Islands.
1890	Cambridge Island, Patagonia.	2	Canaveral, Cape, Florida, U. S.
1	Cambyna Island, Banda Sea.	3	Cancalle, France.
2	Camden Harbor, Maine.	4	Canche River, France.
3	Camel Island, China Sea.	5	Canoun Island, Yucatan.
4	Camel's Hump, Africa, W. Coast.	6	Candelaria, Teneriffe.
5	Camels Island, Philippine Islands.	7	Candelaria Bay, Central America.
6	Cameron, Cape, Honduras.	8	Candelaria Reefs, S. Pacific.
7	Cameron Mt., Van Dieman's Land.	9	Candia (or Crete), Grecian Archipel.
8	Cameroon River, Upper Guinea.	1940	Candlemas Isl., Sandwich Islands.
9	Cameroons, Cape, Africa, W. Coast.	1	Candulo Island, Philippine Islands.
1900	Cameroons Mt., Africa, W. Coast.	2	Candy, Cape, Celebes, N. Coast.
1	Camiguin Island, Babuyanes Islands.	3	Canea, Candia.
2	Camiguin Island, Philippine Islands.	4	Canet, Cape, Spain.
3	Caminha, Portugal.	5	Cangrejo Peak, Central America.
4	Camotes, Islands, Philippine Islands.	6	Canister West, I., Mergui Archip'go.
5	Campanella Point, Italy, W. Coast.	7	Canje Creek.
6	Campbell, Cape, New Zealand.	8	Canna Island, Scotland.
7	Campbell Island, Caroline Islands.	9	Cannac Rock, S. Pacific.
8	Campbell Island, S. Pacific Ocean.	1950	Cannes, France, S. Coast.
9	Campbell Town, Van Dieman's Land.	1	Canning Island, E. Coast Greenland.
1910	Campbell's Isl., North Carolina, U. S.	2	Canning's Rook, Gaspar Strait.
1	Campbelton, Scotland.	3	Cano Island, Central America.
2	Campeche, Yucatan.	4	Canoas Point, New Grenada.
3	Campeche, Gulf of, Mexico.	5	Canoe Cove, West Indies.
4	Campo Bello Island, Maine, U. S.	6	Canonicut I., Narraganset Bay, U.S.
5	Campo Marino, Italy.	7	Causado Port, Africa, W. Coast.
1916	Campo Moro, Cape, Corsica.	1958	Canso, Cape, Nova Scotia.

Nos.	CAN	Nos.	CAP
1959	Canso, Gut of, Nova Scotia.	2001	Cape Barrow, British America.
1960	Canso, Gut of, North Entrance.	2	Bathurst, British America.
1	Canso Harbor, Nova Scotia.	3	Bauld, Newfoundland.
2	Cantaros Mountains, Portugal.	4	Bear.
3	Canterbury, England.	5	Béarn, South France.
4	Cantick Head, Scotland.	6	Beata, Hayti.
5	Cantin Cape, Africa, N. W. Coast.	7	Beaufort, Russian America.
6	Cantire, Mull of, Scotland.	8	Beaufort, British America.
7	Canton, China.	9	Bexley, British America.
8	Canton River, China.	2010	Bianco, Corfu.
9	Canton Island, Philippines.	1	Bianco, Corsica.
1970	Canton Packet Shoal, Gilolo Passage.	2	Bianco, Cyprus.
1	Canton Pulo, Cochin China.	3	Bianco, Sicily.
2	Cap Island, Indian Ocean.	4	Blanco, Africa, West Coast.
3	Cap Island, S. W. Sumatra.	5	Blanco, Asia Minor.
4	Cap Rock, Corea.	6	Blanco, Central America.
5	Capas, Pulo, Cochin China.	7	Blanco, Majorca.
6	Cape Acworth, Prince of Wales L'nd.	8	Blanco, Morocco.
7	Aden, S. Coast Arabia.	9	Blanco or Oxford, Oregon, U.S.
8	Agulhas, South Africa.	2020	Blanco or St. Jorge, Patagonia.
9	Alexander, British America.	1	Blanco, Peru.
1980	Alright.	2	Blanco, Spain.
1	Alwight.	3	Blanco, Syria.
2	Amber (or Ambro), Madagasc'r.	4	Blanco, Tunis.
3	Ambriz, West Africa.	5	Blanco de Santa Maria, California, U. S.
4	Anamoor, Asia Minor.	6	Boeo, Sicily.
5	Anderson, Behring's Strait.	7	Bojador, West Africa.
6	Anguilla, Newfoundland.	8	Bojador, Luzon.
7	Ann, Massachusetts, U. S.	9	Bolinao, Luzon.
8	Ann Harbor, Mass., U. S.	2030	Bolthead, England.
9	Apollonia (or Appolonia), Guinea Coast.	1	Bolus Head, Ireland.
1990	Arago, Oregon, U. S.	2	Bon, North Africa.
1	Argos.	3	Bonavista, Newfoundland.
2	Arnheim, Australia.	4	Boruca, S. Central America.
3	Arrowsmith, Australia.	5	Bougainville, N. W. Australia.
4	Arruba (or Arubah), Persia.	6	Bougainv'le, Van Dieman's L'd.
5	Bainetta, Hayti.	7	Breton Island, British America.
6	Banks, Australia.	8	Breton, Cape Breton Island.
7	Barbas, West Africa.	9	Brett, New Zealand.
8	Bardistan, Persia.	2040	Broyle Harbor.
9	Barfleur, France.	1	Bueno, Cuba.
2000	Baring, British America.	2042	Burela, Spain, West Coast.

Nos.	CAP	Nos.	CAP
2043	Cape Busios.	2086	Cape Chicibicoa.
4	Buzo, Candia.	7	Chignecto, Nova Scotia.
5	Cabaleria, Minorca.	8	Chudleigh, Labrador.
6	Cabron, Samana, W. India.	9	Churchill, British America.
7	Caccia, Sardinia.	2090	Clear, Ireland.
8	Calvi, Corsica.	1	Cleveland, Australia.
9	Camarat, France.	2	Coadera, South America.
2050	Camaron, Honduras.	3	Coast Castle, W. Coast Africa.
1	Cambodia, Siam.	4	Cockburn.
2	Cameroons, Guinea.	5	Cod, Massachusetts, U. S.
3	Campanella, W. Italy.	6	Cod Bay, Massachusetts, U. S.
4	Campbell, New Zealand.	7	Cod Harbor, Mass., U. S.
5	Canaveral, Florida, U. S.	8	Cod Light House, Mass., U. S.
6	Candy, Celebes.	9	Colonna, Greece.
7	Canso, Nova Scotia.	2100	Colonni, Samos I., Gr. Arch'go.
8	Cantin, Morocco.	1	Colony, Africa.
9	Capricorn, Australia.	2	Colville, New Zealand.
2060	Capstan.	3	Comete, West Indies.
1	Carbon, Algiers.	4	Comorin, India.
2	Carbonaro, Sardinia.	5	Conception, California, U. S.
3	Carmel, Syria.	6	Cormorant.
4	Cartaret, France.	7	Cornwall, S. W. England.
5	Carthage, North Africa.	8	Corrientes, Africa, E. Coast.
6	Carvoeiro, S. Coast Portugal.	9	Corrientes, Buenos Ayres.
7	Carvoeiro, W. Coast Portugal.	2110	Corrientes, Central America.
8	Carysfort, Falkland Islands.	1	Corrientes, S. Coast Cuba.
9	Carysfort, Florida.	2	Corrientes, W. Coast Mexico.
2070	Cassepour.	3	Corso, Corsica.
1	Castlereagh, South America.	4	Creux, E. Spain.
2	Cataluña, Majorca.	5	Crillon, Japan.
3	Catastrophe, Australia.	6	Cruz, Cuba.
4	Catharine, W. Africa.	7	Cullera, E. Spain.
5	Catoche, Yucatan.	8	Dame Marie (or Donna Maria), St. Domingo.
6	Cavaliere, Turkey.		
7	Cavallo, Italy.	9	Dartuch, Minorca.
8	Caxines, Algiers.	2120	Dean.
9	Cevera, N. Coast Spain.	1	Deceit.
2080	Cevera, S. Coast Spain.	2	Delgado, E. Africa.
1	Charles, Virginia, U. S.	3	Denbigh, Russian America.
2	Charles, Labrador.	4	Deseada,(or Desire), Patagonia.
3	Charles Harbor.	5	Desire, Nova Zembla.
4	Chatham, Australia.	6	Desolation, Greenland.
2085	Chatte, Anticosti Island.	2127	Desolation, South America.

Nos.	CAP	Nos.	CAP
2128	Cape Despair.	2170	Cape Figari, Sardinia.
9	Direction, Australia.	1	Finisterre, France.
2130	Direction, Van Dieman's Land.	2	Finisterre, Spain.
1	Disappointment, N. W. Coast America.	3	Fino, W. Italy.
		4	Flattery, Washington, U. S.
2	Disappointment, Georgia Isl'nd, S. Atlantic.	5	Flattery, Australia.
3	Discord, Greenland.	6	Flemish.
4	D'Or.	7	Flinders, Australia.
5	East, Asia, Behring's Strait.	8	Florida, Florida, U. S.
6	East, Madagascar.	9	Florida Lt. House, Florida, U.S.
7	East, New Zealand.	2180	Formenton, Majorca.
8	Egmont, Prince Edward's Id.	1	Formosa, W. Africa.
9	Elizabeth, E. Asia.	2	Foulweather, Oregon.
2140	Elizabeth, Russian America.	3	Foulwind, New Zealand.
1	Elizabeth, Maine, U. S.	4	Fourchee, Nova Scotia.
2	Elizabeth Lt. Ho., Maine, U. S.	5	Fox, Anticosti Island.
3	Emineh, Turkey in Europe.	6	François, Hayti.
4	Engaño, Hayti.	7	Freels, Newfoundland.
5	Engaño, Luzon.	8	Frehel, France.
6	English.	9	Frio, Brazil.
7	Enragé, New Brunswick.	2190	Frio, W. Africa.
8	Espartel (or Spartel), N.W. Afr.	1	Galera, N. Coast S. America.
9	Espichel, Portugal.	2	Galera, Trinidad Island.
2150	Espiritu, Santo, Philippine Is.	3	Gallo, Sicily.
1	Espiritu, Santo,Terra del Fuego.	4	Gallo, Greece.
2	Estaca, N. Spain.	5	Gamaley, Japan.
3	Fair, Australia.	6	Garoupe, S. Coast France.
4	Fairweather, Falkland Islands.	7	Garupi, Brazil.
5	Falcon, Sardinia.	8	Gaspé, Canada.
6	False, N. W. Africa.	9	Gata, de, Spain.
7	False, W. Africa.	2200	Gatto, Cyprus.
8	False, Central America.	1	George, South Georgia Island.
9	False, Hayti.	2	Ghir (or Gheer), Morocco.
2160	Farewell, Greenland.	3	Gloucester, Australia.
1	Farewell, New Zealand.	4	Gloucester, Admiralty Islands, S. Pacific.
2	Faro, Sicily.	5	Gloucester, New Britain.
3	Farquhar, W. Australia.	6	Gloucester, Terra del Fuego.
4	Fartak (or Fartash), Arabia.	7	of Good Hope, Africa.
5	Fear, North Carolina, U. S.	8	of Good Hope, China.
6	Fear River, N. Carolina, U. S.	9	Good Success, Terra del Fuego.
7	Ferrat, Morocco.	2210	Gracias a Dios, Central Amer.
8	Ferrato, Sardinia.	2211	Grafton, Australia.
2169	Ferro, Algiers.		

Nos.	CAP	Nos.	CAP
2212	Cape Granitola, Sicily.	2255	Cape Leuwin, Australia.
3	Gregory, W. Coast N. America.	6	Le Heve, France.
4	Grim, Van Dieman's Land.	7	Leuca, West Italy.
5	Grimington, Labrador.	8	Leveque, N. W. Australia.
6	Grisnez, France.	9	Lewis, Greenland.
7	Guardafui, East Africa.	2260	Licosa, West Italy.
8	Haldiman.	1	Londonderry, N. W. Australia.
9	Hamrah, Algiers.	2	Lookout, North Carolina, U. S.
2220	Hancock, N. W. America.	3	Lookout, Oregon, U. S.
1	Hanglip, S. Africa.	4	Lookout, Patagonia, E. Coast.
2	Hatteras, North Carolina, U. S.	5	Lopez, West Coast Africa.
3	Hawke, East Australia.	6	Lopez Bay, W. Coast Africa.
4	Haytien, Hayti.	7	Magdelaine, Canada East.
5	Henlopen, Delaware, U. S.	8	Maize.
6	Henry, Virginia, U. S.	9	Malabar, Massachusetts, U. S.
7	Hillsborough, Australia.	2270	Malek, Candia.
8	Hogan.	1	Manambatoo, Madagascar.
9	Honduras, Central America.	2	Matala, Candia.
2230	Horn, South America.	3	Matapan, Greece.
1	Horn, False, South America.	4	May, Delaware Bay, U. S.
2	Howe, Australia.	5	Maysi, Cuba.
3	Howe, West, Australia.	6	Mayumba, West Africa.
4	Humos, Chile.	7	Melville, Australia.
5	Hurd, Canada.	8	Melville, Greenland.
6	Icy, Russian America.	9	Mendocino, California.
7	Inman.	2280	Mesurado, West Africa.
8	Isabella, British America.	1	Milazzo, Sicily.
9	Island, New Jersey, U. S.	2	Mirik, West Africa.
2240	Jack Shoal.	3	Miseno, South Italy.
1	Jellison Harbor, Maine, U. S.	4	Mondego, Portugal.
2	Jerémie, Hayti.	5	Monte Christi, Hayti.
3	John.	6	Monse, India.
4	Jude.	7	Mount, West Africa.
5	Katakolo, Greece.	8	Mount River, West Africa.
6	Khersonese, Russia.	9	Nabon, Persia.
7	Krio, Candia.	2290	Nao, Spain.
8	Krio, Cyprus.	1	Naturaliste, Australia.
9	La Hague, France.	2	Nau, South Italy.
2250	Lahon, Africa.	3	Naze, Norway.
1	La Hume, Newfoundland.	4	Naze, England.
2	Lastres, Spain.	5	Naze, West Africa.
3	La Vela.	6	Neddock, Maine, U. S.
2254	Lean, Ireland.	2297	Negrais, Bay of Bengal.

Nos.	CAP	Nos.	CAP
2298	Cape Negro, North Africa.	2341	Cape Pillar, Terra del Fuego.
9	Negro, West Africa.	2	Pillar, Van Dieman's Land.
2300	Negro, Brazil, East Coast.	3	Pine, Newfoundland.
1	Negro Harbor, N. Coast Africa.	4	Poge (or Pogue), Mass., U. S.
2	Nelson, Australia.	5	Porcupine.
3	Nicholas.	6	Porpoise, Maine, U. S.
4	Norman.	7	Porpoise Harbor, Maine, U. S.
5	Noir, Terra del Fuego.	8	Portland, Cape Breton Island.
6	North, Norway.	9	Portland, Van Dieman's Land.
7	North, South America.	2350	Powles.
8	North, Prince Edward's Isl'nd.	1	Preston, Australia.
9	North, Cape Breton Island.	2	Prince of Wales, Russian Amer.
2310	North, New Zealand.	3	Prior, Spain.
1	North, Iceland.	4	Prospect.
2	Northumberland, Australia.	5	Pula, Sardinia.
3	Noun (or Noon), West Africa.	6	Quebra.
4	Nuyts, Australia.	7	Race, Newfoundland.
5	Observation.	8	Race Rocks.
6	Orange, Terra del Fuego.	9	Radstock. Australia.
7	Oropesa, Spain.	2360	Raphael, Hayti.
8	Ortegal, Spain.	1	Ray, Newfoundland.
9	Ortegal, New Zealand.	2	Red.
2320	Otway, Australia.	3	Resolution, British America.
1	Palinuro, West Italy.	4	Rivers, Celebes Island.
2	Palliser, New Zealand.	5	Roca, Portugal.
3	Palliser, New Britain.	6	Roger Harbor.
4	Palmas, West Africa.	7	Romain, South Carolina, U. S.
5	Palos, Spain.	8	Romano, Florida, U. S.
6	Parry, East Greenland.	9	Romania, Malacca.
7	Parry, West Greenland.	2370	Romanzoff, Russian America.
8	Pasqua.	1	Rosier (or Rozier), Canada E.
9	Passaro, Sicily.	2	Rouge Harbor.
2330	Patience, Saghalien Island.	3	Roxo, West Africa.
1	Pecora, Sardinia.	4	Roxo, Karamania.
2	Pellew, Australia.	5	Roxo, Mexico.
3	Peloro, Sicily.	6	Roxo, Porto Rico.
4	Pembroke.	7	Roxo, Hayti.
5	Peñas, Spain.	8	Round.
6	Peñas, Terra del Fuego.	9	Runaway, New Zealand.
7	Pera, Majorca.	2380	Sable, Florida, U. S.
8	Perpetua, Oregon, U. S.	1	Sable, Nova Scotia.
9	Pierre de Gros.	2	Sable Island, Nova Scotia.
2340	Pila, Cyprus.	2383	Sacratif, South Spain.

Nos.	CAP	Nos.	CAP
2384	Cape St. Andrew, Sicily.	2427	Cape St. Vincent, Madagascar.
5	St. Andrew, Madagascar.	8	St. Vincent, Portugal.
6	St. Ann, West Africa.	9	St. Vincent, Terra del Fuego.
7	St. Anthony, Arabia.	2430	Salimone, Candia.
8	St. Augustine, Brazil, E. Coast.	1	Salines, Martinique.
9	St. Augustine, N. Coast S. Am.	2	Salinas, Majorca.
2390	St. Blas, Florida, U. S.	3	Samana, Samana Island, W. I.
1	St. Francis, Newfoundland.	4	Sambro, Nova Scotia.
2	St. Francis, South Africa.	5	San Antonio, Brazil.
3	St. George, Australia.	6	San Antonio, Buenos Ayres.
4	St. George, Newfoundland.	7	San Antonio, Cuba.
5	St. George, Nova Scotia.	8	San Antonio, Spain.
6	St. George, Florida, U. S.	9	San Blas, Florida.
7	St. George, Hayti.	2440	San Blas, Panama.
8	St. Gregory, Newfoundland.	1	San Diego, South America.
9	St. James, Cambodia, China Sea.	2	San Francisco, Ecuador.
2400	St. John, Africa.	3	San Juan, Porto Rico.
1	St. John, Candia.	4	San Juan de Guia, North Coast S. America.
2	St. John, Newfoundland.	5	San Julian, Patagonia.
3	St. John, Terra del Fuego.	6	San Lorenzo, Ecuador.
4	St. Lawrence, Cape Breton Id.	7	San Marco, Sicily.
5	St. Lewis.	8	San Marco, Sardinia.
6	St. Lucas, California Peninsula.	9	San Nicolo, Sardinia.
7	St. Martha.	2450	San Vito, Sicily.
8	St. Martha Grande.	1	Sandwich, Australia.
9	St. Mary, Venezuela, W. Africa.	2	Sandy, Australia.
2410	St. Mary, Senegambia, W. Afr.	3	Santa Catalina, Central America.
1	St. Mary, Madagascar.	4	Santa Ines Medio.
2	St. Mary, Newfoundland.	5	Santa Lucia, Patagonia.
3	St. Mary, New Ireland.	6	Santa Lucia, E. Africa.
4	St. Mary, Nova Scotia.	7	Santa Lucia, Windward Islands.
5	St. Mary, Uruquay.	8	Santa Maria, Uruquay.
6	St. Michael, Labrador.	9	Santa Maria, Buenos Ayres.
7	St. Nicholas, Hayti.	2460	Santa Maria, Spain.
8	St. Pablo.	1	Santa Maria di Leuca, W. Italy.
9	St. Paul, W. Africa.	2	Santa Pola, Spain.
2420	St. Roman, N. Coast S. America.	3	Sassoso, Candia.
1	St. Roque, E. Brazil.	4	Saunders, New Zealand.
2	St. Sebastian, Madagascar.	5	Schelky.
3	St. Sebastian, Spain.	6	Sedano, Java.
4	St. Sebastian, Terra del Fuego.	7	Sernella, Spain.
5	St. Sebastian, S. Africa.	2468	Seven Capes, W. Africa.
2426	St. Thomas, Brazil.		

Nos.	CAP	Nos.	CAP
2469	Cape Seven Capes, Candia.	2512	Cape Townshend, Australia.
2470	Seymour, New South Shetlands.	3	Trafalgar, Spain.
1	Shield, Australia.	4	Tribulation, Australia.
2	Shilling, W. Africa.	5	Tryon.
3	Shipounsky, E. Asia.	6	Turner.
4	Shirreff, New South Shetland Is.	7	Vancouver, Russian America.
5	Shoalwater, Washington, U. S.	8	Van Dieman, North Australia.
6	Sicie, South Coast France.	9	Vani, Milo.
7	Sidera, Candia.	2520	Varella, Cochin China.
8	Sidmouth, Australia.	1	Vaticano, Italy, West Coast.
9	Sidmouth, Loochoo Is.	2	Verde, West Africa.
2480	Sierra Leone, W. Coast Africa.	3	Verde Islands.
1	Silleiro, Spain.	4	Verga, S. W. Africa.
2	Skillo, Greece.	5	Victoria, Patagonia.
3	Skropha, Greece.	6	Victory.
4	Small Point, Maine, U. S.	7	Vidio, Spain.
5	South, Van Dieman's Land.	8	Villano, Spain.
6	Spada, Candia.	9	Virgin, Patagonia.
7	Spartel, West Africa.	2530	Virgins.
8	Spartimento, Italy.	1	Voltaire, Australia.
9	Spartivento, Italy.	2	Voltas, South Africa.
2490	Spartivento, Sardinia.	3	Watchman.
1	Spear, Newfoundland.	4	West, New Zealand.
2	Split, Nova Scotia.	5	Whittle, Canada.
3	Split Harbor, Maine, U. S.	6	Wrath, Scotland.
4	Sterns, Denmark.	7	York, Australia.
5	Sunday.	8	York, Greenland.
6	Talabo, Celebes.	9	Zambrona, West Italy.
7	Tarkhan, Crimea.	2540	Zibeeb, North Africa.
8	Tate.	1	Capel Bank, N. E. Australia.
9	Temple.	2	Caper's Island.
2500	Tennez, Algiers.	3	Caplin Bay.
1	Testa, Sardinia.	4	Caplin Bay, Newfoundland.
2	Teulada, Sardinia.	5	Capodietta Bay.
3	Three Points, Yucatan.	6	Capo d'Istria.
4	Three Points, West Africa.	7	Capones Point, Philippines.
5	Tiburon, W. Coast S. America.	8	Capraia Island, West Italy.
6	Tiburon, Hayti.	9	Capraria Island, Balearic Islands.
7	Tindaro, Sicily.	2550	Caprera Island, Corsica.
8	Tiñoso, Spain.	1	Capri Island, West Italy.
9	Torres, Spain.	2	Capri Island, Adriatic.
2510	Tortosa, Spain.	3	Capricorn Is., E. Coast Australia.
2511	Town, Cape of Good Hope.	2554	Capsali, Ionian Islands.

165

Nos.	CAP	Nos.	CAR
2555	Capstan Rocks.	2598	Cariaco, Gulf of, Venezuela.
6	Captain's Island.	9	Cariaco Island, Windward Islands.
7	Capucin Point, Seychelle Archip'go.	2600	Cariati, West Italy.
8	Capul Island, Philippine Islands.	1	Caribana P'nt, N. C'st Isth. Panama.
9	Cara Island, W. Coast Scotland.	2	Caribana Port.
2560	Caracas, Venezuela.	3	Caribbean Sea.
1	Caracas Islands, Caribbean Sea.	4	Caribbee Islands.
2	Caracoles.	5	Caribon Channel.
3	Caracoles Point, S. W. Panama.	6	Caribon Harbor.
4	Caragao Island, Philippine Islands.	7	Caribon Island, Lake Superior.
5	Caramulo Mount, Portugal.	8	Caribon Reef.
6	Carandaga Island, Philippine Is.	9	Carimata Island, China Sea.
7	Caranja Island, British India.	2610	Carimata Passage, China Sea.
8	Cararang Island, Philippine Is.	1	Carimon Java Id., Malay Archip'go.
9	Caratasca Lagoon, Central America.	2	Carimon Great Id., Malay Arch'go.
2570	Caraumilla Point, Chili.	3	Carimon Little Id., Malay Arch'go.
1	Caravel Rock, Martinique.	4	Carlet Island.
2	Caravellas, Brazil.	5	Carlingford, Ireland.
3	Caravellas Bay, Brazil.	6	Carlisle, England.
4	Carbon Cape, Algiers.	7	Carlisle Bay.
5	Carbonière Island.	8	Carleton Road.
6	Cardamum Island, Lacadive Is.	9	Carlö Island, Gulf of Bothnia.
7	Cardamum Reefs, Lacadive Is.	2620	Carlopago, Austria.
8	Cardenas, Cuba.	1	Carlos, St., Bay, Florida.
9	Cardiff, South Wales.	2	Carlos, San, Port, Falkland Islands.
2580	Cardigan, South Wales.	3	Carlscrona, Sweden.
1	Cardigan Bay, South Wales.	4	Carlshamn, Sweden.
2	Cardigan Bay, Prince Edward's Id.	5	Carlshoff Island, S. Pacific Ocean.
3	Cardigan Island, Coast of Wales.	6	Carlso Island, Baltic.
4	Cardigan Shoal.	7	Carmel Cape, Syria.
5	Cardiva Island, Maldive Islands.	8	Carmel Mount, Syria.
6	Cardon Isl'nd, Coast Cent'l America.	9	Carmen Island, Gulf of California.
7	Cardon Point, New Grenada.	2630	Carmen Island, Coast of Yucatan.
8	Cardoz Mount, Brazil.	1	Carmen Town.
9	Careenage.	2	Carmichael Pond.
2590	Careenage Harbor.	3	Carnasa Island, Philippine Islands.
1	Careening Bay, Australia.	4	Carnatic Shoal, China Sea.
2	Careening Island, West Indies.	5	Carnicobar Islands, Bay of Bengal.
3	Carenera Chico.	6	Carnom Point, Gulf of Siam.
4	Carentan, France.	7	Carn's Reef, N. E. Australia.
5	Carey's Islands, Baffin's Bay.	8	Carnsore Point, Ireland.
6	Cargados Garajos Is., Indian Ocean.	9	Carolina, North, United States.
2597	Cariaco, Venezuela.	2640	Carolina, South, United States.

12

166

Nos.	CAR	Nos.	CAS
2641	Carolina City.	2684	Casas River.
2	Caroline Islands, North Pacific.	5	Cascaes Bay, Portugal.
3	Caroline Islands, South Pacific.	6	Cascade Point, New Zealand.
4	Caroline Bay.	7	Cascajal Isles.
5	Caronia, Sicily.	8	Cascapedia Bay.
6	Carpathian Mountains, Europe.	9	Casco Bay, Maine, U. S.
7	Carpentaria, Gulf of, Australia.	2690	Cashe's Ledge, Maine, U. S.
8	Carr Island, Feejee Islands.	1	Caskets, English Channel.
9	Carr Rock, E. Coast Scotland.	2	Casma Bay, Peru.
2650	Carranza Point, Chili.	3	Caspian Sea.
1	Carrasco Mount, Peru.	4	Cassandra Cape, Greece.
2	Carreira Islands, E. Coast Spain.	5	Cassidaigue Rock, France, S. Coast.
3	Carreta Point, Central America.	6	Cassini Island, N. W. Australia.
4	Carretas Head, Peru.	7	Cassis, France, South Coast.
5	Carreto Harbor.	8	Casta Bay.
6	Carriacon, Caribbee Islands.	9	Castana Bay.
7	Carriage Harbor.	2700	Castaguetto Fort, West Italy.
8	Carrical, India.	1	Castelamare, West Italy.
9	Carrickarede Rock, Ireland.	2	Castelhanos Point, Brazil.
2660	Carrickfergus, Ireland.	3	Castellated Rock, China, E. Coast.
1	Carril, Spain.	4	Castel Volturno, West Italy.
2	Cartagena, New Grenada.	5	Castiglione, West Italy.
3	Cartagena, Spain.	6	Castilla Cape, Honduras.
4	Cartago Lagoon.	7	Castillo Island.
5	Cartago Bay, Central America.	8	Castillos Rock, Rio de la Plata.
6	Cartago Mount, Central America.	9	Castine, Maine, U. S.
7	Carteret Cape, N. W. France.	2710	Castle Harbor.
8	Carteret Id., Solomon Is., S. Pacific.	1	Castle Island, Labrador.
9	Carteret Port, Cocos Id., S. Pacific.	2	Castle Island, New Zealand.
2670	Carteret Shoal, North Pacific.	3	Castle Island Passage.
1	Carthage.	4	Castle Peak, Borneo.
2	Carthage Cape, North Africa.	5	Castle Point, New Zealand.
3	Carva Grande Shoals.	6	Castle Choco, Panama.
4	Carvœiro Cape, Portugal.	7	Castle Pinkney, S. Carolina, U. S.
5	Carwar Head.	8	Castle Thunder.
6	Carysfort Cape, Falkland Islands.	9	Castle of San Juan d'Ulloa.
7	Carysfort Cape, Florida, U. S.	2720	Castlereagh Cape, Tierra del Fuego.
8	Carysfort Island, South Pacific.	1	Castleton, Isle of Man.
9	Carysfort Reef, Florida, U. S.	2	Castleton Light, Isle of Man.
2630	Carysfort Reef Light-house, Florida.	3	Castries Bay, Tartary.
1	Casa de Muertos Islands.	4	Castries Port, Sta. Lucia Island.
2	Casamanza, West Africa.	5	Casuarina Island, S. E. Africa.
2683	Casamanza Rock, West Africa.	2726	Casuarina Mount, Australia.

Nos.	CAS	Nos.	CEI
2727	Casuarina Point, S. W. Australia.	2770	Caxo de Muertos Islands, W. Indies.
8	Casuarina Reef, South Australia.	1	Caxones, Central America.
9	Cat Cays, Bahamas.	2	Cay Biscayne, Florida, U. S.
2730	Cat Cove.	3	Cay Bivoras, Florida, U. S.
1	Cat Island, Massachusetts, U. S.	4	Cay Diana.
2	Cat Island, Mississippi, U. S.	5	Cay Grande Roques.
3	Catalina Island, Gulf of California.	6	Cay Holandes, Florida, U. S.
4	Catalina Harbor.	7	Cay Marquese, Florida, U. S.
5	Catalina, Sta. Island, Mexico.	8	Cay Moa.
6	Catalina, Sta. Island, Solomon Is.	9	Cay Piedras.
7	Catalinia.	2780	Cay Largo, Florida, U. S.
8	Catalinita.	1	Cay Larantados.
9	Catanduanes Island, Philippines.	2	Cayaguaneque Port.
2740	Catania, Sicily.	3	Cayamas Port.
1	Catastrophe Cape, S. Australia.	4	Caycos Islands.
2	Catch Harbor.	5	Caycos Passage.
3	Catel, Mindanao.	6	Caye a Raimiers.
4	Catfish Point.	7	Cayenne, French Guiana.
5	Catharina Islands, North Pacific.	8	Cayes.
6	Catherina Reef, China Sea.	9	Cayes St. Louis.
7	Catherine Islands, South Pacific.	2790	Cayeux, France.
8	Catherine Point, Tierra del Fuego.	1	Caymans, West Indies.
9	Catherine, St., Cape, West Africa.	2	Cayman, Great, West Indies.
2750	Catherine, St., Island, S. E. Brazil.	3	Cayman, Little, West Indies.
1	Cato Bank, N. E. Australia.	4	Caymites, Hayti.
2	Catoche Cape, Central America.	5	Cayo, Louisiana, U. S.
3	Catt Island, West Indies.	6	Cayo Islands, West Africa.
4	Cattegatt.	7	Cayo Blanco, Cuba.
5	Cattow Island, Tonga Island.	8	Cayo Romano, Cuba.
6	Catwyk, Great, Island, China Sea.	9	Cayte River.
7	Caution Cape, W. Coast N. America.	2800	Cazza Island, Adriatic.
8	Cavaliere Cape, Karamania.	1	Cazziola Island, Adriatic.
9	Cavallo Port, Texas.	2	Ceara, Brazil.
2760	Cavaillon Bay.	3	Cebellos Harbor.
1	Cavanas.	4	Cedar Hummock.
2	Cavelli Island, Philippine Islands.	5	Cedar Inlet.
3	Cavite, Luzon Island.	6	Cedar Island.
4	Cavite, Point de, Mindanao Island.	7	Cedar Islands.
5	Cavoli Island, Coast of Sardinia.	8	Cedar Keys, Florida, U. S.
6	Cawee, Great, I., Gulf St. Lawrence.	9	Cedros Island, W. Coast Mexico.
7	Cawoor, Sumatra.	2810	Cefalu, Sicily.
8	Caxine Cape, North Africa.	1	Ceicer de Mer, China Sea.
2769	Caxo Island, Grecian Archipelago.	2812	Ceicer de Terra, Cochin China.

168

Nos.	CEL	Nos.	CHA
2813	Celebes Island, Malay Archipelago.	2856	Champion Bay, Australia.
4	Celebes Sea.	7	Champlain, Lake.
5	Centinel, Venezuela.	8	Champoton.
6	Cephalonia, Ionian Islands.	9	Chance Harbor.
7	Ceram Island, Malay Archipelago.	2860	Chance Island, Merqui Archipelago,
8	Ceram Laut Island, Malay Arch'go.	1	Chandeleur Islands, Louisiana, U. S.
9	Cerberus Rock.	2	Chandeleur Is. Light, Louisi'na, U.S.
2820	Cerberus Shoal.	3	Chandeleur Sound.
1	Cerigo Island, Grecian Archipelago.	4	Chandler's Reach.
2	Cerigotto Island, Grecian Archip'go.	5	Chandler's River, Maine, U. S.
3	Cerralbo Island, California.	6	Chaneral Island, Chili.
4	Cerro Azul, Peru.	7	Chang-chi Island, S. E. China.
5	Cerro de Cuebas, Trinidad.	8	Change Island Tickle.
6	Cerro del Mecate, E. Coast Mexico.	9	Channel Islands, English Channel.
7	Cerros Island, W. Coast Mexico.	2870	Chanoury Point, Scotland.
8	Cervera Cape, East Spain.	1	Chao Islands, Peru.
9	Cesareo, Port, East Italy.	2	Chaoul, India.
2830	Cesenatico, East Italy.	3	Chapeau Rouge, Cape, Newfoundl'd.
1	Cestos, West Africa.	4	Chapel Island, China.
2	Cette, South France.	5	Chapman's Point.
3	Ceuta, Morocco.	6	Chaptico.
4	Ceylon.	7	Charbar, Indian Ocean.
5	Chabon.	8	Charente, France.
6	Chabrol Island, Loyalty Islands.	9	Charles, Cape, Virginia, U. S.
7	Chacachacare Island, Trinidad.	2880	Charles Island, Galapagos Islands.
8	Chacalacas River.	1	Charles Island, Spitsbergen.
9	Chacon Cape, Russian America.	2	Charles Fort, Belgium.
2840	Chagaraumas Bay.	3	Charleston, South Carolina, U. S.
1	Chagles.	4	Charleston, Leeward Islands.
2	Chagos, Great, Bank, Indian Ocean.	5	Charlestown, Massachusetts, U. S.
3	Chagre, Central America.	6	Charlotte.
4	Chain Island, South Pacific.	7	Charlotte Bank, China Sea.
5	Chak-chak, Port, East Africa.	8	Charlotte Bank, South Pacific.
6	Chaleur Bay, Gulf of St. Lawrence.	9	Charlotte Harbor, Florida, U. S.
7	Chalky Bay, New Zealand.	2890	Charlotte Harbor, Labrador.
8	Challenger Bank, Gulf of Oman.	1	Charlotte Island, South Pacific.
9	Chalmers, Port, W. C'st N. America.	2	Charlotte Port.
2850	Chamalacon River.	3	Charlotte Town, Prince Edward's I.
1	Chamatla River, Mexico.	4	Chase Island, South Pacific.
2	Chame Point, Central America.	5	Chateau Bay, Labrador.
3	Chamisso Island, Alaska, U. S.	6	Chateaudin Road.
4	Chamisso Port, Caroline Islands.	7	Chatham, England.
2855	Champigny Is., Buccaneer's Arch'go.	2898	Chatham, Massachusetts, U. S.

169

Nos.	CHA	Nos.	CHI
2899	Chatham Bay, Florida, U. S.	2942	Chica Mola River, Central America.
2900	Chatham Cape, Australia.	3	Chicarene Point, Central America.
1	Chatham Cape Rocks, Australia.	4	Chichester, England.
2	Chatham Harb., Massachus'tts, U. S.	5	Chichia Island, Feejee Islands.
3	Chatham Island, Galapagos Islands.	6	Chichiriviche Harbor.
4	Chatham Island, New Zealand.	7	Chickaseen.
5	Chatham Islands, North Pacific.	8	Chicken Head, Orkney Islands.
6	Chatham Islands, South Pacific.	9	Chico Bank.
7	Chatham Port, Andaman Island.	2950	Chicobea Island, Feejee Islands.
8	Chatham Port, Alaska, U. S.	1	Chidleigh Cape, Hudson's Strait.
9	Chatte Cape, Anticosti Island.	2	Chidleigh Cape, Labrador.
2910	Chauchat Rocks, China.	3	Chignecto Bay, New Brunswick.
1	Chaume, La, West France.	4	Chignecto Cape, New Brunswick.
2	Chausey Islands, English Channel.	5	Chihuahua, Mexico.
3	Chauveau, West France.	6	Chikhok Island, China.
4	Chaves, Amazon River.	7	Chilca Point, Peru.
5	Chnyapiren Mount, Patagonia.	8	Chilca Port, Peru.
6	Chayos Archipelago.	9	Childers Rock, China.
7	Chedabucto Bay, Nova Scotia.	2960	Chili, South America.
8	Cheduba Island, Bay of Bengal.	1	Chiloe Island, Coast of Chili.
9	Cheesemans.	2	Chiltepee River.
2920	Che-fow, China.	3	Chimanas Islands.
1	Che-lang-piah Point, China.	4	Chimmo, China.
2	Chelindreh, Karamania.	5	Chimney Hill, Egypt.
3	Chelsea.	6	Chimney Island, China.
4	Chelsieu Rocks, China.	7	China.
5	Cheraw River, South Carolina, U. S.	8	China Sea.
6	Cherbourg, France.	9	Chincha Islands, Peru.
7	Cheribon, Java.	2970	Chin-chew, China.
8	Chermaier Peak, Java.	1	Chinchorro Bank, Gulf of Mexico.
9	Cherokee River.	2	Chiucoteague, Virginia, U. S.
2930	Cherry Island, Fejee Islands.	3	Chincoteague Shoals, Virginia, U. S.
1	Cherry Point.	4	Chin-Hae, China.
2	Cherrystone Inlet.	5	Chin-Hae Fort, China.
3	Chesapeake Bay, United States.	6	Chin-Kiang, China.
4	Chesconessix River, Maryland, U. S.	7	Chin-San Island, China.
5	Chester, England.	8	Chioggia, Italy.
6	Chester River, Maryland, U. S.	9	Chios, Asia Minor.
7	Chesterfield Bank, Madagascar.	2980	Chipana Bay.
8	Cheviot Hill, England.	1	Chira.
9	Chiapa Point, Corsica.	2	Chirambira Point.
2940	Chicacole, Coromandel.	3	Chiriqui, Central America.
2941	Chicago, Illinois. U. S.	2984	Chiriqui Lagoon, Central America.

Nos.	CHI	Nos.	CLA
2985	Chiswell Islands, Alaska, U. S.	3028	Chung-shan Island, China.
6	Chiti Cape, Cyprus.	9	Chupara Point, Trinidad Island.
7	Chittae, Lacadive.	3030	Chupara River.
8	Chittagong, India.	1	Church Creek.
9	Chittagong River, India.	2	Churchill Cape, Hudson's Bay.
2990	Chitwa, Ceylon.	3	Chusan, China.
1	Choco.	4	Chusan Island, China.
2	Choctaw Point, Alabama, U. S.	5	Chuspa.
3	Choctawachee Bay, Florida, U. S.	6	Cica Mount, Greece.
4	Choiseul Bay, Choiseul Island.	7	Cienfuegos.
5	Choiseul Island, Solomon Islands.	8	Cies Islands, Portugal.
6	Choiseul Port, Madagascar.	9	Cimbrishamn, Sweden.
7	Chonos Archipelago, Patagonia.	3040	Cincinnati, Ohio, U. S.
8	Chookea Island, China.	1	Cingue Isles Bay.
9	Chopowansic.	2	Cintra, Mount, Portugal.
3000	Choptank.	3	Cintra, Down of, West Africa.
1	Choptank River, Maryland, U. S.	4	Ciotat, Port, South France.
2	Chosan Port, Corea.	5	Circassia.
3	Chotank.	6	Circular Head, Van Dieman's Land.
4	Choumay Cape, Cochin China.	7	Circular Reef, South Pacific Ocean.
5	Chowry, Nicobar Islands.	8	Circumcision Island, Patagonia.
6	Christchurch, England.	9	Cirella Island, West Italy.
7	Christian, Fort, St. Thomas.	3050	Cirencester Bank, Gaspar Strait.
8	Christiana Island, Candia.	1	Cisargas Islands, West Spain.
9	Christiana Island, Grecian Archi'go.	2	Cispata Harbor, Central America.
3010	Christiania, Norway.	3	Citta Nuova, Illyria.
1	Christianopel, Sweden.	4	Civita Vecchia, Italy.
2	Christiansand, Norway.	5	Civita Vecchia, Dalmatia.
3	Christiansö, Sweden.	6	Cizópol, Turkey.
4	Christianstad, Santa Cruz Island.	7	Claire Island, New Hebrides Is.
5	Christiansund, Norway.	8	Clair, St., Island, Sea of Japan.
6	Christina, Santa Island, S. Pacific.	9	Clapp's Island.
7	Christinestad, Russia.	3060	Clack's Island, Australia.
8	Christmas Harb'r, Kerguelen's Land.	1	Clara, Madeiras.
9	Christmas Island, Indian Ocean.	2	Clara, Santa, Id., Juan Fernandez.
3020	Christmas Island, N. Pacific Ocean.	3	Clara, Santa, Island, Peru.
1	Christmas Sound.	4	Clare Island, Ireland.
2	Christopher, St., Island, W. Indies.	5	Clarence Cove, Fernando Po.
3	Christoval, St., Island, Solomon Is.	6	Clarence Island, Madagascar.
4	Chub Cut.	7	Clarence Island, South Pacific.
5	Chuburna.	8	Clarence Port, Alaska, U. S.
6	Chuluwan Island, East Africa.	9	Clarence Strait, Australia.
3027	Chung-chi Point, China.	3070	Clarence Strait, Persian Gulf.

Nos.	CLA	Nos.	COC
3071	Clark's Bank, Marquesas Islands.	3114	Cob Point.
2	Clarke Bank, Torres Strait.	5	Cobequid Bay, Nova Scotia.
3	Clarke Island, Van Dieman's Land.	6	Cobija, Bolivia.
4	Clarke's Point, Rhode Island, U. S.	7	Cobija Bay, Bolivia.
5	Clarke's Shoal, Buccaneer's Arch'go.	8	Cobija Peak, Bolivia.
6	Claro Babuyan, Babuyanes Islands.	9	Cobourg, Canada.
7	Classet Cape, W. Coast America.	3120	Coca Key, Cuba.
8	Clatiste Harbor.	1	Cocal Island, S. Pacific Ocean.
9	Clay Island.	2	Coche Island.
3080	Clear, Cape, Ireland.	3	Cochin, India.
1	Clearbottom Bay.	4	Cochin China.
2	Clearwater Point, Gulf St. Lawrence.	5	Cochinos Bay.
3	Cleaveland Shoal, W. Coast Africa.	6	Cochinos Island.
4	Cleft Island, South Australia.	7	Cochrane Cape, Kiu-Siu Island.
5	Cleft Rock, China.	8	Cockburn Cape, Australia.
6	Clemente, St., Island, California.	9	Cockburn Harbor.
7	Cleopatra Shoal, Newfoundland.	3130	Cockburn Island, South Pacific.
8	Clerk's Rocks, Sandwich Islands.	1	Cockburn Mount, S. E. Africa.
9	Clerke Island, South Pacific Ocean.	2	Cockburn Reef, N. E. Australia.
3090	Clermont Tonnere Island, S. Pacific.	3	Cockell's Islands, Buccaneer's Arch.
1	Cleveland, Ohio, U. S.	4	Cockle Light, England.
2	Cleveland Cape, Australia.	5	Cockle's Creek.
3	Clew Bay, Ireland.	6	Cockpit Point.
4	Clifford Islands, Corea.	7	Coco Island, Philippine Islands.
5	Cliffy Island, Australia.	8	Cooo, Great, Island, Andaman Is.
6	Clipperton Rock, N. Pacific Ocean.	9	Coco, Little, Island, Andaman Is.
7	Cloates Point, Australia.	3140	Coco Point, British Guiana.
8	Cloch, Scotland.	1	Cocoa Island, Indian Ocean.
9	Clogher Head, Ireland.	2	Cocoa Island Reefs, Indian Ocean.
3100	Clonakilty, Ireland.	3	Cocoa Islands, North Pacific.
1	Clonard Cape, Corea.	4	Cocoa-nut Island, Java Sea.
2	Clopper's Bay, Texas.	5	Cocoa-nut Island, Sandwich Is.
3	Cloudy Bay, New Zealand.	6	Cocoa-nut Island, Torres Strait.
4	Clove Island, China Sea.	7	Cocoa-nut Point, Gilolo.
5	Clove Sound.	8	Cocos Bay.
6	Cloven Cliff, Nova Zembla.	9	Cocos Island, Ladrones.
7	Club Heads.	3150	Cocos Island, N. Pacific Ocean.
8	Clump Island, Dampier Strait.	1	Cocos Island, New Ireland.
9	Clute Island, S. Pacific Ocean.	2	Cocos Island, S. Pacific Ocean.
3110	Clyde, Scotland.	3	Cocos Islands, Sooloo Islands.
1	Clyde River.	4	Cocos Islands, South Pacific.
2	Coast Castle, Cape, W. Africa.	5	Cocos Islands, Sumatra.
3113	Coaster's Harb., Rhode Island, U. S.	3156	Cocos Point, Panama.

Nos.	COC	Nos.	CON
3157	Cocuzza Mount, W. Italy.	3200	Colnett, Cape, California.
8	Cod, Cape, Massachusetts.	1	Colnett, Cape, New Caledonia.
9	Cod, Cape, Harbor, Massachusetts.	2	Colnett Island, Japan Islands.
3160	Cod, Cape, Light, Massachusetts.	3	Colombia, United States of, S Amer'a.
1	Cod, Harbor.	4	Colombier, Cape.
2	Cod's Head, Ireland.	5	Colombo, Ceylon.
3	Coddle's Harbor.	6	Colon, or Aspinwall.
4	Codera Cape, Venezuela.	7	Colonella, E. Italy.
5	Coetivy Island, Almirante Islands.	8	Colonia, Uruguay.
6	Coffin, Cape, Celebes.	9	Colonel's Island.
7	Coffin Island, Madagascar.	3210	Colonna, Cape, Greece.
8	Coffin Island, Nova Scotia.	1	Colonsay Island, Scotland.
9	Coffin Island, South Carolina, U. S.	2	Coloras Islands.
3170	Coffin's Island.	3	Colorado, U. S.
1	Coffin's Patches, Florida, U. S.	4	Colorado Banks, Cuba.
2	Cofre del Perote. Mexico.	5	Colorado Reefs, Cuba.
3	Cohansey Creek, New Jersey.	6	Colorado River, Buenos Ayres.
4	Cohasset Rocks.	7	Colorado River, Texas.
5	Coiba Island, North Pacific.	8	Colquhoun, Mt., W. Africa.
6	Coimbra, Portugal.	9	Columbia, District of.
7	Colares Island.	3220	Columbia, South Carolina, U. S.
8	Colberg, Prussia.	1	Columbia, British.
9	Colbert Island, Buccaneer's Arch'go.	2	Columbia River, Washington Ter.U.S.
3180	Cold Spring.	3	Columbian Rock, Gaspar Strait.
1	Cole's Cave, South Carolina.	4	Columbiano.
2	Coles' Island, Australia.	5	Columbier Island.
3	Coles' Point, Peru.	6	Columbine Shoals.
4	Coleraine, Ireland.	7	Columbretes Islands, E. Spain.
5	Coley Rock, W. Africa.	8	Colville, Cape, New Zealand.
6	Colima, Mt., W. Coast Mexico.	9	Comayagua, Central America.
7	Colindiba River.	3230	Comfort, Cape, Solomon Islands.
8	Colinet Bay.	1	Comino, Cape, Sardinia.
9	Colio Island, China.	2	Commerson Island, S. Pacific.
3190	Coll Island, Scotland.	3	Commodore's Island.
1	Collao, Cham Islands, Cochin China.	4	Comodo Island, Celebes Islands.
2	Collao, Cham False, Cochin China.	5	Comorin, Cape, India.
3	Callao Han Island, Cochin China.	6	Comoro Island, Mozambique Channel.
4	Collato, Cape, South Africa.	7	Comowine River.
5	Collerton River.	8	Concedo Point, Hayti.
6	Collier's Bay.	9	Conceicao.
7	Collins Shoal, Gulf of St. Lawrence.	3240	Concepcion, Bahamas.
8	Collomandoo Atoll, Maldive Islands.	1	Concepcion, Chili.
3199	Colne, England.	3242	Conception Bay, Newfoundland.

173

Nos.	CON	Nos.	COR
3243	Conception Island.	3286	Cooper, Port, New Zealand.
4	Conception Point, California.	7	Cooper's Island.
5	Conception Point, Mexico.	8	Coordomeat Islands, Red Sea.
6	Conch Reef.	9	Coosaw River, South Carolina.
7	Conchagua, Gulf of, Central America.	3290	Cope, Cape de, Spain.
8	Conchée, La, Rock, N. W. France.	1	Copeland, Ireland.
9	Condé Peninsular.	2	Copeland Light, Ireland.
3250	Condillac Island, South Pacific.	3	Copename River, Guiana.
1	Condore, Pulo, Islands, China Sea.	4	Copenhagen, Denmark.
2	Cone, The, Mergui Archipelago.	5	Copiapo, Chili.
3	Cone Island, China Sea.	6	Copinsha Island, Orkney Islands.
4	Cone River, Virginia, U. S.	7	Copnahow Head, Scotland.
5	Coney Island, New York.	8	Copper Harbor, Lake Superior.
6	Confites Cay, Cuba.	9	Copper Island, North Pacific.
7	Conflict Reefs, West Africa.	3300	Coppermine River, British America.
8	Congo River, S. W. Africa.	1	Coquet Island, North Sea.
9	Congoon, Persia.	2	Coquille Harbor.
3260	Conical Hill, India.	3	Coquille Island, North Pacific.
1	Connauticut Island.	4	Coquimbo, Chili.
2	Connecticut. U. S.	5	Coquin Sound, Davis Strait.
3	Connecticut River, U. S.	6	Coral Bank, Nicobar Isles.
4	Conney Bay.	7	Coral Island, Coast of Brazil.
5	Connire Bay.	8	Coral Reef, Marquesas Islands.
6	Consequina Point, Central America.	9	Coral Reef, Tonga Islands.
7	Constant Bank, Almirante Islands.	3310	Coral Rocks, China Sea.
8	Constantine Cape, Russian America.	1	Corbin Bay.
9	Constantinople, Turkey.	2	Corbin Harbor.
3270	Constitution Road, Bolivia.	3	Corchuna, Spain.
1	Contessa, Gulf of, Turkey.	4	Corcobado, Mt., Patagonia.
2	Contoy Island, Gulf of Mexico.	5	Cordouan, France.
3	Contrarietés Island, Solomon's Is.	6	Corea, China.
4	Conway, North Wales.	7	Corea, Straits of.
5	Conway Bay, Galapagos Islands.	8	Corean Archipelago, Yellow Sea.
6	Conway Cape, Australia.	9	Core Nowaret, Red Sea.
7	Conway Cape, China.	3320	Corentyn River, Guiana.
8	Conway Reef.	1	Corfu, Ionian Isles.
9	Conway Rock, Bass Strait.	2	Coringa, India.
3280	Cook Bay.	3	Coringa Shoal, Australia.
1	Cook Port.	4	Corinth, Greece.
2	Cook's Harbor.	5	Corisco Island, Bight of Biafra.
3	Cook's Islands, South Pacific.	6	Cork, Ireland.
4	Coomfidah, Arabia.	7	Corkewetchepe Bay, Gulf St. Law'ce.
3285	Coopang, Timor Island.	3328	Cormachiti, Cape, Syria.

Nos.	COR	Nos.	CRA
3329	Cormorant Point.	3371	Corso Island, Patagonia.
3330	Corn Islands, Gulf of Honduras.	2	Corsoer, Denmark.
1	Cornejo Point, Peru.	3	Corunna, Spain.
2	Corner, Cape, New Guinea.	4	Corvo, Azores.
3	Corner Inlet, Australia.	5	Coscio di Donna Rock, Sardinia.
4	Cornfield Harbor.	6	Cosire, Red Sea.
5	Cornwall, England.	7	Cosmoledo Is., Mozambique Chan'l.
6	Cornwall, Cape, England.	8	Cosnay Island, Greek Archipelago.
7	Cornwall, Cape, Torres Strait.	9	Costa Rica, Central America.
8	Cornwallis.	3380	Coster Cape, Loyalty Islands.
9	Cornwallis Cape, Choiseul Island.	1	Cotaringan River, Borneo.
3340	Cornwallis Island, Baffin's Bay.	2	Côte Blanche Bay, Louisiana, U. S.
1	Cornwallis Island, New Orkneys.	3	Cotrona, Malta.
2	Cornwallis Islands, North Pacific.	4	Cotteral's Key.
3	Cornwallis Islands, (Gaspar Rico,) North Pacific.	5	Coubre, Point de la, France.
		6	Cougalga Island, Aleutian Isles.
4	Cornwallis Mount, New Guinea.	7	Coulaba Island, Indian Ocean.
5	Cornwallis Port, Andaman Islands.	8	Coulomb Point, Australia.
6	Cornwallis Shoals, China Sea.	9	Coumong Harbor, Cochin China.
7	Corny Point, Australia.	3390	Country Harbor, Nova Scotia.
8	Coro, Columbia.	1	Coupang, Timor Island.
9	Coro River.	2	Coupe, Point de la, Jersey Island.
3350	Coroa Grande Shoal, Brazil.	3	Courland.
1	Coromandel, India.	4	Courtland Bay.
2	Coromandel Harbor, New Zealand.	5	Courtown Bank, Central America.
3	Coronados Rocks, California.	6	Coutances, France.
4	Coronation Island, New Orkneys.	7	Cove Bay.
5	Coronation Islands, Alaska, U. S.	8	Cove Point, Maryland.
6	Corouge Island, Gulf of Martaban.	9	Cove Rocks, South Africa.
7	Corral, Fort, Patagonia.	3400	Coveland, British India.
8	Corregidor Island, Philippine Is.	1	Covell Islands, North Pacific.
9	Corrientes, Parana River.	2	Coventry Rock, Australia.
3360	Corrientes Cape, Buenos Ayres.	3	Coversea Skerries, Scotland.
1	Corrientes Cape, Cuba.	4	Cow Head.
2	Corrientes Cape, Mexico.	5	Cow Keys, Florida.
3	Corrientes Cape, Central America.	6	Cowes, England.
4	Corrientes Cape, South Africa.	7	Cowman's Shoal, Banca Strait.
5	Corrubedo Cape, Portugal.	8	Coxcomb Point.
6	Corsair Bay, Venezuela.	9	Coy Inlet.
7	Corseules, Port, France.	3410	Cozumel Island, Gulf of Mexico.
8	Corsewall Point, Scotland.	1	Crab Island, British Guiana.
9	Corsica.	2	Crab Island, Leeward Islands.
3370	Corso Cape, Corsica.	3413	Crab Island, Venezuela.

Nos.	CRA	Nos.	CUB
3414	Craddock Creek.	3457	Croix, St., Bay, East Asia.
5	Crag Island, China Sea.	8	Croix, St., Island, South Africa.
6	Craggy Island, Bass Strait. .	9	Croker Island, Low Archipelago.
7	Craig Harriet, Corean Archipelago.	3460	Croker Island, Australia.
8	Cranberry Isl'nd, Gulf St. Lawrence.	1	Croker Cape, Australia.
9	Crane Island.	2	Cromarty, Scotland.
3420	Craney Island, Virginia.	3	Cromer, England.
1	Craney Island Flats.	4	Cromwell's Ledge.
2	Craney Island Light-house.	5	Cronstadt, Russia.
3	Cranganore River, India.	6	Crooe, Sumatra.
4	Crapeaud Road.	7	Crooked Island, Bahamas.
5	Cras, Cape le, Bougainville Island.	8	Crooked Island Passage.
6	Crawford Cape, Baffin's Bay.	9	Crook Haven, Ireland.
7	Craw Point, Ceram Island.	3470	Croque Harbor.
8	Crawfish Key.	1	Crosby Light, England.
9	Crawford Island, Gulf of Guinea.	2	Cross Cape, Russian America.
3430	Crawford Reefs, China Sea.	3	Cross Cape, West Africa.
1	Creighton Shoal.	4	Cross Hill, Ascension Island.
2	Crelogh Rocks, Ireland.	5	Cross Island, Magdalen Islands.
3	Cremalire Cove.	6	Cross Island, Nova Scotia.
4	Crescent Chain, China Sea.	7	Cross Rip.
5	Crescent City, California.	8	Cross, Port, Island, South France.
6	Crescent Island, Corean Archip'go.	9	Crow Harbor.
7	Crescent Island, Low Archipelago.	3480	Crow Harbor, Georgia, U. S.
8	Crespo Island, North Pacific.	1	Crow Inlet.
9	Cresta del Gallo Island, Philippines.	2	Crow Isles.
3440	Crete.	3	Crown Island, South Pacific.
1	Cretin Islands, New Guinea.	4	Crozer Mount, North Pacific.
2	Creux, Cape de, Spain.	5	Crozet's Islands, S. Indian Ocean.
3	Cricq, Cape St., Australia.	6	Cruz Harbor.
4	Crillon Cape, Sagalin.	7	Cruz, Cape de, Cuba.
5	Crimea, Black Sea.	8	Cruz, Point de.
6	Crimon Island, Java Sea.	9	Cruz, Santa, Africa.
7	Crio Cape, Asia Minor.	3490	Cruz, Santa, Canary Islands.
8	Crio Cape, Candia.	1	Cruz, Santa, Leeward Islands.
9	Croatan Sound, North Carolina, U. S.	2	Cruz, Santa, Island, California.
3450	Croc Harbor, Labrador.	3	Cruz, Santa, Island, Mexico.
1	Croce, Cape Santa, Sicily.	4	Cruz, Santa, Island, South Pacific.
2	Crocker's Reef.	5	Cruz, Santa, Islands, Philippines.
3	Crocodile Islands, Australia.	6	Cruz, Santa, Port, Patagonia.
4	Crocodile Point.	7	Crystal Head, Australia.
5	Crocodile Rock, Bass Strait.	8	Cuagua Islands.
3456	Croisic, France.	3499	Cuba.

Nos.	CUB	Nos.	DAM
3500	Cubagua Islands.	3543	Curlew Harbor.
1	Cuckold Creek.	4	Curnaw.
2	Cuddalore, Hindostan.	5	Current Basin, New Zealand.
3	Cuidad Bolivar, Venezuela.	6	Current Island, Celebes.
4	Cuidadella, Minorca.	7	Current Island, N. Pacific.
5	Cuidado Reef.	8	Currituck Inlet, North Carolina.
6	Culebra, West Indies.	9	Currituck Sound, North Carolina.
7	Culebra Island, Virgin Islands.	3550	Curtis Island, Bass Strait.
8	Culebra Islet, Philippine Islands.	1	Curtis Island, N. W. Australia.
9	Culebras Point, Peru.	2	Curtis Islands, South Pacific.
3510	Culebras Shoal, Tonga Islands.	3	Curtis Point.
1	Culiacan River, Mexico.	4	Curtis Port, Australia.
2	Culincan Shoals, Mexico.	5	Curzola Island, Adriatic.
3	Culili Point, Luzon.	6	Cutch, Hindostan.
4	Cullen, Scotland.	7	Cuthbert Point, Australia.
5	Cullera, Spain.	8	Cuttehunk Island, Massachusetts.
6	Cullera, Cape, Spain.	9	Cuttehunk Light, Massachusetts.
7	Culpepper Island, Galapajos Islands.	3560	Cutter Harbor.
8	Culver Point, Australia.	1	Cutwell Harbor.
9	Cumana, Venezuela.	2	Cuvier, Cape, Australia.
3520	Cumarebo Bay.	3	Cuvier Island, New Zealand Islands.
1	Cumbahee Bank.	4	Cuxhaven, Prussia.
2	Cumbahee River.	5	Cuyos Islands, Philippines.
3	Cumberland.	6	Cyclops, Mount, New Guinea.
4	Cumberland Arm.	7	Cyprus, Asia Minor.
5	Cumberland Bay, Juan Fernandez Id.	8	Cyrene, North Africa.
6	Cumberland. Cape, New Hebrides.	9	Dacres, Cape.
7	Cumberland Entrance, Australia.	3570	Daedalus Shoal.
8	Cumberland Harbor, Cuba.	1	Daery.
9	Cumberland Island, Georgia, U. S.	2	Dagelet Island.
3530	Cumberland Island, Low Archipel'go.	3	Dagerort.
1	Cumberland Islands, N. E. Australia.	4	Da Guia.
2	Cumberland Sound, Georgia.	5	Dale Point.
3	Cumbræ, Scotland.	6	Dalhousie Island.
4	Cumbrian Break, Bashee Islands.	7	Dalmatia.
5	Cunningham Point, Buccaneer's Arch.	8	Dalmy.
6	Cup-chi Point, China.	9	Dalrymple Bay.
7	Cupola, Cape, New Guinea.	3580	Dalrymple Island.
8	Curaçoa, West Indies.	1	Dalrymple Port.
9	Curaçoa Little, West Indies.	2	Dalrymple Rock.
3540	Cure Island, North Pacific.	3	Dalupiri Island.
1	Curieuse Island, Seychelle Arch.	4	Damaun.
3542	Curioso, Cape, Patagonia.	3585	Dame Marie, Cape.

Nos.	DAM	Nos.	DEE
3586	Damariscotta River, Maine, U. S.	3629	Datoo Point.
7	Damietta.	3630	Datoo Pulo, Borneo.
8	Damascus, Asiatic Turkey.	1	Datoo Pulo, China Sea.
9	Dames Point, Florida, U. S.	2	Dauphin Island.
3590	Dammer Islands.	3	Dauphin Port.
1	Dampier Island.	4	Daurus Head.
2	Dampier Straits, Eastern Archipelago.	5	Dauss Island.
3	Dampier's Archipelago, W. Australia.	6	Davis Bank.
4	Damnable Harbor.	7	Davis Cove.
5	Dana Pulo.	8	Davis Straits.
6	Dana's Peak.	9	Davey Port.
7	Dande's Peak.	3640	David Sandbank.
8	Dane's Island.	1	David Shoals.
9	Danger Island, Chagos Group.	2	David's, St.
3600	Danger Island, New Guinea.	3	David's, St., Islands.
1	Dangerous Island.	4	Davilacan Bay.
2	Dangerous Island Reef.	5	Dawbaide.
3	Dangerous Island Point.	6	Dawson Islands.
4	Danger Point, Australia.	7	Day Island.
5	Danger Point, Cape Colony.	8	Dayagan Point.
6	Danger Point, Celebes.	9	Daylight Point.
7	Danholm Island, Baltic.	3650	Dead Islands Harbor.
8	Dantzic, Germany.	1	Deadman.
9	Dantzic Cove.	2	Deadman Island.
3610	Daniel Island.	3	Deadman's Harbor.
1	Danube River.	4	Deal.
2	Danville, Cape.	5	Deal Island.
3	Daond Ras.	6	Dear Island.
4	Dardanelles.	7	Debil Shoal.
5	Dar el Beida.	8	Deblois Island.
6	Darien, Georgia, U. S.	9	Debarda Caire.
7	Darien, Gulf of, U. S. Colombia.	3660	Deboyne Islands.
8	Darnley Island.	1	Deccan, Hindostan.
9	Daros Island.	2	Deception, Cape.
3620	Dars Head.	3	Deception Island.
1	Dartmouth, England.	4	Decrow Point.
2	Dartmouth, British America.	5	Dee, Scotland.
3	Dartmouth, Nova Scotia.	6	Deep Bay.
4	Dartuch, Cape.	7	Deep Creek, Virginia.
5	Darwin Peak.	8	Deep Harbor.
6	Darwin Port.	9	Deep Water Shoals, James River, U.S.
7	Dassen Island, South Africa.	3670	Deep Water Sound.
3628	Das Bocas.	3671	Deep Water Creek.

Nos.	DEE	Nos.	DIA
3672	Deer Harbor.	3715	Derby Cape.
3	Deer Island, Maine, U. S.	6	Dernier Island, Louisiana, U. S.
4	Defence Fort.	7	Deschamps Peak.
5	De Galle, Point de, Ceylon.	8	Derwent, Van Dieman's Land.
6	Degérando Cape.	9	Deseata, Caribbee Isles.
7	De Gras Cove.	3720	Deseada.
8	Debert's Bay.	1	Deseada Cape.
9	Delagua Bay, S. E. Africa.	2	Deseado Cape.
3680	Delambre.	3	Desecho Island.
1	Delaware Bay, United States.	4	Desert Mount Rock, United States.
2	Delaware River, United States.	5	Desertos, Atlantic Ocean.
3	Delaware Breakwater, U. States.	6	Desire Port.
4	Delaware City, United States.	7	Desirade.
5	Delaware Heads.	8	Des Sac Islands.
6	Del Boqueron.	9	Desolado Cape.
7	Delesdernier Point.	3730	Desolate Bay.
8	Delhi River.	1	Desolation, Cape, Davis' Strait.
9	Delisle de la Croyère, Cape.	2	Desolation, Cape, South America.
3690	Deliverance Cape.	3	Despair Rock.
1	Deliverance Island.	4	Destretto.
2	Dellys.	5	Detached Reef.
3	De Lobos Island.	6	Detour, Lake Michigan.
4	Delphi Mount.	7	Detroit, Michigan, U. S.
5	Del Rincon Bay.	8	Detroit River, United States.
6	Delute Harbor.	9	Devicotta, British India.
7	Demerara, British Guiana.	3740	Devil Bay.
8	Demerara River.	1	Devil Island.
9	Denbigh Island.	2	Devil Peak.
3700	Denia, Spain.	3	Devil Point.
1	Denmark.	4	Dhalac Bank.
2	Denis Cape.	5	Dhalac Island.
3	Denis Island, Low Archipelago.	6	Dhaulle Shoal.
4	Denis Island, Seychelles.	7	Devonport, England.
5	Denis, St.	8	Dewees Point.
6	D'Entrecasteaux Point, W. Australia.	9	Diagon Bay.
7	D'Entrecasteaux Channel.	3750	Diamond Harbor, British India.
8	D'Entrecost Islands.	1	Diamond Island, Chagos.
9	D'Entrecost Point.	2	Diamond Island, Faero Islands.
3710	D'Entrecost Reef.	3	Diamond Island, Peru.
1	De Peyster Islands.	4	Diamond Island Rocks.
2	Depuch Island.	5	Diamond Reef.
3	Dequez.	6	Diamond Shoal, Cape Hatteras, U. S.
3714	Derna, North Africa.	3757	Diamond Point, Bahamas.

Nos.	DIA	Nos.	DOM
3758	Diamond Point, Sandwich Islands.	3801	Disappointment, Cape.
9	Diamond Point, Sumatra.	2	Disappointment Island.
3760	Diana Bank.	3	Disaster Island.
1	Diana Peak.	4	Discovery Banks.
2	Dibbah.	5	Discovery Port.
3	Dice's Head.	6	Discovery Reef, N. W. of Borneo.
4	Diceras, Mt.	7	Discovery Reef, Paracele.
5	Didicas Rocks.	8	Dislocation Harbor.
6	Didi-houa Islands.	9	Discourse Shoal.
7	Dido.	3810	Dispatch Rock.
8	Dieffenbach, Mt.	1	Diu Head.
9	Diego Garcia.	2	Dividing Creek.
3770	Diego Islands.	3	Divis, Mt.
1	Diego Rameirez Islands, S. Pacific.	4	Division, Mt.
2	Diego, San, Cape.	5	Divy Point.
3	Diego, San, Point.	6	Dix Cove, West Africa.
4	Diego, St.	7	Dixon Rock.
5	Dieman, Straits of.	8	Djimaja Island.
6	Dieppe.	9	Dnieper River, Russia.
7	Digby, Cape.	3820	Dnister River, Russia.
8	Digges Islands.	1	Doa Pulo.
9	Digue, La, Island.	2	Dobbo Harbor.
3780	Dildo Harbor.	3	Doboy Inlet.
1	Dill Point.	4	Doboy Sound.
2	Dilian Island.	5	Docan Pulo.
3	Dillon Bay.	6	Doctor's Island.
4	Dilly, Mt.	7	Dodd Island.
5	Dilly Town.	8	Doddington Rock.
6	Dinan, France.	9	Dog Island, Banda Sea.
7	Dindirg Pulo.	3830	Dog Island, Florida, U. S.
8	Dingle Bay, Ireland.	1	Dog Island, West Indies.
9	Dingwall, Scotland.	2	Dog Island, Mississippi, U. S.
3790	Dino Island.	3	Dog River.
1	Diogo.	4	Dog Rocks.
2	Diomede Islands.	5	Doif.
3	Dionisio, San, Islands.	6	Dolgoi Ness.
4	Dios Keys.	7	Dollabarats Shoal.
5	Disco Island, Davis Straits.	8	Dolphin Head, British Honduras.
6	Dirk Hartogs Island.	9	Dolphin Head, Jamaica W. I.
7	Direction, Cape.	3840	Doly Point.
8	Direction Island, Indian Ocean.	1	Domairah Island.
9	Direction Island, Sumatra.	2	Domar Pulo.
3800	Disappointment Bay.	3843	Dome, Mt.

Nos.	DOM	Nos.	DUB
3844	Dome of St. Paul's, England.	3887	Dourga Strait.
5	Domea.	8	Douro, Portugal.
6	Domesness.	9	Douro, Pulo.
7	Domingo, St.	3890	Dove Island.
8	Domingo, St., Cay.	1	Dover, England.
9	Domingo, St., Island.	2	Dover Point.
3850	Doming, San.	3	Dover, Straits of, Europe.
1	Dominica, Leeward Islands.	4	Downs, England.
2	Dominica, Marquesas.	5	Downs Point.
3	Don, Cape.	6	Down Patrick.
4	Donaghadee.	7	Down Patrick, Head.
5	Donda, Cape.	8	Dowsing, Inner.
6	Dondra Head.	9	Doyle.
7	Donegal, Ireland.	3900	Doyle Reef.
8	Donkin, Cape.	1	Dragomesti Bay.
9	Donnington Cape.	2	Dragon Bay.
3860	Doobelloo.	3	Dragon's Mouth.
1	Dorchester, Cape.	4	Dragoman Island.
2	Dorchester Heights, Boston, U. S.	5	Dragoman Id. Light, Mediterranean.
3	Dorei Port.	6	Drake's Bay, California, U. S.
4	Doris Cove.	7	Drake's Island.
5	Doro, Cape.	8	Drapano, Cape.
6	Dorre Island.	9	Draper's Island.
7	Dorset, Cape.	3910	Drogheda, Ireland.
8	Dos Hermanos.	1	Dromedary, Mt.
9	Double, Mt.	2	Dronthiem, Norway.
3870	Double Island, Australia.	3	Druid Shoal.
1	Double Island, Gulf of Martaban.	4	Drum Flat.
2	Double Island, Torres Straits.	5	Drum Point.
3	Double Headed Shot Keys, W. I.	6	Drummond's Island, S. Pacific.
4	Double Peak.	7	Drummond's Point.
5	Double Peak Island.	8	Drunken Man's Cay.
6	Double Point.	9	Dry Bank L. H.
7	Doubt Rock.	3920	Dry Harbor.
8	Doubtful Bay.	1	Dry Lands.
9	Doubtful Harbor.	2	Dryander, Mt.
3880	Doubtful Island.	3	Dry Tortugas Island, Florida, U. S.
1	Doubtful Islands.	4	Dry Tortugas Fort.
2	Douglas, Isle of Man.	5	Duarte Islands.
3	Douglas, Cape.	6	Du Bouchage Island.
4	Douglas Island.	7	Du Four Rock.
5	Douglas Islands.	8	Dublin, Ireland.
3886	Douglas Town, St. Lawrence.	3929	Dubus, Fort.

Nos.	DUC	Nos.	EAG
3930	Ducato, Cape.	3973	Dungeness Point.
1	Ducie Island.	4	Dunk Island.
2	Duck Key.	5	Dunkins Reef.
3	Duck Island.	6	Dunkirk, France.
4	Duck Harbor.	7	Dunkirk, Lake Erie.
5	Dudgeon Island.	8	Dunmore.
6	Dudley Digges, Cape.	9	Dunnet Head, Scotland.
7	Dufaure Island.	3980	Dunorling Head.
8	Duff Islands.	1	Dunvegan Head.
9	Duhaertach Rock.	. 2	Duperré, Cape.
3940	Duke of Gloucester Islands.	3	Duperrey Island.
1	Duke of York Island.	4	Duperrey Islands.
2	Dulce, Gulf of, Central America.	5	Duportail Islands.
3	Dulce River.	6	Durand Reef.
4	Dulcigno.	7	Durazzo, Turkey.
5	Dumali Point.	8	Durel's Ledge.
6	Dumaran Island.	9	Durnford Noss.
7	Dumfries, Virginia, U. S.	3990	Durnford Point, N. W. Africa.
8	Dumfries, Scotland.	1	Durnford Point, South Africa.
9	Dumoulin Islands.	2	Dumford Port.
3950	Dumpling Hill.	3	Dumer Island.
1	Dumpling North.	4	D'Urville Island, Caroline Islands.
2	Dumpling Rocks.	5	D'Urville Island, New Zealand.
3	Dunaff Head.	6	D'Urville Island, New Guinea.
4	Dunbar, Scotland.	7	D'Urville Point.
5	Duncan, Michigan, U. S.	8	Dusky Bay.
6	Duncan Island.	9	Dussejour, Cape.
7	Duncan Islands, North Pacific.	4000	Dutch Island.
8	Duncan Rock.	1	Dutch Id., Harbor, Rhode Island,U.S.
9	Duncannon, Ireland.	2	Dutch Key.
3960	Duncannon Fort.	. 3	Duythen Point.
1	Duncansby Head.	4	Dwaalder Island.
2	Dundalk, Ireland.	5	Dwarka.
3	Dundas, Cape, Melleville Island.	6	Dwina River, Russia.
4	Dundas, Cape, New Orkneys.	7	Dyer Island.
5	Dundas Islands.	8	Dyer's Cape.
6	Dundee, Scotland.	9	Dyer's Bay.
7	Dundee Rock.	4010	Dyer's Cove.
8	Dundraw Bay.	1	Dyer's Rocks.
9	Dungarvan.	2	Dysker Rocks.
3970	Dungeness Island.	3	Dzizia.
1	Dungeness Light.	4	Eagle Harbor.
3972	Dungeness Reef.	4015	Eagle Island, Almirant.

13

Nos.	EAG	Nos.	ELK
4016	Eagle Island, Australia.	4059	Egmont Islands.
7	Eagle Island, Ireland.	4060	Egmont, Mt.
8	Eagle Islands, Chagos.	1	Egmont, Port.
9	Eartholms.	2	Egypt.
4020	East Cape, Madagascar.	3	Eider.
1	East Cape, New Zealand.	4	Eight Feet Rock.
2	East Domino.	5	Eimeo Island.
3	East Main Fort.	6	Ekarma Island.
4	Easter Group.	7	Ekholm.
5	Easter Island.	8	Elaghin Channel.
6	Eastern Fields.	9	Elato Islands.
7	Easy, Port.	4070	Elato, Mt.
8	Ebrilles Reef.	1	Elba.
9	Ebro River.	2	Elbe.
4030	Echiquier Islands.	3	Elbow Cay.
1	Echo Rock.	4	Elbow Cays.
2	Eclipse Islands.	5	Eldad Reef.
3	Eddom Sheikh Island.	6	Elena, St., Point.
4	Eddystone Light.	7	Elena, St., Port.
5	Eddystone Point.	8	Elephant Bay.
6	Eddystone Rock, Falkland Islands.	9	Elephant Island, S. Africa.
7	Eddystone Rock, Solomon Islands.	4080	Elephant Island, S. Shetlands.
8	Eden.	1	Elephant Point, Bengal.
9	Eden Island.	2	Elephant Point, Ceylon.
4040	Eden, Mt.	3	Elephant Point, Gulf of Martaban.
1	Edgar, Port.	4	Elephant Point, New Guinea.
2	Edgecumbe, Cape.	5	Elephant Rock.
3	Edgecumbe, Island.	6	Eleuthera Island.
4	Edgecumbe, Mt.	7	Elias, St., Mt.
5	Edinburgh.	8	Elicalpeni Bank.
6	Edisto Inlet.	9	Eliot, Mt.
7	Edomo, Port.	4090	Eliott, Lady, Island.
8	Ee-ki-mah.	1	Elivi Islands.
9	Een Islands.	2	Eliza Reef.
4050	Egg Harbor.	3	Elizabeth, Cape, Maine, U. S.
1	Egg Island.	4	Elizabeth, Cape, Russian America.
2	Egg and Royal Islands.	5	Elizabeth, Cape, Sagalin.
3	Eggrund.	6	Elizabeth Id., Admiralty Islands.
4	Egina Island.	7	Elizabeth Id., Marshall Islands.
5	Egmont.	8	Elizabeth Id., Society Islands.
6	Egmont, Cape.	9	Elizabeth Id., South Pacific.
7	Egmont Cay.	4100	El Kraan.
4058	Egmont Island.	4101	El Kraing.

Nos.	ELL	Nos.	ESP
4102	Ellen Shoal.	4145	Enos.
3	Ellice Islands.	6	Enragé Cape.
4	Ellis Bay.	7	Enskar Beac.
5	Elmina.	8	Enskar Light.
6	Elmo, St., Low Archipelago.	9	Entrada Point.
7	Elmo, St., Malta.	4150	Entry Bank.
8	Elmore Islands.	1	Entry Island, Magdalen Islands.
9	Elphinstone Bay.	2	Entry Island, New Zealand.
4110	Elphinstone Rock.	3	Eoa Island.
1	Elsineur.	4	Eourupig Islands.
2	Embarbaken, Cape.	5	Epiphanius Cape.
3	Embleton.	6	Erandza Island.
4	Emden.	7	Erebus Mount. ·
5	Emeneh, Cape.	8	Eregup.
6	Emerald Island.	9	Erekli
7	Emery Point.	4160	Eris Kay Island.
8	Emu Bay.	1	Ernest Island.
9	Encarnacion Island.	2	Ernest Mount.
4120	Ende Bay.	3	Eroen Cape.
1	Endeavor River.	4	Eroob.
2	Endeavor Reef, Australia.	5	Errakong Island.
3	Endeavor Reef, Bass Strait.	6	Erris Head.
4	Enderbury Island.	7	Erromango Island.
5	Enderby Island, Australia.	8	Erronan Island.
6	Enderby Island, South Pacific.	9	Esarme Cape.
7	Enderby Islands.	4170	Escala, La.
8	Enderby's Land.	1	Escape Point.
9	Endymion Rock.	2	Escarseo Point, Cumana.
4130	Engano Cape, Indian Archipelago.	3	Escarseo Point, Mindoro.
1	Engano Cape, St. Domingo.	4	Eschholtz Islands.
2	Engano Island, New Guinea.	5	Escombrera Island.
3	Engano Island, Sumatra.	6	Escudo Island.
4	Engelbolm.	7	Escumenac Point.
5	England.	8	Esha Ness Skerr.
6	England Pulo.	9	Eskimaux Cape.
7	Englefield Cape, Baffin's Bay.	4180	Esky Adalia.
8	English Bank, Gulf of Mexico.	1	Esmeralda River.
9	English Bank, River Plate.	2	Espada Point.
4140	English Harbor.	3	Espanola Point.
1	English River.	4	Espardell Island.
2	English Company's Islands.	5	Espenberg Cape.
3	English and Welsh Grounds.	6	Esperance Bay.
4144	Ennis Tuskar Rock.	4187	Esperance Cape.

Nos.	ESP	Nos.	FAL
4188	Esperance Rock.	4231	Facheux.
9	Espichel Cape.	2	Facile Harbor.
4190	Espiritu Santo Bay.	3	Faero Islands.
1	Espiritu Santo Cape.	4	Faeander, Norway.
2	Espiritu Santo Island.	5	Fair Cape, East Australia.
3	Espiritu Santo Islands.	6	Fair Foreland.
4	Esprit, St., Islands.	7	Fair Head.
5	Esprit, St., Shoal.	8	Fair Island, North Scotland.
6	Esquimault Harbor.	9	Fairfax Mount.
7	Esquimaux Islands.	4240	Fairlie Rock.
8	Essequibo River.	1	Fairway Rock, Indian Archipelago.
9	Essington, Port.	2	Fairway Rock, N. W. Coast America.
4200	Estaca Point.	3	Fairweather Cape, Patagonia.
1	Esteiras Cape.	4	Fairweather Mount, Patagonia.
2	Estepona.	5	Fairweather Cape, N. W. C'st Amer.
3	Estevan, San.	6	Fairweather M'nt, N. W. C'st Amer.
4	Estrella Bay.	7	Fairweather Island, United States.
5	*Etal Islands.	8	Fairy Island.
6	Etang Harbor.	9	Fairy Queen.
7	Etaples.	4250	Faith Island.
8	Etches, Port.	1	Faiti.
9	Eten Hill.	2	Faka' afo.
4210	Etna Mount.	3	Fakkeberg.
1	Etoile Island.	4	Falcon Cape, Maleares.
2	Eufemia, St.	5	Falcon Cape, Morocco.
3	Eunieh.	6	Falcone Cape.
4	Euphrates Shoal.	7	Falconera Island.
5	Europa Island.	8	Falkenberg.
6	Europa Point.	9	Falkland Islands, S. A.
7	Europe Shoal.	4260	Falkner's Island, United States.
8	Eurotas River.	1	Fall Island.
9	Eustatius, St.	2	Fallskar.
4220	Evangelists.	3	Falmouth Bank.
1	Evening Reef.	4	Falmouth Harbor.
2	Evéque Point.	5	Falmouth, England.
3	Exmouth.	6	Falmouth, Jamaica, W. I.
4	Exmouth Gulf.	7	Falmouth, Nova Scotia.
5	Exploring Islands.	8	Falmouth, Van Dieman's Land.
6	Exuma Island.	9	Falmouth, Virginia, U. S.
7	Eye Island.	4270	False Bank.
8	Eyemouth.	1	False Bay.
9	Eyries Mount.	2	False Cape, Africa.
4230	Faaborg, Denmark.	4273	False Cape, Cape Horn.

185

Nos.	FAL	Nos.	FER
4274	False Cape, Honduras.	4317	Farsey.
5	False Cape, Sierra Leone.	8	Fartak, Cape.
6	False Cape, St. Domingo.	9	Fastnet Rock.
7	False Hook, Entr'ce to N. York Bay.	4320	Fataka.
8	False Point.	1	Fatchiou Island.
9	Falster Island, Baltic.	2	Fatou-hiva.
4280	Falsterbo, St., Sweden.	3	Fatsizio.
1	Falulo Breakers.	4	Fatteye Tanjong.
2	Famagousta, Island of Cyprus.	5	Favignana.
3	Famine Port.	6	Favorite Cove.
4	Fanadik Island.	7	Favorite Shoal.
5	Fanafute Islands.	8	Fayal, Azores, North Atlantic.
6	Fanantara.	9	Fayeou, East Island.
7	Fanar Bournou.	4330	Fayeou, West Island.
8	Fanfoue Island.	1	Fead Islands.
9	Fannet Point.	2	Fear, Cape, U. S.
4290	Fanning Head.	3	February Point.
1	Fanning Island.	4	Fecamp, France.
2	Fanny Shoal.	5	Federal Point, North Carolina, U. S.
3	Fano Island.	6	Feejee Islands, South Pacific.
4	Fano Light.	7	Felalisse Island.
5	Fanoualei.	8	Felices Islands.
6	Farallon de Medinilla.	9	Felicudi Island.
7	Farallon de Torr.	4340	Felipe, San, Cays.
8	Farrallon Sucio.	1	Felix, Cape, Arctic Ocean.
9	Farrallones, N. W. Coast America.	2	Felix, Cape, Sumatra.
4300	Farrallones Point.	3	Felix Harbor.
1	Farewell, Cape, Greenland, Davis St.	4	Felix, St., Island.
2	Farewell, Cape, New Zealand.	5	Felix Isles, South Pacific.
3	Farewell Island.	6	Fell's Point, Baltimore Harbor, U. S.
4	Farilhoens.	7	Feluk Ras.
5	Farne Island.	8	Fenerive.
6	Faro Island, Mediterranean.	9	Fenwick's Island, U. S.
7	Faro Island, Sweden.	4350	Fer, Point au.
8	Faro, South Portugal.	1	Fermer Beet.
9	Faro, Sicily.	2	Fermo.
4310	Faro, Mount.	3	Fermosa Harbor.
1	Far-out Head.	4	Fernandina, Florida, U. S.
2	Farquhar, Cape.	5	Fernando Noronho, Brazil.
3	Farquhar Group.	6	Fernando Po.
4	Farquhar Islands.	7	Fernando, San.
5	Farroilep Islands.	8	Fernando, San, Point.
4316	Farsah, Ras.	4359	Fernando, St., Fo.

Nos.	FER	Nos.	FLA
4360	Ferrajo, Porto.	4403	Fiorentina.
1	Ferrana Point.	4	Fiorenza, St.
2	Ferrat, Cape.	5	Firando Port.
3	Ferrato, Cape.	6	Fire Island, Long Island, U. S.
4	Ferrier's Bank.	7	Fire Island Light.
5	Ferro, Cape.	8	First Point.
6	Ferro Island, Algiers, Africa.	9	First Point Island.
7	Ferro Island, Canaries, N. A.	4410	Fisher, Cape.
8	Ferrol, Spain.	1	Fisher's Island, Pescadores.
9	Ferrol Bay.	2	Fisher's Island, South Pacific.
4370	Ferrol Islands.	3	Fisher's Id., Long Island Sound, U.S.
1	Ferrolle Point.	4	Fisher's Island Sound.
2	Ferryland Head.	5	Fisher's Islands.
3	Ferry Reef.	6	Fisher's Rock.
4	Fetish Town.	7	Fisherman's Islands.
5	Fetlah Island.	8	Fisherman's Bank.
6	Fetou hougo.	9	Fisherman's Harbor.
7	Feys Island.	4420	Fisherman's Point.
8	Fianona.	1	Fisga Point.
9	Fidji Islands.	2	Fishing Rip, Nantucket, U. S.
4380	Fiddle Shoal.	3	Fishing-ship Harbor.
1	Fidonisi, Gulf of Odessa.	4	Fish Shoal.
2	Field Island.	5	Fitfiel Head.
3	Fife, Scotland.	6	Fitz Roy Island.
4	Fifeness.	7	Fitz Roy Rock.
5	Fifteen Point Church.	8	Fiume.
6	Figari, Cape.	9	Fiumicino.
7	Figo Island.	4430	Five-fathom Bank Light Vessel, U. S.
8	Figo, Mountain.	1	Five-fathom Shoal.
9	Figueira, Portugal.	2	Five-fingers.
4390	Figueira, Island.	3	Five Islands Harbor.
1	Figuier, Cape.	4	Five Mile Point, Connecticut, U. S.
2	Filly, England.	5	Fjäderäg, Guat Island.
3	Filsund.	6	Fladda huna.
4	Finale.	7	Fladstrand.
5	Fincham Island.	8	Flag Hill.
6	Finger Peak.	9	Flamborough Head, England.
7	Finisterre, Cape.	4440	Flamenco.
8	Finland, Russia.	1	Flamengo Bay.
9	Finland, Gulf of.	2	Flanders, Belgium.
4400	Finngrund.	3	Flamen Isles, Scotland.
1	Finocchiarola.	4	Flannen Isles.
4402	Finoso.	4445	Flat Bay.

Nos.	FLA	Nos.	FOR
4446	Flat River.	4489	Florida, Gulf of, U. S.
7	Flat Island, Australia.	4490	Florida Reefs, U. S.
8	Flat Island, Borneo.	1	Florida, Straits of, U. S.
9	Flat Island, Natunas.	2	Flotte, Cape, de.
4450	Flat Island, New Zealand.	3	Flushing, England.
1	Flat Island, Sumbaroa.	4	Flushing, Netherlands.
2	Flat Islands.	5	Fluted, Cape.
3	Flat Point, Borneo.	6	Fly Entrance.
4	Flat Point, Ceram.	7	Flying-fish Shoal.
5	Flat Point, New Zealand.	8	Flynn's Knoll, New York Bay.
6	Flat Point, Sumatra.	9	Foerder Light.
7	Flat Rocks.	4500	Fogo Island, Cape de Verdes.
8	Flatholm Island.	1	Fogo Island, East Africa.
9	Flattery, Cape, Australia.	2	Fogo Peak.
4460	Flattery, Cape, North America.	3	Fogo Harbor, Newfoundland.
1	Flaxman Island.	4	Foken Island.
2	Flechas Point.	5	Fokai Point.
3	Fleetwood, England.	6	Foleto Point.
4	Flekkefiord, Norway.	7	Folger Shoal.
5	Flekkero Island.	8	Folkstone, England.
6	Flemish Bank.	9	Folly Island, South Carolina, U. S.
7	Flensburg.	4510	Folly Island, Maine, U. S.
8	Flesh Point.	1	Fond du Lac.
9	Fleurieu, Cape.	2	Fond La Grange Bay.
4470	Fleur de Lis Harbor.	3	Fong Islands.
1	Flinders Bay.	4	Fonseca.
2	Flinders, Cape.	5	Foo-choo-foo, China.
3	Flinders Group.	6	Fool's Rock.
4	Flinders Island, Australia.	7	Fonoue Fous.
5	Flinders Entrance.	8	Fontane, Cape.
6	Flinders Island, Furneaux.	9	Foneland, North England.
7	Flinders Point.	4520	Foneland, South England.
8	Flinders Shoal.	1	Fortak.
9	Flint, North Wales.	2	Footoona.
4480	Flint Island.	3	Foguet Island.
1	Florence, Italy.	4	Foradada.
2	Flores Island, Azores.	5	Forbes Island.
3	Flores Island, Indian Archipelago.	6	Forcados River.
4	Flores Island, Rio de la Plata.	7	Ford, Cape.
5	Flores Head.	8	Foreland Islands.
6	Flores Sea, South Pacific.	9	Forenas.
7	Florida, Cape, U. S.	4530	Forester Island.
4488	Florida Coast, U. S.	4531	Forfana Island.

Nos.	FOR	Nos.	FRI
4532	Forked, Cape.	4575	Fort Point Cove.
3	Forked Harbor.	6	Fort Royal.
4	Forlorn Hope.	7	Fort St. Louis.
5	Formly Light, England.	8	Fort Taylor, Key West, U. S.
6	Formentera Island, Mediterranean.	9	Fortified Island.
7	Formenton, Cape.	4580	Fortune Bay.
8	Formica di Bura.	1	Fortune River.
9	Formiche.	2	Fouchee Harbor.
4540	Formigas.	3	Foul Hole.
1	Formigas Shoal.	4	Fowey, England.
2	Formosa, Cape.	5	Fowey Rocks, Florida Reefs, U. S.
3	Formosa Island.	6	Fowler's Bay, South Australia.
4	Formosa, Mt.	7	Fowling Point.
5	Formosa Channel.	8	Fox Harbor.
6	Fornelles Port.	9	Fox Island.
7	Forrest, Cape.	4590	Fox Island Thoroughfare.
8	Forrester's Island.	1	Fox Island Harbor.
9	Fort Amherst.	2	Fox Island Passage.
4550	Fort Amsterdam.	3	Fox Point.
1	Fort Cameron, U. S.	4	Foyle Lough, Ireland.
2	Fort Capron, Florida, U. S.	5	Franca Villa, Brazil.
3	Fort Carroll, Maryland, U. S.	6	Franca Villa, France.
4	Fort Caswell, U. S.	7	France.
5	Fort Diamond, New York Bay, U. S.	8	France, North Coast of.
6	Fort Ellsworth.	9	France, South Coast of.
7	Forteau Bay.	4600	Frank Island, Miss. Delta, U. S.
8	Fort Erie, Canada West.	1	François Bay.
9	Fort Fisher, N. Carolina, U. S.	2	Franklin Island, Maine.
4560	Fort George.	3	Franklin Point.
1	Fort Hamilton, New York Bay, U. S.	4	Franklin Sound.
2	Forth, Scotland.	5	Fredericia.
3	Forth Shoal.	6	Frederickshall, Norway.
4	Fort Jefferson, Dry Tortugas.	7	Frederickstadt, North Sea.
5	Fort Lafayette, New York Harbor.	8	Freeman's Bay.
6	Fort Lauderdale.	9	Freestone Point.
7	Fort Livingston.	4610	Frejus, France.
8	Fort Macon.	1	French Cove.
9	Fort Madison.	2	French Keys.
4570	Fort Mifflin, Delaware River, U. S.	3	French Reef.
1	Fort Monroe, Virginia, U. S.	4	Friar's Head.
2	Fort Moultrie, Charleston, S. C., U. S.	5	Friar's Point.
3	Fort Norfolk, Virginia, U. S.	6	Friendship Cape.
4574	Fort Pierce, Florida, U. S.	4617	Friendship Island.

Nos.	FRI	Nos.	GAL
4618	Friendly Islands.	4661	Gadd's Rock.
9	Frigate Island, Corgados.	2	Gadsden's Point.
4620	Frigate Island, Seychelles.	3	Gaeta.
1	Frindsbury Reef.	4	Gafrani Islands.
2	Frio Cape, Brazil.	5	Gag.
3	Frio Island.	6	Gagliano.
4	Frio Cape, West Africa.	7	Gagy.
5	Friesland, Netherlands.	8	Gaidaro Island.
6	Frisbees Ledge.	9	Gaidaro Rock.
7	Frying Pan Shoals, Coast N. C., U. S.	4670	Gajo, Port.
8	Froward Cape.	1	Galantry Point.
9	Frozen Cay.	2	Galapagos Islands.
4630	Fuego Island.	3	Galatro Mount.
1	Fuencaliente.	4	Galeota Point.
2	Fuengiro.	5	Galera Point, Chili.
3	Fuenterabia.	6	Galera Point, Colombia.
4	Fuerte Island.	7	Galera Point, Mindanao.
5	Fuerteventura, Canary Isles.	8	Galera Point, New Grenada.
6	Fuga.	9	Galera Point, Trinidad.
7	Fuglöe.	4680	Galera, Port.
8	Fuglöe Island.	1	Galeta Point.
9	Fuglöe Skerry.	2	Galiola Rock.
4640	Fuh-yaou Island.	3	Galion Island.
1	Fulanga Island.	4	Galita Island.
2	Fülehük Light.	5	Gallant, Port.
3	Funchal, Madeira.	6	Galle, Point de.
4	Funen.	7	Gallego Island.
5	Fundy, Bay of.	8	Gallegos Cape.
6	Funk Island.	9	Gallegos Port.
7	Furneaux Island.	4690	Gallen Head.
8	Furneaux Islands.	1	Galley Head.
9	Fury Harbor.	2	Galli Rocks.
4650	Fury Point.	3	Gallinara Island.
1	Gabbard.	4	Gallinas Point.
2	Gabia Mount.	5	Gallinas River.
3	Gabiniere.	6	Gallipoli, Naples.
4	Gable Cape.	7	Gallipoli, Turkey.
5	Gabo Island.	8	Gallo Cape.
6	Gaboon River.	9	Gallo, Cape di.
7	Gabriel, St., Cape.	4700	Galloper.
8	Gabriel, San, Island.	1	Galloway, Mull of.
9	Gad Amaze Reefs.	2	Galong Bay.
4660	Gadd Light.	4703	Galt Reef.

Nos.	GAL	Nos.	GEO
4704	Galveston Bay and Island.	4747	Gay Head.
5	Galvez Fort.	8	Gaya, Pulo, Borneo, N. E.
6	Galway.	9	Gaya, Pulo, Borneo, N. W.
7	Gamaley Cape.	4750	Geby.
8	Gambia River.	1	Gedé Mount.
9	Gambier Mount.	2	Geelvink Cape.
4710	Gambier's Islands, Australia.	3	Gefle.
1	Gambier's Islands, Low Archip'go.	4	Gellibrand Point.
2	Gambroon.	5	Gennargentu Mount.
3	Gamla Carleby.	6	Genoa.
4	Gammon Point.	7	Genoa Gulf.
5	Ganges' Bank.	8	Genoves, Port.
6	Ganges River.	9	Gente Hermosa.
7	Ganjam.	4760	Geographe Rock.
8	Gannet Island.	1	Geographe Shoals.
9	Gannet Islands.	2	Geology Point.
4720	Gannet Rock, Maine, U. S.	3	George and Abercrombie.
1	Gannet Rock, Nova Scotia.	4	George Cay.
2	Gantheaume.	5	George Fort, North America.
3	Gantheaume Point.	6	George Fort, Prince Edward's Isl'd.
4	Gap Island.	7	George Fort, Scotland.
5	Gap Rock.	8	George Island.
6	Garden Bay.	9	George IV., Port.
7	Garden Island.	4770	George, St., Brazil.
8	Gardner Bank.	1	George, St., Grenada.
9	Gardner Island, Galapagos.	2	George, St., Ionian Islands.
4730	Gardner Island, New Ireland.	3	George, St., Cape, Australia.
1	Gardner Island, North Pacific.	4	George, St., Cape, Cape Breton.
2	Gardner Island, South Pacific.	5	George, St., Cape, Indian Ocean.
3	Gardner Mount.	6	George, St., Cape, Newfoundland.
4	Garnot Island.	7	George, St., Cape, New Ireland.
5	Garoupe Cape.	8	George, St., Island, Azores.
6	Garret Denys.	9	George, St., Island, Florida, U. S.
7	Garrow Island.	4780	George, St., Island, India.
8	Garry Cape.	1	George, St., Island, Mozambique.
9	Gaspar Island and Strait.	2	George, St., Island, Alaska, U. S.
4740	Gaspar Rico.	3	George, St., Island, Solomon Isl'ds.
1	Gaspé Cape.	4	George, St., Point.
2	Gasses Pulo.	5	George, St., Shoals.
3	Gata Cape.	6	George, St., d'Arbor Island.
4	Gatcombe Head.	7	George Town, British Guiana.
5	Gato, Island del.	8	George Town, Malacca Strait.
4746	Gatto Cape.	4789	George Town, South Carolina, U. S.

Nos.	GEO	Nos.	GON
4790	George Town, Van Dieman's Land.	4833	Glasgow Port.
1	George Town Head.	4	Glass Island.
2	Georgia Island.	5	Glatton's Rock.
3	Georgia Straits.	6	Glenan Islands.
4	Georgia, United States.	7	Glenelg.
5	Georgio, St., Port.	8	Glennie Islands.
6	Gepirhuk.	9	Glorioso Island.
7	Geraka Point.	4840	Glosholm Light.
8	Gerftsius Island.	1	Gloucester Cape, Australia.
9	Geriah Point.	2	Gloucester Cape, New Britain.
4800	Germain, St.	3	Gloucester Cape, South Pacific.
1	Geronimo, San, Island.	4	Gloucester Cape, Tierra del Fuego.
2	Gerran.	5	Gloucester Island, Australia.
3	Gervaise Cape.	6	Gloucester Island, Low Archip'go.
4	Ghar, Ras el.	7	Gloucester Shoal.
5	Gharah Island.	8	Gloup Holm.
6	Ghelenjik.	9	Glover Reef.
7	Ghir Cape.	4850	Gluckstadt.
8	Giant's Causeway.	1	Goa.
9	Gianuti Island.	2	Goapnauth Point.
4810	Gibbon's Mount.	3	Goat Island, Massachusetts, U. S.
1	Gibraltar.	4	Goat Island, Philippines.
2	Giedserodde.	5	Goazacoalcos Bar.
3	Giens.	6	Gobeah Cape.
4	Gigantangan Island.	7	Gobernador Mount.
5	Gigantes Islands.	8	Godeim, Ras.
6	Giglio Island.	9	Godrevy Island.
7	Gilbert Archipelago.	4860	Goede Hoop Cape.
8	Gilbert Island.	1	Goedereede.
9	Gilibanta.	2	Gogah.
4820	Gilles sur Vie.	3	Golconda Reef.
1	Gillman Cape.	4	Gold Coast.
2	Gilolo.	5	Golden Mount.
3	Ginger Island.	6	Goldown's Bl. River.
4	Gioja.	7	Goleta.
5	Giorgio, St., Mount.	8	Gollonsier.
6	Giourapoulo.	9	Golovatcheff Cape.
7	Gipps' Reef.	4870	Golovine Bay.
8	Giraglia Island.	1	Gomany, Ras.
9	Girdleness.	2	Gomenitza.
4830	Girgenti.	3	Gomera.
1	Glarenza Cape.	4	Gomona.
4332	Glasgow.	4675	Gonaive Island.

192

Nos.	GON	Nos.	GRE
4876	Gonaives.	4919	Gozo Island.
7	Gonzales Head.	4920	Gozzo Island.
8	Good Hope Cape, Africa.	1	Grabusa.
9	Good Hope Cape, China.	2	Gracias à Dios Cape.
4880	Good Hope Island, Low Archip'go.	3	Graciosa, Azores.
1	Good Hope Island, South Pacific.	4	Graciosa, Madeiras.
2	Good Success Bay and Cape.	5	Grado.
3	Goodman Island.	6	Grafton Cape.
4	Goodwin.	7	Grafton Island.
5	Goold Island.	8	Graham Moore Cape.
6	Goonung Apee.	9	Graham's Shoal.
7	Goonung Api, Banda Islands.	4930	Grain Coast.
8	Goonung Api, Flores Sea.	1	Grainger Shoal.
9	Goonung Loose.	2	Grambousa Island.
4890	Goonung Marass.	3	Grampus Islands.
1	Goonung Tella River.	4	Gran Bajo de Esperanza.
2	Goose Cape, Newfoundland.	5	Gran Sasso d'Italian.
3	Goose Island, Connecticut, U. S.	6	Grand Duke Alexander.
4	Goose Island, Furneaux Islands.	7	Grand, Le, Cape.
5	Gooty River.	8	Grand Manan.
6	Goram Island.	9	Grand, Port, Mauritius.
7	Gorda Cay.	4940	Grand, Port, Skyros.
8	Gordewar Point.	1	Grande Island.
9	Gordon Reef.	2	Graude Mount.
4900	Gore Cape.	3	Grande Point.
1	Gore Point.	4	Grane.
2	Gore, Port.	5	Grange.
3	Goree Island.	6	Granitola Cape.
4	Goreloy Island.	7	Grant Island and Point.
5	Gorgona Island, Mediterranean.	8	Granville.
6	Gorgona Island, Peru.	9	Grape Cay.
7	Goro.	4950	Grasholm Island.
8	Goro Island.	1	Grave, Pointe de.
9	Gothland.	2	Gravelines.
4910	Gottenburg.	3	Gravois Point.
1	Gotto Islands.	4	Gray's Harbor.
2	Gottaka Sando.	5	Great Fish Bay.
3	Gouap Island.	6	Great Fish Point and River.
4	Gough's Island.	7	Great Island, South Pacific.
5	Goulburn Islands.	8	Great Island, Spitzbergen.
6	Goulding Cay.	9	Greece.
7	Govan's, St., Head.	4960	Green Cape.
4918	Gower Island.	4961	Green Cay.

Nos.	GRE	Nos.	GUI
4962	Green Island, Australia.	5005	Gros, Cape.
3	Green Island, Calarnianes.	6	Grosnez, Cape.
4	Green Island, Gulf of St. Lawrence.	7	Grosso, Cape.
5	Green Island, Hudson's Straits.	8	Grosvenor Shoal.
6	Green Island, Nova Scotia.	9	Grottamare.
7	Green Point.	5010	Grouin du Cou.
8	Greenhill Island.	1	Gruesco Point.
9	Greenhithe.	2	Guadalcanar Island.
4970	Greenland.	3	Guadalupe Island.
1	Greenly Islands and Mountain.	4	Guadeloupe.
2	Greenock.	5	Guadiana River.
3	Greenwich.	6	Guahan Island.
4	Grego, Cape.	7	Guaianeco Islands.
5	Gregory, St., Cape.	8	Guajaba Island.
6	Greig, Cape.	9	Guam Island.
7	Greig Island.	5020	Guanape Hill.
8	Greig Shoal.	1	Guanica Point.
9	Grekova Rock.	2	Guantanamo.
4980	Grenada.	3	Guarachina Point.
1	Grenadeer Huen.	4	Guarapari.
2	Grenville, Cape.	5	Guaratiba Point.
3	Grenville Island.	6	Guaratuba River.
4	Grenville Point.	7	Guardafui, Cape.
5	Greville, Cape.	8	Guardia Island.
6	Grey, Cape.	9	Guardiani Island.
7	Grey Hook.	5030	Guardias Viejas.
8	Grey Town,	1	Guarmey Bay.
9	Gribbin's Head.	2	Guascama Point.
4990	Gribœrne.	3	Guasco, Port.
1	Griefswaldoe.	4	Guase Island.
2	Griffin Rocks.	5	Guatemala.
3	Griffith Island.	6	Guatulco, Port.
4	Grigan Island.	7	Guayama River.
5	Grim, Cape.	8	Guayaquil.
6	Grimness Head.	9	Guaymas.
7	Grimsey Island.	5040	Guayra, La.
8	Grisnez, Cape.	1	Gueguen River.
9	Grivizza Island.	2	Guei Chew Island.
5000	Groais Island.	3	Guerande.
1	Groene Islands.	4	Guerite Rock.
2	Groix, Island de.	5	Guernsey.
3	Grönskäi Light.	6	Guguan Island.
5004	Groote Eylandt.	5047	Guia, Point de.

Nos.	GUI	Nos.	HAM
5048	Guiana.	5091	Hague, Netherlands.
9	Guilder Rocks.	2	Hague, Cape la.
5050	Guinapac Rocks.	3	Ha Ha.
1	Guinchos Cay.	4	Ha Ha Bay.
2	Guinea, Gulf of.	5	Ha Ha Harbor.
3	Gull Island.	6	Hai-ling-shan Island.
4	Gull Rock.	7	Hai-mun.
5	Gull Stream.	8	Hainan Head, China.
6	Gun Cay.	9	Hainan Island.
7	Gung Island.	5100	Haipong Island.
8	Gunner's Islands.	1	Halcyon Island.
9	Gurupi, Cape.	2	Haleimah, Ras.
5060	Gut of Canso.	3	Hain's Point.
1	Gutzlaff Islands.	4	Hakodadi, Japan.
2	Guy Rock.	5	Haley's Cove.
3	Guyaquil.	6	Half Island Cove.
4	Gwa.	7	Half Moon Cay.
5	Gwadel, Cape.	8	Half Moon Shoal.
6	Gwetter.	9	Half Moon Reef, Texas, U. S.
7	Haano Island.	5110	Half Port Bay.
8	Haarlem, Netherlands.	1	Halfway Island.
9	Habeeba Islands.	2	Halfway Reef.
5070	Habile, Mount.	3	Halfway Rock.
1	Habitant's Bay.	4	Halibut Point.
2	Hacha.	5	Halibut Island.
3	Hack Cove.	6	Halgan Island.
4	Haddock Harbor.	7	Halifax, Nova Scotia.
5	Hadlock Harbor.	8	Halifax Bay, East Australia.
6	Hackluyt's Harbor.	9	Haliguen Port.
7	Hackluyt's Islands.	5120	Hall, Cape.
8	Had, Ras al.	1	Hall Island, Gilbert Archipelago.
9	Haddington, Mount.	2	Hall Island, Hudson's Straits.
5080	Haddington, Port.	3	Hall Point.
1	Hadid, Ras.	4	Hall, Sir J., Group.
2	Hae Chow.	5	Hallands Waderö.
3	Haerlem Islands.	6	Hallowell, Cape.
4	Hae-tan Island.	7	Halmstadt, Sweden.
5	Hafoon, Ras.	8	Halsey Island.
6	Hafringi.	9	Hamburg.
7	Hagemeister Island, Low Archep'go.	5130	Hammamet.
8	Hagemeister Island, N. W. America.	1	Hammerfest.
9	Hag's Head.	2	Hamilton, Canada West, N. A.
5090	Hagget's Cove.	5133	Hammond's Island.

194

Nos.	HAM	Nos.	HAW
5134	Hammond, Cape.	5176	Harp Island, New Zealand.
5	Hampton, Fort.	7	Harpswell Sound, Maine, U. S.
6	Hampton, Virginia, U. S.	8	Harrington.
7	Hampton Bar, Virginia.	9	Harrison Cape.
8	Hampton Roads, Virginia.	5180	Harshall's Nist.
9	Hamrah, Ras al.	1	Hart Island.
5140	Hanalae Bay.	2	Hartford, Connecticut, U. S.
1	Handa Island.	3	Hartland Point.
2	Handkerchief Sh'l, Vineyard Sound, United States.	4	Hartlepool, England.
		5	Hartwell Reef.
3	Hangklip Cape.	6	Haruku Island.
4	Hangman Hill.	7	Harvey Reefs.
5	Hango, Gulf of Finland.	8	Harvey Rocks.
6	Hannah Shoal.	9	Harvey's Islands.
7	Hano Island.	5190	Harwich.
8	Hanover, Germany.	1	Hasborough.
9	Hanover Island.	2	Haski Island.
5150	Hanse Towns, Germany.	3	Hastings Island.
1	Hantsholmen, Ireland.	4	Hastings Harbor.
2	Hants' Harbor.	5	Hastings Rock.
3	Hapaee Islands.	6	Hatchett's Reef.
4	Haradskar.	7	Hat Island.
5	Harbinger Rocks.	8	Hat Cay.
6	Harbor, Grace, Newfoundland.	9	Hatteras Cape, N. Carolina, U. S.
7	Harbor Island.	5200	Hatteras Cove.
8	Harbor of Mercy.	1	Hatteras Inlet.
9	Harburg, Hanover.	2	Hatton's Headland.
5160	Harding's Rock, Massachus'ts, U. S.	3	Haulbowline Island.
1	Hardy Point.	4	Haul-off Rock.
2	Hardy Port.	5	Hausaez Islands.
3	Hardy, Sir C., Islands, Australia.	6	Haute Island, Maine, U. S.
4	Hardy, Sir C., Islands, S. Pacific.	7	Haute Island, New Brunswick.
5	Hare Bay.	8	Hautfond.
6	Hare Island.	9	Hautfond Shoals.
7	Hare Harbor.	5210	Havaii.
8	Hare Ears Point.	1	Havana, Cuba.
9	Hargose.	2	Hav-flue.
5170	Haring's Island.	3	Havre, Cape le.
1	Harlingen, Netherlands.	4	Havre Rock.
2	Harmeel Island.	5	Havre de Grace, Maryland, U. S.
3	Harnish Island.	6	Hawaii, Sandwich Islands.
4	Haro Cape.	7	Hawan Road.
5175	Harp Island, Formosa.	5218	Hawke's Nest.

Nos.	HAW	Nos.	HER
5219	Hawke Bay, Labrador.	5261	Helena, St., Bay.
5220	Hawke's Bay, New Zealand.	2	Helena, St., Point.
1	Hawke Channel, Florida, U. S.	3	Helgoland, North Sea.
2	Hawkesbury Island.	4	Heliers, St.
3	Hawkin's Reef.	5	Hell Gate, Long Island Sound, U. S.
4	Hawlool.	6	Hellyer Rocks.
5	Hay Cape, Australia.	7	Helsingborg, Sweden.
6	Hay Cape, Baffin's Bay.	8	Helsingfors, Russia.
7	Haycock Island, Indian Archip'go.	9	Helsingkall.
8	Haycock Island, Philippines.	5270	Helvetius Cape.
9	Haycock Island, Xulla Islands. .	1	Helvoetsluys, Netherlands.
5230	Haycock Hill.	2	Helwick Head.
1	Hayle, England.	3	Hemos Island.
2	Hayti, W. I.	4	Hempstead, Long Island, U. S.
3	Haytien Cape.	5	Hen and Chickens, Delaware Entrance, U. S.
4	Hazard's Point.		
5	Hazy Island.	6	Hender Island.
6	Head Harbor.	7	Henderville Island.
7	Head Harbor, Maine, U. S.	8	Henderson Island, Maine, U. S.
8	Head of the Great Australian Bight.	9	Heneagua Island.
9	Head of the Passes, Mississippi Riv., United States.	5280	Henley Island.
		1	Henley Ledges.
5240	Health Islands.	2	Henne Bay.
1	Heart's Content Harbor.	3	Henlopen Cape, United States.
2	Heath Point.	4	Henrietta Mar, Cape.
3	Heaux de Brehat.	5	Henry Cape, United States.
4	Heawandoo Island.	6	Henry Cape, Anticosti.
5	Heawandoo Island, Pholo.	7	Henry Cape, Louisiades.
6	Hebrides, West of Scotland.	8	Henry Cape, Queen Charlotte's I.
7	Heckla Mount.	9	Henry Port.
8	Hedge Fence, Massachusetts, U. S.	5290	Henslow Cape.
9	Hedge Hog Mount.	1	Henuaka.
5250	Heemskerk Mount.	2	Heraclea, Greek Archipelago.
1	Hegadis.	3	Heraclia Island.
2	Heiden Island.	4	Heraiki.
3	Heilhornet.	5	Herbert Island.
4	Hekueru.	6	Hereford, New Jersey, U. S.
5	Hela Light.	7	Hereheretua.
6	Hela Point, Prussia.	8	Herekino Road.
7	Helanea Island.	9	Heretua.
8	Helder, Netherlands.	5300	Hergests Rocks.
9	Helen Shoal.	1	Herm Island.
5260	Helena, St.	5302	Herins Bay.

Nos.	HER	Nos.	HOG
5303	Hermanos Island.	5346	Hillsborough Bay, Prince Edw'd's Id.
4	Hermit Island.	7	Hillsborough Inlet, Florida.
5	Hermitage Bay.	8	Hillsborough, Cape.
6	Hermite Island.	9	Hilo, Hawaiian Islands.
7	Hermogenes Island.	5350	Hilongos Point.
8	Hermonist Island.	1	Hilton Head, South Carolina, U. S.
9	Hernöklubb.	2	Hinchinbroke Rocks.
5310	Hernosand.	3	Hind Island.
1	Herpin Rock.	4	Hioga, Japan.
2	Herradura Point.	5	Hippa Island.
3	Herradura de Coquimbo.	6	Hippolite Rock.
4	Herschel, Cape.	7	Hirshan Islands.
5	Herschel Island.	8	Hirtsholmen.
6	Herring Cove, Massachusetts, U. S.	9	Hitchinbroke, Cape, Cape Breton Id.
7	Herring Cove, Nova Scotia.	5360	Hitchinbroke, Cape, N.W. Coast Am.
8	Herring Gut Harbor, Maine.	1	Hitchinbroke Island.
9	Herring Island.	2	Hispaniola.
5320	Herring Neck Harbor.	3	Hiva-Oa.
1	Hesselo, Denmark.	4	Hoa.
2	Heve, Cape.	5	Hoa-pin-su Island.
3	Heyskar Islands.	6	Hobart Town, Van Diemen's Land.
4	Heyst.	7	Hobbies.
5	Hinou.	8	Hoborg, Baltic.
6	Hibbs Point.	9	Hoe, Point du.
7	Hibernia Shoal.	5370	Hocky Island.
8	Hicaron Island.	1	Hodeidah.
9	Hickman's Harbor.	2	Hoedic Island.
5330	Hidden Harbor.	3	Hodgkin's Cove.
1	Hidden Island.	4	Hog Bay.
2	Hieres Islands, Mediterranean.	5	Hog Channel.
3	Hierro.	6	Hog Island, Bay of Boni.
4	High Brothers.	7	Hog Island, Indian Ocean.
5	High Clay Peak.	8	Hog Island, Java.
6	High Island, Buccaneers.	9	Hog Island, Sumatra.
7	High Island, Hudson Strait.	5380	Hog Islands.
8	High Island, Natunas.	1	Hog Point.
9	High Island, New Zealand.	2	Hog Nose.
5340	High Island, South Pacific.	3	Hog Fish Cut.
1	Highland Bay.	4	Hog Inlet.
2	Highlands of Navesink, U. S.	5	Hog Island Harbor, Mass., U. S.
3	Higuey.	6	Hog Island, Virginia, U. S.
4	Higgin's Point.	7	Hogland, Virginia, U. S.
5345	Hilliard's Harbor.	5388	Hogland, Gulf of Finland.

Nos.	HOG	Nos.	HOR
5389	Hog Id. Light House, Virginia, U. S.	5432	Hong Kong China.
5390	Hogan Island.	3	Honga-Hapai.
1	Hogoleu.	4	Honolulu, Sandwich Islands.
2	Hogsten.	5	Hood, Cape.
3	Hogsties, Bahamas.	6	Hood Island, Galapagos.
4	Hogsty Reef.	7	Hood Island, Low Archipelago.
5	Hoibraken.	8	Hood Island, Marquesas.
6	Hoievarde.	9	Hood Island Point, Australia.
7	Hokianga Harbor.	5440	Hood Island Point, Kafferland.
8	Holandes Channel.	1	Hood Port.
9	Holandes Point.	2	Hoo-e-tou Point.
5400	Holbeck, Denmark.	3	Hoogly, British India.
1	Holborne Island.	4	Hook Light, Ireland.
2	Holburn Head.	5	Hook Sound.
3	Holderness Island.	6	Hooper's Straits, Chesap'ke Bay, U. S.
4	Hole in the Wall, Bahamas.	7	Hooping Harbor.
5	Hollow's Bird Island.	8	Hope, Cape.
6	Holland.	9	Hope Island, North Pacific.
7	Holland Bank.	5450	Hope Island, South Pacific.
8	Holland Cove.	1	Hope Island, Spitzbergen.
9	Holland Harbor.	2	Hope Harbor.
5410	Holland Point.	3	Hope Point.
1	Holland's Island, Maryland, U. S.	4	Hope, West Island.
2	Holland's Straits.	5	Hope's Adventure, Cape.
3	Hollin's Harbor, Nova Scotia.	6	Hopedale.
4	Holmes' Harbor.	7	Hopper Island.
5	Holmes' Hole, Vineyard Sound.	8	Horaine Rock.
6	Holsteinburg.	9	Horcon Bay.
7	Holt Island.	5460	Hor Hadeea.
8	Holuthuria Shoals.	1	Hormigas Rocks.
9	Holy Island, England.	2	Horn, Cape.
5420	Holyhead, North Wales.	3	Horn Head.
1	Holmo Gadd, Gulf of Bothnia.	4	Horn Island.
2	Holywood Harbor.	5	Horn Islands.
3	Home Islands.	6	Horn, Mount.
4	Home Island Reef.	7	Horn Point.
5	Honda River.	8	Horne Islands.
6	Honden Island.	9	Horne's Neck.
7	Honduras.	5470	Horned Hill.
8	Honduras, Bay of.	1	Horner Peak.
9	Honduras, Cape.	2	Horno's Island.
5430	Hone-Cope, Harbor.	3	Hornos.
5431	Honfleur, France.	5474	Hornsudde.

Nos.	HOR	Nos.	HUN
5475	Horsburgh Atoll.	5518	Huanchaco Road.
6	Horsburgh, Cape.	9	Huasco, Chili.
7	Horsburgh Island.	5520	Hubbah, Ras el.
8	Horse Hammock.	1	Hubert's Cove.
9	Horsehead Shoals.	2	Huddart's Shoal.
5480	Horse Island.	3	Huddiksvall.
1	Horse Shoe, Nova Scotia.	4	Hudson Bay.
2	Horse Shoe Point.	5	Hudson Island.
3	Horse Shoe Reef, Barrier Reefs.	6	Hudson Island.
4	Horse Shoe Reef, Feejee Islands.	7	Hudson River, United States.
5	Horta.	8	Hudson's Straits.
6	Horton, Nova Scotia.	9	Huechucucuy Head.
7	Hospital Key.	5530	Hue Fo River.
8	Hospital Rock.	1	Hue Harbor, Cochin China.
9	Hotham Cape, Arctic Ocean.	2	Huero Island.
5490	Hotham Cape, Australia.	3	Hughlett's Point.
1	Houa-Houa Bay.	4	Hull, England.
2	Houa-Houna.	5	Hull Island.
3	Hougue, La.	6	Hull Islands.
4	House Harbor.	7	Hull's Cove, Maine, U. S.
5	Hout Point.	8	Humber, England.
6	Houtjes Bay.	9	Humber River.
7	Houtman Rocks.	5540	Humboldt Bay, California, U. S.
8	How Harbor.	1	Hummock Island, Furneaux Is.
9	Howakel Island.	2	Hummock Island, Mela-co-si-mah Is.
5500	Howard Shoal.	3	Hummock Island, Philippines.
1	Howe, Lord, Island.	4	Humm of Kenn.
2	Howe, Lord, Islands.	5	Humphrey Island, Low Archip'go.
3	Howe Island.	6	Humphrey Island, South Pacific.
4	Howe Cape, S. W. Australia.	7	Hune, Cape La.
5	Howe Cape, S. E. Australia.	8	Hungary.
6	Howell's Point.	9	Hungry Hill.
7	Howick's Group.	5550	Hunger's Creek.
8	Howth Baily Light.	1	Hunstanton Point, England.
9	Howtha.	2	Hunter Cape.
5510	Hoyambre Cape.	3	Hunter Island, Marshall Islands.
1	Hoy Island, Scotland.	4	Hunter Island, South Pacific.
2	Hoylake, England.	5	Hunter Island, Van Dieman's Land.
3	Huacanec Island.	6	Hunter Port, East Australia.
4	Huacho Bay, Peru.	7	Hunter Port, South Pacific.
5	Huafo Island.	8	Hunter & Albatross Islands.
6	Huaheine Island.	9	Hunter's Reef.
5517	Huamblin Island.	5560	Hunting Creek.

Nos.	HUN	Nos.	INN
5561	Hunting Islands, S. Carolina, U. S.	5604	Ildefonso Islands, Tierra del Fuego.
2	Huntington Harb., Long Isl'nd, U. S.	5	Ildefonso, St., Cape.
3	Huon Islands.	6	Ilfracombe.
4	Huon River.	7	Ilha das Rollas.
5	Hurd Island, East Africa.	8	Ilha Grande Bay.
6	Hurd Island, South Pacific.	9	Ilheo, d'.
7	Hurm Lake.	5610	Illack Island.
8	Hurricane Bay.	1	Illuluck.
9	Hurst.	2	Imalaguan.
5570	Hussey Sound.	3	Imbros.
1	Hutchinson Island.	4	Immor Island.
2	Hvalöe.	5	Imperieuse Shoal.
3	Hvidingsöe, Norway.	6	Inaccessible Islands, New Orkneys.
4	Hwang-ching-tao Island.	7	Inaccessible Islands, S. Atlantic.
5	Hyannis, Massachusetts, U. S.	8	Inagua Islands.
6	Hydra, Greece.	9	I-nah-Kwoh.
7	Hydra Rock.	5620	Inch Keith.
8	Hypocrite Passage.	1	Indefatigable Island.
9	Iana River.	2	Independence Island.
5580	Ianthe Shoal.	3	Inderabia Island.
1	Ibayat Island.	4	India.
2	Ibbetson Cape.	5	Indian Ocean.
3	Ibbetson Islands.	6	Indian Head, Australia.
4	Ibo Island.	7	Indian Head, Buenos Ayres.
5	Ibugos.	8	Indian River.
6	Icacos Point, Cuba.	9	Indigirka River.
7	Icacos Point, Honduras.	5630	Indio Point.
8	Icacos Point, Trinidad.	1	Indispensable Reef.
9	Ice Sound.	2	Indjeh Boornou Cape.
5590	Iceland.	3	Indramayu Point.
1	Ickulaka Reef.	4	Indrapour Point.
2	Icy Cape.	5	Indus River.
3	Ida Mount, Asia Minor.	6	Ine Islands.
4	Ida Mount, Candia.	7	Infanta Cape.
5	Idjeng Mount.	8	Infiernillo Rock.
6	Ifelouk Islands.	9	Inhambane Bay.
7	Igloolik Island.	5640	Inhampura River.
8	Ignacio, St., Island and Point.	1	Iniue.
9	Iguape River.	2	Inman Cape.
5600	Ihrum Cap.	3	Innis Murray.
1	Ikourangi Mount.	4	Innisgort.
2	Ilchester Shoal.	5	Innishowen Head.
5603	Ildefonso Islands, California.	5646	Innistrahal.

Nos.	INS	Nos.	JAQ
5647	Inscription, Cape.	5690	Iujah Point.
8	Inspection Hill.	1	Ives, St.
9	Inverarity Shoal.	2	Iviza.
5650	Inverness.	3	Ivory Coast.
1	Investigator Reefs.	4	Jabo, Cape.
2	Inyack, Cape.	5	Jaboug Point.
3	Ioanni Point.	6	Jacinto, Port San.
4	Iona Island.	7	Jackee Pulo.
5	Ionian Islands.	8	Jackson's Arm.
6	Iphigenia Rocks.	9	Jackson Port.
7	Ipsera.	5700	Jackson Point.
8	Ipswich Bay.	1	Jackson Shoal.
9	Iquique.	2	Jacksonville, Florida.
5660	Ireland.	3	Jack Taylor's Reef.
1	Irene, Cape.	4	Jacmel.
2	Irish Rock.	5	Jacob's Harbor Head.
3	Irois Fort.	6	Jacquemel.
4	Iron, Cape.	7	Jacquinot Island.
5	Irvine.	8	Jacquinot Point.
6	Isaac, Gt., Rock.	9	Jaffa, Joppa, Palestine.
7	Isabel, Cape.	5710	Jaffrabad, India.
8	Isabel Island, California.	1	Jaffatin, Great, Island.
9	Isabel Island, Solomon Islands.	2	Jagenos Island.
5670	Isabella, Cape.	3	Jageson's Island.
1	Isabelle Point.	4	Jago, St., Cuba.
2	Ischia Island.	5	Jagua Bay.
3	Isbailoh Rocks.	6	Jaguribe River.
4	Isla, Cape.	7	Jahleel Point.
5	Islamabad River.	8	Jamaica, Antilles.
6	Islay.	9	James Bay.
7	Isle of Man.	5720	James Island.
8	Isle of Wight.	1	James River, U. S.
9	Isleta.	2	James, St., Cape, Cochin China.
5680	Ismid.	3	James, St., Cape, Queen Charlotte Id.
1	Isolette, Cape.	4	Janeiro, Rio de, Brazil.
2	Istapa.	5	Jane's Island.
3	Itabayana Mountains.	6	Jane's Table Land.
4	Itacolomi Point.	7	Janena Edjaya River.
5	Italy.	8	Jan Mayen Island.
6	Itapacoroya Point.	9	Janvrin Harbor.
7	Ithaca.	5730	Janvrin Shoal.
8	Itourup Island.	1	Japan.
5689	Itsoumo, Cape.	5732	Jaquemel, Cape, Hayti.

Nos.	JAQ	Nos.	JOH
5733	Jaquet Bank.	5776	Jericoacoara.
4	Jara Head.	7	Jermain, Cape.
5	Jara Island.	8	Jernain Island.
6	Jaragua River.	9	Jerningham Point.
7	Jardinellos.	5780	Jersey, Channel Islands.
8	Jardines, Cuba.	1	Jershöft.
9	Jardines, North Pacific.	2	Jerusalem, Palestine.
5740	Jarvis Island.	3	Jervis Bay, New South Wales.
1	Jask, Cape.	4	Jervis, Cape.
2	Jason Islands.	5	Jervis Island.
3	Jatibnica River.	6	Jesso Island.
4	Jaulo Island.	7	Jesus Maria, Island.
5	Java.	8	Jestico Harbor.
6	Java Head.	9	Jewnee, Ras.
7	Java Sea.	5790	Jibbel Dthubbah.
8	Javinal Point.	1	Jibsh Ras.
9	Jayua Island.	2	Jidda, Jeddah, Arabia.
5750	Jean Ravel Road.	3	Jigat Point.
1	Jean, St., de Luz.	4	Jijghinsk Island, Okchotsk Sea.
2	Jebel Antar.	5	Jintotolo Island.
3	Jebel Hadid.	6	Jintotolo Point.
4	Jebel Kinkeri.	7	Joao, St., Island.
5	Jebel Sarsar.	8	Joano.
6	Jebel Searjan.	9	Joatinga Point.
7	Jebel Soubah.	5800	Jobano.
8	Jebel Teer.	1	Jobie Island.
9	Jebel Thelj.	2	Joe Flogger Shoal.
5760	Jebel W. Lehuma.	3	Joe's Hole.
1	Jebel Zawan.	4	Johanna.
2	Jebel Zoogur Island.	5	Johanna, Island, Mozambique Chan.
3	Jeddah (Jidda), Arabia.	6	John Baptist Fort.
4	Jedderens Reef.	7	John's Bay.
5	Jeddo (Yeddo), Japan.	8	John Point.
6	Jedore Harbor.	9	John Begg Rock.
7	Jeffrey's Bank.	5810	John de Nova Island.
8	Jegogan Harbor.	1	John, St., Cape, Africa.
9	Jei, Ras.	2	John, St., Cape, Candia.
5770	Jenichesk.	3	John, St., Cape, Newfoundland.
1	Jekyl Island.	4	John, St., Cape, Terra del Fuego.
2	Jerabou.	5	John, St., Point.
3	Jerba Island.	6	John's, St., Antigua, W. I.
4	Jerbourg.	7	John's, St., New Brunswick.
5775	Jeremie.	5818	John's, St., Newfoundland.

Nos.	JOH	Nos.	KAD
5819	John's, St., Highland, W. Coast India.	5861	Juan, St., Bay, Venezuela.
5820	John's, St., Island, Greece.	2	Juan, St., Mount.
1	John's, St., Island, Red Sea.	3	Juan, St., Port.
2	John's, St., Island, South Pacific.	4	Juan, Cape.
3	John's, St., Island, Virgin Isles.	5	Juan, St., da Nova.
4	John's, St., Point.	6	Juan, San, Island.
5	John's, St., River, Florida.	7	Juan, San, Port.
6	John's, St., River, Gulf St. Lawrence.	8	Juan de Guia, Cape.
7	John's, St., River, Kafferland.	9	Juan de Nicaragua, Central America.
8	John's, St., River, Pega.	5870	Juan Baptiste Island.
9	Johnson Harbor.	1	Juanica.
5830	Johnson Reef.	2	Juba River, East Africa.
1	Joinville Island.	3	Jubal Island.
2	Jolbos Island.	4	Juby, Cape.
3	Jolly Island.	5	Judge and Apostle Rocks.
4	Jolvos Island.	6	Judge Rocks.
5	Jomalie Island.	7	Judge and Clerk.
6	Jomfrueland.	8	Judgment Rock.
7	Jomonjol Island.	9	Judith Point, Rhode Island, U. S.
8	Jonas, St., Island.	5880	Jugurnaut.
9	Jones' Harbor.	1	Jui Mountain.
5840	Jones' Island.	2	Julian Mountain.
1	Jones' Point, Potomac River, U. S.	3	Julian, St.
2	Jootsima.	4	Julian, St., Island.
3	Jordan's Point, James River, Va., U.S.	5	Julian, St., Mountain.
4	Jose, St., Island.	6	Julian, St., Port.
5	Jose, San.	7	Juliana Bay.
6	Jose, San, Island.	8	Julie.
7	Josef Pobre Point.	9	Julo Island.
8	Josef, San, Port.	5890	Junkseilon, Indian Ocean.
9	Joseph, St., Islands.	1	Jupiter Inlet, Florida, U. S.
5850	Joseph, St., Bay.	2	Jupiter Inlet L. H., Florida, U. S.
1	Jouvency Island.	3	Jura Island.
2	Joujou River.	4	Jurien Island.
3	Jourimin Islands.	5	Jururu Port.
4	Joyi.	6	Jussari.
5	Juan de Fuca Straits, N. W. Coast America.	7	Just au Corps.
		8	Jutland, Denmark.
6	Juan del Pozo.	9	Jykill Island, Georgia, U. S.
7	Juan Fernandez Islands.	5900	Kabes.
8	Juan d'Olio.	1	Kabruang.
9	Juan Louis Key.	2	Kadahboo Bluff.
5860	Juan, St., Bay, California.	5903	Kadija.

Nos.	KAE	Nos.	KAY
5904	Kae-choo Bank.	5947	Kantavu.
5	Kaffa.	8	Kao Island.
6	Kafferland.	9	Kapenouare Island.
7	Kagul, Cape.	5950	Karababa.
8	Kaholawe.	1	Karábournú, Cape, Asia Minor.
9	Kahowawa.	2	Karábournú, Cape, Karaman.
5910	Kaiagatch.	3	Karábournú, Cape, Turkey.
1	Kaifa.	4	Karadash Bournou, Cape.
2	Kaipara Harbor.	5	Karaghinsky Island.
3	Kakava Island.	6	Karakakoa Bay.
4	Kakulimah Mountain.	7	Karakita.
5	Kalaeko.	8	Karamania.
6	Kalampunian Island.	9	Karang Mountain.
7	Kalautan River.	5960	Karang Takat.
8	Kalao.	1	Karavi Island.
9	Kalemaas.	2	Karawang Point.
5920	Kalgalaksha.	3	Karek Island.
1	Kaliagri, Cape.	4	Kari-kari.
2	Kalibia.	5	Karkena Islands.
3	Kalingal Island.	6	Karki.
4	Kalkoon Islands.	7	Karo Island.
5	Kalla Rock.	8	Kastrosikia.
6	Kallbaden.	9	Kastro Tornese.
7	Kalmar.	5970	Katafanga Island.
8	Kalomata.	1	Katakolo, Cape.
9	Kaloyeri Rocks.	2	Katang Rock.
5930	Kalpeni Islands.	3	Katchall Island.
1	Kalymno.	4	Kater, Cape.
2	Kamasoun Island.	5	Kater Island.
3	Kambara Island.	6	Ka-tih-neaou Island.
4	Kame, Cape.	7	Katiu.
5	Kamoudi Pulo.	8	Katomun, Cape.
6	Kampong Outa.	9	Kattaunie, Ras.
7	Kamtchaksky, Cape.	5980	Kattaro.
8	Kanaga Island.	1	Kattou, Ras.
9	Kanais, Ras al.	2	Katwyk.
5940	Kanary, Grand.	3	Kauai.
1	Kandabou Island.	4	Kaula.
2	Kandalaksha.	5	Kavahi Island.
3	Kangaroo Island.	6	Kaven Island.
4	Kangelang.	7	Kawa Kawa.
5	Kanin Noss, Cape.	8	Kawia Harbor.
5946	Kanneeoongan Point.	5989	Kayes Island.

Nos.	KAZ	Nos.	KIN
5990	Kazantip Cape.	6033	Ketoy Island.
1	Keatlama.	4	Keu-sau Mount.
2	Keats Point.	5	Keyn Island.
3	Keats Port.	6	Keyser's Peak.
4	Kedgeree.	7	Khabaroff Cape.
5	Keelah.	8	Khania.
6	Keeling Islands.	9	Kharamamoukotan Island.
7	Keenapoussan Island.	6040	Khelb, Ras.
8	Keerweer Cape.	1	Khelidonia Islands.
9	Keffing, Great, Island.	2	Kherson.
6000	Kega Point.	3	Khersones Cape.
1	Keiskama River.	4	Khina Island.
2	Keith's Reef.	5	Khitouk Cape.
3	Kejsarsklubb.	6	Khore Jeramah.
4	Kekik Island.	7	Khubber Island.
5	Kelang.	8	Khyle, Ras al.
6	Kelly Harbor.	9	Khynzyr Cape.
7	Kelung Island and Harbor.	6050	Ki Islands.
8	Kema.	1	Kia.
9	Kemin Island.	2	Kiahow Harbor.
6010	Kemmi.	3	Kiama, Port.
1	Kenain.	4	Kibatch Point.
2	Kendall Cape.	5	Kibliyah Island.
3	Kendarie Bay.	6	Kidnappers Cape.
4	Kendrick Island.	7	Ki-Doulan.
5	Kenmare.	8	Kiel.
6	Kenn Island.	9	Kiephali Cape.
7	Kenn Reef.	6060	Kieri Cape.
8	Kennedy Island.	1	Kikiay Island.
9	Kent Islands.	2	Kila Point.
6020	Kentish Knock.	3	Kilcradan.
1	Kephali Cape.	4	Kilda, St.
2	Kephken Adassi Island.	5	Kildyum Island.
3	Keppel Cape.	6	Kilidromi.
4	Keppel Island.	7	Kilios.
5	Keppel Islands.	8	Killala.
6	Kerempeh Cape.	9	Kill Devil Hills.
7	Keresoun.	6070	Killibegs.
8	Kerets Cape.	1	Killingholme.
9	Kerguelen's Land.	2	Kinabataugan Point.
6030	Kerki Mount.	3	Kinbourn.
1	Kermadec Islands.	4	King Cape, East Asia.
6032	Kertch.	6075	King Cape, Niphon.

Nos.	KIN	Nos.	KOS
6076	King Charles Cape.	6119	Knobens.
7	King George Island.	6120	Knocklayd.
8	King George's Is., Hudson's Bay.	1	Knox Island.
9	King George's Is., Low Archip'go.	2	Knuckle Point.
6080	King George's Sound.	3	Knysna River.
1	King George Town, Bight of Biafra.	4	Koamaro Cape.
2	King George Town, Ivory Coast.	5	Kodiak Island.
3	King Island, Bass Strait.	6	Koh Dud Island.
4	King Island, Alaska, U. S.	7	Koh Kong Island.
5	King William Cape.	8	Koka Shoal.
6	King William Town.	9	Koks Island.
7	King's Island.	6130	Kokskar.
8	King's Point.	1	Kola.
9	King's Sound.	2	Kolah.
6090	Kingsmill Islands.	3	Kolgaupia Cape.
1	Kingstou, China Sea.	4	Kolguyev Island.
2	Kingston, St. Vincent Island.	5	Kolioutchin Island.
3	Kingstown.	6	Kolovrat Mount.
4	Kini Balu.	7	Kona Cape.
5	Kinkwa-zan Island.	8	Konig Cape.
6	Kinnaird's Head.	9	Konigsberg.
7	Kinsale.	6140	Konouchin Cape.
8	Kioustenje.	1	Konoupoli Point.
9	Kirkness.	2	Kooe Mubarrack.
6100	Kirkwall.	3	Koo-kien-san Island.
1	Kirton Shoal.	4	Koolab.
2	Kish Light.	5	Koolewatte Head.
3	Kishm Island.	6	Koomisang Island.
4	Kiska Island.	7	Koor Island.
5	Kismayo Island.	8	Koo-re-mah.
6	Kissa.	9	Koraka Cape.
7	Kiswahara.	6150	Korgo Island.
8	Kittan.	1	Koro Island.
9	Kiu-siu Island.	2	Koron.
6110	Kizil Ermak Cape.	3	Korotuna Island.
1	Kizimkaz.	4	Kors Fiord.
2	Kjer Cape.	5	Korsö Light.
3	Klampis Point.	6	Korsoren.
4	Klapp Island.	7	Koruma Island.
5	Klobat Mount.	8	Kos.
6	Kluchevski.	9	Ko-si-chang Islands.
7	Knivskjaerodden.	6160	Ko-sima Island.
6118	Knob Cape.	6161	Koslof.

Nos.	KOT	Nos.	LAG
6162	Kotama Island.	6205	Kwing Island.
3	Kotubdea Island.	6	Kwyhoo Island.
4	Kotzebue Sound.	7	Kyangle Island.
5	Koulassien.	8	Kyholm.
6	Koumi, Cape.	9	Kyk Down.
7	Kounelo, Cape.	6210	Kyook Phoo.
8	Kouri, Cape.	1	Laage Island, N. W. of Banca.
9	Koussie River.	2	Laage Island, Sumatra.
6170	Koutalai Island.	3	Laarat.
1	Koutousoff, Cape.	4	Labée, Cape.
2	Koutousoff Island.	5	Labenki Island.
3	Koutousoff Islands.	6	Labiche Island.
4	Kouzomen.	7	Labillardière, Cape.
5	Kowie River.	8	Laborde Islet.
6	Krakatoa.	9	Labrador.
7	Kramtchenko Islands.	6220	Labrador, Cape.
8	Krio Nero.	1	Labuan Island.
9	Krithina Mountain.	2	Lacadive Islands.
6180	Krléougoun, Cape.	3	Lacepede Islands.
1	Krompa Island.	4	Lacotta, Pulo.
2	Kronotsky Peak and Cape.	5	Lacrosse Island.
3	Kronprindsens Island.	6	Lacul.
4	Kronstadt.	7	Ladd Reef.
5	Krusenstern, Cape, N. Coast Amer.	8	Ladda, Pulo.
6	Krusenstern, Cape, Kotzebue Sound.	9	Ladrone, Grand.
7	Krusenstern Island.	6230	Ladrones.
8	Krusenstern Islands.	1	Lady Grey, Cape.
9	Krusenstern Rock.	2	Laers Island.
6190	Kuching Hill.	3	Lagartos.
1	Kukewári.	4	Lage Rock.
2	Kullen Light.	5	Lage de Santos.
3	Kumi Island.	6	Laghi, Cape.
4	Kumpal Island.	7	Lagoon Island.
5	Kunashire Island.	8	Lagoon Reef.
6	Kunna.	9	Lagoondy, Pulo.
7	Kurauchee.	6240	Lagos, Africa.
8	Kuria Island.	1	Lagos, Portugal.
9	Kuria Muria Islands.	2	Lagosta Island.
6200	Kuriat, Cape.	3	Lagostas, Cape.
1	Kurile Islands.	4	Lagostini Rocks.
2	Kuryah Islands.	5	Lagrandière Island.
3	Kusha Island.	6	Lagskar.
6204	Kweeshan Islands.	6247	Lagoa City.

Nos.	LAG	Nos.	LEA
6248	Lagoa River.	6291	Lankayan Island.
9	Laguna, Port.	2	Lannes, Cape.
6250	Lahaina.	3	Lanrick's Shoal.
1	Lahaye, Cape.	4	Lantao Peak.
2	Lahou, Cape.	5	Lantinga, Pulo.
3	Laou Shoal.	6	Lanzarote.
4	Lai-chow.	7	Lapland.
5	Lakahia Mountain.	8	Larack Island.
6	Lakemba Island.	9	Larnaca.
7	Lakemba Pass.	6300	Larne Rock.
8	Lakor.	1	Laseine Islands.
9	Lalang Besar Island.	2	Lassoa Point.
6260	Lalla Rookh Shoal.	3	Lastang Island.
1	Lamanchiri Hill.	4	Lastres.
2	Lamarche, Cape.	5	Latakia.
3	Lamarck Island.	6	Latham's Island.
4	Lamas River.	7	Latouche Treville, Cape.
5	Lamay Island.	8	Latta Islands.
6	Lamb Head.	9	Latte Island.
7	Lambay Island.	6310	Laughlan Islands.
8	Lambayeque Rd.	1	Laurel Bank.
9	Lambert, Cape.	2	Laurel Shoal.
6270	Lamintao Point.	3	Laurent du Var.
1	Lammas Mountain.	4	Laurie Island.
2	Lamo Bay.	5	Lauriston.
3	Lamock Islands.	6	Laurot Islands.
4	Lampedusa Island.	7	Laut, Great Pulo.
5	Lampion Island.	8	Lava Island.
6	Lampon, Port.	9	Lavenskar.
7	Lam-yit Island.	6320	Lawn Island.
8	Lancaster.	1	Lawrence, St., Bay.
9	Lançoes Grandes.	2	Lawrence, St., Cape.
6280	Lançoens Grandes.	3	Lawrence, St., Island, Indian Ocean.
1	Landfall Island, Andamans.	4	Lawrence, St., Alaska, U. S.
2	Landfall Island, S. America.	5	Lawrence, St., R. and G.
3	Languard Fort.	6	Lax Island.
4	Landskrona.	7	Lay, Cape.
5	Landsort Light.	8	Layken Point.
6	Langanaes, Cape.	9	Laysan Island.
7	Langle Bay.	6330	Lazareff Island.
8	Langley.	1	Lazaro, St., Cape.
9	Lango Island.	2	Leading Bluff.
6290	Languin.	6333	Leander Shoal.

Nos.	LEA	Nos.	LIG
6334	Leasowe Light.	6377	Leron Harbor.
5	Leat, Pulo.	8	Lerwick.
6	Lebany Bay.	9	Leschenbault Cape.
7	Lebert Island.	6380	Lessina Island.
8	Lebida.	1	Lessoe Island.
9	Ledo Cape, Brazil.	2	Lesson Island.
6340	Ledo Cape, West Africa.	3	Lesueur Cape.
1	Leeuwin Cape.	4	Lesueur Island.
2	Leeward Islands.	5	Lesueur Mount.
3	Leewarden Shoal.	6	Leton Rocks.
4	Lefchimo.	7	Le-tsin.
5	Leffouw.	8	Letti.
6	Lefouka Island.	9	Leübu River.
7	Legarto Head.	6390	Leuconna Hummocks.
8	Legendre Island.	1	Leucung Island.
9	Leghorn.	2	Levanso Island.
6350	Legiep Islands.	3	Leven Island.
1	Le Grand Cape.	4	Leven Point.
2	Leguwan Islands.	5	Leven Port.
3	Leighton Rock.	6	Leven, St., Point.
4	Leith.	7	Leveque Cape.
5	Lejon, Grand, Rock.	8	Levita Island.
6	Leköe.	9	Levuka.
7	Lema, Great.	6400	Lewa.
8	Le Maire & Tasman's Islands.	1	Lewis, Butt of.
9	Leman & Ower Light.	2	Lewis, St., Cape.
6360	Lemnos.	3	Leyden.
1	Lena River.	4	Leyte Island.
2	Lengua de Vaca Point.	5	Liakhov Islands.
3	Lenin Islands.	6	Liant Cape.
4	Leno, Point de.	7	Libagao Island.
5	Leopard Reef.	8	Libarran Island.
6	Leopold Cape.	9	Libau.
7	Leopold Island.	6410	Libby Island.
8	Leopold Islands.	1	Liberia.
9	Lepanto.	2	Libertad.
6370	Lepers Island.	3	Lichtenfeld.
1	Lepreau Cape.	4	Licosa Cape.
2	Lepsina Island.	5	Lido, Port.
3	Lera Point.	6	Lien Chew.
4	Lerang Point.	7	Lieskov Island.
5	Lerina.	8	Lighthouse Reef.
6376	Lero.	6419	Ligitan Island.

Nos.	LIG	Nos.	LON
6420	Liguanea Island.	6463	Little Hope Island.
1	Lignano, Port.	4	Lively Island.
2	Lihou Cape.	5	Lively Rock.
3	Lima.	6	Liverpool.
4	Limasagua Island.	7	Liverpool Island.
5	Limasol.	8	Liverpool Port.
6	Limbarra Peak.	9	Liverpool River.
7	Limbe Island.	6470	Livingston Island.
8	Limbones Point.	1	Lizard.
9	Limeburner Shoal.	2	Lizard Island.
6430	Limeni.	3	Lloyd, Port.
1	Limerick.	4	Loa River.
2	Linacapan Island.	5	Loango River.
3	Linago Island.	6	Lobetobie.
4	Linaro Cape.	7	Lobito.
5	Lincoln Island.	8	Lobo Point, Peru.
6	Lincoln Port.	9	Lobo Point, Philippines.
7	Lindsay Island.	6480	Lobos Cape.
8	Lindy River.	1.	Lobos Cay.
9	Lingayen.	2	Lobos de Afuera Islands.
6440	Lingen Island.	3	Lobos de Tierra.
1	Linguetta Cape.	4	Lobos Island, Canaries.
2	Linitan Island.	5	Lobos Island, Gulf of California.
3	Linné Peak.	6	Lobos Island, River Platte.
4	Linosa Island, Grecian Archip'go.	7	Lobos Island, Vera Cruz.
5	Linosa Island, Malta.	8	Lobos Rocks.
6	Liong-soy Point.	9	Locos Island.
7	Lipari Islands.	6490	Loevenstern Cape.
8	Lippu.	1	Lofoden.
9	Lipso.	2	Lofty Mount.
6450	Liptrap Cape.	3	Logito River.
1	Lisbon.	4	Logounor Island.
2	Lisburne Cape, North America.	5	Loguno Peak and Cape.
3	Lisburne Cape, New Hebrides.	6	Loheia.
4	Liscomb Harbor.	7	Lökö.
5	Lise, Island du.	8	Loma Point.
6	Lisiansky Island.	9	Lomas Point.
7	Lismore Island.	6500	Lomblem.
8	Lissa Island.	1	Lombock.
9	Lissan al Kahpeh.	2	London Breakers.
6460	Listersteen.	3	London Reefs.
1	Litke Island.	4	London Shoal.
6462	Little Fish Bay.	6505	Londonderry.

Nos.	LON	Nos.	LUC
6506	Londonderry Cape.	6549	Louan.
7	Long Hill.	6550	Louasappe.
8	Long Island, Bahamas.	1	Lough Ryan.
9	Long Island, New York, U. S.	2	Louis, Cape.
6510	Long Island, Gaspar Strait.	3	Louis, Port, Falkland Islands.
1	Long Island, Hudson's Bay.	4	Louis, Port, France.
2	Long Island, New Britain.	5	Louis, Port, Mauritius.
3	Long Island, New Zealand.	6	Louis-Philippe, Cape.
4	Long Island, S. Pacific.	7	Louisa Shoal, Borneo.
5	Long Island, Torres Strait.	8	Louisa Shoal, Philippines.
6	Long Point.	9	Louisburg.
7	Long Nose.	6560	Louisiana.
8	Longone, Port.	1	Loup Head.
9	Longships Light.	2	Lousiade Archipelago.
6520	Longstone Light.	3	Loutzee Rock.
1	Loo's Shoal.	4	Lovisa.
2	Loochoo Island.	5	Low Archipelago.
3	Loodatoo.	6	Low Black Point.
4	Looe Cay.	7	Low Island, Natunas.
5	Looe Island.	8	Low Island, Spitzbergen.
6	Looké, Port.	9	Low Islands.
7	Lookers-on Bay.	6570	Low Point.
8	Looki-ong Island.	1	Low Port.
9	Lookout, Cape, Hudson's Bay.	2	Lowestoft.
6530	Lookout, Cape, Mexico.	3	Lowly Point.
1	Lookout, Cape, North Carolina.	4	Lowry, Cape.
2	Lookout Point, E. Australia.	5	Lowther Island.
3	Lookout Point, N. E. Australia.	6	Loyalty Isles.
4	Lookout Point, North Carolina.	7	Loyro Mountain.
5	Lookout Reef.	8	Lozin, Pulo.
6	Lookout Rock.	9	Luabo River.
7	Lopatka, Cape.	6580	Luban Island.
8	Lopez, Cape.	1	Lubeck, Java Sea.
9	Lorenzo, San.	2	Lubeck, Prussia.
6540	Lorenzo, San, Island.	3	Lucapin.
1	Lorenzo, St., Cape.	4	Lucar, San.
2	Loretto.	5	Lucas, St., Cape.
3	Lornel Point.	6	Luce, St.
4	Los, Isles de.	7	Lucea Harbor.
5	Los, Isle de, Naranjos Islands.	8	Lucepara Island.
6	Los, Isle de, Reyes.	9	Luceparas.
7	Lot's Wife.	6590	Lucia, St.
6548	Lottin Island.	6591	Lucia, St., Cape, Kafferland.

Nos.	LUC	Nos.	MAG
6592	Lucia, St., Cape, S. America.	6635	Macclesfield Shoal.
3	Lucia, St., Cape, Windward Islands.	6	McCluer Island.
4	Luckipoor.	7	McCluer Inlet.
5	Lucky Bay.	8	McCluer Point.
6	Luconia Shoal.	9	McDonnel Cove.
7	Lucrecia Point.	6640	M'Diarmid Island.
8	Luffan, Ras.	1	Maceio.
9	Lui Chew.	2	Macgowen Reef.
6600	Luis, San, Harbor.	3	Machado, Cape.
1	Luis, San, de Apra Island.	4	Machias Bay.
2	Luko, Cape.	5	Machias, Seal Islands.
3	Lundy Island.	6	Machichaco, Cape.
4	Lur, Ras el.	7	M'Kean Island.
5	Lurcher Rock.	8	Mackenzie Islands.
6	Lusancy Islands and Reefs.	9	Mackenzie River.
7	Luz.	6650	Mac Leay Island.
8	Luxa River.	1	McLeod Bank.
9	Luzon Island and Point.	2	M'Nutt's Island.
6610	Lyakhovski Island.	3	Macoripe Point.
1	Lydia Island, Caroline Islands.	4	Macour Island.
2	Lydia Island, Marshall Islands.	5	Macquarrie, Fort.
3	Lynas Point Light.	6	Macquarrie Harbor.
4	Lynedoch Shoal.	7	Macquarrie Island.
5	Lynber Reef.	8	Macquarrie, Port, Australia.
6	Lynn Shoal.	9	Macquarrie, Port, New Zealand.
7	Lynn's Well Light.	6660	Macquereau Point.
8	Lynx Island.	1	Macronisi Island.
9	Lyra Island.	2	Maccullah.
6620	Lyra Shoal.	3	Madagascar.
1	Lyserort.	4	Madalena Island, Marquesas.
2	Maatsuyker Islands.	5	Madalena Island, Sardinia.
3	Mabbere, Ras.	6	Madame Island, Cape Breton Island.
4	Mabo, Cape.	7	Madame Island, Madagascar.
5	Mabudis.	8	Madeira.
6	Macao.	9	Madona Island.
7	Macapá.	6670	Madras.
8	Macarska.	1	Madre de Dios A.
9	MacAskill Islands.	2	Madura.
6630	Macas River.	3	Maestra, Point della.
1	Macassar.	4	Maestre de Campo Island.
2	Macassar, St.	5	Mafamede Island.
3	Macasse Point.	6	Magdor.
6634	Macauley Island.	6677	Magadoxa.

Nos.	MAG	Nos.	MAN
6678	Magdalen, Cape.	6721	Malaguash Harbor.
9	Magdalen Islands.	2	Malalabon Point.
6680	Magdalen Shoal.	3	Malamocco, Port.
1	Magdalena Bay.	4	Malan, Ras.
2	Magdalena Hook.	5	Mala Pasqua Cape.
3	Magdalena River.	6	Malavi Island.
4	Magellan Straits.	7	Malayta Island.
5	Magua, Port.	8	Malcolm Atoll.
6	Magnetic Island, Australia.	9	Malcolm Point.
7	Magnetic Island, Guatemala.	6730	Malden Island.
8	Magnetic Pole.	1	Mal di Ventre.
9	Magoari Cape.	2	Mal di Vetro.
6690	Magon-hai.	3	Maldive Islands.
1	Maharag Island.	4	Maldonado.
2	Mahato Island.	5	Malé Atoll.
3	Mahé Island.	6	Maleddam Point.
4	Mah-Koondoo Island.	7	Malespina Cape.
5	Mahmur.	8	Malfatano, Port.
6	Mahon.	9	Malin Head.
7	Mahon's Ditch.	6740	Malivi.
8	Maiana.	1	Mallawallee Island.
9	Maiden Rocks.	2	Mallicollo Island, New Hebrides.
6700	Maine.	3	Mallicollo Island, South Pacific.
1	Maitea Island.	4	Mallison's Island.
2	Maitresse Island.	5	Malmo.
3	Majambo Bay.	6	Malo, St.
4	Majorca.	7	Maloncon Island.
5	Majunga Point.	8	Malora.
6	Makalara Island.	9	Malora Island.
7	Maker's Ledge, S.	6750	Malorn.
8	Makin.	1	Malpelo Island.
9	Makri.	2	Malpelo Point.
6710	Makri Cape.	3	Malta.
1	Makrino Mount.	4	Mamalakje Island.
2	Maksimon Island.	5	Mambahenanan.
3	Makuimu.	6	Mamburao River.
4	Makumba Island.	7	Mammelle, W.
5	Mala Point, Gulf of Genoa.	8	Mamori Cape.
6	Mala Point, Panama.	9	Mampava Point.
7	Malabar Coast.	6760	Mana Island.
8	Malabriga.	1	Mana Point.
9	Malacca.	2	Mana River.
6720	Malaga.	6763	Manacles.

15

Nos.	MAN	Nos.	MAR
6764	Manado.	6807	Manoel Cape.
5	Managua Paps.	8	Manoel Luiz Shoal.
6	Manalipa Island.	9	Man-of-War Bay, Bahamas.
7	Manama.	6810	Man-of-War Bay, Tobago.
8	Manambatoo Town.	1	Man-of-War Bay, Virgin Islands.
9	Manambatoo Village.	2	Manono Island.
6770	Manamec Island.	3	Manook Manook.
1	Mananhar.	4	Manoombing Hill.
2	Manapar Point.	5	Manooroo.
3	Manas-wari Island.	6	Manouran, Pulo.
4	Manby Point.	7	Manovolko Island.
5	Mancap, Pulo.	8	Mansfield Island.
6	Mandalike Island.	9	Mansfield Shoal.
7	Mandarin's Cap.	6820	Mansular Islands.
8	Mandhar Cape.	1	Mantaleugom Mount.
9	Mandinga.	2	Manua Island.
6780	Mandvee.	3	Manukau Harbor.
1	Mandri, Port.	4	Manuwangi.
2	Maudro Island.	5	Manvers, Port.
3	Manfredonia.	6	Manza, Sta.
4	Manga.	7	Manzanilla Bay.
5	Mangaia Island.	8	Manzanilla Cays.
6	Mangaloon Island.	9	Manzanilla Point, Panama.
7	Mangalore.	6830	Manzanilla Point, Venezuela.
8	Manga Noui Island.	1	Maouna Island.
9	Manga Noui Mount.	2	Mapare Island.
6790	Manglares Point.	3	Maplin.
1	Mango Island.	4	Maraca Island.
2	Mangrove Point.	5	Maracaybo.
3	Mangs Islands.	6	Maradong, Pulo.
4	Mangai Islands.	7	Maragusan Point.
5	Manguinba Point.	8	Maraki.
6	Manguirin, Port.	9	Marambaya Island.
7	Manhegan Island.	6840	Maranham.
8	Manhii.	1	Marargiu Cape.
9	Manicani Island.	2	Marathon Cape.
6800	Manifold Cape.	3	Marathonisi.
1	Manila.	4	Maratua Island.
2	Manipa Island.	5	Marble Island.
3	Manna Point.	6	Marblehead.
4	Manning Point.	7	Mar Chiquito.
5	Mannu Cape.	8	Marco, St., Cape, Sardinia.
6806	Manoel Rodriguez Shoal.	6849	Marco, St., Cape, Sicily.

Nos.	MAR	Nos.	MAR
6850	Marcos, St., Fort.	6893	Marka.
1	Marcos, St., Point.	4	Markana Islands.
2	Marcouf Islands.	5	Marken Island.
3	Marcus Island.	6	Marköe.
4	Mare, Point, della.	7	Marlborough Cape.
5	Marescot Mountain.	8	Marmagoa.
6	Mare Island, California, U. S.	9	Marmora Island.
7	Margaret Island.	6900	Marmorice.
8	Margaret Islands.	1	Maro Reef.
9	Margareta Island.	2	Maronea.
6860	Margaret's Bay.	3	Marowyne River.
1	Margarita Island, California.	4	Marqueen Islands.
2	Margarita Island, Cumana.	5	Marquesa Point.
3	Margate.	6	Marquesas.
4	Maria, Cape.	7	Marquis de Traverse Islands.
5	Maria di Leuca, St., Cape.	8	Marquis of Huntly Bank.
6	Maria Island, Gulf of Carpentaria.	9	Marsa Ougrah.
7	Maria Island, Low Archipelago.	6910	Marsa Sousa.
8	Maria Island, Van Dieman's Land.	1	Marsa Zafran.
9	Maria, Sta., Cape.	2	Marsa Zeitoun.
6870	Maria, Sta., Island.	3	Marsala.
1	Maria Theresa Reef.	4	Marsden Point.
2	Maria Van Diemen Cape.	5	Marseille.
3	Mariagalante.	6	Marsh, Cape.
4	Maria Gorda Bay.	7	Marshall.
5	Mariana Islands.	8	Marshall Islands.
6	Maricaban Island.	9	Marstrand Light.
7	Maricas Islands.	6920	Marta, Sta.
8	Marie Louise Island.	1	Marta, Sta., Cape.
9	Mariel, Port.	2	Martaban.
6880	Marienleuchte.	3	Martahoolah Peak.
1	Marière, Pulo.	4	Martha's Vineyard.
2	Marigot Bay.	5	Martin de Biarritz.
3	Marigot, Fort.	6	Martin, St., Cape.
4	Mariguana Island.	7	Martin, St., Cove.
5	Marinduque Island.	8	Martin, St., Island, Aracan.
6	Marino Cays.	9	Martin, St., Island, Leeward Islands.
7	Marino San.	6930	Martin, St., Port, Africa.
8	Marion and Crozet's Islands.	1	Martin, St., Port, France.
9	Maritimo Island.	2	Martin's, St., Scilly Islands.
6890	Mariupol.	3	Martin Vas.
1	Mark House.	4	Martinez Peak.
6892	Mark's, St.	6935	Martinique.

Nos.	MAR	Nos.	MAY
6936	Martyr's Islands.	6979	Matamoras, Mexico.
7	Marua Island.	6980	Matana Island.
8	Marutea.	1	Matanani Islands.
9	Mary Ann Island.	2	Matanilla.
6940	Mary Ann Shoal.	3	Matanzas.
1	Mary Jones Bay.	4	Matapan, Cape.
2	Mary, St., Cape, Madagascar.	5	Mataro.
3	Mary, St., Cape, Newfoundland.	6	Matchian.
4	Mary, St., Cape, New Ireland.	7	Mateemo Island.
5	Mary, St., Cape, Nova Scotia.	8	Matelotas Islands.
6	Mary, St., Cape, River Plate.	9	Maternillas Point.
7	Mary, St., Cape, Senegambia.	6990	Matthew, St., Island.
8	Mary, St., Cape, W. Africa.	1	Matthew's Island.
9	Mary, St., Cays.	2	Matthew's Rock.
6950	Mary, St., Island, Azores.	3	Mathias' Island.
1	Mary, St., Island, Madagascar.	4	Matia.
2	Mary, St., Island, S. Africa.	5	Matifou, Cape.
3	Mary, St., Island, Scilly Islands.	6	Matilda Island.
4	Mary, St., Rocks, Labrador.	7	Matinicus Island.
5	Mary, St., Rocks, Malabar Coast.	8	Matounda Point.
6	Mary's Bay.	9	Matsou Island.
7	Maryland.	7000	Matthew Point.
8	Maryport.	1	Matthew's, St., Island.
9	Masafuera Island.	2	Matthew's, St., Island, Philippines.
6960	Masbate Island.	3	Mattos, Island, dos.
1	Masella.	4	Matty Island.
2	Mason, Port.	5	Matuku Island.
3	Maspa Point.	6	Matura.
4	Massachusetts.	7	Maude Reef.
5	Massachusetts Bay.	8	Mauger Cay.
6	Massarina Island.	9	Maui.
7	Masse Island.	7010	Mauiti.
8	Massowah Island.	1	Mauki.
9	Masthead Islet.	2	Maulamat Island.
6970	Mastic Point.	3	Maule River.
1	Masulipatam.	4	Maulmain.
2	Mataatu Harbor.	5	Maunbané Point.
3	Matabella Islands.	6	Maupiti Island.
4	Matagorda Bay.	7	Maura, Sta.
5	Mataina.	8	Mauritius.
6	Matala, Cape.	9	Maurizio, Port.
7	Matalqui, Cape.	7020	Mausoleum Island.
6978	Matamawi, Cape.	7021	May, Cape.

Nos.	MAY	Nos.	MES
7022	May Island.	7065	Mele, De la.
3	May Point.	6	Meleda Island.
4	Maya.	7	Meleka Cape.
5	Mayaguez Bay.	8	Melilla.
6	Mayé Mount.	9	Melinda.
7	Mayo.	7070	Mellish Cays.
8	Mayo Pulo.	1	Melmore Point.
9	Mayor Cape.	2	Melville Cape, Australia.
7030	Mayotta.	3	Melville Cape, S. Shetlands.
1	Maysi Cape.	4	Melville Island, Australia.
2	Mayumba Bay.	5	Melville Island, Barrow's Strait.
3	Mazagan.	6	Melville Island, Low Archipelago.
4	Mazatlan.	7	Melville Islands and Bay.
5	Mazeewy Island.	8	Melville Peninsula.
6	Mazeira Island.	9	Melville, Port, Loochoo Islands.
7	Mazimba.	7080	Melville, Port, South Africa.
8	Mazzara.	1	Memel.
9	Mbenga Island.	2	Memory Rock.
7040	Meac Sima Islands.	3	Menai Island.
1	Meangis Islands.	4	Mendana Island.
2	Mecatina Islands.	5	Mendocino Cape.
3	Medano Island.	6	Mendoza Island.
4	Medano Point.	7	Mentchikoff Islands.
5	Medas Islands.	8	Merat Island.
6	Medemblik.	9	Mercury Bay.
7	Mednoi Island.	7090	Mercury Island.
8	Medrano Rocks.	1	Meredith Cape.
9	Meedenblik.	2	Mergui.
7050	Meek Point.	3	Merite Island.
1	Meganom Cape.	4	Merjee River.
2	Megara.	5	Merlera.
3	Mehedia, Africa, N. W.	6	Mermaid Shoal.
4	Mehediah, Barbary.	7	Meroe Island.
5	Meh-heb-bakah.	8	Merope, S. Shoal, China.
6	Meia-co-si-mah.	9	Merope, Indian Archipelago.
7	Meichow Island.	7100	Merrimac River.
8	Meklong River.	1	Mertens Cape.
9	Mel, Island do.	2	Mesa, Island de la.
7060	Mel, Point do.	3	Mesa Point.
1	Melamo Cape.	4	Messa River.
2	Melancias Mount.	5	Messalonghi.
3	Melbourne.	6	Messina.
7064	Melbourne Island.	7107	Mesurada Cape.

218

Nos.	MET	Nos.	MIS
7108	Metcalfe Island.	7151	Milazzo Cape.
9	Metchignie Bay.	2	Milestone Rock.
7110	Methana.	3	Mileto.
1	Mette Island.	4	Milford.
2	Mette Ras.	5	Milford Haven.
3	Mevenklint.	6	Milla.
4	Mew Bay.	7	Mills Islands.
5	Mewstone.	8	Milner.
6	Mexiana Island.	9	Milo.
7	Mexico.	7160	Miloradovitch Island.
8	Mexico Point.	1	Min River.
9	Mexillones Mount.	2	Mindanao Island and Point.
7120	Meyo.	3	Mindoro.
1	Mezen.	4	Minerva Cay.
2	Mezzaluna Point.	5	Minerva Island.
3	Miadi.	6	Minerva Reef, Low Archipelago.
4	Miatao Islands and Strait.	7	Minerva Reef, South Pacific.
5	Michael, St., Azores.	8	Minerva Rock.
6	Michael, St., Philippines.	9	Mingan Islands.
7	Michael, St., Bank.	7170	Mingan Patch.
8	Michael, St., Cape.	1	Minicoy.
9	Michael, St., Gulf.	2	Minorca.
7130	Michael, St., Head.	3	Mino Sima Island.
1	Michael, St., Mount.	4	Minow Island.
2	Miculle Reef.	5	Minquiers Rocks.
3	Midday Reef.	6	Minstrel Shoal.
4	Middelburg.	7	Mintao, Pulo.
5	Middelburg Island.	8	Minto Hill.
6	Middle Island, Bay of Boni.	9	Miquelon.
7	Middle Island, Sumatra.	7180	Miramichi Bay.
8	Middle Island, Mergui Archip'go.	1	Mira por vos.
9	Middle Island, Recherche Arch'go.	2	Mirik Cape.
7140	Middleton Cape.	3	Mirs Bay.
1	Middleton Point.	4	Mirza Helaib.
2	Middleton Reef.	5	Misaki Cape.
3	Middleton Shoal.	6	Misamis.
4	Midway Islands, N. Pacific Ocean.	7	Miscow Island.
5	Miguel, San, Bay.	8	Miseno Cape.
6	Miguel, San, Island, Admiralty Is.	9	Mispalu Islands.
7	Miguel, San, Island, Low Arch'go.	7190	Misratah Cape.
8	Miguel, San, Island, Mexico.	1	Mississippi River.
9	Mikhailoff.	2	Mississippi Sound.
7150	Mikoulkin Cape.	7193	Mistake Point.

Nos.	MIS	Nos.	MON
7194	Misteriosa Bank.	7237	Moleques.
5	Mita Point.	8	Molewal House.
6	Mitchell Group.	9	Molfetta.
7	Mitiéro Island.	7240	Molino Point.
8	Mitre, Cape.	1	Molky Rocks.
9	Mitre Island.	2	Moller Island, Low Archipelago.
7200	Mitre, the.	3	Moller Island, N. Pacific.
1	Mitylene.	4	Moller, Port.
2	Mizen Head.	5	Molokai.
3	Moa.	6	Molonta Island.
4	Moa, Cape.	7	Moloque Atoll.
5	Moala Island.	8	Molyneaux Harbor.
6	Moar Mountain.	9	Moma Bank.
7	Moar, Pulo.	7250	Mombaza.
8	Moarree, Ras.	1	Mona Island.
9	Moarro Island.	2	Monaco.
7210	Mobile.	3	Monastir.
1	Mocamba, Port.	4	Monat Point.
2	Mocha.	5	Monchique Mountains.
3	Mocha Island.	6	Monckton Fort.
4	Moco Moco.	7	Moncœur Islands.
5	Moco Moco Point.	8	Mondego, Cape.
6	Modeste Island.	9	Mondigo Mountain.
7	Modon.	7260	Mondoleh Island.
8	Moduda Island.	1	Mondrain Island.
9	Moela Light.	2	Monemvasia.
7220	Moen Island.	3	Money Shoal, N. Australia.
1	Moffen Island.	4	Money Shoal, N. W. Australia.
2	Mogador.	5	Monfalcone.
3	Moghady Island.	6	Monfeea Island.
4	Mogmog Island.	7	Monganui Harbor.
5	M'gotes Point.	8	Mongó Mountain.
6	Mohammed, Ras.	9	Mongon, Cape.
7	Mohillah.	7270	Mongon Mountain.
8	Moikepää Beacon.	1	Mongulho River.
9	Moilah.	2	Monich Islands.
7230	Mokau River.	3	Monito Island.
1	Moko hinou Islands.	4	Monjes.
2	Mokungai Island.	5	Monjos Islands.
3	Mola, Adriat.	6	Monk Rock.
4	Mola, Italy.	7	Monkonrushy Island.
5	Mola, Cape.	8	Monmouth Island.
7236	Mole Island.	7279	Monneron Island.

Nos.	MON	Nos.	MOR
7280	Monodendri.	7323	Monument Island.
1	Monolitho, Cape.	4	Monze Cape.
2	Monomy Point.	5	Moolegee Islands.
3	Monopin Hill.	6	Moor Island.
4	Monopoli.	7	Moora Point.
5	Monrovia.	8	Moore Point.
6	Monsiá Mountain.	9	Moose, Fort.
7	Montague, Cape.	7330	Mootapilly Shoal.
8	Montague Island, Australia.	1	Mopelia.
9	Montague Island, China.	2	Mopiha.
7290	Montague Island. New Hebrides.	3	Morant Cays.
1	Montague Island, Alaska.	4	Morant Point.
2	Montague Island, Sandwich Islands.	5	Morant Port.
3	Montague, Port.	6	Morea Castle.
4	Montague Rocks.	7	Morebat, Cape.
5	Montalivet Islands.	8	Morell Island.
6	Montaran Islands.	9	Moreno Mountain.
7	Montauk Point.	7340	Moresby Point.
8	Mont de Trigo.	1	Moresses.
9	Monte Altissimo.	2	Moreton, Cape.
7300	Montebello Islands.	3	Morgan, Cape.
1	Monte Christi Bay.	4	Moriarty Bank.
2	Monte Circello.	5	Morjovetz Island.
3	Monte Junto.	6	Morlaix.
4	Monte Moreno.	7	Mornington Island.
5	Monte Stello.	8	Morocco.
6	Monte Ventoso.	9	Moro tiri Islands.
7	Monte Video, China.	7350	Morotoi Island.
8	Monte Video, Patagonia.	1	Morrison Mountain.
9	Monte Video, River Plate.	2	Moro de Puercos.
7310	Montecristo Island.	3	Morro di Porco Cape.
1	Montego Bay.	4	Morro Island.
2	Montemont Islands.	5	Morro Mesas.
3	Monterey.	6	Morro of Barcellona.
4	Monteverde Islands.	7	Morro of Sama.
5	Montgomery Islands.	8	Morro of Seiba.
6	Montpelier.	9	Morro Point.
7	Montrose.	7360	Morro San Juan.
8	Monts Point.	1	Morro Solar.
9	Montserrat.	2	Morro St. Paulo.
7320	Montufar Point.	3	Morro Tibao.
1	Montuosa Island.	4	Morros, Point de los.
7322	Monty, Cape.	7365	Mort Point.

Nos.	MOR	Nos.	MYP
7366	Mortigliano Point.	7409	Mudge Point.
7	Mortlock Islands, Caroline Islands.	7410	Mugeres Island.
8	Mortlock Islands, S. Pacific.	1	Muiron Island.
9	Morty.	2	Muleje.
7370	Morundum Island.	3	Muletas Archipelago.
1	Moruptange Light.	4	Mulgrave Fort.
2	Mosal Island.	5	Mulgrave Islands.
3	Moscos Islands.	6	Mulgrave Port.
4	Mosque Point.	7	Mull Head.
5	Mosquito Lagoon.	8	Mull Island.
6	Mossel Bay.	9	Mulu Island.
7	Mostaganem.	7420	Mulu Mountain.
8	Mostaza.	1	Mumbles Light.
9	Motane.	2	Mumbolithe Reef.
7380	Mother Rock.	3	Muncoda Point.
1	Motir.	4	Mundanny, Ras.
2	Motou-aro, Cape.	5	Munro Mountain.
3	Motouheka Island.	6	Murcielagos Island.
4	Motouhora Island.	7	Murder Island.
5	Motou-iti.	8	Murderer's Bay.
6	Motou Kawa Islands.	9	Muro, Cape.
7	Motril.	7430	Murot Hill.
8	Motutunga.	1	Murr Islands.
9	Moudiuga Island.	2	Murray Island.
7390	Moudros.	3	Murray Islands.
1	Moul Head.	4	Murray River.
2	Mount, Cape, and River.	5	Murray's Sound.
3	Mourache, Cape.	6	Murry Islands.
4	Mourcheflo.	7	Mùsa, Port.
5	Mourilleu Group.	8	Musgrave Islands.
6	Mourodonos, Cape.	9	Mushaab, Ras.
7	Mourondava.	7440	Mushabeah Island.
8	Mourovia.	1	Muskat.
9	Mousa Island.	2	Musquillo Islands.
7400	Mouse Island.	3	Musquito Cays.
1	Mouse Light.	4	Musquito Inlet.
2	Mowee Island.	5	Musquitos Point.
3	Mowna Loa Mount.	6	Mussendom, Cape.
4	Moxacar.	7	Muta, Pt. de.
5	Mozambique.	8	Muzon, Cape.
6	Moze Island.	9	Myconi Island.
7	Muck Island.	7450	Myggenoes Island.
7408	Mucksa, Cape.	7451	Mypurra Island.

Nos.	MYS	Nos.	NAZ
7452	Mysole.	7495	Nanuku Island.
3	Mysory Island.	6	Nao, Cape.
4	Nabend, Ras.	7	Napakiang.
5	Nacascolo, Port.	8	Naples.
6	Nachvack Bay.	9	Napoli di Romania.
7	Nadiejda, Cape.	7500	Naranjo Port.
8	Nadiejda Rocks.	1	Narbonne.
9	Nagaeff, Cape.	2	Narborough, Cape.
7460	Nagel Island.	3	Narborough Island, Galapagos.
1	Nahkiainen Shoal.	4	Narborough Island, Patagonia.
2	Nain.	5	Narcondam.
3	Nàirai Island.	6	Narcissus Island.
4	Nairsa.	7	Nareenda Bay.
5	Naitamba Island.	8	Nargen Island.
6	Nàkkehoved.	9	Narsapour.
7	Nakutipipi.	7510	Nasca Point.
8	Nalsoe Island.	1	Nash Point.
9	Namacpacan Point.	2	Nash's Island.
7470	Nambu, Cape, and Port.	3	Nassau.
1	Nameless Island.	4	Nassau, Cape, British Guiana.
2	Namequo Island.	5	Nassau Cape, Nova Zemblia.
3	Naminie.	6	Nassau Island.
4	Nam-ki Island.	7	Nata, La.
5	Namoa.	8	Natal Bay.
6	Namoa Island.	9	Natal Cape, and Port.
7	Namolipifian Group.	7520	Natashquan Point.
8	Namolouk Islands.	1	Natunas.
9	Namouka.	2	Naturaliste.
7480	Namounouyto Group.	3	Nau, Cape.
1	Namourek Islands.	4	Nauset Harbor, Massachusetts, U. S.
2	Namouyin Islet.	5	Nautilus Island.
3	Nam-quan.	6	Nautilus Rock.
4	Namuka Island.	7	Nautilus Shoal.
5	Namurek.	8	Navalo, Port.
6	Nancy, Pulo.	9	Navarin, Cape.
7	Nanek River.	7530	Navarino.
8	Nangasaki.	1	Navasa Island.
9	Nanka Islands.	2	Navesink Lights.
7490	Nankin.	3	Navidad Port.
1	Nanouki.	4	Navigator's Island.
2	Nanouti.	5	Navula Point.
3	Nantes.	6	Naxos Island.
7494	Nantucket Island.	7537	Nazaire, St., Port.

Nos.	NAZ	Nos.	NIC
7538	Nazareth River.	7581	New Hebrides.
9	Naze Light.	2	New Ireland.
7540	Neah, Port.	3	New Island, Falkland Islands.
1	Necker Island.	4	New Island, Tierra del Fuego.
2	Needle Rock.	5	New Jersey.
3	Needles Light.	6	New London.
4	Negapatam.	7	New Orkneys.
5	Negombo.	8	New Orleans.
6	Negrais Cape.	9	New Point Comfort.
7	Negril Points.	7590	New Providence Island.
8	Negro Cape, Brazil.	1	New S. Shetland.
9	Negro Cape, West Africa.	2	New Year Island, Australia.
7550	Negro River.	3	New Year Island, Marshall Is.
1	Negropont.	4	New Year Islands.
2	Negros Island.	5	New York.
3	Negros Islands.	6	New York Island.
4	Neiafou.	7	New Zealand.
5	Neill, Port.	8	Newark Island.
6	Nelson.	9	Newarp.
7	Nelson Port.	7600	Newbury, Port.
8	Nelson's Cape.	1	Newcastle, Australia.
9	Nelson's Island.	2	Newcastle, England.
7560	Nengo-Nengo.	3	Newenham Cape.
1	Nepean Island, South Pacific.	4	Newfoundland.
2	Nepean Island, Torres Strait.	5	Newhaven.
3	Nepean Point.	6	Newport, England.
4	Neptune Islands.	7	Newport, Ireland.
5	Nerva.	8	Newport, Rhode Island.
6	Netherland Island.	9	Newry.
7	Neuf, De, Island.	7610	Nganaiti.
8	Neuse River, North Carolina, U. S.	1	Ngarik.
9	Nevil Island.	2	Nhao Island.
7570	Nevis.	3	Nhatrang Bay.
1	New Amsterdam.	4	Nias, Pulo.
2	New Bedford.	5	Niau Island, Feejee Islands.
3	New Britain.	6	Niau Island, Low Archipelago.
4	New Brunswick.	7	Nicaragua.
5	New Caledonia.	8	Nicaria.
6	New Dungeness Point.	9	Nice.
7	New Grenada.	7620	Nicero.
8	New Guinea.	1	Nicholson, Port.
9	New Hanover.	2	Nicholson Shoal.
7580	New Haven, United States.	7623	Nickerie, Fort.

Nos.	NIC	Nos.	NOR
7624	Nicobar Islands.	7667	Niua-foou.
5	Nicolao Reef.	8	Niua-tabou-tab.
6	Nicolao, St., Port.	9	Niukalofa.
7	Nicolas, St.	7670	Nobflure Island.
8	Nicolas Gat.	1	Noble Island, Australia.
9	Nicolas Island.	2	Noble Island, New Zealand.
7630	Nicolas Mole.	3	Noel, Port.
1	Nicolas Point.	4	Noesa Comba.
2	Nicolayev.	5	Noesa Laut.
3	Nicolo, St., Mount.	6	Noesa Seras.
4	Nicolo, St., Port.	7	Noessaniva Point.
5	Nicols Island.	8	Nogou-laoudzala.
6	Nicoya Gulf.	9	Noir Cape.
7	Niddingen.	7680	Noirmoustier.
8	Niedlingen.	1	Noja Spit.
9	Nielson Reef.	2	Noli.
7640	Nieuport.	3	Nomali Mount.
1	Nightingale Island, Cochin China.	4	Noman's Land.
2	Nightingale Island, S. Atlantic.	5	Nomo Cape.
3	Nightingale Rocks.	6	Nona.
4	Nihiru Island.	7	Noncowry Island.
5	Niihau.	8	Noo, Ras.
6	Nikolai Point.	9	Nootka Sound.
7	Nikolo, St.	7690	Nordskaren.
8	Nila.	1	Nordwyk Light.
9	Nile.	2	Nore Light.
7650	Nillandoo Atolls.	3	Norfeo Cape.
1	Nimrod Group.	4	Norfolk, Virginia, U. S.
2	Nimrod's Entrance.	5	Norfolk Island.
3	Nine-feet Reef.	6	Norfolk Mount.
4	Nine Islands of Carte.	7	Norman Island.
5	Ninepin Island.	8	North Berwick.
6	Ninepin Rock, China.	9	North Bluff.
7	Ninepin Rock, Indian Ocean.	7700	North Cape, Amazon.
8	Ninfas Point.	1	North Cape, Iceland.
9	Ning Po.	2	North Cape, Indian Archipelago.
7660	Ninipo Point.	3	North Cape, Norway.
1	Ninth Island.	4	North Carolina.
2	Nio Island.	5	North Island, Cargados.
3	Nipa Nipa Point.	6	North Island, Eastern Archipelago.
4	Niphon Island.	7	North Island, Seychelles.
5	Nisao Point.	8	North, Lord, Island.
7666	Nitendi.	7709	Northumberland Cape.

Nos.	NOR	Nos.	OLD
7710	Northumberland Inlet.	7753	Nuyts Reefs.
1	Northumberland Islands.	4	Ny Carleby.
2	Northumberland Shoal.	5	Nyeborg Light.
3	North-west Island.	6	Nygrund.
4	Norwalk Island.	7	Nyhamn.
5	Norway.	8	Nysted.
6	Norway Islands.	9	Oahu.
7	Noshe Barracouta.	7760	Oaitupu.
8	Noss Head, Scotland.	1	Oalan Island.
9	Noss Head, Shetland.	2	Oatafu.
7720	Noss Beh Island.	3	Oban.
1	Noss Veh Island.	4	Obe Gulf.
2	Nossa Sen., Mountain.	5	Obispo.
3	Nostra Senhora de Desterro.	6	O'Brien Island.
4	No-te-perderas Mountain.	7	Oby Island.
5	Norto, Cape.	8	Oby, Pulo.
6	Nottingham Island.	9	Ocean Island, N. Pacific.
7	Noun, Cape, and River.	7770	Ocean Island, S. Pacific.
8	Neup Head.	1	Ocean Islands.
9	Nourse River.	2	Ocili Harbor.
7730	Nouvelle, La.	3	Ockseu Islands.
1	Nova Redonda.	4	Ocracock Inlet.
2	Nova Scotia.	5	Oddy Sand.
3	Nova Zemblia.	6	Odemira.
4	Novosilzoff, Cape.	7	Odensholm.
5	Now Chow.	8	Odessa.
6	Nuala.	9	Oe, Mull of.
7	Nuevo G. and Hds.	7780	Oeno Island.
8	Nugu Ongea Reef.	1	Oetablas Island.
9	Nukahiva.	2	Offak Harbor.
7740	Nukufetau.	3	Ofo-Langa.
1	Nukulau Island.	4	Ofoo Island.
2	Nuku Levu Reef.	5	Ogle Point.
3	Nukumubasanga Island.	6	Obeteroa Island.
4	Nukunono.	7	Ohoura Mountain.
5	Numba Island.	8	Okatootaia.
6	Nuniwak Island.	9	Oki Islands.
7	Nús, Ras.	7790	Okosir Islands.
8	Nusa Baron Island.	1	Okotsk.
9	Nusa Cambangan.	2	Oland.
7750	Nusa Nessing.	3	Olango Island.
1	Nusa Tello Islands.	4	Old Fort Island.
7752	Nuyts Point.	7795	Old Head.

Nos.	OLD	Nos.	ORT
7796	Old Matacumba Island.	7839	Opotiki.
7	Old Point Comfort, Virginia, U. S.	7840	Oraitilipou Bank.
8	Old Proprietor Shoal.	1	Oran.
9	Old Providence.	2	Orange Bay.
7800	Old Catalina Islands.	3	Orange Cape.
1	Old Topsail Inlet.	4	Orange Cays.
2	Olenea Island.	5	Orange Fort.
3	Olensk River.	6	Orange Island.
4	Oleron Island.	7	Orange Peak.
5	Olifant's River.	8	Orange River.
6	Olimarao Islands.	9	Orani.
7	Olinda Point.	7850	Oran-Souari, Cape.
8	Olive Island.	1	Orchila.
9	Ollap Island.	2	Ord of Caithness.
7810	Olutaya Islet.	3	O'Reilly Island.
1	Olutorsky, Cape.	4	Orford, Cape, North America.
2	Olympus, Mt., Asia Minor.	5	Orford, Cape, New Britain.
3	Olympus, Mt., Grecian Archipelago.	6	Orfordness, Australia.
4	Oman Gulf.	7	Orfordness, England.
5	Ombay.	8	Orient, L'.
6	Ombrone River.	9	Orinoco.
7	Omega Shoal.	7860	Oristano.
8	Ommanney, Cape.	1	Orizaba, Mountain.
9	Omoa.	2	Orkney, Islands.
7820	Onaseuse Island.	3	Orlando, Cape.
1	Oneata Island.	4	Orleana Shoal.
2	Oneehow Island.	5	Orlovsk.
3	Onega.	6	Orme's Head.
4	Onemene River.	7	Ormsbee Shoal.
5	Ongea Island.	8	Ormuz Island.
6	Ono Island.	9	Orne.
7	Ono Islands.	7870	Ornellas, Mt.
8	Onoune Islet.	1	Oroloug.
9	Ons Island.	2	Orontes Reef.
7830	Ontario Reef.	3	Oropesa, Cape.
1	Ontong Java Islands.	4	Orosenga Island.
2	Ooglit Islands.	5	Orotava.
3	Oologan Point.	6	Orote Islet.
4	Oomel Grushe.	7	Orrengrund.
5	Oparo Island.	8	Orskär Light.
6	Open Bay.	9	Ortegal Cape.
7	Ophir Mountain.	7880	Ortiz Bank.
7838	Oporto.	7881	Ortona.

Nos.	ORU	Nos.	PAG
7882	Oruba Island.	7925	Ouroup Island.
3	O Sima Island.	6	Oury Island.
4	Os Ilheos.	7	Outao.
5	Osborne, Cape.	8	Outer Rep Island.
6	Osborne Reef.	9	Ouwer Ouwer Point.
7	Oscar, Fort.	7930	Oval Mountain.
8	Osnaburgh Island.	1	Ovalau Island.
9	Osprey Shoal.	2	Ovalu Island.
7890	Ossa.	3	Oven, The.
1	Ossa Mountain.	4	Ovo Island, Archipelago.
2	Ossa Skerry.	5	Ovo Island, Greece.
3	Ostend.	6	Owen, Port.
4	Ostergarnsholm.	7	Owen Shoal.
5	Osterley Shoals.	8	Owers Light.
6	Oster Yökel.	9	Owharree Harbor.
7	Ostro, Point.	7940	Owhyhee Island.
8	Otago Point.	1	Owl's Head Bay.
9	Otaha Island.	2	Oxia Island.
7900	Otaheite Island.	3	Oxö Light.
1	Otchakov.	4	Oyolava.
2	Otdia.	5	Oyster Bay.
3	Otea Island.	6	Oyster Island.
4	Oteavamea.	7	Oyster Rocks.
5	Otihi.	8	Ozernoi, Cape.
6	Otoohoo Island.	9	Ozy Point.
7	Otoque Islands.	7950	Pabbay Island.
8	Otou, Cape.	1	Pacasmayo Point.
9	Otranto.	2	Pacence, Ras.
7910	Otway, Cape.	3	Pachacamac Islands.
1	Otway Port.	4	Pacific.
2	Ouap Island.	5	Packerort.
3	Ouda River.	6	Padang Head.
4	Oudou-oudou.	7	Padaran, Cape.
5	Ouessant Island.	8	Paddeway Bay.
6	Ougamok Island.	9	Paddipholo Atoll.
7	Ouleay Islands.	7960	Padre, Port del.
8	Ouliouthy Islands.	1	Padron Point.
9	Oumnack Island.	2	Padstow.
7920	Ounalashka Island.	3	Pagoda, Cape.
1	Ounalga Island.	4	Pagoda Island.
2	Ounekotan Island.	5	Pagoda Point, E. Africa.
3	Ounimack.	6	Pagoda, Gulf of Martaban.
7924	Oura Island.	7967	Pagon Island.

228

Nos.	PAG	Nos.	PAO
7968	Paguayan.	8011	Palomos Island, Spain.
9	Pagvilao Island.	2	Palompon, Port.
7970	Paho River.	3	Palopa.
1	Paihea Mission.	4	Palos.
2	Pailluri, Cape.	5	Palos, Cape de.
3	Paimbœuf.	6	Palumban Islands.
4	Pajaro Island.	7	Paman, Cape.
5	Pajaros Islets.	8	Pamanoukan Point.
6	Pak Chan River.	9	Pemaroong Island.
7	Pakefield Light.	8020	Pampatan.
8	Palabi Island.	1	Pamlico Sound.
9	Palais, Port de.	2	Pan de Azucar.
7980	Palaon Bay.	3	Pan de Guaijaibon.
1	Palapa, Port.	4	Pan de Matanzas.
2	Palawan Island.	5	Panagatan Shoal.
3	Palozzo, Port.	6	Panagia, Cape.
4	Palembang Point.	7	Panagia Nisi.
5	Palermo.	8	Panama.
6	Palermo Port.	9	Panaon Island.
7	Pali, Cape.	8030	Panaria Island.
8	Palinurus Reefs.	1	Panay Island.
9	Palinurus Shoal.	2	Pancha Island.
7990	Palliser, Cape, New Britain.	3	Pandagitan.
1	Palliser, Cape, New Zealand.	4	Pandan Point.
2	Palm Islands.	5	Pandora Entrance.
3	Palma, Canaries.	6	Pandora Reef, Solomon Islands.
4	Palma Majorca.	7	Pandora Reef, S. Pacific.
5	Palmajola Island.	8	Panga.
6	Palma Marina.	9	Pangani Point.
7	Palmarola Island.	8040	Panghu Island.
8	Palmas.	1	Pangootaran.
9	Palmas Cape.	2	Pango-Pango.
8000	Palmas Island.	3	Panjang, Pulo, Gulf of Siam.
1	Palmas Point.	4	Panjang, Pulo, N. Coast Java.
2	Palmer Shoal.	5	Panjang, New Guinea.
3	Palmerston, Cape.	6	Panjang, N. W. of Banca.
4	Palmerston Islands.	7	Panjangan Island.
5	Palmetto Point.	8	Panka Point.
6	Palmiras Point.	9	Pantai River.
7	Palmo, Cape.	8050	Pantar.
8	Palmyra Point.	1	Pantellaria Island.
9	Palmyras Island.	2	Panumbangam.
8010	Palomos Island, Africa.	8053	Pao Mount.

Nos.	PAO	Nos.	PAT
8054	Paoom Islands.	8097	Pass Cavallo.
5	Papa Island.	8	Pass Christian Light.
6	Papado Bay.	9	Pass Fourchon, Louisiana, U. S.
7	Papas Cape.	8100	Passage Island, Banda Sea.
8	Papeete Harbor.	1	Passage Island, Feejee Islands.
9	Paposa.	2	Passage Island, Madagascar.
8060	Paps of Bio Bio.	3	Passage Island, Philippines.
1	Paquiqui Cape.	4	Passage Island, South China.
2	Para.	5	Passage Island, S. E. China.
3	Paracca Village.	6	Passage Island, Sumatra.
4	Paracels.	7	Passage Island, West Indies.
5	Parahyba River.	8	Passage, Port.
6	Parahyba do Norte River.	9	Passamaquoddy Bay.
7	Parallel Peak.	8110	Passandava Bay.
8	Paramaribo.	1	Passaro Island.
9	Paramatta.	2	Passarouan.
8070	Paranaan Point.	3	Passe, Island de.
1	Paranagua Bay.	4	Passier.
2	Parang, Pulo, Indian Archipelago.	5	Passig Island.
3	Parang, Pulo, Java Sea.	6	Passion Rock Island.
4	Parasan Island.	7	Passy Cape.
5	Parcelar Hill.	8	Patagonia.
6	Parece Vela.	9	Patahecock Island.
7	Paredes, Point de.	8120	Patani Cape.
8	Parenzo.	1	Patapsco River.
9	Parga.	2	Patchitan Bay.
8080	Pargo Point.	3	Patchusan Island.
1	Parigy.	4	Paternoster Islands.
2	Parina Point.	5	Paternoster Point.
3	Paris.	6	Paternosters, Great.
4	Parmesang Hill.	7	Paternosters, Little.
5	Paros Island.	8	Paterson Cape.
6	Parry Cape, America, N. Coast.	9	Paterson Island.
7	Parry Cape, Greenland.	8130	Paterson, Port.
8	Parry Island.	1	Patience Cape.
9	Parry Islet.	2	Patiro Cape.
8090	Parry's Group.	3	Patmos.
1	Partridge Island.	4	Patook River.
2	Partridge Point.	5	Patras.
3	Pasanhan.	6	Patrick, St., Head.
4	Pasha Harbor.	7	Patrocinio Island.
5	Pasley Cape.	8	Patta.
8096	Pass a l'Outre, Mississippi Delta.	8139	Patten Point.

16

Nos.	PAU	Nos.	PEN
8140	Paul de Loando.	8183	Peel, England.
1	Paul, St., Cape.	4	Peel Island.
2	Paul, St., Cathedral.	5	Pegasus, Port.
3	Paul, St., Harbor.	6	Pegu.
4	Paul, St., Rocks.	7	Peignes Rocks.
5	Paul, St., Island, Indian Ocean.	8	Pei-ho River.
6	Paul, St., Island, Low Archip'go.	9	Peking, China.
7	Paul, St., Island, North America.	8190	Pela Point.
8	Paul, St., Island, Alaska, U. S.	1	Pelado Rock.
9	Paumben Point.	2	Pelagisi.
8150	Pauna Point.	3	Pelagosa Islands.
1	Pauroma River.	4	Pelée Island.
2	Pawen Island.	5	Pelelew Island.
3	Paximades Islands.	6	Pelew Islands.
4	Paxo Island.	7	Pelican Point.
5	Payta.	8	Peling Island.
6	Peacock Island.	9	Pelion Mount.
7	Peaked Island.	8200	Pellew Cape.
8	Pearce Cay.	1	Pellew, Sir E., Islands.
9	Pearce Point, Australia.	2	Pellinge, Great.
8160	Pearl Island.	3	Pelly Islands.
1	Pearl Lagoon.	4	Pelorus Rock.
2	Pearl Rocks.	5	Pelsart Group.
3	Pearl & Hermes Reef.	6	Pelung Cape.
4	Pearson Shoal.	7	Pemba Island.
5	Pearson's Islands.	8	Pembrey.
6	Pecora Cape.	9	Pembroke.
7	Pedaso.	8210	Pembroke Cape, Falkland Islands.
8	Pedder Islands.	1	Pembroke Cape, Southampton Isl'd.
9	Pedestal Point.	2	Penang Island.
8170	Pedir Point.	3	Penantipode Island.
1	Pedra Blanca.	4	Penas Cape, Spain.
2	Pedra Branca.	5	Penas Cape, Tierra del Fuego.
3	Pedro Bank.	6	Pencarrow Head.
4	Pedro Bluff.	7	Penda Shoal.
5	Pedro de Roda.	8	Pendulum Islands.
6	Pedro Nalasco Island.	9	Penedo de San Pedro.
7	Pedro Point, Jamaica.	8220	Penguin Island.
8	Pedro Point, Sumatra.	1	Penguin Islands.
9	Pedro, St., Bay.	2	Penguin Point.
8180	Pedro, St., Island.	3	Penha Grande.
1	Peejow Village.	4	Peni Island.
8182	Peel, Australia.	8225	Peniscola.

Nos.	PEN	Nos.	PIA
8226	Penlan Point.	8269	Peru Island.
7	Penmaquid Harbor, Maine.	8270	Pervo-ousmotrennaia.
8	Penmarc'h Rocks.	1	Pesanda Islands.
9	Penna Point.	2	Pesaro.
8230	Pennant Point.	3	Pescador Island.
1	Pennee, Pulo.	4	Pescadores Islands, Formosa.
2	Pennsylvania.	5	Pescadores Islands, N. Pacific.
3	Pennsylvania Island.	6	Pescadores Point.
4	Pennsylvania Shoals.	7	Pescaro.
5	Penobscot Bay.	8	Peschichi.
6	Penobscot River.	9	Pe-shan Islands.
7	Penrose Rocks.	8280	Petalies Islands.
8	Penrhyn Cape.	1	Peter and Paul Ch.
9	Penrhyn Island.	2	Peter, St., Island, Antarctic Ocean.
8240	Pensacola Bay.	3	Peter, St., Island, N. Pacific.
1	Pentecote Island.	4	Peter's, St., Islands.
2	Pentire Point.	5	Peterhead.
3	Pentland Skerries.	6	Petersburgh, St.
4	Penzance.	7	Petersburg, Virginia.
5	Pepe Cape.	8	Petit Manan.
6	Pepin Island.	9	Petite Terre.
7	Pera Cape.	8290	Petracciato.
8	Pera Head.	1	Petrie Reef.
9	Pera Pulo.	2	Petrolo Point.
8250	Perallo Point.	3	Phanari Cape.
1	Percy Island.	4	Pheleohe Island.
2	Percy Islands.	5	Phenix Island.
3	Perdido Bay, Alabama.	6	Philadelphia.
4	Peregrine Point.	7	Philip Cape.
5	Perez Island.	8	Philip Island, Caroline Islands.
6	Perim Island, Arabia.	9	Philip Island, Low Archipelago.
7	Perim Island, India.	8300	Philip Island, South Pacific.
8	Pernambuco.	1	Philip Broke Cape.
9	Pernau.	2	Philip de Benguela.
8260	Peron Islands.	3	Philippeville.
1	Peros Banbos Islands.	4	Philippine Islands.
2	Perpendicular Point.	5	Phillip Island.
3	Perpetua Cape.	6	Phillip Port.
4	Perpignan.	7	Phineka.
5	Persian Gulf.	8	Phipps Cape.
6	Perth.	9	Phoowa Moloku Island.
7	Pertominsk.	8310	Phuyen Harbor.
8268	Peru.	8311	Piana Island.

Nos.	PIA	Nos.	PLA
8312	Pianosa Island, Adriatic.	8355	Pinheira Point.
3	Pianosa Island, Italy.	6	Pinnacle Island, Formosa.
4	Pic de l'Etoile.	7	Pinnacle Island, Japan.
5	Pichidanque Bay.	8	Pinon Island.
6	Picholo Point.	9	Pinos Island.
7	Pickering Peak.	8360	Pinos Point.
8	Pic Lamanon.	1	Pinque Island.
9	Pico.	2	Pinunko.
8320	Pico Fragos.	3	Pinxter Point.
1	Pico Ruivo.	4	Pio Quinto, Port.
2	Picos Point.	5	Piombino.
3	Picton Harbor.	6	Piperi Island, Grecian Archip'go.
4	Piedra de Mar.	7	Pipon Islands.
5	Piedras Cay.	8	Piræus.
6	Piedras, Cay de.	9	Pirano.
7	Piedras Point.	8370	Pirate Cay.
8	Pierre au Vrack.	1	Pirate Islands, Gulf of Tonquin.
9	Pierre, St.	2	Pirate Islands, Philippines.
8330	Pierre, St., Island, Anambas.	3	Pisa.
1	Pierre, St., Island, Indian Ocean.	4	Pisagua River.
2	Pierre, St., Island, Newfoundland.	5	Pisan.
3	Pierson Cape.	6	Pisang, Pulo, Indian Archipelago.
4	Pietro, St., Island.	7	Pisang, Pulo, Pitt Passage.
5	Pigali Island.	8	Pisang, Pulo, Strait of Malacca.
6	Pigeon Island, Dampier Strait.	9	Pisang, Pulo, Sumatra.
7	Pigeon Island, Ceylon.	8380	Piscataqua River, New Hampshire.
8	Pigeon Island, Malabar Cape.	1	Piscataway, Maryland.
9	Pigott Point.	2	Pisco.
8340	Pih-ki-shan Islands.	3	Piscopia.
1	Pih-quan Peak.	4	Pise Island.
2	Pih-seang Islands.	5	Piserarr.
3	Pilier Island.	6	Pisonia Island.
4	Pillar Cape, Magellan Strait.	7	Pisura River.
5	Pillar Cape, Van Dieman's Land.	8	Pitcairn Island.
6	Pillau.	9	Pitea.
7	Pinckney, Fort.	8390	Pitt Bank.
8	Pine Cape.	1	Pitt Cape.
9	Pine Peak.	2	Pitt Island, Gilbert Archipelago.
8350	Pines Cape.	3	Pitt Island, South Pacific.
1	Pines Island, Cuba.	4	Pitt Island, S. Shetland.
2	Pines Island, New Caledonia.	5	Pitt Passage.
3	Ping-hae Bay.	6	Pittie.
8354	Ping-hai.	8397	Placa Islands.

Nos.	PLA	Nos.	POR
8398	Placentia Harbor.	8441	Poll Rock.
9	Placer de Jagua.	2	Polla Rock.
8400	Pladda Lights.	3	Pollock Cove.
1	Plaintain Islands.	4	Pollock Reef.
2	Plaka, Cape.	5	Pollock Rock.
3	Plana Cays.	6	Pollux Rock.
4	Plana Island, Archipelago.	7	Pomba Bay.
5	Plana Island, Spain.	8	Pomo Rock.
6	Planier Island.	9	Ponafidin Island.
7	Plata Island.	8450	Ponchang Kacheel Island.
8	Plate Island.	1	Pond, Cape.
9	Plate River.	2	Pond, Mount.
8410	Platform Point.	3	Pondicherry.
1	Platte Island.	4	Ponghou Islands.
2	Pleasant Cape.	5	Pon-Kan River.
3	Pleasant Island.	6	Pontang Point.
4	Pleasant River.	7	Pontiana River.
5	Pleinmont.	8	Pontchartrain Lake, Louisiana.
6	Plettenburg Bay.	9	Ponza Island.
7	Plouguerneau.	8460	Poole.
8	Plum Island.	1	Popa, Pulo.
9	Plumb Island.	2	Popo.
8420	Plummer Island.	3	Pora Islands.
1	Plymouth, England.	4	Porcelli Rocks.
2	Plymouth, Mass., U. S.	5	Porcos Islands.
3	Plymouth, Montserrat.	6	Pori Island.
4	Plymouth, New.	7	Poriam Point.
5	Pnaougoun, Cape.	8	Porirua Harbor.
6	Pocklington Shoal.	9	Poromoushir Island.
7	Poge, Cape.	8470	Poros Island.
8	Poggy Islands.	1	Porquerolles Island.
9	Poivre Islands.	2	Porpoise, Cape.
8430	Pol de Léon.	3	Portage Island.
1	Pola.	4	Port-au-Prince.
2	Pola Island.	5	Portendik.
3	Pola, Sta., Cape.	6	Portitski.
4	Policandro Island.	7	Portland, England.
5	Policastro.	8	Portland, Maine, U. S.
6	Polignano.	9	Portland Cape, Cape Breton.
7	Polillo Island.	8480	Portland Cape, Van Dieman's.Land.
8	Polino Island.	1	Portland Island.
9	Polior Island, and Shoal.	2	Portland Islands.
8440	Poliwero, Cape.	8483	Portland Point, Hudson's Bay.

Nos.	POR	Nos.	PRO
8484	Portland Point, Jamaica.	8527	Poverty Bay.
5	Portland Rock.	8	Powell's Islands.
6	Portlock Reef.	9	Poyas Peak.
7	Port-on-Craig.	8530	Pozzuoli.
8	Port Patrick.	1	Prasliu Island,
9	Port Royal, Jamaica.	2	Praslin, Port, New Ireland.
8490	Port Royal, S. Carolina.	3	Praslin Port, Solomon Islands.
1	Port Royal Harbor.	4	Prasso Nisi, Cape.
2	Porto Bello.	5	Pratas Shoal.
3	Porto Cabello.	6	Pratt Shoal.
4	Porto Fino, Cape.	7	Praubilah Point.
5	Porto Grande.	8	Prawle Point.
6	Porto Novo, Coromandel.	9	Praya, Port.
7	Porto Novo, Gold Coast.	8540	Precelly Top.
8	Porto Re.	1	Predpriatié Island.
9	Porto Rico Island.	2	Premiera Rocks.
8500	Porto Santo.	3	Preparis Island.
1	Porto Santo Island.	4	Preston, Cape.
2	Porto Seguro.	5	Prevesa.
3	Porto Vecchio.	6	Priaman.
4	Portrush.	7	Price, Cape.
5	Portsmouth, England.	8	Prieto, Cape, Solomon Islands.
6	Portsmouth, New Hampshire, U. S.	9	Prieto, Cape, Spain.
7	Portugal.	8550	Prim Point.
8	Portugalete.	1	Prince Island.
9	Possession, Cape, S. Shetlands.	2	Prince Edward Island.
8510	Possession, Cape, Tierra del Fuego.	3	Prince Edward Islands.
1	Possession Island, New Guinea.	4	Prince of Wales' Bank.
2	Possession Island, Torres Straits.	5	Prince of Wales' Cape.
3	Possession Mount.	6	Prince of Wales' Island.
4	Possession, North Island.	7	Prince of Wales' Sound.
5	Possidi, Cape.	8	Prince Regent Haven.
6	Post Horse Reef.	9	Prince Regent's River.
7	Post Office Bay.	8560	Prince William Henry Island.
8	Post Orange.	1	Prince's Bay.
9	Postilions.	2	Prince's Island, Bight of Biafra.
8520	Potol Point.	3	Prince's Island, Strait of Sunda.
1	Pottbakker Island.	4	Princess Harbor.
2	Pouhia-i-wakadi.	5	Princess Island.
3	Pouinipet Island.	6	Printian, Pulo.
4	Poulkova.	7	Prior, Cape.
5	Poulouhot Island.	8	Prise, Isle de la.
8526	Poulousouk Island.	8569	Procida Island.

Nos.	PRO	Nos.	QUI
8570	Procofieff Island.	8613	Quade.
1	Prodano Island.	4	Quadra Island.
2	Præstöe.	5	Quail Island, Australia.
3	Proisdo Island.	6	Quail Island, Cape Verde Islands.
4	Promontory Porer Cape.	7	Quail Island, Madagascar.
5	Protection, Port.	8	Quamannu Bay.
6	Proti Island.	9	Quarken.
7	Proudfoot Shoal.	8620	Quebec.
8	Provençal Island.	1	Queda.
9	Providence.	2	Quedal Cape.
8580	Providence Island, Indian Ocean.	3	Queen Charlotte C., New Caledonia.
1	Providence Island, New Guinea.	4	Queen Charlotte Cape, S. Pacific.
2	Providence Islands.	5	Queen Charlotte Island.
3	Prudhoo Island.	6	Queen Charlotte Islands.
4	Prussia.	7	Queen Charlotte Sound.
5	Psyche's Islands.	8	Queen's Cape.
6	Pubnico Harbor.	9	Queen's Mount.
7	Pudding-pan Hill.	8630	Queimada Islands.
8	Pueblo, Port.	1	Quelpaert.
9	Puget Cape.	2	Quemado Mount.
8590	Puget Sound.	3	Quemoy Island.
1	Puig das Aguilas.	4	Querimba Island.
2	Puka Puka.	5	Qui Quick.
3	Pulicat.	6	Quibo.
4	Pullam Island.	7	Quicara.
5	Pulo Laut, Little Islands.	8	Quickme.
6	Pulpit Rock.	9	Quicombo Bay.
7	Puna Island.	8640	Quilan Cape.
8	Punnecoil.	1	Quilca.
9	Puntas Arenas.	2	Quillates Cape.
8600	Purcell Island.	3	Quillebœuf.
1	Purdies Islands.	4	Quillimane River.
2	Purdy Islands.	5	Quiloa.
3	Purvis Cape.	6	Quiloan.
4	Puysegur Point.	7	Quimper River.
5	Pyagik Cape.	8	Quinatancan Island.
6	Pyghella Island.	9	Quinhone Harbor.
7	Pylstaart Island.	8650	Quiniluban.
8	Pyramid Island, Bass Strait.	1	Quintin, St.
9	Pyramid Island, Cochin China.	2	Quiros.
8610	Pyramid Point.	3	Quiros Cape.
1	Pyramid Rock.	4	Quirpon Island.
8612	Quaco.	8655	Quistholm.

Nos.	QUI	Nos.	REA
8656	Quita Sueno Bank.	8699	Ramirez Bank.
7	Quitta.	8700	Ramos Islands.
8	Quoddy Head.	1	Ramsey Island.
9	Quoin.	2	Ramsgate.
8660	Quoin Island.	3	Ranai Island.
1	Quoin Point.	4	Ranay Mount.
2	Quoin, Great.	5	Rangazvak.
3	Quorra River.	6	Ranger Island.
4	Quoy Cape.	7	Ranger Rock.
5	Rabbit Islands, Grecian Archip'go.	8	Rangoon.
6	Rabbit Islands, Philippines.	9	Raoul Cape.
7	Rabi Island.	8710	Raoul Island, Kermadec Islands.
8	Race Cape.	1	Raoul Island, South Pacific.
9	Race Point.	2	Raour Island.
8670	Rachado Cape.	3	Rapel Shoal.
1	Rachlin Island.	4	Raper Cape.
2	Racket, Pulo.	5	Raphti, Port.
3	Radack Islands.	6	Rapurapu Island.
4	Radstock Cape.	7	Raraka.
5	Rafael Cape.	8	Raroia.
6	Rafael, San, Island.	9	Rarotonga Island.
7	Raft Point, Australia, N. W.	8720	Rasa Island.
8	Raft Point, Buccaneer's Archip'go.	1	Rasalgett.
9	Ragged Island.	2	Rasca Point.
8680	Ragged Island, Great.	3	Rashau Island.
1	Ragged Islands.	4	Rat Island.
2	Ragged Point, Borneo.	5	Rathbone Island.
3	Ragged Point, Timor.	6	Rathlin O'Birne Islands.
4	Raggedy Point.	7	Ratmanoff Island.
5	Ragusa.	8	Rattray Point.
6	Raiatea Island.	9	Raukoko Island.
7	Raieffsky Island.	8730	Raukura.
8	Raine Island.	1	Raven Island.
9	Rajah Bassa.	2	Ravenna.
8690	Rajah Point.	3	Rawson Shoal.
1	Rajah, Pulo.	4	Ray Cape.
2	Rajapour Harbor.	5	Raza.
3	Rakau-manga-manga.	6	Raza Island, Brazil.
4	Raleigh Mount.	7	Raza Island, South Africa.
5	Ralick Islands.	8	Razat Cape.
6	Ramas Cape.	9	Razzoli Island.
7	Rame Head, England.	8740	R'dresser, Ras.
8698	Rame Head, Kafferland.	8741	Rea Head.

Nos.	REA	Nos.	RIF
8742	Realejo.	8785	Rennell Island.
3	Reaumur Peak.	6	Renyang Island.
4	Reccan, Ras.	7	Repon Island.
5	Reccan River.	8	Repulse Bay.
6	Recherche Archipelago.	9	Repulse Islands.
7	Recherche Bay.	8790	Resolution Bay.
8	Recherche, Cape.	1	Resolution Island.
9	Recif, Cape.	2	Resolution Cape.
8750	Recif Island.	3	Resolution Port.
1	Redang Islands.	4	Rest Bay.
2	Redcar.	5	Restoration Island.
3	Red Head, Baffin's Bay.	6	Return Reef.
4	Red Head, Scotland.	7	Retymo.
5	Red Island.	8	Revel.
6	Red Point.	9	Reville.
7	Red Sea.	8800	Revsnig. Cape.
8	Redonda Mountain.	1	Rewa Roads.
9	Redondo Island.	2	Rey Island.
8760	Redondo Rock, Bass Strait.	3	Reyes, Point de los.
1	Redondo Rock, Galapagos.	4	Rezo.
2	Reed Island.	5	Rhe Island.
3	Reef Island.	6	Rhenea.
4	Reevesby Island.	7	Rhinns of Isla.
5	Refsnœs.	8	Rhode Island.
6	Refsudden Light.	9	Rhodes.
7	Refuge, Port.	8810	Rhone River.
8	Reggio.	1	Riackah Island.
9	Reid Rocks.	2	Riah, Pulo.
8770	Reid's Islands.	3	Ribadeo.
1	Reierskar Rock.	4	Rica de Oro Rock.
2	Reikianes, Cape.	5	Rica de Plata.
3	Reikiavig.	6	Rich Island.
4	Reinga, Cape.	7	Richardson, Cape.
5	Reirson Island.	8	Riche Island.
6	Reitoue.	9	Richibucto Harbor.
7	Rembang.	8820	Richmond, Virginia, U. S.
8	Remedios Point.	1	Richmond Bay, Hudson's Bay.
9	Remire Island.	2	Richmond Bay, Prince Edw. Island.
8780	Renard Islands.	3	Richmond Islands.
1	Rendezvous Harbor.	4	Ricord, Cape.
2	Rendezvous Island.	5	Ridge Shoal.
3	Rennel, Cape.	6	Ridley Island.
8784	Rennel Island.	8827	Rifunsherry Island.

Nos.	RIG	Nos.	RON
8828	Riga.	8871	Rochefort.
9	Riguy Cape.	2	Rochelle.
8830	Riley, Cape.	3	Rochelois Shoal.
1	Riley, Point.	4	Roches Douvres.
2	Rimini.	5	Rock, Cape.
3	Rimitara Island.	6	Rockabil Islands.
4	Rimsky Korsakoff Islands.	7	Rockal.
5	Ringdove Shoal.	8	Rockingham Bay.
6	Rio Doce.	9	Rocks Island.
7	Rio Grande, Guatemala.	8880	Rocky Bank.
8	Rio Grande, Mexico.	1	Rocky Cape.
9	Rio Grande do Norte.	2	Rocky Head.
8840	Rio Grande do Sul.	3	Rocky Point, Aracan.
1	Rio Janeiro.	4	Rocky Point, New Zealand.
2	Rio Nunez.	5	Rocky Point, Sumbawa.
3	Rio Point del.	6	Rocky Point, Van Dieman's Land.
4	Rio Tronto.	7	Rodkallen Rocks.
5	Riou Island.	8	Rodney, Cape.
6	Riou Point.	9	Rodney Point.
7	Riow.	8890	Rodoni, Cape.
8	Risk Point.	1	Rodosto.
9	Ritchie's Reef.	2	Rodrigue.
8850	Ritidian Point.	3	Roebuck Point.
1	River Charlotte Shoal.	4	Roeeness Hill.
2	River, Fort.	5	Rohamba Point.
3	Rivers, Cape.	6	Roissy Island.
4	Rivoli.	7	Rokbo.
5	Rixhöft.	8	Roldan Mountain.
6	Rizzuto, Cape.	9	Rolfs Islands.
7	Roa Poua.	8900	Rollin Cape.
8	Roan Island.	1	Roma.
9	Roanoke Island, N. Carolina, U. S.	2	Roman Cape.
8860	Roanoke River.	3	Roman, San, Cape.
1	Robben Island, Sagalin.	4	Romania Point.
2	Rob Roy Rock.	5	Romano, Cape.
3	Robert's Island.	6	Romanzoff, Cape.
4	Roca, Cape.	7	Romanzoff Island, Low Archipelago.
5	Roca de Plata.	8	Romanzoff Island, Marshall Islands.
6	Roca Partida, N. Pacific.	9	Romberg, Cape.
7	Roca Partida, Vera Cruz.	8910	Rome.
8	Rocas.	1	Rona Island.
9	Roche Bonne.	2	Ronaldsay Island.
8870	Roche Point.	8913	Roncador Cay.

239

Nos.	RON	Nos.	RUM
8914	Roncador Reefs.	8957	Rottum Island.
5	Rondo.	8	Rottumah Island.
6	Rondo, Pulo.	9	Rouabouki Island.
7	Rönne.	8960	Roug Islands.
8	Ronakar.	1	Rouge Harbor.
9	Rooke Island.	2	Reuib.
8920	Roque, St., Cape.	3	Roumelia.
1	Roquepiz.	4	Roumiantsov Cape.
2	Roques, Los.	5	Round Cape.
3	Rosa Point.	6	Round Hill, Australia.
4	Rosa, Sta., Bay.	7	Round Hill, Rhode Island.
5	Rosa, Sta., Island, Florida.	8	Round Island, Corea.
6	Rosa, Sta., Island, Mexico.	9	Round Island, Feejee Islands.
7	Rosa, Sta., Island, N. Pacific.	8970	Round Island, Indian Ocean.
8	Rosa, Sta., Shoal.	1	Round Island, Recherche Arch'go.
9	Rosalie Rock.	2	Roupat, Pulo.
8930	Rosalind Bank.	3	Routh Rock.
1	Rosaretta Reef.	4	Roux Cape.
2	Rosario Channel.	5	Rover Island.
3	Rosario Island.	6	Rover Shoal.
4	Rosario Islands.	7	Rovigno.
5	Rose Island.	8	Rovouma Cape.
6	Roseau.	9	Roway, Ras.
7	Rosemary Island.	8980	Rowley Shoals.
8	Roseness.	1	Roxo Cape, Gulf of Guinea.
9	Roseto.	2	Roxo Cape, Karamania.
8940	Rosetta.	3	Roxo Cape, Mexico.
1	Rosily Island.	4	Roxo Cape, Porto Rico.
2	Rosiugyn.	5	Roxo Cape, St. Domingo.
3	Ross Bay.	6	Royal Bishops.
4	Ross Island.	7	Royal Captain, Shoal.
5	Rossel Island.	8	Royal, Fort.
6	Rossell Sea Mk.	9	Royal, George, Shoal.
7	Rosso Cape.	8990	Royalist Shoal.
8	Rost Island.	1	Royau, Port.
9	Rostock.	2	Ruatan Island.
8950	Rota.	3	Rugen.
1	Rota Island.	4	Rugged Islands.
2	Rotch Island.	5	Rugged Point.
3	Rothakar.	6	Rum Cay.
4	Rottee.	7	Rum Island.
5	Rottenest Island.	8	Rumby Mounts.
8956	Rotterdam.	8999	Ru More.

Nos.	RU	Nos.	SAL
9000	Ru Stor.	9043	Sacrificios Island.
1	Run, Pulo.	4	Saddle Group.
2	Runawai Cape.	5	Saddle Hill, Andamans.
3	Rundlestone Beacon.	6	Saddle Hill, British Honduras.
4	Runebrake Shoal.	7	Saddle Hill, New Zealand.
5	Runo Island.	8	Saddle Hill, Tartary.
6	Rupert's House.	9	Saddle Island, China.
7	Rurick Islands.	9050	Saddle Island, China Sea.
8	Rurick Rock.	1	Saddle Island, Corea.
9	Rurutú Island.	2	Saddle Island, Indian Archipelago.
9010	Rusa Linguete.	3	Saddle Island, Labrador.
1	Rusa Raji.	4	Saddle Island, New Orkneys.
2	Russia.	5	Saddle Island, Philippines.
3	Russian Promontory.	6	Saddle Island, Strait of Gaspar.
4	Russki Zavorot Cape.	7	Saddle Island, Strait of Malacca.
5	Rybatchy Island.	8	Saddle of Payta.
6	Rye.	9	Saddleback Island.
7	Ryk Islands.	9060	Saddleback Ledge.
8	Ryvingen Island.	1	Sado Island.
9	Saavedra Cape.	2	Sadras.
9020	Saba.	3	Safety Beacon.
1	Sabanilla, Port.	4	Safi.
2	Sabanoon.	5	Sagalin.
3	Sabbskar.	6	Sahul Bank.
4	Sabelo Point.	7	Said Point.
5	Sabina Shoal.	8	Saigon.
6	Sabine City.	9	Sail Rock.
7	Sabine Pass.	9070	Saints, The.
8	Sabine Pass Light-house.	1	Sal.
9	Sabine River.	2	Sal Cay.
9030	Sable Cape, Florida.	3	Sal Rocks.
1	Sable Cape, Nova Scotia.	4	Salaberria Reef.
2	Sable Island, Cape Breton.	5	Salamanca Peak.
3	Sable Island, Indian Ocean.	6	Salang Island.
4	Sable Reef.	7	Salango Island.
5	Sables d'Olonne.	8	Salangore.
6	Sabtan Island.	9	Salanketa Point.
7	Sabuda, Pulo.	9080	Salavako Island.
8	Sacken Island.	1	Salawatty.
9	Saco Harbor.	2	Salaway Point.
9040	Sacquoy Head.	3	Salayer Island.
1	Sacratif Cape.	4	Sala y Gomez.
9042	Sacrifice Rock.	9085	Salcombe.

Nos.	SAL	Nos.	SAN
9086	Saldanha Bay.	9129	Samarang Islands.
7	Salem, Mass., U. S.	9130	Samasana Island.
8	Salem, N. Jersey, U. S.	1	Sambas River.
9	Sale Macowa.	2	Samboangan.
9090	Salerno.	3	Sambro Island.
1	Salibabos Islands.	4	Samoa Islands.
2	Salice Island.	5	Samos.
3	Salina Island.	6	Samothraki Island, Grecian Archip.
4	Salinas, Brazil.	7	Samothraki Island, Ionian Islands.
5	Salinas, Peru.	8	Samoy.
6	Salinas, Yucatan.	9	Sampanmango Point.
7	Salinas Island.	9140	Samsoun.
8	Salinas, Cape.	1	Samsoun Mountain.
9	Salinas Point, St. Domingo.	2	Samur Island.
9100	Salinas Point, W. Africa.	3	Sansapu Harbor.
1	Salinas Point, Yucatan Island.	4	San Blas Harbor.
2	Salingar Island.	5	Sancassee Island.
3	Salisbury Island.	6	Sancori, Pulo.
4	Sallabanka Islands.	7	Sand Bay.
5	Sallahtook Point.	8	Sand Cey.
6	Sallee.	9	Sand Island, Alabama.
7	Salleolookit Rock.	9150	Sand Island, Gaspar St.
8	Salmadina Shoal.	1	Sandakan Bay.
9	Salmon Cove.	2	Sandalwood Bay.
9110	Salo Light.	3	Sandalwood Island.
1	Salomon, Cape.	4	Sanday Island.
2	Salomon Islands.	5	Sandbuys Shoals.
3	Salomon Sweert, Cape.	6	Sanderson Hope.
4	Salonika.	7	Sandhead.
5	Salou.	8	Sandkallen.
6	Salt's White Rocks.	9	Sandoway.
7	Saltees Light.	9160	Sandown Castle.
8	Salut Islands.	1	Sandspit Light.
9	Salvador Islands.	2	Sandwich Bay.
9120	Salvador Port.	3	Sandwich, Cape.
1	Salvages.	4	Sandwich Island, New Hebrides.
2	Samalga Island.	5	Sandwich Island, S. Pacific.
3	Samana, Cape.	6	Sandwich Islands, N. Pacific.
4	Samana Cay.	7	Sandwich Island, S. Atlantic.
5	Samanco Bay.	8	Sandwich, Port, New Hebrides.
6	Samar Island.	9	Sandwich, Port, S. Africa.
7	Samarang.	9170	Sandy, Cape.
9128	Samarang Island.	9171	Sandy Cay.

Nos.	SAN	Nos.	SCA
9172	Sandy Hook.	9215	Sarakino.
3	Sandy Island, Australia.	6	Sarawak River.
4	Sandy Island, Borneo.	7	Sardina, Cape.
5	Sandy Island, Madagascar.	8	Sardinia.
6	Sandy Island, Meia-co-sim.	9	Sariguan Island.
7	Sandy Island, Great.	9220	Saritch, Cape.
8	Sangald.	1	Saritchev, Cape.
9	Sangallan Island.	2	Sarmiento Mountain.
9180	Sangar, Cape.	3	Sarytcheff Peak.
1	Sangboys Island.	4	Sasseno Island.
2	Sangian Sira Point.	5	Sasso, Cape.
3	Sanguin River.	6	Satahoual Island.
4	Sanguinares Islands.	7	Satellite Rock.
5	Sanguir.	8	Sau.
6	Sanho, Cape.	9	Saugor Island.
7	Sannagh Island.	9230	Saul, Port.
8	Sannana Bay.	1	Saumarez, Sir, Banks.
9	Sansego Island.	2	Saunders, Cape.
9190	San-shan-tow Islands.	3	Saunders Island, Sandwich Islands.
1	Santa Bay, and Island.	4	Saunders Island, Society Islands.
2	Santander.	5	Savage, Great.
3	Santapilly Rocks.	6	Savage Island.
4	Santiago, Barra de.	7	Savage Islands.
5	Santiago, Cape.	8	Savage Point.
6	Santiago de Tolu.	9	Savaii Island.
7	Santiago Point.	9240	Savannah River.
8	Santiago de Cuba.	1	Savannah la Mar.
9	Santjang, Cape.	2	Savona.
9200	Santona.	3	Savu.
1	Santorin Island.	4	Savu, New.
2	Santos.	5	Savu Savu Point.
3	Santos Island.	6	Sawa Bay.
4	Sanxette, Fort.	7	Saya de Malba Bank.
5	Sanyabel Island.	8	Saylee Point.
6	Saona Island.	9	Saypan Island.
7	Sapaca Point.	9250	Scala.
8	Saparooa Island.	1	Scalambra, Cape.
9	Sapata, Pulo.	2	Scalanuova.
9210	Sapello Sound.	3	Scaletta.
1	Sapey, Cape.	4	Scara Island.
2	Saphonidi.	5	Scarborough.
3	Sapienza Island.	6	Scarborough Shoal.
9214	Sapoudi.	9257	Scarp Island.

Nos.	SCA	Nos.	SEM
9258	Scarpanto Island.	9301	Searah Island.
9	Scarpenton Island.	2	Searle, Cape.
9260	Scatary Island.	3	Seaton.
1	Schank, Cape.	4	Sebastian Bay.
2	Schank Island.	5	Sebastian, St., Brazil.
3	Schanz Islands.	6	Sebastian, St., Spain.
4	Schapen Island.	7	Sebastian, St., Cape, Madagascar.
5	Schenas.	8	Sebastian, St., Cape, S. Africa.
6	Scherschel.	9	Sebastian, St., Cape, Spain.
7	Schetky, Cape.	9310	Sebastian, St., Cape, Tier. del Fuego.
8	Scheveningen Light.	1	Sebastian, St., Island.
9	Schiedam Islands.	2	Sebenico.
9270	Schiermonik.	3	Se Beero.
1	Schoomagen Islands.	4	Seberget Island.
2	Schouten Island.	5	Sebooko.
3	Schouten Mountain.	6	Secassie.
4	Schouwen.	7	Secreti Islands.
5	Schubert, Cape.	8	Sedano, Cape.
6	Scilly Islands, England.	9	Sedarie Reef.
7	Scilly Islands, S. Pacific.	9320	Sededap Island.
8	Scio.	1	Seeal Point.
9	Scituate.	2	Seeall Islands.
9280	Scoresby, Cape.	3	Seemeesa.
1	Scotchwell Harbor.	4	Segelskar.
2	Scotland.	5	Segna.
3	Scott, Cape.	6	Segoro Wedji Bay.
4	Scott Islands.	7	Seguam Island.
5	Scott Reef.	8	Seguin Island.
6	Scylla.	9	Sein, Island de.
7	Sea Bear Bay.	9330	Seir Abonaid.
8	Seaconnet Point.	1	Seir Beni Yass.
9	Sea Dog Rock.	2	Seiva Point.
9290	Seagull Group.	3	Selang Point.
1	Seahorse Bank.	4	Selio, Pulo.
2	Seahorse Point.	5	Sellada Mountain.
3	Seahorse Shoal.	6	Selonda Island.
4	Sea Klip Rocks.	7	Selouan Island.
5	Seal, Cape.	8	Selsea Bill.
6	Seal Island, Nova Scotia.	9	Semerara Islands.
7	Seal Island, S. Africa.	9340	Semione Island.
8	Sealer's Ledge.	1	Semiru Mountain.
9	Sea Lion Islands.	2	Semitsch Islands.
9300	Seals Islands.	9343	Sempo Island.

Nos.	SEN	Nos.	SHA
9344	Senegal.	9387	Seven Heads.
5	Senegambia.	8	Seven Islands, Caroline Islands.
6	Senetoso Point.	9	Seven Islands, Celebes.
7	Seniavin Islands.	9390	Seven Islands, France.
8	Senna.	1	Seven Islands, Gulf of St. Lawrence.
9	Senning Skar Rock.	2	Seven Islands, Lapland.
9350	Sentina Point.	3	Seven Islands, N. W. of Banca.
1	Sentinel Islands.	4	Seven Islands Bay.
2	Sentinela Island.	5	Seven Mountains Island.
3	Separation Point.	6	Seven Stars.
4	Sependong Island.	7	Seven Stones Light.
5	Sequeiras Island.	8	Severn Fort.
6	Sercq Island.	9	Severn Shoal.
7	Serdz Kamen, Cape.	9400	Severndroog Island.
8	Seringapatam, Elizabeth Shoal.	1	Seychelle Archipelago.
9	Seringapatam Reef.	2	Seyer Islands.
9360	Serle Island.	3	Seymour, Cape.
1	Sermattan.	4	Shab el Jurmah.
2	Sernella, Cape.	5	Shabler, Cape.
3	Seroua.	6	Shab Shaybah.
4	Serpent's Island.	7	Shab Subbah.
5	Serpho Islands.	8	Shab Umbarrack.
6	Serra Island.	9	Shadwan Island.
7	Serrana Bank.	9410	Shadwell Point.
8	Serranilla Bank.	1	Shag Island.
9	Serrantes Mountain.	2	Shag Rocks, Labrador.
9370	Servi Island.	3	Shag Rocks, S. Atlantic.
1	Seakar Island.	4	Shaggy Rocks.
2	Sesola Rock.	5	Shahah.
3	Sestri di Levante.	6	Shahbunder Shoal.
4	Se Tappo.	7	Shalbet Island.
5	Settang River.	8	Sha-lui-tien Island.
6	Sette Bocche.	9	Shallop Creek.
7	Settee River.	9420	Shampee Islands.
8	Settra Kroo.	1	Shang-ta.
9	Setubal.	2	Shannon Island.
9380	Seubeli Par.	3	Shannon River.
1	Seulement Point.	4	Shantar Islands.
2	Sevastopol.	5	Shan Tung.
3	Sevedo, Port.	6	Sharja.
4	Seven Brothers Mountain.	7	Shark Head.
5	Seven Capes, Cape, Africa.	8	Shark's Bay.
9386	Seven Capes, Cape, Candia.	9429	Shark's Point.

Nos.	SHA	Nos.	SIL
9430	Sharp Island.	9473	Shortland Bluff.
1	Shaum.	4	Shortland Islands.
2	Shaw's Peak.	5	Shreveport, Louisiana, U. S.
3	Sha-wei-shan.	6	Shrinky Island.
4	Shea Islands.	7	Shugra.
5	Shebar River.	8	Shut-in Island.
6	Sheep Head.	9	Sialat Point.
7	Sheepscot Bay, Maine, U. S.	9480	Si Ameel Island.
8	Sheerness.	1	Siam.
9	Sheid, Ras.	2	Siao.
9440	Sheikh Shaib Island.	3	Siao-kin-Tao.
1	Sheik, Munsoud Ras.	4	Siayan.
2	Sheipoo.	5	Sibago.
3	Shelburne Harbor.	6	Sibay Island.
4	Shepherd's Harbor.	7	Sibbald's Bank.
5	Shernrow Island.	8	Siberia, New.
6	Sherbédat, Ras.	9	Sibuyan Island.
7	Sherboro Island.	9490	Sicayah Point.
8	Sherburne Reef.	1	Sicie Cape.
9	Sherm Rhabuc.	2	Sicily.
9450	Sherm Yembo.	3	Sidera Cape.
1	Sherriff Harbor.	4	Sidmouth Cape, Australia.
2	Shetland Islands.	5	Sidmouth Cape, Loochoo Islands.
3	Shiant Islands.	6	Sidmouth Rock.
4	Shiashkotan Island.	7	Sidney Island.
5	Shield Cape.	8	Sidon.
6	Shields.	9	Sierra Cape.
7	Skilling Cape.	9500	Sierra Bermeja.
8	Ship Channel.	1	Sierra de Mijas.
9	Ship Harbor.	2	Sierra de San Antonio.
9460	Ship Island.	3	Sierra Leone Cape.
1	Ship Rock.	4	Sierra Ventana.
2	Shipounsky Cape.	5	Sievero-Vostotchni Cape.
3	Shipwash.	6	Sigayan Point.
4	Shirreff Cape.	7	Sighajik.
5	Shishkoff Cape.	8	Siglenaes.
6	Shoal Bay.	9	Sigri Cape and Port.
7	Shoal Point.	9510	Siguljon Island.
8	Shoalwater Cape.	1	Sihuatenejo.
9	Shoe Island, Dampier Strait.	2	Si-ki Rock.
9470	Shoe Island, Gaspar Strait.	3	Sikokf Island.
1	Shoe Island, South Pacific.	4	Sikyno Island.
9472	Shoreham.	9515	Silam.

17

Nos.	SIL	Nos.	SMI
9516	Silhouette Island.	9559	Sitchin Island.
7	Silino Island.	9560	Sitengon.
8	Silla de Caraccas.	1	Sitka, Alaska, U. S.
9	Sillah Islands.	2	Six Fathom Bank.
9520	Silleiro Cape.	3	Six Islands.
1	Silonay Island.	4	Skafus.
2	Silungun Mount.	5	Skagsudde.
3	Silva Shoal.	6	Skala Cape.
4	Silver Bank and Cay.	7	Skal Svee.
5	Silvi.	8	Skantzoura Island.
6	Sima Cape.	9	Skaw, The.
7	Simao.	9570	Skelda Ness.
8	Simara Island.	1	Skeleton Point.
9	Simmambaya.	2	Skelligs.
9530	Simon's Bay.	3	Skergriatish Rock.
1	Simon's, St., Island.	4	Skerki Shoals.
2	Simonoff Island.	5	Skerries.
3	Simpson Island.	6	Skerryvore Rocks.
4	Simpson Port.	7	Skiathos Island.
5	Simusir Island.	8	Skiddy Ielands.
6	Sinai Mount.	9	Skinosa Island.
7	Sinam, Pulo.	9580	Skird Rocks.
8	Sines Cape.	1	Skopelos Island.
9	Singapore.	2	Skopo Mount.
9540	Single Island.	3	Skraaven.
1	Sinigaglia.	4	Skuddesnœs.
2	Sinkel.	5	Skyro Poulo.
3	Sinkep, Pulo.	6	Skyros Island.
4	Sinope.	7	Slade Point.
5	Sicellands Reef.	8	Sledge Island.
6	Sipadan Island.	9	Sleepers.
7	Sipang, Tanjong.	9590	Slieve Donard.
8	Siphanto Island.	1	Slieve Sneacht.
9	Sir Isaac Point.	2	Sligo.
9550	Sirangani, East Indies.	3	Slinger's Bay.
1	Siren Island.	4	Slipper and Table Rocks.
2	Sirik Point.	5	Sloping Island.
3	Sirius Rock.	6	Slyne Head.
4	Sisal.	7	Smalls Rocks.
5	Sisiran, Port.	8	Smeerenberg.
6	Sisters, Andamans.	9	Smith Island, Hudson's Bay.
7	Sisters, Furneaux.	9600	Smith Island, Maryland.
9558	Sisters, Two.	9601	Smith Island, North Carolina.

Nos.	SMI	Nos.	SOV
9602	Smith Island, S. Shetlands.	9645	Souga Island.
3	Smith Point, Australia.	6	Sonserol Islands.
4	Smith Point, N. America.	7	Soo-Au.
5	Smith Shoal.	8	Soogoot Point.
6	Smith's Knoll.	9	Sooladdie Island.
7	Smith's, Sir J., Group.	9650	Sooloo Island.
8	Smoky, Cape.	1	Sooloo Islands.
9	Smyrna.	2	Soonmeany.
9610	Smyth Islands.	3	Soosoo.
1	Smyth's Islet.	4	Sor H.ugoen.
2	Snake and Madagascar Shoals.	5	Sordi Island.
3	Snap Rock.	6	Sorell, Cape.
4	Snapper Bank.	7	Sorelle.
5	Snapper Island.	8	Sorisa Point.
6	Snares, Kurile Islands.	9	Soroen Island.
7	Snares, New Zealand.	9660	Sorol Islands.
8	Sneefeldsyökel.	1	Sorrento.
9	Snowdon.	2	Sorsogon, Port.
9620	Society Islands.	3	Sosnovetz.
1	Socoa.	4	Sosonova.
2	Socorro Island.	5	Sotoang Group.
3	Socotra.	6	Souffriere.
4	Soda Island.	7	Sough Island.
5	Soderarm Light.	8	Souirah.
6	Soderhamm.	9	Soulima River.
7	Soderskar.	9670	Soumenap.
8	Sofala River.	1	Soumshou Island.
9	Sohar.	2	Sourabaya.
9630	Soimonoff, Cape.	3	Souroutou.
1	Sojoton Point.	4	Sous River.
2	Sola Island, Cumana.	5	South Sand Head.
3	Solander Islands.	6	Southampton.
4	Solitary Island, Australia.	7	Southampton Island, and Cape.
5	Solitary Island, Indian Ocean.	8	Southeast Pass, Mississippi Delta.
6	Solitary Island, S. Pacific.	9	South Pass, Mississippi Delta.
7	Solombo.	9680	Southwest Pass, Mississippi Delta.
8	Solomon Islands.	1	Southerness Light.
9	Solor.	2	Southern, Port.
9640	Solta Island.	3	Southern Thule Islands.
1	Solway Firth.	4	Southwold.
2	Sombrero.	5	Souvela, Cape.
3	Sombrero Rock.	6	Souvorov, Cape.
9644	Sommers Island.	9687	Sovel Island.

Nos.	SOW	Nos.	STO
9688	Sow and Pigs.	9731	Stampalia Island.
9	Soya, Cape.	2	Standia Island.
9690	Spada, Cape.	3	Stanford Light.
1	Spain.	4	Stapodia.
2	Spain, Port.	5	Star Bank and Reefs.
3	Spalatro.	6	Star Island.
4	Spauberg, Cape.	7	Starbuck Island.
5	Sparo.	8	Start Light.
6	Spartel, Cape.	9	Start Point.
7	Spartimento Point.	9740	Stasida.
8	Spartivento, Cape, Naples.	1	Staten Hoek.
9	Spartivento, Cape, Sardinia.	2	Staten Island.
9700	Spathi, Cape.	3	Staunton Island.
1	Speakers' Bank.	4	Stauro, Cape.
2	Spear Cape.	5	Stavers Island.
3	Speiden Island.	6	Stavri, Cape.
4	Spencer, Cape, New Brunswick.	7	Stavronisi Island.
5	Spencer Cape, New Guinea.	8	Stead's Entrance.
6	Spencer Cape, Alaska.	9	Steenboom, Cape.
7	Spencer Cape, Spencer Gulf.	9750	Steep Point, Australia.
8	Spencer Gulf.	1	Steep Point, Peru.
9	Spencer Point, Alaska.	2	Steep-to Island.
9710	Spezzia.	3	Stefano, St.
1	Spezzia Island.	4	Steffens Klint.
2	Sphagia Island.	5	Stephen, St., Island.
3	Sphakia.	6	Stephens, Cape, New Britain.
4	Spitzbergen.	7	Stephens, Cape, Solomon Islands.
5	Spodsbierg Light.	8	Stephens Island, New Zealand.
6	Spratly's Sandy Island.	9	Stephens Island, Torres Strait.
7	Sprogo.	9760	Stephens, Port, Falkland Islands.
8	Spurn Lights.	1	Stephen's Port, Australia.
9	Squally Island.	2	Stettin.
9720	Square Handkerchief.	3	Stewart, Cape.
1	Square Island.	4	Stewart Island.
2	Srednoy.	5	Stewart Islands, Australia.
3	Staalburghuk.	6	Stewart Islands, Solomon Islands.
4	Staberhuk.	7	Stewart, Port.
5	Stack South Light.	8	Stickney Island.
6	Stadtland.	9	Stilo, Cape.
7	Stag Rocks.	9770	Stirrup Cays.
8	Stag Shoal.	1	Stockholm.
9	Stags.	2	Stockton.
9730	Stamfanes Islands.	9773	Stokes, Cape.

Nos.	STO	Nos.	SWA
9774	Stolbovoi, Cape.	9817	Sugarloaves, Two.
5	Stonehaven.	8	Suick.
6	Stoneskar.	9	Sulaban Point.
7	Stonington.	9820	Sulisker Island.
8	Stono Inlet, South Carolina, U. S.	1	Sullivan's Island, S. Carolina, U. S.
9	Stony Island.	2	Sulphur Island, Loochoo Islands.
9780	Storah.	3	Sulphur Island, N. Pacific.
1	Stor Jungfrun.	4	Suluan Island.
2	Storkalle Shoal.	5	Sumatra.
3	Storm Bay.	6	Sumbawa.
4	Storm Island.	7	Sumbelan.
5	Stornaway Light.	8	Sumburgh Head.
6	Stor Rebben.	9	Sunda Strait.
7	Stour Rorny.	9830	Sunday Island.
8	Stralsund.	1	Sunderland.
9	Stranraer.	2	Sunderland. N.
9790	Strathy Head.	3	Sunk Light.
1	Strogonov, Cape.	4	Supé Bay.
2	Stromboli.	5	Surat.
3	Stromness.	6	Surdy Island.
4	Strongylo Island.	7	Surigao Islands.
5	Stronsa Island.	8	Surinam River.
6	Strumble Head.	9	Surop.
7	Struys Point.	9840	Surville, Cape.
8	Stuart Island.	1	Surville Point.
9	Styrsudd Head.	2	Susah.
9800	Styx.	3	Sutrauha.
1	Suadiva Atoll.	4	Suva Harbor.
2	Snakin.	5	Suwarrow Islands.
3	Subec, Port.	6	Svalferort Light.
4	Submarine Volcano.	7	Svartklubb Light.
5	Succadana.	8	Sveaborg.
6	Success Breakers.	9	Svenoe Langö.
7	Suckling, Cape.	9850	Svenska Hogarne.
8	Suda.	1	Sviatoi, Cape.
9	Suderoe Island.	2	Sviatoi Noss.
9810	Suellaba Point.	3	Svingleboen.
1	Suez.	4	Svinöe.
2	Suffrein Bay.	5	Swaine, Cape.
3	Sugarloaf, Great.	6	Swaine's Reefs.
4	Sugarloaf Island.	7	Swallow Shoal.
5	Sugarloaf Point.	8	Swan Islands, Honduras Coast.
9816	Sugarloaf Rocks.	9859	Swan's Islands, Van Dieman's Land.

Nos.	SWA	Nos.	TAL
9860	Swan Islands, West Indies.	9903	Tabooan Island.
1	Swan Port.	4	Tabou-sima.
2	Swan Point.	5	Tabutha Island.
3	Swan River.	6	Ta-Chu-shan.
4	Swanji.	7	Tae Islands.
5	Swansea.	8	Taeuga.
6	Swede Islands.	9	Tafou Point.
7	Sweden.	9910	Taftsness.
8	Sweers Island.	1	Tagai Islands.
9	Swin, Middle Light.	2	Taganrog.
9870	Swinemünde.	3	Tagapula Island.
1	Syang.	4	Tagh-Kiniagh Island.
2	Sydenham Island.	5	Tagliamento River.
3	Sydney.	6	Taglo Point.
4	Sydney Bay.	7	Tagloe Bay.
5	Sydney Harbor.	8	Tagolana Point.
6	Sydney Shoal.	9	Tagolanda.
7	Sylph's Rocks.	9920	Tagomago Island.
8	Sylva Bank.	1	Tahaa.
9	Symi Island.	2	Tahanea.
9880	Symonds Harbor.	3	Ta-He-Shan.
1	Symplegades Islands.	4	Tah Faroon Rocks.
2	Syra Island.	5	Tahiti.
3	Syracuse.	6	Tahoora Island.
4	Syria.	7	Tahou-aita.
5	Ta Group.	8	Tahourowa Island.
6	Tabarca.	9	Tahow.
7	Tabasco River.	9930	Taichow Islands.
8	Tabe-ouni.	1	Taichow River.
9	Tablas Island.	2	Tain.
9890	Table Bay.	3	Tairo Island.
1	Table, Cape, New Zealand.	4	Tajourah, Ras al.
2	Table, Cape, Van Dieman's Land.	5	Takhtalu, Mountain.
3	Table Head.	6	Takli, Cape.
4	Table Hill, China.	7	Tako Mountain.
5	Table Hill, Formosa.	8	Takurea.
6	Table Island, New Zealand.	9	Takutea.
7	Table Island, Pescadores.	9940	Talamone.
8	Table Island, Straits of Gaspar.	1	Talantam Bank.
9	Table, Little, Island.	2	Talbot, Cape.
9900	Tabo, Cape.	3	Talcahuano.
1	Tabocannee Rock.	4	Talenading Islands.
2	Taboga Island.	9945	Talinay Mountain.

Nos.	TAL	Nos.	TEA
9946	Talyabo, Cape.	9989	Tappanooly Bay.
7	Taman.	9990	Taptee Light.
8	Tamana Island.	1	Tarafal Bay.
9	Tamandaré.	2	Tarawa.
9950	Tamar, Cape, Falkland Island.	3	Tarbert Light.
1	Tamar, Cape, Tierra del Fuego.	4	Tarbetness.
2	Tamara Island.	5	Tarento.
3	Tamareed.	6	Tarifa.
4	Tamatam Island.	7	Tarkhan-kout, Cape.
5	Tamatave.	8	Tarpaulin Cove, Massachusetts, U. S.
6	Tamboretes Islands.	9	Tarragona.
7	Tambove Bay.	01	Tartary.
8	Tampa Bay.	2	Tasman's Head.
9	Tampat Tuan Point.	3	Tatakoto.
9960	Tampico.	4	Tatau Mountain.
1	Tamquam River.	5	Tatnam, Cape.
2	Tam-sui Harbor.	6	Tatukoka.
3	Tanaga Island.	7	Tauranga Bay.
4	Tanakeka Island.	8	Tavernier Cay.
5	Tan Chew Island.	9	Tavolara Island.
6	Tancook Island.	010	Tavoy.
7	Tanega Sima.	1	Taw.
8	Tangier.	2	Tawally.
9	Tangtang.	3	Tawee Islands.
9970	Tanjong Api.	4	Taweree.
1	Tanjong Batoo.	5	Tawiti Rahi Islands.
2	Tanjong Burram.	6	Taya.
3	Tanjong Datou.	7	Taya Islands.
4	Tanjong Maletayor.	8	Taya, Pulo.
5	Tanjong Po.	9	Taypu Point.
6	Tanjong Salatan.	020	Taytao, Cape.
7	Tanjong Sambar.	1	Tchandjour Mountain.
8	Tanjong Sednrie.	2	Tchaouda, Cape.
9	Tanjong Sipang.	3	Tchaplin, Cape.
9980	Tanjong Slokko.	4	Tchatirdag.
1	Tankar.	5	Tcherina.
2	Tanna Island.	6	Tchikotan Island.
3	Taormina.	7	Tchilachap.
4	Taouhwa Island.	8	Tchina Point.
5	Taouw.	9	Tchirinkotan Island.
6	Tapamanoa Island.	030	Tchouka-kore Point.
7	Tapeantana.	1	Tchoukotsky, Cape.
9988	Tapoute-ouea.	032	Tea-boura Island.

252

Nos.	TEA	Nos.	THR
033	Teay.	076	Terra Nuova.
4	Tebounkou.	7	Terrapore Point.
5	Tebruk.	8	Terre Négre.
6	Tecla Mountain.	9	Terribles.
7	Tedlès, Cape.	080	Terron Point.
8	Tees, River.	1	Ter Schelling.
9	Tefelneh, Cape.	2	Testa, Cape, della.
040	Tega, Pulo.	3	Testigos Islands.
1	Tegal Mountain.	4	Tetas de Cabra.
2	Tehor.	5	Tetrina.
3	Tehuantepec.	6	Tetuan.
4	Teiara.	7	Tetuaroa Island.
5	Teignmouth Shoal.	8	Tetukota.
6	Teignouse.	9	Teulada, Cape.
7	Tejupan River.	090	Tewara, Cape.
8	Tekareka.	1	Texas.
9	Teku.	2	Texel Island.
050	Telabo Island.	3	Teynga Island.
1	Telaguir Islands.	4	Thaddeus, St., Cape.
2	Telibon Island.	5	Thames River.
3	Tematu Leiwuwau.	6	Tha-roa.
4	Temo Island.	7	Thaso Island.
5	Temuel, Cape.	8	Thatchu Island.
6	Templar Bank.	9	Theressa.
7	Tenasserim Island.	0100	Thermia Island.
8	Tendra Island.	1	Thetis.
9	Tenedos Island.	2	Thirsty Sound.
060	Tenerife Island.	3	Thistle Island, Australia.
1	Ten Fathom Hole.	4	Thistle Island, Corea.
2	Tenimber Islands.	5	Thomé, St., Cape.
3	Tennez, Cape.	6	Thomas, St., Island, Bight of Biafra.
4	Ten Pound Island.	7	Thomas, St., Island, N. Pacific.
5	Tenth Island.	8	Thomas, St.. Island, W. Indies.
6	Tequepa Point.	9	Thompson's Island.
7	Terawiti, Cape.	0110	Thoresby Mountain.
8	Teroera.	1	Thoroylen Island.
9	Termination Island.	2	Thorshavn.
070	Termini.	3	Thouin, Cape.
1	Terminos Laguna.	4	Thousand Islands.
2	Termoli.	5	Three Alike Islands.
3	Ternate.	6	Three Brothers, Australia.
4	Ternay Bay.	7	Three Brothers, Celebes.
075	Terracina.	0118	Three Hill Island, New Hebrides.

Nos.	THR	Nos.	TOF
0119	Three Hill Island, N. Pacific.	0162	Tilla.
0120	Three Hummock Island.	3	Tillen Head.
1	Three Islands, Borneo.	4	Tillicherry.
2	Three Islands, S. Pacific.	5	Tillongchong.
3	Three Kings, Cochin China.	6	Tillongchool.
4	Three Kings, New Zealand.	7	Timbalier Bay, Louisiana. U. S.
5	Three-peaked Island.	8	Timbalier Island.
6	Three Points, Cape, Australia.	9	Timboor Island.
7	Three Points, Cape, Br. Honduras.	0170	Timoan, Pulo.
8	Three Points, Cape, Cumana.	1	Timor.
9	Three Points, Cape, Gold Coast.	2	Timor Laut.
0130	Three Points, Cape, Madre de Dios.	3	Timour, Cape.
1	Three Points, Cape, Patagonia.	4	Tinakoro.
2	Three Sisters.	5	Tindjil, Pulo.
3	Three Sisters, Tree Island.	6	Tindle and Walls Islands.
4	Threshold Point.	7	Tingaro.
5	Thunoe.	8	Ting-hae, E. China.
6	Thurbat Ali.	9	Ting-hae, S. E. China.
7	Thurso.	0180	Tingy, Pulo.
8	Thwart-the-Way, New Guinea.	1	Tinhosa Islands.
9	Thwart-the-Way, Strait of Sunda.	2	Tinian Island.
0140	Tiao-yu-su Island.	3	Tinker Rock.
1	Tiberun, Cape, St. Domingo.	4	Tino Island.
2	Tiberun, Cape, Isthmus of Panama.	5	Tinos Island.
3	Tiburon Island.	6	Tinoso, Cape.
4	Ticao Island.	7	Tintagel.
5	Ticopia.	8	Tiokea.
6	Tidore.	9	Tiompan Head.
7	Tiega, Pulo.	0190	Tiouters.
8	Tien Pak.	1	Tiraght Rock.
9	Tierra del Fuego.	2	Tirahn Islands.
0150	Tigalda Island.	3	Tirandie Islands.
1	Tiger Island, Cochin China.	4	Tirey Island.
2	Tiger Island, S. Pacific.	5	Tiritan.
3	Tiger Islands, and Shoals.	6	Titan Island.
4	Tiger Point.	7	Titangonya Island.
5	Tigil.	8	Titter Head.
6	Tigre.	9	Toau.
7	Tijioca Point.	0200	Tobago.
8	Tike.	1	Tobin, Cape.
9	Tikehau.	2	To-doo Island.
0160	Tiki-tiki.	3	Todos Santos, Bay.
0161	Tikoma Island.	0204	Tofua Island.

Nos.	TOF	Nos.	TOW
0205	Tofua Mountain.	0248	Torre del Greco.
6	Toiro Point.	9	Torre della, Cape.
7	Token Beasys.	0250	Turre della Testa.
8	Tokolebo Bay.	1	Torrens Mountain.
9	Toku Island.	2	Torre Nueva.
0210	Tokumalou Bay.	3	Torres Island, Caroline Islands.
1	Tola Island.	4	Torres Island, Hudson's Bay.
2	Tolaga Bay.	5	Torres Port.
3	Tolboukhin.	6	Torres Straits.
4	Tolmeitah.	7	Torres, Great West.
5	Tolstoy, Cape.	8	Torricelli Mountains.
6	Tomb, Little and Great.	9	Tortola.
7	Tombe, Ras ul.	0260	Tortosa, Spain.
8	Tomelin Island.	1	Tortosa, Syria.
9	Tomkins, Fort.	2	Tortuga Island, Cumana.
0220	Tom Shot's Point.	3	Tortuga Island, Gulf of California.
1	Tonga Islands.	4	Tortuga Island, St. Domingo.
2	Tongatabou Island.	5	Tortuga Shoals.
3	Tongeon Mountain.	6	Tortugas.
4	Tong-ting Island.	7	Tory Channel.
5	Tonin, Cape.	8	Tory Island.
6	Tonin Islands.	9	Tosa, Cape, Japan.
7	Tonnerre Point.	0270	Tosa, Cape, Spain.
8	Touquin River.	1	Totoia Island.
9	Tonsang Harbor.	2	Toty, Pulo.
0230	Tonyn Islands.	3	Toua Manado Island.
1	Tood Bataha.	4	Toua Nuin Island.
2	Toojoo Pulo.	5	Toubai Island.
3	Toor.	6	Toubouai Island.
4	Tootomy, Cape.	7	Toucques.
5	Topolo-polo, Cape.	8	Toué-toué.
6	Toppers Hoodjie.	9	Touhoua Island.
7	Torat Bay.	0280	Toukoukemou Island.
8	Torbjornskar.	1	Toulon.
9	Torinana.	2	Toupoua Island.
0240	Torment Point.	3	Touquet Point.
1	Tornea.	4	Toura Kira, Cape.
2	Torngrund.	5	Touri, Cape.
3	Toro Point.	6	Tova Island.
4	Toro Rock.	7	Tova Reef.
5	Torpoy Islands.	8	Tower Island.
6	Torquay.	9	Tower Rocks.
0247	Torr Point.	0290	Towers' Island.

Nos.	TOW	Nos.	TSC
0291	Town Point.	0334	Triangles, Macassar Strait.
2	Townshend, Cape.	5	Triboli.
3	Townshend Fort.	6	Tribulation, Cape.
4	Townshend Harbor, Maine, U. S.	7	Trichindore.
5	Townshend Harbor, S. America.	8	Trieste.
6	Tracy Island.	9	Trieste Island.
7	Trade Town.	0340	Trikeri Island.
8	Trafalgar, Cape.	1	Trincomalee.
9	Trafalgar Mountain.	2	Trindelen Light.
0300	Traill Island.	3	Trindelen Shoal.
1	Traitor's Head.	4	Trinders Shoal.
2	Traitor's Islands.	5	Tringany River.
3	Tranen Islands.	6	Trinidad Bay, California, U. S.
4	Trani.	7	Trinidad, Cuba.
5	Trano Island.	8	Trinidad, N. Atlantic.
6	Tranquebar.	9	Trinidad Island, S. Atlantic.
7	Trapani.	0350	Trinity Cape, and Island.
8	Traps.	1	Trinity Harbor.
9	Trau.	2	Triple Island.
0310	Treasury Islands.	3	Tripoli, Africa.
1	Trebizonde.	4	Tripoli, Syria.
2	Treble Island.	5	Tristan d'Acunha.
3	Tree Island, Aracan.	6	Triton Bay.
4	Tree Island, E. Archipelago.	7	Triton Island.
5	Tree Point, Australia.	8	Trobriand Islands.
6	Tree Point, Borneo.	9	Troja, Cape.
7	Trees, Cape.	0360	Tromelin Island.
8	Trees Island.	1	Trompetto.
9	Tregal Rocks.	2	Tromsöe.
0320	Tregrosse Islets.	3	Trondhiem.
1	Treguier.	4	Tronta, Point del.
2	Tremiti Islands.	5	Tropez, St.
3	Tremouille Islands.	6	Troubadour.
4	Tréport.	7	Troubridge Hill.
5	Tres Forcas, Cape.	8	Troughton Island.
6	Tres Irmaos.	9	Troup Head.
7	Tres Marias Islands.	0370	Trouwers Island.
8	Tres Montes, Cape.	1	Truant Island.
9	Treurenberg.	2	Truxillo, Honduras.
0330	Trevandrum.	3	Truxillo, Peru.
1	Trevose Head.	4	Tsaregradskoe.
2	Triagoz.	5	Tschesmé, Cape.
0333	Triangles, Gulf of Mexico.	0376	Tschichagoff, Cape, Japan.

Nos.	TSC	Nos.	UND
0377	Tschichagoff, Cape, Alaska.	0420	Turtle Islands, Indian Archipelago.
8	Tschichagoff Island.	1	Turtle Islands, N. W. Australia.
9	Tschirikoff, Cape.	2	Turtle Reef.
0380	Tschirikoff Island.	3	Turtle-backed Island.
1	Tsing-hac-wei.	4	Tusihau, Cape.
2	Tsis Island.	5	Tusima Island.
3	Tsung Ming Island.	6	Tuskar Rock.
4	Tsus-sima.	7	Tusket Islands.
5	Tubanaiella Island.	8	Tuspam Shoal.
6	Tubarao Point.	9	Tutoya.
7	Tucacas.	0430	Tutuila.
8	Tucapel Head.	1	Tuxtla.
9	Tucker Island.	2	Tresteen.
0390	Tucker's Island.	3	Twin Rocks.
1	Tulau Island.	4	Twin Peaks.
2	Tuloop, Ras.	5	Twins, China.
3	Tulour Island.	6	Twins, Mergui Archipelago.
4	Tumbelan Islands.	7	Two Bays, Cape.
5	Tumbora Mountain.	8	Two Brothers, Borneo.
6	Tungaty.	9	Two Brothers, Java Sea.
7	Tung-chuh.	0440	Twofold Bay.
8	Tungences Light.	1	Two Groups Island.
9	Tung-ying Islands.	2	Tyfore.
0400	Tunis.	3	Tylon Island.
1	Tupinier Island.	4	Tyn, Ras al.
2	Turacoon Island.	5	Tynemouth.
3	Turatte Point.	6	Typa Island.
4	Turfeie.	7	Typinsan Island.
5	Turivassu Point.	8	Tyre.
6	Turkey.	9	Unfato.
7	Turkey Islands.	0450	Udirik.
8	Turk's Islands.	1	Udsire.
9	Turnabout Island.	2	Udvœr Islands.
0410	Turnagain, Cape.	3	Uist Islands.
1	Turneffe.	4	Ukyera Reef.
2	Turner Point.	5	Ularoa Island.
3	Turon, Cape.	6	Uleaborg.
4	Turon Island.	7	Ulietea Island.
5	Turret Island.	8	Ulkogrunni.
6	Turtle Island, Bay of Biafra.	9	Umata Bay.
7	Turtle Island, Cochin China.	0460	Umea.
8	Turtle Island, Feejee Islands.	1	Unda Point.
0419	Turtle Islands, Gulf of Guinea.	0462	Underoo.

Nos.	UND	Nos.	VAU
0463	Underwood, Port.	0506	Valiente Peak.
4	Unie Bay.	7	Valientes Island.
5	Union Bay.	8	Valparaiso.
6	Union, Port de la.	9	Valsche Cape.
7	United States.	0510	Vancouver, Fort.
8	Unsang Point.	1	Vancouver Island.
9	Upolu.	2	Vancouver Port.
0470	Upright Cape.	3	Vanderlin Island.
1	Upright Point.	4	Vanderschelling Islands.
2	Upstart Cape.	5	Van Dieman's Land.
3	Uracas.	6	Van Diemen Cape.
4	Urajarao Island.	7	Van Diemen's Inlet.
5	Urcas.	8	Vandö.
6	Urck.	9	Vandola Island.
7	Urh-Taou.	0520	Vandotena Island.
8	Urhud.	1	Vanguard Shoal, China Sea.
9	Usborne, Port.	2	Vanguard Shoal, Sweden.
0480	Ushant.	3	Vanikoro Island.
1	Ushishir Islands.	4	Vannes.
2	Ustica Island.	5	Vansittart Shoals.
3	Utila Island.	6	Vanua Levou Island.
4	Utiroa Town.	7	Vanua Vatou Island.
5	Utiroa Harbor.	8	Varano.
6	Utklipporna.	9	Varela Cape.
7	Uto.	0530	Varela, Pulo.
8	Utrecht, Fort.	1	Varela False Cape.
9	Uya.	2	Varellah, Pulo.
0490	Vache Island.	3	Vares Cape.
1	Vaches Cape.	4	Varna.
2	Vado.	5	Varne Shoal.
3	Væröe Island.	6	Vashon Cape.
4	Vago Island.	7	Vashon Head.
5	Vaigatch Island.	8	Vasto Ammone.
6	Valdez Peninsula.	9	Vathi.
7	Valdez Port.	0540	Vathy, Port.
8	Valdivia.	1	Vaticano Cape.
9	Valencia.	2	Vatoa Island.
0500	Valentia.	3	Vatoo Madre.
'1	Valentine Peak, Van Dieman's L'd.	4	Vatou Lele Island.
2	Valentine Peak, Mozambique Ch.	5	Vatou Rera Island.
3	Valery, St., sur Somme.	6	Vavao Island.
4	Valery, St., en Caux.	7	Vavitou Island.
0505	Valetta.	0548	Vaux's Tomb.

Nos.	VAY	Nos.	VIT
0549	Vayng Islands.	0592	Victoria, Seychelles.
0550	Ve Skerries.	3	Victoria Harbor.
1	Vega Shoal.	4	Victoria Land.
2	Vela Cape.	5	Victoria Point.
3	Vela Rete Rocks.	6	Victoria Port.
4	Velas Cape.	7	Victoria Reef.
5	Velez Malaga.	8	Victoria Shoal.
6	Velthoens.	9	Victory Bank.
7	Vendeloos Bay.	0600	Victory Cape.
8	Vendres, Port.	1	Victory Island.
9	Venere, Port.	2	Vidal Cape.
0560	Venetico Island, Asia Minor.	3	Vido Island.
1	Venetico Island, Greece.	4	Vieja Island.
2	Venezuela.	5	Vieque Island.
3	Venice.	6	Vierge Island.
4	Ventenat Cape.	7	Vieste.
5	Ventimiglia Point.	8	Vigia.
6	Ventry Head.	9	Vigo.
7	Venus Point.	0610	Vigten Islands.
8	Ver, Point de.	1	Villa do Conde.
9	Vera Cruz.	2	Villa Franca.
0570	Veragrund.	3	Villano Cape.
1	Verd Cape.	4	Villaret Cape.
2	Verde Cay.	5	Villariuo Point.
3	Verde, Cape de.	6	Vincent, St.
4	Verde Island.	7	Vincent, St., Cape, Madagascar.
5	Verde Point.	8	Vincent, St., Cape, Portugal.
6	Verga Cape.	9	Vincent, St., Island.
7	Verlegen Hook.	0620	Vincent, St., Port.
8	Vermont, U. S.	1	Vine Shoal.
9	Vermilion Bay.	2	Vingorla Rocks.
0580	Vernon Islands.	3	Vineyard Sound, Mass., U. S.
1	Verraders.	4	Viper Shoals.
2	Verruer Point.	5	Viradores Islands.
3	Vertes Islands.	6	Viraquera Point.
4	Vestal Shoal.	7	Virgenes Cape.
5	Vesuvius Mount.	8	Virgin Cape.
6	Vetergnach.	9	Virginia, U. S.
7	Viana.	0630	Virgin Islands.
8	Viareggio.	1	Virgin Gorda.
9	Vicksburg, Mississippi, U. S.	2	Virgin Rocks.
0590	Victor Gulley.	3	Vischer Island.
0591	Victoria, China.	0634	Viti Islands.

Nos.	VIT	Nos.	WAR
0635	Viti Levou.	0678	Wai-taki Bay.
6	Vito, St., Cape, Naples.	9	Waitera River.
7	Vito, St., Cape, Sicily.	0680	Waitengi Port.
8	Vivero.	1	Waiwongy Island.
9	Vizagnpatam.	2	Wakain Island.
0640	Vliegen Island.	3	Wakaroa Bay.
1	Vlieland Light.	4	Wake Island.
2	Vliko Port.	5	Wakuru Island.
3	Vogel Sang Island.	6	Walden Island.
4	Vohemar Point.	7	Waldgrave Islands.
5	Volcan Viejo.	8	Wales.
6	Volcano Bay.	9	Walker Bank.
7	Volcano Island, Andamans.	0690	Walker, Cape.
8	Volcano Island, Japan.	1	Walker Island, N. Pacific.
9	Volcano Island, S. E. of Japan.	2	Walker Island, Van Dieman's Land.
0650	Volcano Island, S. Pacific.	3	Wallabi Group.
1	Volo.	4	Waller's Shoals.
2	Volos Island.	5	Wallis Island.
3	Volta River.	6	Wallis Islands, S. Pacific.
4	Voltaire, Cape.	7	Wallis Islands, Torres Straits.
5	Voltas, Cape.	8	Walney Island.
6	Vonizza.	9	Walpole Island.
7	Vordate.	0700	Walsingham, Cape.
8	Voronov, Cape.	1	Walsorarne Islands.
9	Vosmaer Bay.	2	Walter Bath, Cape.
0660	Vostok Island.	3	Walton.
1	Vourla Scala.	4	Walvisch Bay.
2	Vries Island.	5	Wamoukou River.
3	Vulcan Island.	6	Wan-chow-foo.
4	Vulcano Island.	7	Wanganui Harbor.
5	Vuna Island and Point.	8	Wanganui River.
6	Wadde Fellingk.	9	Wanga-parawa, Cape.
7	Waderoe Island.	0710	Wangari Bay.
8	Wady Jumaul Island.	1	Wangaroa Harbor.
9	Wager Island.	2	Wangeroog.
0670	Wager River.	3	Wangy Wangy.
1	Wahaay Harbor.	4	Warberg.
2	Waia Island.	5	Ward's Islands.
3	Wai Apou.	6	Wardhuys Island.
4	Waigamele Point.	7	Wardlaw, Cape.
5	Waigeou.	8	Warnemunde.
6	Waikato Harbor.	9	Warning Mountain.
0677	Waimea.	0720	Waroo Bay.

Nos.	WAR	Nos.	WHI
0721	Warr Reef.	0764	Wells Reef.
2	Warren Point.	5	Wellstead Rock.
3	Warrender, Cape.	6	Wenman Island.
4	Warrender Port.	7	Wessel's Islands.
5	Warrior Island.	8	Wessels.
6	Warsaw Sound, Georgia, U. S.	9	Westall Point.
7	Wasa.	0770	Western Port.
8	Waseen Peaks.	1	Western Reef.
9	Washington, D. C.	2	Westerwyk.
0730	Washington, N. Carolina.	3	Westmanna Islands.
1	Washington Island, Marquesas.	4	Westminster Hall.
2	Washington Island, N. Pacific.	5	Weston, Cape.
3	Washington Sound.	6	Westpoint, New York.
4	Wassia.	7	Westport.
5	Watcher, N.	8	Wetang.
6	Watcher, S.	9	Wetta.
7	Watchman, Cape.	0780	Wexford.
8	Watceo Island.	1	Weyland Point.
9	Water Cay.	2	Weymouth.
0740	Water Island.	3	Weymouth, Cape.
1	Water Islands.	4	Whale Cove.
2	Water Volcano.	5	Whale Rock.
3	Waterford.	6	Whale Sound.
4	Waterhouse Island.	7	Whalefish Islands.
5	Waterlandt Island.	8	Whale's Back.
6	Watling's Island.	9	Whang-ho.
7	Waxway Island.	0790	Whidbey Islands.
8	Way, Pulo, Gulf of Siam.	1	Whitby.
9	Way, Pulo, Sumatra.	2	White Bear Point.
0750	Waygat Island.	3	White Bluff Head.
1	Weda.	4	White, Cape.
2	Weda Islands.	5	White Dogs.
3	Wedge Island.	6	White Head, Maine, U. S.
4	Wednesday Island.	7	White Head, Peru.
5	Weeks Reef.	8	White Head Island.
6	Wegg's, Cape.	9	White Island, Asia.
7	Wegg's Island.	0800	White Island, Massachusetts.
8	Wei-hai-wei Harbor.	1	White Island, New Zealand.
9	Welle Island.	2	White Rock, China Sea.
0760	Wellesley Islands.	3	White Rock, Falkland Islands.
1	Wellesley Shoal.	4	White Rock, Indian Archipelago.
2	Wellington.	5	White Rock, Tartary.
0763	Wellington, Cape.	0806	White Rock Islet.

Nos.	WHI	Nos.	WYT
0807	White Sea.	0850	Woahoo Island.
8	Whitehaven.	1	Woerden Castle.
9	Whitsun Island. .	2	Wolf Beacon.
0810	Whitsunday Island.	3	Wolf Island.
1	Whittle Cape.	4	Wolf Islands.
2	Whydah.	5	Wolf Rock, England.
3	Whytootackie Island.	6	Wolf Rock, Gilolo.
4	Wiborg.	7	Wolfe's Monument.
5	Wickham Cape.	8	Wolkonsky Island.
6	Wicklow.	9	Wollaston Land.
7	Widau Light.	0860	Wood Island, Labrador.
8	Wigwam Point.	1	Wood Island, Maine, U. S.
9	Wilberforce Cape.	2	Woodah Island.
0820	Wiles Cape.	3	Wood's Hole, Massachusetts, U. S.
1	Willaumez Island.	4	Woodin's Channel.
2	William Cape.	5	Woodlark Islands.
3	William, Port, Falkland Islands.	6	Woodle Island.
4	William, Port, New Zealand.	7	Woody Cape.
5	William Rock.	8	Woody Island, China Sea.
6	William's Island.	9	Woody Island, Indian Archipelago.
7	Williamston.	0870	Woody Island, Madagascar.
8	Willoughby Cape.	1	Woody Island, Paracels.
9	Willoughby's Spit.	2	Woody Island, North.
0830	Wilmington, Delaware, U. S.	3	Woody Head.
1	Wilmington, North Carolina, U. S.	4	Woody Hill.
2	Wilson Cape.	5	Woody Point.
3	Wilson's Island, Low Archipelago.	6	Woosung.
4	Wilson's Island, South Pacific.	7	Workington.
5	Wilson's Islands.	8	Worms Head.
6	Windau.	9	Wostenholme Cape.
7	Windsor River.	0880	Wostenholme Island.
8	Windward Islands.	1	Wowony Island.
9	Wine Cooper's Point.	2	Wrath Cape.
0840	Wingo Light.	3	Wreck Island.
1	Winkova.	4	Wreck Reef.
2	Winter Harbor.	5	Wreck Rock.
3	Winter Island.	6	Wright Rock.
4	Winterton.	7	Wukido Island.
5	Wisby.	8	Wyadda Island.
6	Wismar.	9	Wyang Islands.
7	Witt, Mount de.	0890	Wyllie Rocks.
8	Wittgenstein Island.	1	Wyre Light.
0849	Wizard Rocks.	0892	Wytoonee Island.

Nos.	XAC	Nos.	ZEB
0893	Xacro Cape.	0936	York River Harbor, Maine, U. S.
4	Xavier Island.	7	Yorktown, Virginia, U. S.
5	Xeros Island.	8	Youalan Island.
6	Xulla Islands, Bessey.	9	Youghal.
7	Xulla Islands, Mangola.	0940	Younaska Island.
8	Xulla Islands, Talyabo.	1	Young Cape.
9	Xyli Cape.	2	Young Harbor Rock.
0900	Yait Chew Bay.	3	Young Nik's Head.
1	Yakuno Sima.	4	Young's Foreland.
2	Yalanga-lala Island.	5	Young's Reef.
3	Yale College.	6	Ypun Island.
4	Yallab's Point.	7	Ysarog.
5	Yami.	8	Ystad.
6	Yanar.	9	Ytapere Point.
7	Yang-tse Cape.	0950	Ythata Island.
8	Yap Island.	1	Yucatan.
9	Yarmouth.	2	Yucatan Channel.
0910	Yatsoude Point.	3	Yule's Reef.
1	Yazon Cape.	4	Yule's Opening.
2	Yba.	5	Yu-lin-Kan Bay.
3	Yellaboi Island.	6	Yzou Cape.
4	Yellow River.	7	Zafarine Islands.
5	Yembo.	8	Zaffarana, Cape.
6	Yendua Island.	9	Zandvort.
7	Yenikaleh.	0960	Zannone Island.
8	Yenisei Gulf.	1	Zante.
9	Yermoloff Island.	2	Zanzibar Island.
0920	Yeu, Island de.	3	Zapadilla Cays.
1	Yit Islands.	4	Zapara Castle.
2	Yki Island.	5	Zapato Menor.
3	Ykima Island.	6	Zapote Point.
4	Ylin, East, Island.	7	Zapotilan Point.
5	Ylo.	8	Zara.
6	Yloe.	9	Zavodovski Island.
7	Yloylo.	0970	Zavora Point.
8	Yokohama, Japan.	1	Zawani, Point.
9	York Breakers.	2	Zazarine.
0930	York Cape, Baffin's Bay.	3	Zea Island.
1	York, Cape, Island.	4	Zealand Fort, British Guiana.
2	York Factory.	5	Zealand Fort, Formosa.
3	York Harbor.	6	Zebayer Islands.
4	York Island.	7	Zebeed, Ras.
0935	York River, Virginia, U. S.	0978	Zebu Island.

Nos.	ZEM	Nos.	ZUY
0979	Zembra.	0985	Zircoa Island.
0980	Zeewyk Channel.	6	Zirona Piccola Island.
1	Zegin, Ras.	7	Zoarah.
2	Zelée Cape.	8	Zurafa Rock.
3	Zeyla.	9	Zuri Island.
0984	Zinari Island.	0990	Zuyder Zee, German Ocean.

www.ingramcontent.com/pod-product-compliance
Lightning Source LLC
Chambersburg PA
CBHW030342270326
41926CB00009B/922